HYMNS OF THE REPUBLIC

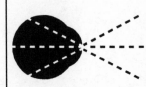

Hymns of the Republic

THE STORY OF THE FINAL YEAR
OF THE AMERICAN CIVIL WAR

S. C. Gwynne

THORNDIKE PRESS
A part of Gale, a Cengage Company

LIBRARY OF CONGRESS CIP DATA ON FILE.
CATALOGUING IN PUBLICATION FOR THIS BOOK
IS AVAILABLE FROM THE LIBRARY OF CONGRESS

ISBN-13: 978-1-4328-7204-5 (hardcover alk. paper)

Published in 2019 by arrangement with Scribner, an imprint of Simon & Schuster, Inc.

Printed in Mexico
1 2 3 4 5 6 7 23 22 21 20 19

To Maisie

I saw battle-corpses, myriads of them,
And the white skeletons of young men, I
saw them,
I saw the debris and debris of all the
slain soldiers of the war,
But I saw they were not as was thought,
They themselves were fully at rest, they
suffer'd not,
The living remain'd and suffer'd, the
mother suffer'd,
And the wife and the child and the
musing comrade suffer'd,
And the armies that remain'd suffer'd.
— Walt Whitman,
"When Lilacs Last in the Dooryard Bloom'd"

Neither party expected for the war the magnitude or the duration which it has already attained. Neither anticipated that the cause of the conflict might cease with or even before the conflict itself should cease. Each looked for an easier triumph, and a result less fundamental and astounding. Both read the same Bible and pray to the same God, and each invokes His aid against the other. It may seem strange that any men should dare to ask a just God's assistance in wringing their bread from the sweat of other men's faces, but let us judge not, that we be not judged.

— Abraham Lincoln,
Second Inaugural Address

CONTENTS

CHAPTER ONE:
THE END BEGINS

ABRAHAM LINCOLN: By spring 1864 it was clear that the nation's fate hinged on the president's success or failure at the November polls.

Washington, DC, had never, in its brief and undistinguished history, known a social season like this one. The winter of 1863–64 had been bitterly cold, but its frozen rains and swirling snows had dampened no spirits. Instead a feeling, almost palpable, of optimism hung in the air, a swelling sense that, after three years of brutal war and humiliating defeats at the hands of rebel armies, God was perhaps in his heaven, after all. The inexplicably lethal Robert E. Lee had finally been beaten at Gettysburg.[1] Vicksburg had fallen, completing the Union conquest of the Mississippi River. A large rebel army had been chased from Chattanooga. Something like hope — or maybe just its shadow — had finally loomed into view.

The season had begun as always with a New Year's reception at the Executive Mansion, hosted by the Lincolns, then had launched itself into a frenzy whose outward manifestation was the city's newest obsession: dancing. Washingtonians were crazy about it. They were seen spinning through quadrilles, waltzes, and polkas at the great US Patent Office Ball, the Enlistment Fund Ball, and at "monster hops" at Willard's hotel and the National.[2] At these affairs, moreover, *everyone* danced. No bored squires or sad-eyed spinsters lingered in the shadows of cut glass and gaslight. No one could sit still, and together all improvised a wildly moving tapestry of color: ladies in lace and silk and crinolines, in crimson velvet and purple

14

moire, their cascading curls flecked with roses and lilies, their bell-shaped forms whirled by men in black swallowtails and colored cravats.

The great public parties were merely the most visible part of the social scene. That winter had seen an explosion of private parties as well. Limits were pushed here, too, budgets broken, meals set forth of quail, partridge, lobster, terrapin, and acreages of confections. Politicians such as Secretary of State William Seward and Congressman Schuyler "Smiler" Colfax threw musical soirees. The spirit of the season was evident in the wedding of the imperially lovely Kate Chase — daughter of Treasury Secretary Salmon P. Chase — to Senator William Sprague. Sprague's gift to Kate was a $50,000 tiara of matched pearls and diamonds. When the bride appeared, the US Marine Band struck up "The Kate Chase March," a song written by a prominent composer for the occasion.[3]

What was most interesting about these evenings, however, was less their showy proceedings than the profoundly threatened world in which they took place. It was less like a world than a child's snow globe: a small glittering space enclosed by an impenetrable barrier. For in the winter of 1863–64, Washington was the most heavily defended city on earth. Beyond its houses and public buildings stood thirty-seven miles of elaborate trenches

15

and fortifications that included sixty separate forts, manned by fifty thousand soldiers. Along this armored front bristled some nine hundred cannons, many of large caliber, enough to blast entire armies from the face of the earth.[4] There was something distinctly medieval about the fear that drove such engineering.

The danger was quite real. Since the Civil War had begun, Washington had been threatened three times by large armies under Robert E. Lee's command.[5] After the Union defeat at the Second Battle of Bull Run in August 1862, a rebel force under Lee's lieutenant Stonewall Jackson had come within twenty miles of the capital while driving the entire sixty-thousand-man Union army back inside its fortifications, where the bluecoats cowered and licked their wounds and thanked heaven for all those earthworks and cannons.[6]

A year and a half later, the same fundamental truth informed those lively parties. Without that *cordon militaire,* they could not have existed. Washington's elaborate social scene was a brocaded illusion: what the capital's denizens desperately wanted the place to be, not what it actually was.

This garishly defended capital was still a smallish, grubby, corrupt, malodorous, and oddly pretentious municipality whose principal product, along with legislation and war

16

making, was biblical sin in its many varieties. Much of the city had been destroyed in the War of 1812. What had replaced the old settlement was both humble and grandiose. Vast quantities of money had been spent to build the city's precious handful of public buildings: the Capitol itself (finished in December 1863), the Post Office Building, the Smithsonian Institution, the US Patent Office, the US Treasury, and the Executive Mansion. (The Washington Monument, whose construction had been suspended in 1854 for lack of funds, was an abandoned and forlorn-looking stump.)[7]

But those structures stood as though on a barren plain. The Corinthian columns of the Post Office Building may have been worthy of the high Renaissance, but little else in the neighborhood was. The effect was jarring, as though pieces of the Champs-Élysées had been dropped into a swamp. Everything about the place, from its bloody and never-ending war to the faux grandiosity of its windswept plazas, suggested incompleteness. Like the Washington Monument, it all seemed half-finished. The wartime city held only about eighty thousand permanent residents, a pathetic fraction of the populations of New York (800,000) and Philadelphia (500,000), let alone London (2.6 million) or Paris (1.7 million).[8] Foreign travelers, if they came to the national capital at all, found it hollow, showy, and vainglorious. British writer Anthony Trollope, who visited the city during the war and thought it a colossal disappointment, wrote:

Washington is but a ragged, unfinished collection of unbuilt broad streets. . . . Of all the places I know it is the most ungainly and most unsatisfactory; I fear I must also say the most presumptuous in its pretensions. Taking [a] map with him . . . a man may lose himself in the streets, not as one loses oneself in London between Shoreditch and Russell Square, but as one does so in the deserts of the Holy Land . . . There is much unsettled land within the United States of America, but I think none so desolate as three-fourths of the ground on which is supposed to stand the city of Washington.[9]

He might have added that the place smelled, too. Its canals were still repositories of sewage; tidal flats along the Potomac reeked at low tide. Pigs and cows still roamed the frozen streets. Dead horses, rotting in the winter sun, were common sights. At the War Department, one reporter noted, "The gutter [was] heaped up full of black, rotten mud, a foot deep, and worth fifty cents a car load for manure."[10] The unfinished mall where the unfinished Washington Monument stood held

18

a grazing area and slaughterhouse for the cattle used to feed the capital's defenders.[11] The city was both a haven and a dumping ground for the sort of human chaff that collected at the ragged edges of the war zone: deserters from both armies, sutlers (civilians who sold provisions to soldiers), spies, confidence men, hustlers, and the like.

Washington had also become the nation's single largest refuge for escaped slaves, who now streamed through the capital's rutted streets by the thousands. When Congress freed the city's thirty-three hundred slaves in 1862, it had triggered an enormous inflow of refugees, mostly from Virginia and Maryland.[12] By 1864 fifty thousand of them had moved within Washington's ring of forts. Many were housed in "contraband camps," and many suffered in disease-ridden squalor in a world that often seemed scarcely less prejudiced than the one they had left. But they were never going back. They were never going to be slaves again. This was the migration's central truth, and you could see it on any street corner in the city. Many would make their way into the Union army, which at the end of 1863 had already enlisted fifty thousand from around the country, most of them former slaves.

But the most common sights of all on those streets were soldiers. A war was being fought, one that had a sharp and unappeasable appetite for young men. Several hundred thousand of them had tramped through the city since April 1861, wearing their blue uniforms, slouch hats, and knapsacks. They had lingered on its street corners, camped on its outskirts. Tens of thousands more languished in wartime hospitals. Mostly they were just passing through, on their way to a battlefield or someone's grand campaign or, if they were lucky, home. Many were on their way to death or dismemberment. In their wake came the seemingly endless supply trains with their shouting teamsters, rumbling wagon wheels, snorting horses, and creaking tack.

Because of these soldiers — unattached young men, isolated, and far from home — a booming industry had arisen that was more than a match for its European counterparts: prostitution. This was no minor side effect of war. Ten percent or more of the adult population were inhabitants of Washington's demimonde. In 1863, the *Washington Evening Star* had determined that the capital had more than five thousand prostitutes, with an additional twenty-five hundred in neighboring Georgetown, and twenty-five hundred more across the river in Alexandria, Virginia. That did not count the concubines or courtesans who were simply kept in apartments by the officer corps. The year before, an army survey had revealed 450 houses of ill repute.[13] All served drinks and sex. In a district called

Murder Bay, passersby could see nearly naked women in the windows and doors of the houses. For the less affluent — laborers, teamsters, and army riffraff — Nigger Hill and Tin Cup Alley had sleazier establishments, where men were routinely robbed, stabbed, shot, and poisoned with moonshine whiskey. The *Star* could not help wondering how astonished the sisters and mothers of these soldiers would be to see how their noble young men spent their time at the capital.[14] Many of these establishments were in the heart of the city, a few blocks from the president's house and the fashionable streets where the capital's smart set whirled in gaslit dances.

This was Washington, DC, in that manic, unsettled winter of 1863–64, in the grip of a lengthening war whose end no one could clearly see.

Of all the parties, gatherings, and balls that season, none would be as indelibly etched into the memories of Washingtonians as a public reception at the White House on the wet, blustery night of Tuesday, March 8. President Lincoln held two such receptions a week — known in the day as levees — where he and his wife, Mary, would stand in the doorway to the Blue Room and greet all comers. The president would shake hands, in a manner that reminded people of someone sawing wood, and say "How do?" and perhaps a few more words, then visitors would be passed along to Mary Lincoln, who greeted them in turn. The Tuesday reception was the more formal one. According to a reporter who was there, the well-dressed attendees were as usual "pour[ing] through the drawing rooms into the great East Room, where they circulate in a revolving march to the music of the Marine Band, stationed in an adjoining room."[15]

Except that this night was different. At about nine thirty, Lincoln was at his usual perch, wearing a collar one size too large, a badly tied necktie, and his habitual expression of bemused melancholy, when a sudden noise and commotion arose at the entrance to the room.[16]

From the small crowd at the door, which had sorted itself into a double file, now emerged a man with a slender build, slightly stooped shoulders, mild blue eyes, and an unexceptional beard, wearing the uniform of a Union soldier.[17] When Lincoln saw him, all sadness vanished from the president's face, and he rushed toward the man.

"Why, here is General Grant!" Lincoln exclaimed. "Well, this is a great pleasure, I assure you!"[18]

As the crowd gaped, the two men chatted amiably, if somewhat awkwardly, for a moment — the stork-like Lincoln was fully eight

22

inches taller than Grant and had to stoop to engage him — whereupon Grant was passed to Secretary of State William Seward, who then presented him to the first lady. As word of the visitor's arrival traveled rocket-like through the Blue Room and into the crowded East Room, utter pandemonium broke loose. A genteel riot ensued, driven by wild cheers and applause so uninhibited that Secretary of the Navy Gideon Welles found it "rowdy and unseemly."[19] As one observer described it, "Laces were torn, crinoline mashed." Within minutes, Seward and his charge, Ulysses S. Grant, war hero of the west and the great hope of the Union, were swallowed by the great surge of the crowd.[20]

As the crowd's behavior suggested, this was no casual visit. Grant had come to Washington because he had just been promoted by act of Congress to a rank — lieutenant general — that had been held only twice in American history, once by George Washington and once by Winfield Scott, hero of the Mexican-American War. In both cases, the commission was honorary. Thus the modest and unassuming Ulysses S. Grant, known to his army friends as Sam, the antithesis of pomp, circumstance, and military grandeur, was about to become the first full-blown three-star general in US history.[21]

The immediate impetus for the promotion had been his victory at Chattanooga, Tennessee, in November, where he had broken General Braxton Bragg's siege and then sent Bragg's forty-thousand-man Confederate army reeling in retreat, thus confirming what Abraham Lincoln had been thinking anyway: that Grant, among a crowded field of often timid, indecisive, and incompetent Union commanders, was the best choice to win the war. But Chattanooga was merely Grant's most recent trophy of war. In 1862 he had swallowed a twelve-thousand-man rebel army whole at Fort Donelson, Tennessee, refusing to offer any terms but *unconditional surrender.* Those words, with their strange, cold, insistent rhythm, had passed immediately into American legend. At Vicksburg, Mississippi, in 1863 he had shocked the nation again by capturing another entire Confederate army, this time containing thirty thousand men. Nor had his attitude toward surrender grown more charitable. When the opposing general had politely suggested a negotiating session to hammer out terms of surrender to "save the further effusion of blood," Grant replied, "The useless effusion of blood you propose stopping by this course can be ended at any time you may choose by an unconditional surrender of the city and the garrison." This was more of the same music that had sounded at Fort Donelson, bright and dissonant, and it was like nothing anyone had ever before heard. Where other commanders temporized

24

and hesitated, Grant simply put his head down and hammered forward, like a battering ram.

A good deal more was attached to Grant than these three victories — including a drinking problem that had gotten him dismissed from the army, his questionable performance at the Battle of Shiloh, and a bizarre episode of anti-Semitism in 1862 — but for now only the winning mattered. Few people of consequence, in the winter of 1863–64, argued against the promotion of "Unconditional Surrender" Grant, the Union general who won. He was the implacable force, the irresistible power from the west, where the soldiery had not formed a habit of losing.

At Lincoln's request Congress had promoted Grant, and now, in March, he had been summoned by Secretary of War Edwin Stanton to Washington to accept his new commission as head of all Union armies. Traveling with his thirteen-year-old son, Fred, his close aide John Rawlins, and another officer, Grant had made his way by boat from Louisville to Cincinnati, then by train to Washington, arriving at the station on the afternoon of March 8. He was one of the most celebrated men in the Western World at that moment, and the focus of fierce, often obsessive, national interest. He was probably more popular in the North than Lincoln himself. Grant was so famous that his full-length portrait, field glasses in hand and flanked by a demolished rebel cannon, hung in a committee room in the Capitol.[22] His likeness was featured on patriotic posters. Oceans of printer's ink had been expended describing his battlefield victories.

But few people in the east knew what he looked like, a problem compounded by his not looking like much at all. He had grown up in Ohio, which was very much part of "the west" in the middle nineteenth century. Though he had attended West Point in New York State, he had been to Washington exactly once in his life and had spent his entire military career, including the Civil War, in the Midwest, the far West, or Mexico.

His arrival in the late afternoon of March 8 was almost comically unceremonious. Due to a logistical error, no one had met his train at the station. To all appearances, he was just another sunburned soldier in an army hat and linen duster, stepping off a passenger car, looking blankly around him for whoever had been appointed to greet him. Thus stranded, Grant's small group took a carriage to the office of army general-in-chief Henry Wager Halleck, in the hope of seeing a familiar face. But Halleck was not there. The group then proceeded to Halleck's residence, but he was not there either. Having failed three times to find anyone who might welcome him, Grant decided he would just go on to Willard's hotel, where he had been told rooms had been reserved for him and his party.

The difference between Grant's arrival and the arrival, nineteen months earlier, of the Union's leading general George McClellan in Washington following his defeat in the Seven Days Battles, east of Richmond, is worth noting.[23] The caravan bearing the baggage of McClellan and his staff consisted of twenty-five six-foot-by-nine-foot wagons, painted dark brown and varnished to a high gleam. The wagons were each drawn by four matched bay horses — both their color and manes had been deliberately coordinated for effect — and each driven by two black attendants in immaculate blue livery. On the side of each wagon, in large gold letters, was the inscription BAGGAGE. HEADQUARTERS. ARMY OF THE POTOMAC. McClellan had arrived like an imperial pasha with one hundred horses and fifty attendants; Grant with only his son and a light suitcase.[24] The lordly McClellan had turned out to be an embarrassment, a timid general who had to be coaxed, cajoled, shamed, and threatened into fighting Confederates and who finally had to be gotten rid of.

Grant's ordeal of anonymity was not quite over. He arrived at Willard's, quietly checked in as "U. S. Grant and son, Galena, Ill.," and, still unrecognized, went down to dinner with

Fred.[25] In the dining room the lightning bolt finally struck. After whispers, more whispers, and a rising commotion, a nearby gentleman banged on his table with a dinner knife, rose, and announced that he had "the honor to inform [the diners] that General Grant was present in the room with them." The crowd of diners rose to their feet, and soon thunderous cheers were rolling through the room. "My father arose and bowed," Fred Grant recalled later, "and the crowd began to surge around him; after that, dining became impossible; and an informal reception was held for perhaps three quarters of an hour; but as there seemed to be no end to the crowd assembling, my father left the dining room and retired to his apartments."[26] Word of Grant's arrival spread quickly. Former secretary of war Simon Cameron soon came to collect him and give him a proper escort to Lincoln's reception, two blocks away.

What Grant faced inside the East Room made the disturbance at Willard's seem tame. He was greeted by more booming cheers, but now the possibility that he might be trampled seemed quite real. Secretary of State Seward solved the problem by having Grant climb up onto a sofa, where, in the description of *Sacramento Daily Union* reporter Noah Brooks,

he could be seen, and where he was secure, at least for a time, from the madness of the multitude. People were caught up and whirled into the torrent which swept through the Great East Room. . . . Many got up on sofas, chairs, and tables to be out of harm's way or to get a better view of the spectacle. It was the only real mob I ever saw in the White House. For at least once, the President of the United States was not the chief figure in the picture. The little, scared-looking man who stood on a crimson-colored sofa was the idol of the hour.[27]

At least sixty minutes passed before Lincoln and a flushed and perspiring Grant were able to hold a conversation.[28] In the meantime the people had gotten a glimpse of Grant and were thrilled by what they saw: a plain and modest man whose clear and impassive blue eyes showed both confidence and determination, a man free of the cant and hollow grandeur that had marked some of his predecessors.[29] With his immense gifts of command and his humble manner, he managed to be transcendently American.

As a westerner — that was how he thought of himself — Grant had learned to despise the intrigue, corruption, infighting, pettifoggery, and personality-driven politics of Washington. Instinctively, he wanted nothing to do with the place. The regular army had enough of all that anyway. He was a straight-ahead fighter, not someone who bent with political winds. He wanted to be measured by battlefield results. Everyone around him agreed with him that he needed to stay away from Washington — both as a place and as an idea. John Rawlins wrote, of his boss's Washington visit, "I am doing everything I can to get him away from here."[30] Grant's sidekick and sometime political conscience William Tecumseh Sherman had advised him, in his letter congratulating him on his promotion, "Do not stay in Washington. . . . For God's sake and for your country's sake, come out of Washington!"[31]

Now, in the presence of the great Lincoln, Grant was vouchsafed a clear view as to why. Though Lincoln had just met Grant, the president was already stage-managing the events of the next day, when Grant would officially accept his new commission. The president spoke to Grant as though the little general might have trouble understanding how such complicated adult matters worked, as one would to a bright middle schooler.

"I shall then make a very short speech to you," Lincoln said, "to which I desire you to make a reply . . . and that you may be properly prepared to do so I have written what I shall say — only four sentences in all — which I will read from my MS. as an example which you may follow and also read your reply, as you are perhaps not as much accustomed to speaking as I, myself — and I therefore give you what I shall say that you may consider it and form your reply." If this wasn't quite patronizing enough — perhaps it had momentarily escaped Lincoln that managing the Union armies in the western theater, from the Alleghenies to the Mississippi River, might require some presentational skills — he then went on to tell Grant exactly what he was to say:

There are two points that I would like to have you make in your answer, 1st, to say something which shall prevent or obviate any jealousy of you from any of the other generals in the service, and 2nd, something which shall put you on as good terms as possible with this Army of the Potomac.[32]

At the ceremony the next day Lincoln read his statement, praising and promoting Grant, and then Grant made his own little speech, which must have entirely lived up to Lincoln's dismal expectations: choppy, disjointed, and delivered in what one observer called a "struggling" fashion. Grant had scribbled it down in pencil on a half sheet of notepaper and seemed to have trouble reading his own writing. "Mr. President, I accept this commission with gratitude for the high honor conferred, with the aid of the noble armies that have fought on so many fields for our common country." And so on. He managed to say little, and, perhaps not coincidentally, *nothing at all of what his boss had told him to say.* Lincoln's secretary, John G. Nicolay, noted dryly at the time that Grant "had either forgotten or disregarded entirely the president's hints to him of the night previous."[33]

Grant took Sherman's advice and got the hell out of Washington as soon as he could. He turned down a dinner invitation from Lincoln, saying, "Dinner to me means a million dollars a day lost to the country," which appealed to Lincoln's fiscal instincts. He also told Lincoln that he had "become very tired of this show business," which also pleased the president, who was by then tired of grandstanding generals. Grant made a brief excursion to Brandy Station in northern Virginia to visit the Army of the Potomac and its commander, General George G. Meade — where brass bands greeted Grant in pouring rain — then took a train to Nashville, where he met with his friend Sherman, to whom he handed command of the Union armies in the west.[34]

When Grant returned east a few days later, it was not to Washington, DC, but to a small town in Virginia called Culpeper Court House. As general in charge of all Union armies, he would not, as his predecessor Major General Henry Wager Halleck had, make his headquarters in the political rat's nest of Washington. Grant would be at the front. Camped across the Rapidan River from him, just a few miles away, was the single most potent military force on the North American continent, the Army of Northern Virginia, commanded by the other towering military genius of the Civil War, a man whom Grant had never faced on a battlefield. Grant's mission was simple yet unprecedented in a war that had until now favored conquering real estate instead of armies, cities instead of people: destroy Robert E. Lee. In Grant's attempt to do that he would unleash, in just a few months, a storm of blood and death that beggared even the killing fields of Gettysburg and Chancellorsville. He would find himself in a world of bitterness, violence, hatred, and retribution that would make the early years of the conflict look innocent and honorable by comparison. He and Lee would soon remake the war into something that neither the country nor its hardened veterans had ever before seen.

CHAPTER TWO:
WITH MALICE TOWARD ALL

NATHAN BEDFORD FORREST: One of the Confederacy's most brilliant generals, he presided over the war's greatest atrocity.

You would have been hard-pressed, in the early spring of 1864, to find a more obscure and militarily irrelevant backwater than Fort Pillow, Tennessee. Located eighty river miles upstream from Memphis on the Mississippi River, it sat on a high bluff and consisted mostly of crude earthworks, just dirt pushed up into walls, with a trench dug at their base.[1] The structures looked like something the Celts might have put up to stop the Romans. The fort had been built in the early war by the cowardly and incompetent Confederate general Gideon Pillow and had lived up to its name ever since, failing repeatedly to protect the interests of whoever occupied it, first the Confederacy and then, after 1862, the Union. Fort Pillow was so unnecessary that in January 1864 Major General William Tecumseh Sherman had shut it down, only to see it rise miraculously again, in spite of his orders, to resume its time-tested function of failing to stop rebel guerrilla raids.

Yet a minor military engagement took place here — a month after Ulysses S. Grant's awkward and portentous arrival in Washington — that would demonstrate better than any other event of that spring the reasons Grant and Lee were about to join their titanic fight. They were not the same reasons the North and the South had fought at the First Battle of Bull Run three years before. Fort Pillow would become both a rallying cry and a line of demarcation, a stark and brutal sign of the revolutionary change that had swept

35

through the war and altered its nature.

Major William F. Bradford, who began Tuesday, April 12, 1864, as second-in-command of the federal garrison at Fort Pillow, didn't see any of that coming. He had thought that things were going rather well. He would have been astonished to learn that he was about to become a grim historical footnote. The thirty-six-year-old officer was both a Tennessean and a Unionist, the sort of soldier his Confederate countrymen sneeringly called a "Tennessee Tory" or "homemade Yankee." A traitor, in short. He came from a well-connected family and had personally recruited a battalion of like-minded young men — many of whom were deserters from rebel units in Tennessee — who had joined the US army as the 13th Tennessee Cavalry.[2] He had little military experience and was not well suited to command. His soldiers had received minimal training. From February to April he had been the ranking officer at the fort.

Bradford's main duties were to hunt down partisan raiders in Union-held western Tennessee, recruit new soldiers, and offer safe haven to escaped slaves who crossed into his lines. But he had another charge, too: make the people of the Confederacy feel the hard hand of their Northern masters. The idea had gained currency in Grant's 1863 Vicksburg campaign and now, in the war's fourth year, was emerging as full-blown federal policy. Ordinary citizens of the South had once been seen as innocent bystanders. In most cases their personal property had been respected and even protected by Union commanders. Now all that had changed. Civilians were the enemy. They were harborers of guerrillas, suppliers of food to the rebel army, owners of the slaves who produced that food, takers of potshots at Union troops. Their land, crops, farm animals, barns, fences, machinery, and slaves were now seen as part of the larger Confederate war-making apparatus. Landowners were thus to be harassed and taught that their perfidy had consequences that extended beyond the maiming and killing of their sons, brothers, and fathers. The new hard-war policy was about retribution, too, or at least that was what the common soldiers who carried it out believed: it was payback for all those dead Union boys, payback for making war necessary in the first place.[3]

Thus Bradford's orders were to "forage liberally," as the euphemism went, which meant using farms near the fort to feed and equip his troops, seizing horses and stores of food, and engaging in what looked to residents very much like looting, pillaging, and persecution.[4] For this, Bradford and his troops were hated by the Tennesseans, and the hatred bore an even sharper edge because they were local boys. They would have been hated even more if they had been the slightest bit effective in hunting down partisan raiders. Other than offering shelter to slaves, deserters, and Unionists, Fort Pillow was the same haphazard military enterprise it had always been.[5]

In late March an event took place that would change the destinies of both Fort Pillow and Major Bradford. This was the arrival of reinforcements: four companies of heavy artillery and a section of light artillery. But these were not ordinary reinforcements. They were *black,* members of the 6th US Colored Heavy Artillery and the 2nd US Colored Light Artillery. They were all escaped slaves who had been recruited in Tennessee — from the same areas that they were now commissioned to occupy and pacify. Though black soldiers had fought in a handful of engagements in 1862 and 1863, their presence in combat situations — authorized formally by President Lincoln in January 1863 — was still relatively new. Few Confederate soldiers had ever faced them. These recruits were under the command of Major Lionel F. Booth, a white officer who outranked Bradford due to seniority and who assumed command of the fort. Thus bolstered, the Union garrison was roughly six hundred strong, about half black and half white.

They would soon be tested. In the early morning of April 12, a force of fifteen hundred Confederate cavalry appeared suddenly at Fort Pillow, as though they had been dropped from the sky. No one had seen them coming. At sunup the rebels surprised the federal pickets, killed some of them, drove the others in, and attacked the fort. By 9:00 a.m. their sharpshooters had killed Major Booth. Though the garrison's defenders repulsed several assaults and the Union gunboat *New Era* had diligently banged away at the antic gray figures on the shore of the Mississippi, by noon the Confederates had forced the federals back into the works atop the bluff and formed a tight noose around the fort. Their success was caused less by ineptness — though these green federal troops did not know what they were doing — than by flaws in the fort's layout, which prevented its defenders from either hiding or effectively returning fire.[6]

But the Union's rapidly deteriorating prospects had another cause, too. Though Bradford — who had assumed command on the death of Booth — did not yet realize it, that morning he was facing one of the South's most brilliant commanders, a born tactical genius whom Major General William T. Sherman, a man not given to idle praise, called "the most remarkable man our Civil War has produced on either side." This man, Nathan Bedford Forrest, was the sort of spectacular military accident that only a desperate war could produce. Unlike the overwhelming majority of Confederate general officers, he had neither education nor elevated birth. He grew up poor in middle Tennessee, the son of a blacksmith who died when Nathan was sixteen and left him to care for a large family. Determined to lift himself out of poverty, Forrest built a small business empire out of land, cotton, and slave trading. He became the largest slave dealer in Memphis.[7] By the start of the war he was one of the richest men in the South. At the time he knew absolutely nothing of warfare or military operations. He had never been in a militia. He had never read a book on military history or tactics. He was barely literate.

No matter. The war's particular needs perfectly matched Forrest's remarkable abilities, and he learned his new trade with astounding speed. He rose in a single year from the rank of private to brigadier general of cavalry. Tall, handsome, humorless, quick to anger, brave to the point of recklessness, he inspired fierce loyalty in his men and was simply better at command than anyone else. He was also better at spotting and exploiting the enemy's weaknesses. In 1862 he began a series of highly destructive raids that would make him one of the most feared cavalry officers of the war and present a military problem that the Union high command would never fully solve. That Booth and Bradford never saw him coming meant only that they had plenty of company.

For someone of Forrest's immense talents, the conquest of the defensively flawed Fort Pillow against a callow commander was relatively simple. Sometime around noon, according to Forrest's aide-de-camp, "It was perfectly apparent to any man endowed with the smallest amount of common sense that to all intents and purposes the fort was ours."[8]

That description apparently did not apply to Major William F. Bradford. He was guilty, from the start of the battle, of wildly excessive optimism. He and Booth had felt so secure that they had failed to fully destroy a set of barracks just outside the fort, thus offering their enemies both cover and a clear line of fire into the inner sanctum.[9] Bradford believed that the New Era, a stern-wheeler outfitted with six howitzers, could somehow equalize his opponents' advantage in numbers, even though it was blindingly clear to Forrest's men that the boat, which had pumped out 282 ineffectual rounds, would have little effect on the battle's outcome.[10] Bradford had also decided, without any corroborating evidence, that three passenger ships that had appeared on the river around noon were carrying Union reinforcements. They turned out to be merely commercial steamers.

At 2:00 p.m. Forrest, a practical soldier who would not shed blood if he did not have to, sent a note to Major Booth (of whose death he was unaware) under a flag of truce, saying:

Your gallant defense of Fort Pillow has entitled you to the treatment of brave men. I now demand the unconditional surrender of your forces, at the same time assuring that you will be treated as prisoners of war. I have received a new supply of ammunition and can take your works by assault, and if compelled to do so you must take the consequences.[11]

This might have seemed like a conventional demand for surrender. But it was not at all. To this point in the war Confederate commanders had largely refused to give black soldiers the usual rights of prisoners of war. Many had been executed; many had been returned to their owners or sold back into slavery. But General Forrest, known to be a man of his word, was for some reason including them in the deal he now offered the Union commander. Bradford, posing as Booth, temporized, consulted his officers, bargained unsuccessfully for more time, and finally delivered his answer, which probably sounded quite gallant to him: "I will not surrender."[12]

This was a spectacularly bad idea. It took the Confederates less than ten minutes to carry the fort's breastworks, killing most of the federal officers as they rushed forward.[13] The valiant Bradford's own response was to run. "Boys, save your lives," he yelled. In minutes battle gave way to rout as the hapless federals, black and white, did the only thing they could do: flee in heart-pounding panic over the earthen walls on the far side of the fort and half tumble, half run down the steep slope to the banks of the Mississippi River.[14] The black recruits had fought bravely to defend the fort. But their white officers had been killed almost immediately, leaving them with no leadership amid the noise, chaos, and swirling white smoke atop the bluff. Several of them later said they had simply followed the white men of Bradford's panicking 13th Cavalry over the earthworks and down the hill.[15]

The escaping men must have felt a moment of elation as they broke free of the murderous fire in the fort and into the clear air of the riverbank, looking prayerfully toward the gunports of the *New Era*. But a moment was all it was. Once outside the walls the federals found themselves caught in a tailor-made killing zone far worse than what they had faced inside. Now they were being shot at from *three* directions: by rebel soldiers above on the slope and parapets and by detachments

Forrest had placed on the riverbanks both above and below the fort. The *New Era,* which Bradford had instructed to open fire with shotgun-like canister if the rebels breached the fort — this had seemed like an excellent idea, too — was easily driven off when Forrest ordered one of the fort's cannons turned on the steamer. There was nowhere to hide, and no way out, except into the Mississippi itself. Many men did plunge into the four-hundred-yard-wide river. But the evidence suggests that most of the besieged federals did the sensible thing: they threw down their weapons and tried to surrender.

That was when the slaughter started — the deliberate shooting by Confederates of unarmed Union soldiers with their hands in the air. The killing seems to have happened spontaneously. No senior officer had given such orders.[16] What happened appeared to be an extemporaneous explosion of rage, fueled by the presence of so many black soldiers, by the very idea that white soldiers would command and fight alongside them, and by the taunting of rebel troops by some of those blacks during the truce.[17] Later, Confederate brigadier general James R. Chalmers tried to explain his troops' behavior to a Union gunboat officer. According to the officer, Chalmers said, "The men of General Forrest's command had such a hatred toward the armed negro that they could not be restrained from killing the negroes after they had captured them. . . . He said it was nothing better than we could expect so long as we persisted in arming the negro."[18]

Indeed, there was something deep-seated and almost primal in white Southerners' fears of what they insisted on calling a "servile insurrection" — as though they could not bring themselves to utter the words "slave revolt." Arming slaves and setting them against their masters had been the animating idea behind John Brown's failed raid at Harpers Ferry in 1859. The horror the raid produced in the South had less to do with its military particulars than with the fact that so many Northerners saw nothing wrong with the idea. People in the North were apparently happy to endorse the disembowelment of Southern white men, women, and children, the rape of white women by black men, and the burning of Southern farms and homes. Such behavior had a precedent, too: Nat Turner's 1831 slave uprising in tidewater Virginia, in which fifty-five white people were hacked and clubbed to death. Now the US government was officially putting Springfield rifles into the hands of escaped slaves and teaching them how to kill white Southerners. As the song had it, John Brown's soul was marching on.

The next twenty minutes saw a straightforward butchery of men who were either trying to surrender, had already surrendered, or had been rendered completely helpless. Many were already wounded when they were shot down or hacked apart with sabers. Many were shot repeatedly, often in the head. Most of the violence was directed at black soldiers, though many whites were not spared.

Confederate sergeant Achilles V. Clark, of the 20th Tennessee Cavalry, described the scene in a letter to his sisters two days later:

> The slaughter was awful. Words cannot describe the scene. The poor deluded negroes would run up to our men, fall upon their knees, and with uplifted hands scream for mercy, but they were ordered to their feet and then shot down. The white men fared but little better. Their fort turned out to be a slaughter pen. Blood, human blood stood about in pools, and brains could have been gathered up in any quantity.[19]

The account of Union officer Mack J. Leaming conveys the same sense of horror: "The scene which followed . . . beggars all description. . . . Our men were shot down without mercy. . . . This [was] wholesale butchery of brave men, white as well as black, after they had surrendered."[20]

One Union surgeon who found himself in the midst of men who were being shot while "crying for quarter" described how twenty men who were asked to "fall into line" to surrender were shot down in place. Though two of them managed to move away, the remaining eighteen men on the ground "were chopped to pieces with sabres."[21] Soldiers who tried to escape by swimming — in numbers so great "they resembled a drove of hogs," according to one observer — either drowned or were shot in the water.[22] When General Forrest later wrote that "the river was dyed with the blood of the slaughtered for 200 yards," he was making an accurate and unembellished observation.[23]

As the massacre progressed and it became clear that surrendering meant certain death, many soldiers, particularly blacks, who had tried to surrender took up their rifles again or tried to flee, which made the scene even more chaotic. An individual's surrender in the heat of battle was a difficult maneuver anyway, especially when fortifications were carried by assault. One moment a soldier was fighting hard and killing his enemies, and the next moment he was begging them not to do the same to him. What, exactly, made him worthy of such instant mercy, such sudden grace?

The carnage did not stop on the battlefield. Wounded men in the field hospital were killed, as were sick soldiers in tents inside the fort. Some were burned alive when their tents were set on fire. Later testimony by individual black soldiers suggested a cruelty so wanton that it almost defies belief: Daniel Tyler, a former slave from Mississippi and a private in the 6th US Colored Heavy Artillery, was shot at point-blank range after he surrendered. He was shot again by another captor and had his eye jabbed out. He was then buried alive with dead soldiers and dug himself out only with the help of a sympathetic rebel. Arthur Edwards, like Tyler a former Mississippi slave and a private in the same unit, was shot after he surrendered, first in the head, then in the shoulder. Half an hour later he was shot in the head again. One of his attackers said, "God damn you, you are fighting against your master!" Private Manuel Nichols, also with the 6th Colored Heavy Artillery, was wounded inside the fort at the beginning of the fight. He surrendered, then was shot again, this time under his left ear. He was later shot yet again in his right arm.[24] These men were among the lucky ones: most of the black soldiers who were shot multiple times did not survive.

What of Major Bradford, whose misguided refusal to surrender had led to the destruction of his battalion? He had fled down the bank to the river's edge, where he stood with his hands in the air "crying at the top of his voice that he surrendered," said one observer. When the rebels continued to fire at him, he

48

escaped briefly into the river, then returned to shore and ran back up the bluff, still holding up his hands and screaming, "I surrender." He survived only because his assailants were poor pistol shots. He finally found a rebel soldier to whom he could surrender.[25] He would escape later that evening, then be recaptured the next day by Confederate soldiers and summarily shot to death.

Forrest and other senior officers managed to stop the bloodletting on the riverbank after thirty minutes. Later testimony, however, suggested that killings of wounded black soldiers and black prisoners continued into the night and even the next morning. (Forrest, who had been lightly wounded, spent the night elsewhere.) By the time the last prisoner was executed, nearly half of the six hundred soldiers in Fort Pillow's garrison were dead. Two-thirds of them were black.[26] The death rate for blacks was nearly double that for whites. The rebels took 168 whites prisoner, and only 58 blacks.[27] Union witnesses had little doubt that the mass killing at Fort Pillow had violated the most basic rules of warfare, or that the violence had been directed overwhelmingly at African Americans.

The story became a sensation in the North. The *Cincinnati Gazette* called the incident "one of the most horrible that has disgraced the history of modern warfare."[28] *Harper's*

Weekly showed rebels bayoneting and shooting unarmed blacks under the headline "The Massacre at Fort Pillow." *Frank Leslie's Illustrated Newspaper* featured the hacking and bludgeoning of helpless Union soldiers.[29] Along with the shock and horror came some pointed questions, too. A number of Northern papers challenged the notion that using black soldiers in combat was a good idea in the first place. The *Chicago Tribune,* while condemning Forrest and his soldiers, suggested that blacks had caused the massacre by running away. The *Portland Advertiser* took an even more biased view, writing, "Dressing a monkey in the uniform of the government . . . cannot convert the monkey into a real soldier and attach to him the rights and immunities of a prisoner of war."[30]

The most inflammatory account of all came, oddly enough, from the US Congress. In May the Joint Committee on the Conduct of the War published sixty thousand copies of a sensational report based on interviews with witnesses. The language was blunt and brutal and impassioned:

> Then followed a scene of cruelty and murder without parallel in civilized warfare. . . . The rebels commenced an indiscriminate slaughter, sparing neither age nor sex, white nor black soldier nor civilian. The officers seemed to vie with each other in the devil-

ish work. Men, women and their children, wherever found, were deliberately shot down, beaten, and hacked with sabres. Some of the children, not more than ten years old, were forced to stand up and face their murderers while being shot. The sick and wounded were butchered without mercy, the rebels even entering the hospital buildings and dragging them out to be shot.

The report chronicled in bloody detail men shot in the river, men burned to death, men nailed to burning tents and buildings, and men deliberately buried alive.[31]

Much of what was in the congressional report was true, especially about the killing of unarmed and wounded soldiers. But parts were not true. In their zeal to indict Forrest and his men, Senate investigators had uncritically believed all the testimony they heard, particularly the most outrageous parts. Though a few civilians died, no evidence suggested that women and children were part of the massacre. (Almost all had escaped by boat.) A few federals did end up being buried alive, but no evidence showed that the practice was systematic. Some had been buried alive because they were pretending — with good reason — to be dead. Though witnesses did report two bodies nailed to wood and burned alive, this was only hearsay; no one actually saw it. Several wounded soldiers were indeed inside tents when they were burned by Confederate troops, but at least some of this was accidental.[32]

Forrest agreed with the authors of the report that a massacre had taken place. There was no getting around the body count. The sticking point, and the question that was pursued through thousands of newspaper articles in both the North and South and investigations by both the US army and Congress, was, What had made the soldiers do it? Had the killing of unarmed men been ordered by General Forrest? Early statements from some witnesses suggested that it had, and this was the first and most shocking conclusion many Northerners came away with: that the "battle" was just premeditated murder.

Forrest, who overnight became a figure of evil incarnate in the North, flatly denied the charge. In his version his opponents had never surrendered and had continued to fight as the battle moved out onto the riverbank. The Union soldiers had brought this savagery on themselves, Forrest insisted, by refusing to stop fighting and by running away. Most of the testimony from participants and observers suggested that this was not true. But neither did any specific evidence suggest that Forrest had ordered his men to shoot unarmed federals. Forrest argued that the high death rate of blacks was due to the innate racial superiority of his white troops. "It is hoped that these facts will demonstrate to the Northern people that negro soldiers cannot cope with Southerners," he wrote in a letter the day after the battle. To Forrest, "slaughter" was simply what happened when white troops faced blacks.[33]

Such arguments carried little weight in the North. The message of the congressional report was clear and easy to understand: Fort Pillow was the single greatest atrocity of the Civil War, proof of the cruelty, moral degeneracy, and savage racism of the Southern soldier.

The war had begun as a fight, undertaken by the United States of America — or what was left of it — to restore the Union. That is what President Abraham Lincoln said the war was about. He said it again and again. Those bright-eyed young men in blue uniforms who marched forth into the mysterious lands of the Confederacy were simply trying to force the eleven prodigal states back inside the commonwealth. Wholeness, completeness, was the goal. Congress, too, agreed that this was the purpose of the war and said so with great clarity in the Crittenden-Johnson Resolution, a measure passed almost unanimously in 1861 saying that the Union government would take no actions against the institution of slavery. What the war was absolutely and incontrovertibly *not* about, said the wise men who wielded most of the power in Washington, was *freeing the slaves.* Thus "victory" in the war and reestablishment of the Union did not mean that slave owners in Alabama or North Carolina would lose either their property or their peculiar social and economic system. Victory meant returning to the status quo, a unified republic under a single federal government. "I have no purpose, directly or indirectly," Lincoln stated in his First Inaugural Address in March 1861, in case his constituents were still unclear about his intentions, "to interfere with the institution of slavery in the states where it exists. I believe I have no right to do so, and I have no inclination to do so."

His position was pure political artifice, of course, a sort of dance through the rhetorical raindrops of the great sectional conflict that had been boiling for fifty years. He was playing to an electorate that included opponents of abolition in places such as New England as well as the residents of border slave states. He needed their support in his war effort, and he would not get it if he even hinted the war was really about abolishing slavery or saving black people so that they could flood Northern job markets with cheap labor.

This flag of convenience infuriated abolitionists, none more so than Lincoln's most visible critic on the subject of slavery, Frederick Douglass. Douglass was one of the most remarkable men of his era. He had escaped bondage in Maryland, moved north to Massachusetts, and made a career as an activist and author. His riveting speeches and the harrowing tales of his own life in two prewar autobiographies did much to change Northern perceptions of the institution of slavery. He was determined, above all, in the first two years of the war, to change Lincoln's mind, to force him to acknowledge publicly the reality Douglass saw: that the war must inevitably be a crusade against slavery.[34] To Douglass and other abolitionists, omitting slavery's abolition from the political equation of the war seemed impractical if not immoral. Douglass insisted that he had "a right to hold Abraham Lincoln sternly responsible for any disaster or failure attending the suppression of this rebellion." Horace Greeley, editor of the *New-York Daily Tribune,* wrote that Lincoln was "disastrously remiss in the discharge of [his] official and imperative duty."[35]

Lincoln abhorred slavery. But he was convinced that the issue could only be properly addressed — whether by compensated emancipation or gradual emancipation or by some far-fetched scheme such as shipping blacks back to Africa (an idea Lincoln loved) — by a pacified, unified, restored Union. Lincoln's reasoning was on display in a public letter to Greeley in which Lincoln demonstrated the sort of verbal acrobatics required to embrace the issue:

> My paramount object in this struggle is to save the Union, and is not either to save or to destroy slavery. If I could save the Union without freeing any slave I would do it, and if I could save the Union by freeing all the slaves then I would do it, and if I could save it by freeing some and leaving others alone I would also do that. What I do about slavery, and the colored race, I do because I believe it helps to save the Union.

Thus Lincoln's great pragmatism, his realpolitik. The subtext here was fully apparent to people of the time: any move to free slaves or to declare that the war was about abolishing slavery would instantly threaten the loyalty of the "border states." These were the deeply divided, politically explosive slave states that had not seceded: Maryland, Delaware, Kentucky, and Missouri. Lincoln considered them crucial to the Union victory. With their roads, railways, and rivers, the border states were critical as gateways to the deeper South. Their population of 2.6 million white people, half as many as in the entire eleven states of the Confederacy, constituted a deep military recruiting pool that could turn the tide of the war. And the industrial effects of border-state defection were potentially staggering. If Maryland and Delaware alone seceded, the Confederacy's manufacturing capacity would instantly double. Just how desperate Lincoln was to keep those states in the Union was evident when he suspended habeas corpus — the sacred American right of an arrested person to appear in court and be informed of the charges against him — in Maryland in the war's first year.

Nor had the Northern population in general yet come around to the idea. At the start of the war most of the people and the politicians in the North were not abolitionists. They were, as a whole, white supremacists who believed in the inalienable superiority of the white race and were profoundly uncomfortable, both economically and socially, with the idea of 4 million former slaves suddenly mixing with whites. They did not advocate universal emancipation. The majority of them did not believe that their fathers and brothers and sons were fighting and dying for the sole purpose of freeing blacks from bondage so they could compete with white people for jobs or, heaven forbid, marry them. The North came only slowly to even a partial enlightenment on the subject of race.

But abolitionism as a movement — based on the principle of immediate freedom for all slaves — had grown with astonishing speed, moving from the margins of politics, where it had resided before the war, to center stage. Abolitionists had once been seen by large sections of the population as fanatics and cranks. Now, in response to this horrifically bloody and expensive war, public opinion was undergoing a radical shift, goaded on by a constant stream of speeches and articles by Douglass and fellow abolitionists such as William Lloyd Garrison.[36]

Lincoln's resolve had thus been put to several tests.

The first came in August 1861, when Union general John C. Frémont placed the state of Missouri under martial law and unilaterally declared that the property and slaves of rebels would be confiscated and their slaves freed. Lincoln angrily revoked the order a week later, prompting screams of protest from the antislavery crowd. Eight months later, Union general David Hunter, commander of the coastal forces in South Carolina, Georgia, and Florida, announced that all slaves in those states were free. Lincoln slapped him down, too, and immediately rescinded the order. William Lloyd Garrison, a leading abolitionist, accused the president of "serious dereliction of duty" and suggested that though he was "six feet four inches high, he is only a dwarf in mind."[37] Nor was Lincoln interested in enforcing Congress's Confiscation Acts, laws that allowed Union seizure of rebel property and freed the slaves belonging to the Confederate army and to Confederate civil and military officials. Lincoln saw the acts as damaging the cause of union with conservatives and, most important, threatening the loyalty of his sacred border states. So he slow-walked the law's promulgation.[38] He wasn't ready to free anyone's slaves. Not yet. Douglass and other abolitionists howled in protest. A month after Lincoln had overruled Frémont, Douglass gave a blistering speech in Rochester, New York, entitled "The American Apocalypse," in which he criticized those politicians who, to unite the North, refused to support the total abolition of slavery.

But Lincoln was listening more closely than anyone imagined, and was changing his mind faster and more completely than almost anyone realized.

While dragging his feet on enforcing the Confiscation Acts and revoking General Hunter's orders, Lincoln was also busy working on the Emancipation Proclamation, a draft of which he delivered to his cabinet in the summer of 1862. He waited only for a victory on the battlefield to formally issue it. When the Union army finally managed to not lose a battle — at Antietam on September 17, 1862 (which it didn't actually win, either, but close was good enough) — Lincoln saw his opportunity.[39]

On September 22 he issued the proclamation, stating that unless the seceded states rejoined the Union by January 1, 1863, all slaves in those states would be "thenceforward and forever free." Lincoln would use his war powers to confiscate enemy property. Slaves in the loyal border states would thus be exempt from the order, an exception that showed how deeply the president was still in thrall to the tortured politics in those states, and one that appalled Douglass and other abolitionists, though they were pleased that Lincoln had at least freed the slaves of the Confederacy.

When the proclamation came into force in January, Lincoln added a single clarifying paragraph to the already revolutionary, nation-transforming text: "I further declare and make known that such persons [former slaves] of suitable condition, will be received into the armed service of the United States to garrison forts, positions, stations, and other places, and to man vessels of all sorts in said service."[40] Blacks had previously been allowed in the army; now they would be able to carry weapons and fight. This was not simply a moral imperative. Lincoln saw it as military necessity. He had to find employment for the five hundred thousand to seven hundred thousand escaped slaves who had sought shelter behind federal lines. He needed to deprive the Confederacy of manpower. In a looming war of attrition, he needed warm bodies at the front. Lincoln believed that black soldiers would win the war, and that is what he told General Grant. "I believe it is a resource which, if vigorously applied now, will soon close the contest," he wrote.[41]

Thus with a stroke of the pen Lincoln had transformed the war from a morally unanchored attempt to reunite a divided nation into a war for the freedom of the nation's 4 million slaves — *a war of black liberation.* Just as radically, he had asserted that an army of black men would be raised from the native soil and would become the instruments of their own deliverance. While the goal of universal abolition hung suspended in the fog of war, the first and most critical phase of Lincoln's emancipation campaign was actually *enlistment:* black men mustering in and putting on uniforms and learning how to march and shoot with their white counterparts. And with enlistment came, quite possibly, true social revolution. "Never since the world began was a better chance offered to a long enslaved and oppressed people," wrote Douglass. "Once let a black man get upon him the brass letters U. S.; let him get an eagle on his button and a musket on his shoulder, and bullets in his pocket, and there is no power on earth or under the earth which can deny that he has earned the right of citizenship in the United States." A black soldier in the army ranks was the best argument in the world against — as Confederate vice president Alexander Stephens put it — "the great truth that the negro is not equal to the white man, that slavery, subordination to the superior race, is his natural and normal condition."[42]

By the time of the Battle of Fort Pillow, black soldiers — both free men and former slaves — had fought in only a handful of engagements. Their experience of the war had been uniformly harsh. They suffered abuse at the hands of white officers: whippings and beatings reminiscent of their days as slaves. They were insulted by common soldiers, given atrocious medical care and discriminatory duties (such as digging latrines), and issued substandard and sometimes worthless weapons. They got nothing like the fair and equal treatment they had been promised.[43]

In the battles and engagements they fought in 1863 and 1864, at Port Hudson, Louisiana; Milliken's Bend, Louisiana; Fort Wagner, South Carolina; and Olustee, Florida, they generally fought bravely — the black regiments who made the doomed assault on Fort Wagner were legendary for their courage — but suffered staggeringly high mortality rates.

This was because rebels concentrated their fire on blacks, shot or bayoneted wounded black soldiers, executed black prisoners, and followed, for the most part, an unofficial Confederate policy of "no quarter for negroes." After the fight at Port Hudson, a war correspondent wrote that no black prisoners were found either in hospitals or in the town.[44] After the fight at Milliken's Bend, senior Confederate officers were furious that any black prisoners had been taken at all, calling it a "disagreeable dilemma."[45] The officers did not know what to do with them other than shoot them or reenslave them, and both of those invited retaliation. Many of the black soldiers who were captured were returned to slavery — even some who had never been slaves in the first place.* Southerners refused to grant them the rights they granted to white soldiers.

Fort Pillow was at once the Civil War's most lurid atrocity and the one that everybody knew about. The war had been far bloodier and more terrible than anyone could possibly have imagined. Men had had their brains and guts splattered across battlefields from Arkansas to Florida. But here was something new.

* The South's policies of reenslavement of escaped slaves extended to the Gettysburg campaign in 1863, during which as many as a thousand blacks were captured — many in Pennsylvania — to be returned to their owners. These captured men were not soldiers but suffered the same fate as many black men in arms.

The images that rocketed through newspapers in the North showed white rebel soldiers hacking wounded, surrendering black soldiers to pieces with sabers. They showed Southern soldiers in a fury killing the thing they had subjugated, the thing that was now rising up against them. There was something at once horrifying and futile about these acts, and perhaps this was the meaning of a war of black liberation. Black soldiers were changing the war's moral and physical logic. By the end of the war 180,000 black men would enlist in the Union army, of whom more than half were former slaves. They made up more than 10 percent of the entire Union army, enough indeed to change the balance of the war.

CHAPTER THREE:
ARMIES OF SPRING

ROBERT E. LEE: His Army of Northern Virginia was the closest thing to an invincible force in American history, but now faced the indomitable Ulysses S. Grant.

On May 2, 1864, General Robert E. Lee assembled his top generals at a signal station atop an elevated ridge known as Clark's Mountain. They arrived on horseback and stood in the bracing air, gazing out at the gently swelling lands of central Virginia. The place was lovely. Spring was exploding in a dozen shades of green. Eight hundred feet below them the Rapidan River shimmered in slanting sunlight. Beyond the river spread a flowered broad meadowland. At first glance one could believe that this expanse was still the old Piedmont, timeless and handsome and lazy, the way it had been before the ravening armies came.

Seen through field glasses, however, the illusion vanished. The banks of Rapidan were riven and scarred with fortifications. The fields in the valley were green, yes, but untended, weed choked, overgrown. Trees had systematically been chopped from the landscape for fuel and to build the thousand things an army needed, from huts to corduroy roads. Houses and fences and barns had vanished into company campfires. Crumbling chimneys and smashed-up cisterns were all that remained of many farms. Livestock had been slaughtered and consumed. The land had been plundered, wrecked, stripped bare.[1]

In place of the Currier-and-Ives Virginia now stood a military colossus containing more people than all but eight American cities and nearly twice the population of Washington, DC, a technological monstrosity that had consumed or overtaken almost everything one could see from the top of the mountain.* The Army of the Potomac, commanded by Grant's subordinate George G. Meade, the general who had won the Battle of Gettysburg, was the largest force ever assembled on the North American continent.

Its presence on the Rapidan was the reason Lee had gathered his commanders from the Army of Northern Virginia together that day, field glasses in hand. Clark's Mountain offered one of the best tactical vantage points of the war, a place from which the entirety of the enemy could be viewed at leisure, down to his latrines, telegraph lines, artillery parks, mule trains, and boxcars.[2] The encampment's conical white tents and log huts sprawled for miles along the river's northern bank, subsuming the towns of Brandy Station, Culpeper, and Stevensburg, while above them thousands of columns of smoke rose languidly into the sky.[3] The sheer scope of it all was jaw-dropping, even to men who were accustomed to managing large armies. To the

* According to the 1860 census, the population of Washington was 75,000. Grant's army contained 120,000 soldiers. The Union camp on the north side of the Rapidan would have included many people in addition to soldiers, from quartermaster and medical personnel to wagon drivers, sutlers, and escaped slaves.

west the rebel generals could see clearly the Union supply line — the curving black scar of the Orange and Alexandria Railroad — over which rolled seemingly endless supplies of fresh troops and supplies. To the east was the blur of deep green scrubland known as the Wilderness. The generals paid particular attention to this piece of the landscape. Almost exactly one year before it had been the scene of Robert E. Lee's greatest victory and one of the great tactical masterpieces in the history of warfare: the Battle of Chancellorsville.

Lee had long ago gotten used to the idea that he would always be outnumbered. But now he could see in agonizing detail the size of Grant's advantage. By his own estimate of the troops in both camps that day, the Union held a twenty-thousand-man edge.[4] He would soon revise that. In the looming fight he would field only 64,000 soldiers against the Army of the Potomac's 120,000. Grant would have all of the reinforcements he needed. Lee could expect few and would have to draw them from existing reserves. If Lee had not faced similar odds before and won, as he had at Fredericksburg and Chancellorsville, a casual observer might have said he had no chance at all.

Lee's own army lay on the steep, wooded riverbank below him. His men had been there all winter, barricaded into a fortress of earth and timber. Except for a brief and bungled Yankee attempt to cross the river in February, the rebels had mainly been staring at the federal pickets across the Rapidan, waiting for the rains to end and the war to start up again in earnest. Though these soldiers were separated by only a thin ribbon of water, they were in other ways worlds apart. The army in blue on the northern shore was the best-fed, best-trained, best-clothed, and best-equipped fighting force in the history of the world. It was supported by a rapidly industrializing nation with good credit and a ready supply of money. For its troops the preceding months had mostly been snug and happy. "This was the most cheerful winter we had passed in camp," recalled George T. Stevens, a surgeon with the 77th New York regiment. "One agreeable feature was the great number of ladies, wives of officers, who spent the winter with their husbands. On every fine day . . . [the] ladies might be seen riding about the camps and over the desolate fields, and their presence added greatly to the brilliancy of the frequent reviews."[5] The men ate a relatively balanced diet that included pork or beef, dried vegetables and dried apples, onions, potatoes, turnips, cabbage, and pickles, and even soft bread instead of the usual rock-hard biscuits known as hardtack. They had sugar. They had plenty of coffee.[6]

There was far less joy on the southern bank.

The men in butternut and gray were raggedly clothed and hopelessly shod and subsisted on a barely digestible mush of salt pork and cornmeal. Salt pork, composed mostly of pig fat, was heavily salted, often bluish in color, and generally issued with hair, dirt, and skin left on. Coffee was made from acorns, or worse. The rebels dreamed of Yankee coffee and exulted whenever they captured some. The Army of Northern Virginia had become the appendage of a failing nation, which was an apt description of the Confederacy in the spring of 1864. A Union naval blockade had choked off inflows of food, medicine, and manufactured products. Exports of cotton, the South's main source of revenue, had fallen by 95 percent. Shortages were acute. As the supplies of food and clothing and seed and farm tools and everything else dwindled, inflation ran wild. From October 1861 to March 1864, prices in the South had risen an average of 120 percent per year. A suit of clothes now cost seven hundred increasingly worthless Confederate dollars; a pair of shoes more than forty. In Richmond, people observed that, where once they took a purse full of money to the market and carried food home in a basket, they now carried in a basket of money and came out with a purse full of food.[7] The nation was as good as bankrupt, bled dry by a war it could not afford and by a war-ravaged economy that was producing a fraction of the goods it once made.[8] The soldiers felt all of this acutely, from their ragamuffin shoes to their dwindling rations, substandard tents, and, most worrisome of all, their impoverished families back home. These and other hardships accounted for the army's shockingly high rate of absenteeism: 10 percent of Lee's army was not there.[9] Some of these men were on "French leave" and might return. Many others had deserted for good.

In spite of all that — amazingly — morale in the Army of Northern Virginia was high. Many of the men had reenlisted. These gaunt, hollow-eyed rebels with sallow skin were, after all, the nearest thing in all of American history to an invincible army. They had dominated the first three years of the war in the east. They had won dramatic victories at First Bull Run, Seven Days, Cedar Mountain, Second Bull Run, Fredericksburg, and Chancellorsville. At Antietam they had fought a drawn battle against an enemy more than twice their size. Five times Union armies had moved toward the Confederate capital at Richmond, and five times Lee and his army had defeated them. He had humiliated and caused to be removed from command a succession of once-glorious Union generals: George McClellan, John Pope, Ambrose Burnside, and Joseph Hooker. (In late fall 1863, George Meade had failed to dislodge

71

Lee at the Battle of Mine Run, though he remained in command.) Gettysburg had been the lone defeat. But Lee and his army did not necessarily see it that way. They had not surrendered. The enemy had not even pursued them after the battle. In their minds *they* had been the ones who had carried the attack deep into the North; *they* had been the assaulting force; *they* had caused the numerically superior Union army to fight a desperate defensive battle it had come tantalizingly close to losing. Lee wrote to his wife the day after the battle, "We failed to drive the enemy from his position." As a matter of hard, objective fact, he was not wrong. His men adored him. "I am sure that there can never have been an army with more supreme confidence in its commander than [the Army of Northern Virginia] had in Gen. Lee," wrote rebel artillerist Edward Porter Alexander. "We looked forward to victory under him as to successive sunrises."[10]

All of which was cold comfort now. Standing atop Clark's Mountain, the handsome, graying, fifty-seven-year-old general could see not only what was in front of him. He could see beyond that to unseen armies in remote parts of Virginia that were also being marshaled against him, and to the immense troop movements that were about to begin whose intent was to place him in a box from which he could not escape and then to destroy him in place. Already, 165,000 Union soldiers assigned to do just that were in the Commonwealth of Virginia. Their purpose and whereabouts were closely held Union secrets, and only the federal high command knew them in detail. Just what Ulysses S. Grant, victor of Vicksburg and Chattanooga and savior of the Union, was going to do as chief of the federal armies was the talk of both nations.

Although Lee had no formal chief of intelligence and only two staff officers to help sort out strategic information, he was able, from his own observations and from reports of spies and scouts and accounts in the press, to piece together an astonishingly accurate picture of where Grant and his armies were going.[11] Since the Army of the Potomac could not attack Lee head-on, it would move by its left, Lee said, to the south and east. As he gazed out with his officers, he pointed to two downstream points on the Rapidan: Germanna Ford and Ely's Ford. The Yankees would cross there, he said. He had also figured out that a Union army would be moving up the James River, well south and east of Lee's present position, to threaten Richmond.[12] He even correctly guessed that another Union force would be attacking rebel armies to the west in Virginia, moving specifically against the Virginia and Tennessee Railroad. All this would happen as he said it would, and all of it would require his attention.

For now he had to worry about what was directly in front of him. Lee had been to Clark's Mountain many times in the past months to see what all those men and horses were doing on the far side of the river. Mostly they had been doing nothing in particular other than consuming and excreting gigantic amounts of food and forage. But that was changing. Activity in the camps was quickening. Just after midnight on the night of May 4, the Union army arose, shook off the last of its winter lethargy, and began its leftward march on the hard, dry roads, just as Lee had predicted. Men remembered the morning's march as one of those perfect moments that often preceded extreme carnage: the air was gentle and warm, the sky was filled with stars; around Stevensburg the roadsides were covered in violets.[13]

Dawn uncovered a spectacular sight: the largest army ever seen on the continent flowing southeast in a rolling sea of blue. The men came on steadily and massively in their divisions and brigades and regiments, their columns stretching for miles, winding down the gently sloping roads to the fords, and, when they got there, tramping loudly across the Rapidan on pontoon bridges at the rate of about three thousand men an hour, exactly where Lee said they would.[14] The movement of such an army seemed less a traditional march than a grand pageant. Tens of thousands of rifle barrels flashed like heliographs in the morning sun, regimental flags snapped, bugles sounded, drums beat the march. With the army were more than sixty thousand horses. Behind them came the army's enormous train, strung out for miles through the woods: 4,300 wagons, 835 ambulances, and a herd of cattle.[15]

The march went off flawlessly, prompting Meade's chief of staff, Andrew Humphreys, to boast, "It was a good day's work in such a country for so large an army, with its artillery and fighting trains, to march twenty miles, crossing a river bridge of its own making, without a single mishap, interruption, or delay." Grant thought the day a "great success."[16]

Still, something about the whole exercise was inescapably odd. Grant had believed that the movement of his army would likely be contested by the enemy. Men on the march were highly vulnerable, as was the army's supply train, which trailed behind it for miles like the tail of a dragon. But Lee had not even tried to stop them. So as the day waned and the army continued to push south of the Rapidan, the time had come to ask, What exactly was Robert E. Lee, perhaps the most aggressive and purely belligerent general in either army, planning to do?

■ ■ ■ ■

Whatever the answer was — Grant would not have to wait long to find out — Lee's actions would be driven by a single, concentrated idea. Though the war had defied all expectations of what was supposed to happen, or of how or when the end might come, by the spring of 1864 a single truth had loomed into view. Both sides acknowledged it, though they could agree on almost nothing else. The truth was that the outcome of all of this bloodshed, the final resolution, now hinged on a single event: *the November presidential election in the North.* The fate of both nations rested on the political fortunes of a single man. Americans had hoped in the past that the warring sides could sit down at a mahogany table somewhere and finally come to their senses and make peace. The war was too terrible and bloody and costly to continue, and for those reasons it would have to stop. Southerners in particular had hoped that the British or French or even the Russians might intervene diplomatically to broker an acceptable peace. Some believed the Union could be restored as it was before the war. Some believed that the peace would be made by two independent, sovereign nations, one slave, one free. Either way, the idea of peace, negotiated peace, seemed always to hang in the air like smoke over a battlefield.

In the end these were all illusions. Abraham Lincoln wasn't going along with any of them, and as long as he was in office, nothing else mattered. He had by then established two simple yet nation-defining requirements for peace talks: first, that there could be no consideration of anything less than a full union of American states; and second, that there could be no slavery in that union. As Fort Pillow had so cruelly illustrated, a line had been crossed. Politicians on both sides spun a good deal of blather around this, but if Confederate president Jefferson Davis and his Congress wanted to talk peace, it would have to be on those terms. Despite growing antiwar sentiment in the South, the men in power in the Confederate government were not in several lifetimes going to agree to Lincoln's stipulations.

So half a century of bitter political fighting had come down to an election, and the main goal of both armies along the Rapidan was to affect its outcome. If the Union won on the battlefield, Lincoln would be reelected, and if Lincoln was reelected, then the North's crushing superiority in money, men, and matériel would soon triumph in the war. The life of the Confederacy — the official one, anyway — would likely be measured in months. If the Union lost on the battlefield, Lincoln would lose at the polls, and the man who beat him would be a Democrat elected for the specific purpose of ending the war. Both sides saw it that way. In the war's new logic, deaths on the battlefield meant votes at Northern polling stations. "Every bullet we can send . . . is the best ballot that can be deposited against [Lincoln's] election," wrote the *Daily Constitutionalist* in Augusta, Georgia, on January 2, 1864. "The battlefields of 1864 will hold the polls of this momentous decision."[17]

Lincoln was in the deepest trouble of his political career. He believed that he would likely lose the coming election. His unpopularity — reflected in the rise of a vigorous antiwar, anti-Lincoln movement — was due in his critics' eyes to a litany of sins: his mismanagement of the war and his failure to win in spite of large expenditures of blood and money; his "despotic" abuse of power by suspending habeas corpus and imposing martial law in volatile border states and jailing political dissidents; and his irresponsible issuance of the Emancipation Proclamation, which had changed the war from a reasonable attempt to restore the union to a misguided exercise in universal black liberation. The latter was for many citizens of the North the most egregious error of all, as antiwar Copperhead Democrats were happy to remind them. "Let every vote count in favor of the *white* man," one Ohio Democrat thundered in the *Dayton Daily Empire,* "and against the abolition hordes who would place negro children in your schools, negro jurors in your jury boxes, and negro votes in your ballot boxes!"[18] But Northerners did not have to be racist to be heartily sick of the war. Lincoln was not wrong about his waning political fortunes. He was fading fast.

Thus as Ulysses S. Grant's enormous army moved out on the early morning of May 4, all bets were on the table. That same day he put virtually every Union soldier in Virginia in motion, a coordinated set of attacks that had no precedent in the war: he sent one army racing up the James River to threaten Richmond, another pushing south through the Shenandoah Valley to threaten Lee's supply lines; yet another in western Virginia was to hit critical infrastructure that included railroads, salt works, and lead mines. Grant believed that he had less than six months to defeat the South, and he was wasting no time.[19] Lee felt a similar urgency. Though he had no illusions that he could win the larger war, by defeating Grant now he might make it stop, and possibly on terms favorable to the Confederacy. So everything was at risk. There would be no more of the aimless drift that had characterized the early war: battles here and there to no particular end except holding or taking real estate, which turned out to be pointless exercises. The movement of all that glorious flashing steel on May 4 was the beginning of the finish fight. Grant versus Lee. The nation, which understood that, waited breathlessly to see what was going to happen. "These are fearfully critical, anxious days," wrote Union diarist George Templeton Strong. "The destinies of the continent for centuries depend in great measure on what is now being done."[20]

CHAPTER FOUR:
A WILDERNESS OF PAIN

ULYSSES S. GRANT: His men likened him to "Thor, the Hammerer" because of his relentlessly aggressive style of fighting.

The worst Union defeat of the Civil War had taken place at the Battle of Chancellorsville in May 1863. Robert E. Lee, with a brilliant assist from Thomas J. "Stonewall" Jackson, had soundly beaten a Union army twice Lee's size under the command of Major General Joseph Hooker. That enormous army had then retreated ignominiously across the Rappahannock River. Two principal lessons were to be learned from such a grand-scale humiliation. First, that Lee and Jackson were smarter, more resourceful, and more daring than any generals on the Union side. And second, that the Union had given away its advantages of size and firepower by allowing the battle to take place in the Wilderness, which was every soldier's idea of the worst place in the world to fight. That woodland, which spread twelve miles by six miles on the southern flanks of the Rapidan and Rappahannock Rivers, was less a forest than a trackless snarl of scrub oak, dwarf pine, cedar, hickory, thorns, and brambles. Brambles, especially. The landscape was a by-product of the local iron industry, which had cut down all of the original trees to make charcoal. In their place had sprung up this ugly, dense, swampy, second-growth brush.

By accident of history — for there is no other way to explain it — the route that Major General George G. Meade had now chosen across the Rapidan River fords led right through the heart of the Wilderness. (Grant had given Meade operational control over the army, at least for a while.) That was not because he wanted to fight a battle there. Fighting there was the last thing he wanted to do. What could be more foolish than a strategy that handed Robert E. Lee back his old advantages of terrain and took away the federal edge in artillery? Thus the idea in the spring of 1864 was to pass through the Wilderness as briskly as possible, then turn in a westerly direction out of the dense brush and into more open country. The objective was to flush Lee from behind his Rapidan earthworks. The plan, concocted by the cautious, temperamental George Meade and his staff, looked good on paper. The only conceivable risk was that the Army of Northern Virginia would ambush the Army of the Potomac in that suffocating thicket. But that could not possibly happen, Meade said. He and his staff knew with certainty that Lee could never move quickly enough to pull off such a maneuver.

That calculation was one of the most fatuous, ill-advised, and costly command errors of the Civil War. Thousands of men would die for it. The Battle of the Wilderness, as it came to be called, turned on it. Something about that tangled woodland, with its unmapped thickets and tortured byways, impaired the judgment of Union commanders.[1]

Lee had seen the Union army moving at an early hour. He had decided that, instead of contesting the river crossing, he would flood the countryside with cavalry, which would tell him where the enemy was and where it was going. By 10:00 a.m. on May 4, he knew that the main body of the Army of the Potomac was headed for the heart of the Wilderness. Lee decided that Grant and Meade had made a serious mistake. He threw his 2nd and 3rd Corps under lieutenant generals Richard S. Ewell and A. P. Hill on the road, heading due east and directly into the guts of Meade's army. Lee's plan was to intercept that army as quickly as possible and pin it in the Wilderness — engaging it but not bringing on a full-scale fight — until his 1st Corps under Lieutenant General James Longstreet arrived to deliver a hammer blow to the Union left. This plan had two problems: first, Lee's troops had gotten a late start and might not arrive in time to catch the Union soldiers in the woods; and second, Lee would have only about a third of his opponent's force with which to hold the enemy in place. But the tactical conceit was breathtaking. If the maneuver succeeded, Lee stood a good chance of rolling up the Union flank just as Stonewall Jackson had done a year before. (Jackson had died from wound-related pneumonia after Chancellorsville.) Like many of Lee's maneuvers, it involved enormous risk.

Meade and Grant were, meanwhile, making a succession of mistakes that Lee would see, grasp, and quickly move to exploit. Having assumed that Lee would not try to hit him in the Wilderness, Meade had then compounded that error by dispatching most of his cavalry — the eyes and ears of the army — on a pointless mission to the east chasing phantom rebels, leaving a scant thirty-five hundred mounted men under an inexperienced commander to cover a ten-mile front.[2] They were not equal to the task. As a result, the Union high command had no idea where most of the rebel army was. Somewhere to the west, they supposed, well out of range.

But that mistake paled in comparison to the one Meade made, with the acquiescence of Grant, in midafternoon. With Lee's army running dead at them, the Union high command made the astonishing decision to order the army to stop marching and make camp — *in the middle of the Wilderness.* The reason was to let the army's supply train catch up, a consideration that, by comparison, had never slowed Stonewall Jackson's victorious armies or hampered Grant in his Vicksburg campaign. But now it stopped Grant's entire spring offensive. Supply-line obsession was just ingrained Union caution and timidity, the old habit from the McClellan days of worrying compulsively about all the things that could possibly go wrong. Like so many Union generals before him, offense unnerved Meade, and in any case he was convinced that Lee's army was still a long way off, digging in behind earthworks. So Meade's hard-marching divisions were allowed to make camp and build fires and eat dinner in the balmy spring air.

While the Union soldiers relaxed and sipped coffee, Lee's corps commanders were pushing their troops hard down two narrow, east-west running roads that pierced the Wilderness, the Orange Turnpike and the Orange Plank Road. The next day Union troops were astounded to find large numbers of rebels in front of them. As the armies prepared to fight, the advantages of Lee's chosen terrain became immediately apparent. Though Meade's army had twice as many soldiers, his division commanders had a brutally difficult time bringing their men forward for combat or moving them into place. One division required more than four hours to cover a mile of ground. Once a brigade of men had been brought up, officers found it nearly impossible to form them into coherent battle lines or to link them with other brigades. At 7:15 a.m. Meade ordered his 5th Corps under Major General Gouverneur Warren — twenty-four thousand men — to charge Ewell's force on the Orange Turnpike. But Warren required more than five hours to get his men into line and even then did not feel prepared to attack. When he did move, it was with only part of the force that should have been available to him, and he did so reluctantly and without the benefit of Union artillery, which was virtually useless because the density of the woods greatly limited the deployment of guns and also made it often impossible for gunners to see what they were shooting at. Thus many of the nominally huge Union advantages were nullified.

The fighting was horrific in the extreme and desperate in a way that shocked even veterans. It was like fighting in darkness, or a darkness pierced by thousands of pieces of flying lead. The men could not see each other, except at close range. Whole regiments were swallowed by the thickets; soldiers in the same army found themselves shooting at one another. Men hacked and scraped their way forward, or whichever way seemed like forward, through thorn-filled swamps and gullies, groping for the precise position of the invisible enemy while bullets ripped through the trees and bushes and everyone around them. The firing was so intense that small trees were cut down, most of them at the murderous height of three to five feet. Much of the fighting was at close quarters, which was the only way you could see the enemy anyway.

To the usual horrors of spurting blood, spilling intestines, and exploding heads was now added a less familiar one: fire. First breastworks, then woodlands, then fields, were aflame, engulfing the wounded, who screamed for help that rarely came and tried to claw and drag themselves out of the inferno. Many were roasted alive. Many men suffocated, and one couldn't tell, from the charred corpses, who had been roasted and who had died sucking air.[3] Fire did something else, too: it blew up the cartridge belts the men carried at their waists. The individual cartridges — powder and bullets in a soft wrapping — made rapid, high-pitched popping sounds when they went off and caused appalling wounds, ripping men's bellies open. Many soldiers preferred suicide to being burned to death or perforated by their own detonating cartridges. They had only to listen to the screams of men being roasted alive to see what lay ahead of them. "I saw one man, both of whose legs were broken," wrote one soldier, "lying on the ground with his cocked rifle by his side and his ramrod in his hand, and his eyes set on the front. I knew he meant to kill himself in case of fire."[4] Observed Grant's aide Horace Porter, "It seemed as though Christian men had turned to fiends, and hell itself had usurped the place of earth."[5]

A change in the soldiers' behavior had also made the fight far more lethal. Entrenchments had become common in the war. In the first two years they had been used mainly when armies were protecting fixed locations.

Later armies built fortifications of wood and dirt when they were on active campaign. But in the Wilderness, and in the series of battles that followed it, the practice of digging in during battle became the rule rather than the exception, and the men quickly refined it to an art. They were like fiddler crabs: whenever they stopped somewhere for more than a few moments, they started digging. Later photographs of Saunders' Field, one of the few cleared areas on the Orange Turnpike, show that Ewell's breastworks had rifle pits two feet deep fronted by stacked, mud-chinked logs as much as five feet high.[6] The works went up quickly, too. "Within one hour there is a shelter against bullets, high enough to cover a man kneeling," wrote one of Meade's staff in a letter home. ". . . When our line advances, there is the line of the enemy, nothing showing but the bayonets, and the battle flags stuck on top of the works."[7]

The result of the first day of fighting was a rout of the federals around the Orange Turnpike in the morning and, ultimately, a tactical victory for Richard Ewell's 2nd Corps. To the south, where the terrain worked equally well in Lee's favor, the Union army fared only slightly better. In the afternoon, thirty-three thousand Union soldiers under Major General Winfield S. Hancock, one of the heroes of Gettysburg, attacked A. P. Hill's sixty-five hundred rebels and failed completely to dislodge them. By 6:00 p.m. on May 5 the battles on both roads were temporarily suspended. The Wilderness that paralyzed the Union had also prevented the Confederacy from winning a dominant victory. Men on both sides collapsed in place and in silence.

The second day saw more of the same furious, close-range fighting along the two roads, the same high levels of casualties, the same fire that swept through woods and field, the same terrifying inability to tell friend from foe. Attacks and counterattacks continued, as the two armies pushed each other up and down the battlefield. Ironically, after being too cautious in the early going, Meade and Grant were too impatient later on: they repeatedly ordered their forces to attack before they were ready, before they had gathered sufficient numbers of men. The battle on the second day was memorable for two brilliant Confederate flank attacks. The first was the one in Lee's battle plan: after Hill had succeeded in pinning the Union army in place, James Longstreet's 1st Corps made a stunning run around the left of the Union 2nd Corps using an old railroad cut, rolling up the left wing of the army and nearly ending the battle right there. But in the Wilderness it was hard to press an advantage. Longstreet was severely wounded by friendly fire in the neck and shoulder — eerily reminiscent of Stonewall Jackson's fate a year earlier — and the offensive ran out of steam. A few hours later, another successful rebel flank attack a few miles north along the Orange Turnpike that had smashed the Union right to pieces and thrown a massive scare through the high command had collapsed, too, when it had run into impenetrable breastworks.

When the smoke finally cleared and the bodies were counted, the magnitude of the Confederate victory became apparent. Though Lee had by no means destroyed the Army of the Potomac as a fighting unit, and he had done little more than stop Grant's grand offensive in its tracks, he had dealt Grant a blow that, measured strictly by casualties, was even worse than the damage the rebel general had inflicted at Chancellorsville. In that battle, Union casualties were fourteen thousand (killed, wounded, missing) over three days, compared to the South's ten thousand. In two days in the Wilderness the Union had lost nearly eighteen thousand to Lee's eleven thousand. Which meant that, numerically speaking, the Union setback was the worst of the war to date. Lee's victory was strictly tactical: the armies ended the fight roughly in the same positions they had occupied at its start. But Grant had been stopped cold. His men had been slaughtered by the thousands.

Grant, in typical fashion, chose not to see it that way. Though his grand offensive had stalled and collapsed, he insisted that this was nothing more than a drawn battle in which Lee had failed to do what he set out to do. Grant observed blandly to his staff that the day "had not been much of a test of strength. . . . I feel pretty well satisfied with the result of the engagement, for it is evident that Lee attempted by a bold movement to strike this army in flank before it could be put into line of battle . . . but in this he has failed."

This was the famously imperturbable Grant, taking what seemed like terrible news and shrugging it off. But on the second day the almost unbearable tension, as he waited for news of what had happened, began to show. He had smoked more than twenty cigars, which was a great deal of smoking even for him. He had nervously whittled his way through countless sticks, which was also a habit with him. But in this case he was so distracted that he had also managed to whittle away most of the fancy "thread" gloves his wife had given him. After the Union flank was turned north of the turnpike in early evening, and courier after courier arrived with news of a Union collapse, one panicked officer approached Grant to tell him that Lee "will throw his own army between us and Rapidan and cut us off completely from our communication." Grant removed the cigar from his mouth and in an uncharacteristically loud and obviously perturbed voice said, "Oh, I am heartily tired of hearing what Lee is going to do. Some of you seem to think he is suddenly going to turn a double somersault and land in our rear and on both of our flanks at the same time. Go back to your command, and try to think what we are going to do ourselves, instead of what Lee is going to do."[8]

Any doubt that Grant was upset was laid to rest later that evening. While acknowledging that Grant had met the bad news "outwardly with calmness and self-possession," one of his aides also described how Grant "withdrew to his tent, and, throwing himself face downward on his cot, gave vent to his feelings in a way which left no room to doubt that he was deeply moved." Which sounds very much like screaming into his pillow. The aide added that Grant "made no effort to conceal from them the gravity of the danger by which the army was being threatened."[9]

Grant then did something that, in a long and bloody and complicated war, no one had yet seen a Union commander in the eastern theater do. History would record it as a turning point in the war and one of the most important moments in Grant's life. To understand what he did, and how he was able to do it, one must understand something of his past.

A Union general once compared Ulysses S. Grant to "Thor, the Hammerer," which was as good a description as any of the man who had suddenly assumed such outsize importance in the Civil War.[10] Hammering was what he did. He came directly at you and smashed into you again and again until you were beaten, then persisted beyond that to the nonexistent terms of your surrender. He had a doggedness that had been absent in all of the previous top Union generals, something flat and implacable and emotionless and, if you were his enemy, downright frightening. He sat in his camp chain-smoking and whittling, holding no councils of war and posting no pins on maps, fighting the war in his head, accepting victories as nothing to get terribly excited about and brushing off grave setbacks as though he had expected them to happen. He hated defensive fighting. His main approach was to punch the enemy in the gut and then afterward worry about what the enemy had been planning to do to him. He was more than simply a blunt instrument, of course. His maneuvers in the Vicksburg campaign, for example — from running the rebel artillery gauntlet on the Mississippi to cutting loose from his supply lines to his looping, indirect assault on the city — were among the most daring and intricate of the war. Still, the effect on his unfortunate adversary was mainly produced by hammering — river strikes and bayou strikes and railroad strikes and rearward strikes and finally the lengthy, pounding siege. He did not stop, and he would not be deterred.

This was the Grant that Abraham Lincoln saw, the one he had promoted to lieutenant general and upon whom he had placed the burden of winning the war. The actual Grant was far more complicated, with a past that, when everything was added together — all of the bad and good and indifferent — amounted to little more than a handful of dust. There was no figuring it. The man who hammered had appeared as if by divine intervention from behind a humble clerk's desk at a leather-goods shop in Galena, Illinois, at the start of the war at the precise moment in history when his country needed him, then had spun transcendent success from abject failure. How he did that was anyone's guess.

He had been a mediocre student at the US Military Academy at West Point, though he was exceptional in two subjects: mathematics and riding. He understood math well enough to teach it. He was one of the best riders his classmates had ever seen. (He had learned to ride long before he had learned to read and by the age of twelve was an accomplished horse trainer.) He was otherwise shy and inconspicuous, having drawn from his loud-mouthed, pushy, self-advancing father the lesson that the most prudent action was to sit in the back row and keep his mouth shut. He did not like calling attention to himself. After graduation Grant served with minor distinction in the Mexican-American War. This can be seen as the high point of his pre–Civil War life. At least nothing had gone horribly wrong.

All that would soon change. After the war he had remained in the army, serving in several posts in the Midwest and New York State, then at Fort Vancouver, in what is now Washington, and later to Fort Humboldt, in Northern California. Since his military duties as quartermaster were relatively minimal, he spent most of his free time thinking up and then putting into play a series of business ventures. In 1852, he was living in the Gold Rush–era West, where it seemed that everyone and his cousin were getting rich and he was certain, as he breathlessly wrote his wife, Julia, back East, that he was going to get rich, too. Just three principal obstacles had to be overcome: he had terrible ideas, abominable luck, and a credulous, trusting personality that was easily duped.

The result was a remarkably consistent string of failures. He invested in a store in San Francisco, then was tricked into trading his equity for an unsecured note by the store's manager, who sold out and departed, taking Grant's $1,500 investment with him. Grant bought hogs and cattle in the fall to sell in the spring, the prices fell, and he lost money. He had heard that people in San Francisco were paying a premium for ice, so he financed an ice shipment from the Northwest. The ship was delayed at sea, the ice melted, and he lost his investment. He tried the same sort of arbitrage with chickens, but this time the chickens died during the voyage. With two of his fellow army officers, he grew potatoes and onions for market and cut timber to sell to steamboats. All three commodities were wiped out when the Columbia River flooded. He and several partners opened a social club and billiard room in San Francisco, losing their entire investment when the agent absconded with it. Observed one of his business associates, "Neither Grant nor myself had the slightest suggestion of business talent. He was the perfect soul of honor and truth, and believed everyone as artless as himself."

But he had still not hit bottom. After the failure of his projects, he found himself marooned in a lonely army fort in a redwood forest on a remote California coast. Bored, lonely, and miserable, missing his wife and family, who had stayed in St. Louis, he began to drink. The US army in those days was awash in liquor. Officers not only drank but drank hard. The more remote the fort, the harder the men tended to drink. In modern terms, it would have been hard to tell the alcoholics from the men who just liked to drink all the time.

Unfortunately, at five feet seven inches tall and 135 pounds, Grant had little tolerance for alcohol. While a couple of drinks might render a normal man happy and garrulous, they transformed Grant from a quiet, self-possessed young man to a speech-slurring, sloppy drunk. For this reason he drank considerably less often than everyone else. But when he did drink — little binges here and there — everyone remembered it. In 1853 he began to drink more than usual, and this started to interfere with his work. When he was visibly drunk at a pay call one day, his commanding officer gave him the choice of resigning or facing a court-martial. Because he could not bear admitting to his wife that he had been brought up on such charges, he left the army.[11]

There was still room to fall. When he returned to his wife and family in St. Louis, he was nearly penniless. He was forced to borrow money from his domineering father. For the next seven years, right up to the brink of the Civil War, his setbacks would become more dramatic. He continued to lose money, at farming now, sometimes because of weather, sometimes because market prices collapsed. He begged, unsuccessfully, for jobs from old army acquaintances. Several times he was reduced to selling firewood on the streets of St. Louis. Army and West Point friends who saw the gaunt, shabbily dressed Captain Grant hawking logs were amazed at what had become of him. A fellow officer who had not seen him since the Mexican-American War, cried, "Great God, Grant! What are you doing?" To which he responded, "Solving the problem of poverty."[12] He tried working as a bill collector, loan negotiator, and real estate salesman in a small firm with his nephew. He had no talent for any of those businesses, either. He was forced to close the company.

A story from this dark period of his life illuminates the man and his troubles. In 1858 a group of army officers were camped at the Planters' Hotel in St. Louis playing brag, a popular card game of the era. They needed another player and somehow dredged up Captain Ulysses S. Grant. One of the players was Major James Longstreet, a Georgian who had been one of Grant's best friends at West Point and a member of his wedding party.[13] Grant had married Longstreet's cousin. The two men were happy to see each other, though Longstreet was upset to see that "Grant had been unfortunate, and . . . was really in needy circumstances."[14]

The following day Longstreet was walking

outside the hotel when he encountered his old army friend again. As he later described it:

I found myself face to face again with Grant who, placing in the palm of my hand a five dollar gold piece, insisted that I should take it in payment of a debt of honor over fifteen years old. I peremptorily declined to take it, alleging that he was out of the service and more in need of it than I.

"You must take it," said he. "I cannot live with anything in my possession which is not mine." Seeing the determination in the man's face, and in order to save him mortification, I took the money, and shaking hands we parted.[15]

This was pure Grant: honest and steadfast and honorable in the face of hardship. To Longstreet — who in May 1864 faced Grant as Robert E. Lee's principal lieutenant in the Army of Northern Virginia — Grant's behavior was fully in keeping with the man he knew. But such integrity didn't help Grant in the slightest. His luck only got worse. By 1859, sixteen years after his graduation from West Point, his prospects for success in commercial life were approaching zero. He was forced to do what he had sworn he would not do: go to work for his overbearing father in the leather-tannery business. He accepted

100

a humble clerkship in Galena, working for modest wages under the supervision of his two younger brothers. There, at the age of thirty-eight, the Civil War found him.

Grant is the most famous success story of the war, the man who failed and failed and failed again, then suddenly succeeded beyond anyone's wildest expectations. What is missing in this conventional view is the man's extraordinary resilience through the bad times, his stubborn ability to weather harrowing and relentless adversity. Longstreet's account is only one example. What stands out in his life are less the defeats than his ability to endure them, less his perpetually declining prospects than his refusal to allow his losses to become shattering moral defeats. After each setback he shouldered resolutely into whatever the next bad idea was. Because he was a smart and resourceful man with a first-rate mind and a keen ability to parse the world around him — no one can doubt this now — Grant must have wondered how he fared so poorly when so many of his West Point and army fellows were succeeding.

But he did not give up. And he did not turn to drink, either, at least not regularly, and not during the worst of his travails after the army. Drink would have been the easiest refuge. Where other men would have understood that they were beaten, Grant somehow concluded that he still had a chance. He was right. It just took twenty years for that to happen. "He was incapable of any attempt to deceive anybody except for a legitimate purpose, as in military strategy," wrote Union general and later secretary of war John M. Schofield. "And above all, he was incapable of deceiving himself."[16] Which meant that he saw clearly what was taking place. Mainly, though, he understood that, no matter what was happening to him, it was the way he thought about it that mattered.

So, too, with the Battle of the Wilderness. In the hours after the final Confederate assaults on the battle's second day, an unnerving calm had settled over the battlefields. "The impressive feature of that memorable night was the silence that succeeded the din of battle," recalled Confederate general John B. Gordon. As the two great armies "rested in hailing distance of each other," the silence was broken only by "the low moans of the wounded, and their calls for help, as the ambulance corps administered to blue and gray alike."[17]

In the Union lines the men had that familiar and disheartening feeling that they were about to turn tail and head back north, or, as the soldiers had it, "skedaddle." "Most of us thought it would be another Chancellorsville," said one Massachusetts soldier, "and that the next day we should recross the

102

river."[18] The enormous number of Union casualties was dreary proof that the new commander had fared no better against Lee than his predecessors. "I do not see that Grant does anything but sit quietly about, whittle, and let [his aide John Rawlins] talk big," wrote Union general Marsena Patrick of his new boss.[19]

Then something happened that instantly changed what the troops thought of themselves, the battle, and even of the war itself. That evening, as the men of Major General Winfield Scott Hancock's 2nd Corps waited behind their earthworks for orders to move, they saw a cluster of horsemen approaching at a trot, fronted, on a powerful horse, by a small, stoop-shouldered man wearing a regulation army hat, plain shirt, and muddy cavalry boots.[20] As the group passed, the soldiers recognized General Grant and his staff. In the same moment they also came to the thundering realization that these riders were heading *south.* South! Toward Richmond. And this changed everything. There had been no defeat after all, just the opening round in the great fight to end the war. This was Grant's way of thinking, and troops by the thousands instantly embraced it. Suddenly every soldier was on his feet, rushing forward, and cheering wildly. They swung their hats and set pine knots and leaves on fire to light Grant's way.[21] Here, finally, was purpose and direction and courage, too, instilled by a man who in his life had steadfastly refused to acknowledge defeat. These feelings swept through the rest of the army like the wildfires that had incinerated their friends. Among them were the black soldiers of the US 9th Corps, who were just as happy as everyone else. As they marched toward the capital of the Confederacy, a burly sergeant prodded the men with the butt of his rifle, saying, "Close up dere, lambs."[22]

They were all going south, to the end of the war.

CHAPTER FIVE:
SHOVELS AND OTHER WEAPONS OF WAR

GEORGE G. MEADE: The Union general who had won at Gettysburg found himself reduced to being Grant's errand boy.

The Battle of Spotsylvania Court House was all about digging.

It involved shooting, too, and men marching and countermarching and attacking each other and the usual abundance of death and suffering. But the battle was about digging first, and the digging determined almost everything that happened. Men had dug holes for protection before — from the dawn of humankind — and they had dug holes in this war, too, most recently in the Wilderness. But not like this. Here what they did changed the outcome of the battle they fought, and the very nature of warfare.[1] Though no battle had turned primarily on fieldworks before Spotsylvania, every major battle that followed, well into the twentieth century, would look like a version of that battle, with honeycombed trenches running to the horizon, and generals calculating, ever more helplessly, how to overrun them. Tactical warfare, which had once embraced grand and sweeping maneuvers in open country, envelopments, and daring flank attacks, was quickly being reduced to prying soldiers from behind thick, artillery-proof fortifications.

But before the men could dig, they had to march.

The successor fight to the Wilderness began as a footrace between two large armies. The distance was ten miles. Grant started out with all the advantages. He knew where he was going, for one thing — though Lee quickly grasped that his opponent's destination was the unremarkable crossroads of Spotsylvania Court House — and his army was closer than Lee's to its destination.[2] If Grant won, his army would be positioned squarely between Lee and Richmond. Lee would then either be forced into a headlong retreat toward the Confederate capital or to attack in the open country where Grant's advantages in numbers and firepower could be brought to bear. The federal high command did not think that Lee could possibly beat them. This was the same group that had been absolutely convinced that Lee could not pin them in the Wilderness.

They lost the race.

They did not lose by much, but close did not count, and the margin of rebel victory was enough to allow Lee's cavalry, and soon enough his infantry, to hold the field. The Union troops followed their botched march — one of their generals said it was the most disgraceful he had ever seen — with a poorly coordinated series of infantry attacks that failed again to put their army between Lee and Richmond. Though they outnumbered the Confederates two to one, as usual they brought only pieces of their huge force to bear.

All of which allowed Robert E. Lee time to lay out his defenses, and this interval changed everything. He ran his lines west to east in a six-mile-long crescent that blocked the approaches to the Spotsylvania crossroads, and thus to roads leading to Richmond. Then he gave orders to entrench.[3] His troops, exhausted from their overnight march, nevertheless needed no prodding to build works that would shield them from bullets and shells. They dug furiously and with astonishing speed and reminded more than one observer of beavers. Trees were felled and stacked lengthwise. Ditches were dug and the dirt thrown on top of the timber. Wooden or stone revetments were built to hold the dirt in place. The works were typically chest high and four to six feet wide.[4] To crown their parapets, soldiers put in place head logs, anchored on both ends, creating an opening three to four inches wide through which they could fire while protecting their heads. They piled brush and sharpened limbs in front of the entrenchments. Any trees left in front of the works were chopped down to open a clear field of fire.[5]

A little to the north, the Yankees, nominally the aggressors, were doing exactly the same thing, digging in just as industriously along lines laid out by engineers, erecting a mirror image of the six-mile fortified wall of the Confederates. They, too, were happy to forgo sleep to build defenses that might prevent their faces, arms, and scrotums from being blown off. This was the first instance in the war that two armies, facing each other in the

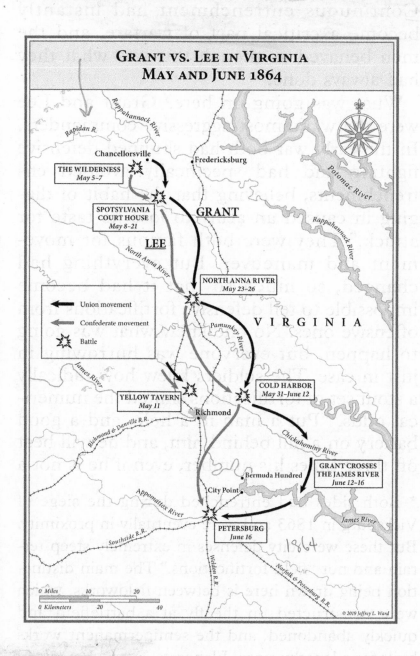

GRANT VS. LEE IN VIRGINIA
MAY AND JUNE 1864

Rapidan R.

Rappahannock River

Chancellorsville

THE WILDERNESS
May 5–7

Fredericksburg

Potomac River

Rappahannock River

SPOTSYLVANIA COURT HOUSE
May 8–21

GRANT

LEE

North Anna River

NORTH ANNA RIVER
May 23–26

Pamunkey River

VIRGINIA

→ Union movement
→ Confederate movement
✸ Battle

James River

YELLOW TAVERN
May 11

Richmond

Richmond & Danville R.R.

COLD HARBOR
May 31–June 12

Chickahominy River

Bermuda Hundred

City Point

GRANT CROSSES THE JAMES RIVER
June 12–16

James River

Appomattox River

Southside R.R.

PETERSBURG
June 16

1864

Weldon R.R.

Norfolk & Petersburg R.R.

| 0 Miles | 10 | 20 |
| 0 Kilometers | 20 | 40 |

© 2019 Jeffrey L. Ward

field at close range, had done such a thing.* Continuous entrenchment had instantly become a critical part of warfare, and the men behaved as though this was what they had always done.

What was going on here? Grant and Lee were the war's most aggressive commanders. In the early war both had shunned defensive fighting and had specifically avoided entrenchments, believing that the habit of digging in caused an army to lose its taste for attack.[6] They were both famous for movement and maneuver. But everything had changed, so much so that it had become impossible to tell defensive fortifications from offensive ones. No one knew what was going to happen, but everyone was burrowing in just in case. The soldiers knew how radically a stout set of fortifications shifted the numerical odds. "Put a man in a hole, and a good battery on a hill behind him, and he will beat off three times his number, even if he is not a

* Both sides had entrenched during the siege of Vicksburg in 1863 and were eventually in proximity. But these were city defenses in extremely steep terrain and not "field fortifications." The main distinction being drawn here is between fieldworks, which were constructed on the fly at a battlefield and quickly abandoned, and the semipermanent works built for a lengthy siege. Elaborate entrenchments in siege warfare were not new.

very good soldier," wrote Meade's aide-de-camp Theodore Lyman.[7]

But tactical advantages did not fully explain the soldiers' manic eagerness to dig. The Battle of the Wilderness had been a particularly horrifying demonstration of the randomness of death. Men lying in semidarkness in a dense wood where nothing could be clearly seen or even heard had seemingly surrendered all control of their lives and destinies to all that lead and iron flying around them. This was deeply unsettling, especially since many of them were religious and saw what happened in the world as the manifestation of the Lord's will. Some believed in a fully deterministic universe in which *everything* happened according to God's plan. Prominent Presbyterian theologian — and Stonewall Jackson's onetime chief of staff — Robert Lewis Dabney offered this remarkable statement of his faith: "Even when the thousand missiles of death, invisible to mortal sight, and sent forth aimless by those who launched them, shoot in inexplicable confusion over the battle-field, His eye gives each one an aim and a purpose according to the plan of His wisdom."[8]

The idea that God directed every bullet was troubling in a war where both combatants were convinced that he was on their side. What did it mean, then, when someone's eighteen-year-old son's head was taken off by a cannonball? Was that an affirmation of faith, or its opposite? Why, if he was fighting on God's side, did God want him decapitated? And why did God's divine plan look like pure chaos? The idea was theologically complex and even prompted a battlefield joke at the Reverend Dabney's expense. At the Battle of Malvern Hill, Jackson's staff had come under fire, prompting Dabney to take refuge behind a gatepost. Later a staff officer approached him and exclaimed, "Why, Dr. Dabney, if the God of battles directs every shot, why do you want to put a gatepost between you and a special providence?" Dabney's riposte: "Why, just here the gatepost is the special providence."[9]

Though nothing was going to stop death and injury or its haphazard distribution across a field of combat, a fortified trench offered the men a way to reduce what had become to many of them an insane degree of chance. Those who believed, like Dabney, that God was directing all of those pieces of airborne death perhaps did not need fortifications. But any sinner — and certainly more than a few of them were among the assembled troops — or anyone who doubted that God was fully on his side, or anyone drawn to the easy nihilism of the battlefield, might be tempted to get a little help. A six-foot-thick mound of earth reinforced by twelve-inch-wide logs and impervious to artillery looked very much like help.

What mainly drove the new mania for entrenchment was the commanding generals' conclusion that it was a good idea. By the spring of 1864 there was simply too much evidence showing what happened to men when they made frontal assaults against fortified positions. But the top brass on both sides had come to this consensus only gradually. As early as June 1862, Union forces under George McClellan had built strong defensive works on the banks of Beaver Dam Creek, just east of Richmond, and the eleven thousand rebels who foolishly attacked them had been torn to pieces. A few days later Union soldiers firing from behind fieldworks at Gaines' Mill had once again inflicted terrible damage. But instead of setting the pattern for future battles, generals on both sides took the reverse lesson. Since McClellan ended up losing the Seven Days Battles to Lee — who had not entrenched — fortifications were seen as either dispensable or possibly not even a good idea. Neither side had entrenched at the Second Battle of Bull Run, though Stonewall Jackson, whose troops fought from behind an unfinished railroad cut, had the perfect opportunity.[10] Lee had not fortified at Antietam, even though he had plenty of time, had his back to the Potomac River, and had fought an almost purely defensive battle.

But military opinion was changing. At the Battle of Chancellorsville in May 1863, Union general Joseph Hooker had built the strongest field fortifications in American history, which reflected a major shift in tactical thinking. Though he had lost the battle — Jackson, in the war's most famous flank march, simply went around the fieldworks — everyone knew they were all but unassailable from a frontal attack. (Indeed, Hooker may have made his works *too* strong. The idea of field fortifications — as opposed to city defenses — was to induce your opponent to attack them head-on.)[11] Gettysburg, in the summer of 1863, had seen moderate and effective use of trenches and breastworks by both sides. In the western theater, men had dug in at Stones River and Chickamauga. At the Battle of Fredericksburg, Lee had watched wave after wave of blue-clad soldiers slaughtered in front of General James Longstreet's trenches. In the Battle of the Wilderness, A. P. Hill's Confederate 3rd Corps offered object lessons to both sides: they first suffered huge losses after failing to entrench, then suffered huge losses later when they attacked a fortified Union position.[12]

Now Lee's army had been given plenty of time to build smartly engineered trenches. "It is a rule," wrote Meade's aide Theodore Lyman, "that when the rebels halt, the first day gives them a good rifle pit; the second, a regular infantry parapet with artillery in position; and the third, a parapet with an abatis in front and entrenched batteries behind." The evolving wisdom was even more gloomy. The officers and men of the Army of the Potomac had begun to believe and would soon be completely convinced that, in the words of one of their generals, "when the enemy had occupied a position six or eight hours ahead of us, it was useless to attempt to take it."[13]

Which changed the rules of combat.

Major General Gouverneur Kemble Warren, a man with a wonderfully elaborate name, was at thirty-four the youngest corps commander in the Army of the Potomac. He was considered by many who knew him to be a horse's ass. Of course that was not what his curriculum vitae said. He had been a brilliant student at West Point, graduating second in his class. He had later been promoted to chief engineer of the Army of the Potomac. At Gettysburg he had set the Union defenses at Little Round Top and had emerged as one of that battle's heroes. He was calm under fire, fierce in combat, serious to the point of being somber, and searingly intelligent. Grant saw him as the officer most likely to replace George Meade, if such a change became necessary. By early 1864 Warren was perhaps the fastest-rising star in the Union army.

He had flourished in spite of a deeply eccentric — many would have said deeply flawed — personality. Though his slovenly attire and abstracted manner reminded some of an absentminded professor, nothing about him was benign. He was by nature morose, unsmiling, rude, abrupt, intolerant, and critical of everyone around him. He was often cruel and startlingly profane to his men and openly disrespectful to his bosses, whom he generally saw as unworthy of their ranks. His own artillery commander was amazed at his temper tantrums and at "the desperate blackguardism they displayed."[14] The provost marshal of the Army of the Potomac called him "loathsome, profane, ungentlemanly & disgusting."[15] After Gettysburg he had been publicly critical of his own high command in testimony before Congress. He was both an annoying micromanager of his own troops and a persistent meddler in other generals' business. That such a man had been entrusted with the Army of the Potomac's 5th Corps, one of the key commands in Grant's campaign to end the war, was odd indeed.

At Spotsylvania on May 8, corps under Warren and Major General John Sedgwick attacked strong rebel entrenchments on an elevated piece of ground called Laurel Hill, and they were sharply repulsed. Two days later Warren received orders to attack Laurel Hill again. This time he had far more men and more time to prepare. But again his assault disintegrated into a bloody, lopsided fight that looked much like what had happened on May 8.[16] He found, too, that his artillery was largely useless against Lee's fortifications: iron shells fired with flat trajectories simply buried themselves in his opponents' log and soil embankments.[17]

One might have thought that a lesson had been learned. Certainly Warren's staff, subordinate officers, and troops believed that the risks of assaulting Laurel Hill had been amply demonstrated. But no minds at headquarters had been changed. Grant — Grant now, not Meade, was controlling movements of troops on the field, having had enough of Meade's dithering in the Wilderness — had drawn no conclusions. There had been many casualties, but casualties did not cause him to lose sleep. He had merely become more suspicious of Warren, who had already performed poorly in the Wilderness.[18]

A few hours later the 5th Corps was yet again ordered to attack the Confederate trenches at Laurel Hill. This time Warren balked. A superb engineer, he knew exactly how strong the rebel works were, in addition to believing that his superiors were idiots. He made only the most nominal effort. Of his three divisions, one did not advance at all, one advanced a short distance and then turned back, and a third engaged the enemy but quickly disintegrated as Warren's men, panicky with fear at what they felt was certain death or wounding, retreated. Warren canceled the attack. His heart had never been in it. "The charge will not be made this evening," said one of his staff officers. "General Warren says the loss of life would be too great to risk it."[19]

Warren and his officers were right: attacking those entrenchments again and again with no hope of success was, taken by itself, madness. But Grant saw a different world. For him, the way to beat Lee was by rapid and continuous assaults all along his lines, keeping him off-balance and preventing him from seizing the initiative. Some of the attacks had no purpose but to pin rebel troops in place so they could not be used as reinforcements elsewhere. In Grant's mind, for some of these attacks to fail and for many men to die in the attempts was perfectly acceptable. This was the true meaning of hammering at the opponent, and the subtext of Grant's accession to power. He didn't mind losing tens of thousands of men. For common soldiers it was the ultimate horror.[20] They were being deliberately and callously sacrificed.

But Warren's ordeal was far from over. In fact the worst of it lay ahead. On May 12 — to his profound amazement — he was ordered to attack Confederate entrenchments at Laurel Hill *for the fourth time.* The idea —

Grant's, naturally — was that Lee had weakened his Laurel Hill defenses to shore up other parts of his battle lines. Warren knew this was not true. So he refused to attack. Though he offered practical reasons why he could not do so, the real reason was that he did not want to sacrifice his men. The high command's patience with its ill-humored commander had run out. Grant considered removing Warren from command. "The order of the major-general commanding is peremptory that you attack at once at all hazards," wrote Meade's exasperated chief of staff, Andrew Humphreys.

Warren now had no choice. He ordered a full-scale attack. His men went forward and came at once under murderous fire from the Confederate trenches. The men went down in bloody waves, first from the entrenched artillery, then from men firing from behind thick, reinforced earthworks and breastworks, the muzzles of their rifles spitting sheets of flame from chinks in the log-reinforced embrasures. Warren and his officers and staff had seen the slaughter coming, and Warren had warned his superiors about it, and he was now forced to watch his men die in front of him. Worse still, that butchery was being carried out by a single attenuated Confederate division — merely five thousand men — against a Union corps of twenty-five thousand men. These pointless mass killings continued until Meade mercifully ordered the 5th Corps back to its own earthworks. Warren had tried to act rationally and humanely under a general whose main strategy was to bludgeon his opponent to death, to outbleed him. And the young major general had failed spectacularly. This was the new war, Grant's war, one in which Warren's sort of sensible, humane restraint had no place.

The Battle of Spotsylvania Court House marked the flameout of Warren's rising star. He would never be trusted again by his superiors. His once-glittering career collapsed rapidly, punctuated by bitter arguments with Meade and General Philip Sheridan and Warren's open disparagement of Grant's man-wasting tactics. Warren faded into irrelevance and in April 1865 was abruptly relieved of command.

By the fourth day at Spotsylvania, General Grant faced a problem of war-changing proportions. His assaults on Lee's fortified lines had all failed, at enormous cost. His other corps commanders were faring no better than Warren, which meant that Grant's overwhelming advantage in numbers had vanished. Lee had figured out yet another way to neutralize his enemy's strength. Was it simply a fact now — as remarkable as it seemed — that men firing from behind heavy cover were invincible? What did it mean for the future of the war if the Army of the Potomac could not carry its opponents' fieldworks?

Grant, a veteran of many campaigns and victor in all of them, had exactly one idea left of how to break the standoff. It had come from a precocious twenty-four-year-old named Emory Upton, who had graduated three years before from the US Military Academy. The young colonel had distinguished himself the previous fall when his brigade had used highly original tactics to carry a fortified rebel bridgehead on the Rappahannock River, capturing a thousand prisoners. Upton, who could think simply about complex matters, was arrogant and dismissive of the wisdom of his elders. "Some of our corps commanders are not fit to be corporals," he had written. "Lazy and indolent, they will not even ride along their lines."[21] His idea, which was as radical as his fiery temperament, was for some reason supported by the generals in charge — perhaps because they had no ideas of their own.

On the evening of May 10, Upton took a handpicked force of five thousand men, packed them into a narrow, dense, blue rectangle — the complete opposite of a normal stretched-out battle line and an enticing target for both artillery and musketry — and threw them at an inverted U-shaped bulge in Lee's battle lines that had been

121

dubbed the Mule Shoe. Their orders were not to shoot their weapons until they were through the wall. The idea was to use massive and sudden force to tear a hole in the Confederate works.

It worked. Brilliantly. Upton's men rushed forward with fixed bayonets and carried the earthworks in minutes, taking hundreds of prisoners as they piled forward. "Numbers prevailed," wrote Upton later, "and like a resistless wave, the column poured over the works." Just like that, they were on the other side of the impenetrable trenches. They pushed on in joy and triumph for nearly three-quarters of a mile, at which point they realized they had a problem. To hold what they had taken, and to keep open the breach they had created, they needed reinforcements, but no other Union troops appeared. This command failure meant that Upton's men were left alone to face a furious Confederate counterattack. They were quickly outnumbered and forced to retreat. Many of them wept for the wasted opportunity, the pointless loss of life.[22]

But Grant, who had not wept for the loss of anything, decided to repeat Upton's tactic, though this time on a colossal scale. On the morning of May 12, twenty thousand Union soldiers swept forward — an entire corps this time, nearly twice the number of men in Pickett's Charge at Gettysburg — and attacked the nose of the Mule Shoe salient, where some forty-five hundred rebel soldiers were stunned to see what was coming at them. No soldiers in this war had ever seen so many men packed into such an enormous, dense, pulsing column; like Upton's charge, it violated all the accepted rules of infantry tactics. These attackers too held their fire until they were over the wall. The federals quickly overwhelmed the works, and thousands of other federal troops soon broke rebel lines nearby. They took three thousand Confederate prisoners. They occupied the trenches. Once again Lee's men counterattacked, but this time the federals did not retreat. Now the opponents came at each other in desperately close quarters, fighting hand to hand with bayonets and rifle butts in some of the most desperate fighting of the war. Men fired point-blank into each other's faces, impaled each other atop the embankments. Trenches filled with rainwater, and the water turned crimson. The men, said one Southerner, "fired without showing their heads above the work, which was certain death. Guns were loaded, held up to the breastwork . . . and the trigger pulled with the thumb."[23] One participant remembered it as an "unmitigated slaughter." Nine thousand men were killed or wounded that day.

In the end the great Union assault failed. Though the rebel embankments were assaulted again and again, and their trenches were thick with bleeding bodies, they had ultimately held; they had been pierced but not broken. By the next morning Lee had redrawn his battle lines, reducing his vulnerability, and was more strongly entrenched than ever.

Amazingly, Grant believed that the fight on May 12 had been a success, or at least that is what he told his superiors. "The eighth day of battle closes," he stated flatly in his dispatch to Union army chief of staff Henry Halleck, "leaving between 3,000 and 4,000 prisoners in our hands for the day's work, including two general officers and 30 pieces of artillery." Grant also believed, against considerable evidence, that Lee's army was badly depleted and on the verge of collapse. He saw Lee's constant entrenchments as proof that his army was "very shaky." Grant was quite mistaken, as he would soon learn. The war would last almost a year longer. But this was vintage Grant, the man who would not acknowledge defeat. He was frustrated, but undeterred.

The Battle of Spotsylvania went on — in a series of fights from May 8 to May 20 — with more federal assaults on the Confederate lines. But nothing changed the fundamental logic of Lee's entrenchments. The fighting at the Mule Shoe and the Bloody Angle would be as close as Grant would come to breaking his enemy's defenses. Grant's other offensives in Virginia were sputtering, too, or failing outright, which meant that Lee would soon be reinforced, which meant that it would be even harder to lever him out of his works. There was nothing left to do but move southward again, toward the Confederate capital, to find some new battlefield where maybe the Army of the Potomac's luck would change.

On May 11, the day before the bloody fighting at the Mule Shoe, Grant had sent a telegram to Washington that became one of the most famous documents of the war. He delivered a mild, broadly optimistic assessment of the campaign: although casualties were high, the results were "very much in our favor." The enemy had suffered heavy casualties, too. Then Grant stated his own intentions: "I . . . propose to fight it out on this line if it takes all summer." He had not thought much about the phrase when he wrote it, burying it in the middle of the report. But when newspapers published it, a shock wave went through the North. Grant would not, like his predecessors in command, back down. He wasn't going anywhere. This was language that, like his matter-of-fact demand for unconditional surrender two years earlier, no one had heard before, and these words created a sensation, too, especially in Washington. Lincoln made them immediately public, and the city erupted "with a tremendous demonstration of joy," in the words of newspaper reporter Noah Brooks. "There was something like delirium in the air. Everybody seemed to think that the war was coming to an end right away."[24]

Even more interesting, Grant's historic turn of phrase, strictly speaking, was not true.

A few days after Grant made that statement, he concluded that he could not possibly fight it out all summer along the "line" represented by Lee's entrenchments at Spotsylvania. That would be foolish, excessively bloody, and a strategy that favored Lee. And sacrificing another twenty thousand fair-haired Union boys to no particular end was politically unacceptable. The presidential election loomed. There had to be at least an apparent purpose. So Grant did the only thing he reasonably could, he moved south, away from the line he had said he would fight it out on all summer. He had neither the heart nor the political capital to do that. Lee, apparently, was the one willing to fight it out on that line all summer.

Nor was it true that, as Grant had put it so succinctly in a letter to Meade on April 9, "Lee's army will be your objective point. Wherever Lee goes, there you will go also." In this case Lee had not gone anywhere and had no plans to go anywhere. If the Union army was to stay with Lee and destroy him and not worry about such outmoded notions as taking and holding cities and other supposedly valuable chunks of real estate, then it should have stayed in its trenches on that wide arc north of Spotsylvania Court House. As Confederate general John B. Gordon later put it, "Lee was not going toward Richmond except as Grant went toward Richmond. He was not going in any direction. He was standing still at Spotsylvania and awaiting the pleasure of General Grant."[25] Grant was going for Richmond, after all. That was because Lee had changed his style of fighting, which had changed the logic of Grant's entire offensive, and of the war itself.

CHAPTER SIX:
ONE ADDITIONAL HORROR

WOUNDED UNION SOLDIERS AT THE BATTLE OF SPOTSYLVANIA COURT HOUSE: They were swept up in the war's greatest medical disaster.

By now killing had become a daily habit, something that had never happened in this war. Most of the battles before the spring of

1864 had been singular and relatively isolated events: opposing armies had hurled large masses of men at each other in fights that had usually lasted only a few days. Then the combat was over and the loser withdrew, the guns went silent, the numbers were tallied, the dead were buried, and the wounded taken to hospitals. The scale of the slaughter guaranteed that it would have to stop, at least for a while. An exhausted army could absorb only so much mayhem, so much tearing of human flesh, before its elaborate infrastructure of supply lines, doctors, ambulances, and field hospitals began to collapse. So before the next big fight came a pause, and a stillness, and an interval of peace. The notable exception had been the Seven Days Battles in front of Richmond, which included five major engagements from June 25 to July 1, 1862, and which indeed caused extreme havoc in the support systems of both armies.

But what had happened at the Wilderness and at Spotsylvania Court House was something different. The two great armies had fought almost continuously for more than two weeks. Other than Grant's shuffle to the southeast, this grinding fight that had already killed or wounded nearly forty thousand men had barely moved at all.[1] Where the Seven Days had ended with a clear rebel victory and a typical five-week intermission, now came no resolution at all, no victorious army holding the field, no loser moving off to lick his wounds, no stillness, no pause for breath. Just more of the same appalling, close-hand combat, the same relentless hammering with no end in sight.

What this meant for the Union side — where by far the greatest numbers of casualties had taken place — was that a system built to handle concentrated outbreaks of violence suddenly became massively overloaded. Then it failed. The result was one of the great and unheralded medical disasters of the Civil War, one that caused horrible suffering for untold thousands of Union soldiers.[2] To understand how it happened, one must understand the uncertain, embattled world of the US Army Medical Department in the days after the fighting began in the Wilderness.

The problems started with bullets. Specifically, .57- or .58-caliber conical chunks of lead known as minié balls, named after the Frenchman who invented them, Claude-Étienne Minié.[3] They caused extremely destructive wounds, far out of proportion to their size. Moving at low velocity, they lost their shape on impact, tumbling through the body's soft flesh and often lacking the speed or power to exit.* A bullet that hit one New York soldier in the cheek was taken out

* Minié balls were first adopted for use by the

130

between his shoulders. A bullet that penetrated another soldier's left waist climbed in a diagonal line to his right shoulder, tearing through kidneys, intestines, stomach, and lungs on the way. One captured Confederate soldier had been badly wounded in four different places — neck, chest, shoulder, and arm — by a single ball. Veterans even cautioned green recruits against crouching down while advancing on the enemy because such a posture could allow a bullet to travel the length of the body.[4] When the bullets hit bone, they often flattened and spread to the width of a silver dollar, while splintering and shattering the bone so badly that it could not be set. Artillery wounds — from shell, shrapnel, and canister — also caused jagged, low-velocity wounds.

A wounded man who was unable to walk away from the fighting posed the medical corps' second problem: how to extract him. The challenge began with the stretchermen, a generally oafish subcategory of soldier who had gotten the job because their commanding officers didn't want them at the front ruining regimental discipline. They gathered up injured men and delivered them to ambulances five hundred yards behind the lines.

American army in the 1850s by then secretary of war Jefferson Davis.

The Wilderness defeated them at every turn. The woods were so dense that stretchers had difficulty passing through. Whole sections of the battlefield were on fire. The lines of demarcation between friend and enemy were often nonexistent, which meant that enemy soldiers were constantly popping up out of nowhere, and bullets didn't distinguish between medical corps and fighting men. Men in agony on the ground, meanwhile, had much else to fear: being trampled by rider-less horses and escaped mules, being crushed by horse-drawn artillery wagons.[5] Or simply being burned alive long before the malingering stretcher-bearers ever showed up.

Those who were carried out were then taken by ambulance to a field hospital — clusters of medical tents in the rear of the army — where surgeons worked to stop bleeding, to clean and suture wounds, and to amputate limbs. The scenes inside the surgeries were among the most gruesome of the war. Men screamed. Their leaking, spurting, puddling blood covered the ground. Hacksaw-wielding doctors stood flanked by oozing piles of arms and legs. The tents reeked, too, both from the slaughterhouse smells of human offal and from open bowel and bladder wounds. The most common surgery was a simple amputation, using a method known as guillotining. After knocking the patient out with chloroform, administered on a sponge, the surgeon used a knife to slice through the soft tissue above the injury and then a saw to sever the bone. He clamped spewing arteries, tied them off with pieces of oiled silk, threw the arm or leg on the pile, and proceeded to his next patient. An accomplished surgeon could complete a full amputation in less than two minutes.[6]

But an amputee or any other patient in a field hospital soon faced an even greater risk than surgery. The Civil War took place just before the discovery of pathogenic microorganisms, which meant that, while surgery itself had become relatively sophisticated, doctors had no idea what caused infection or how to stop it. Field hospitals were massively contaminated with bacteria. Virtually everything that touched the patients was covered with germs. Doctors operated in smocks that were soaked through with pus and blood. Their idea of sterile technique was to wipe their bloody knives with dirty rags. Not surprisingly, infection and disease were bigger killers in the Civil War than bullets and shells. The sick were always among the wounded, too, victims of camp diseases such as typhoid, malaria, and pneumonia. Diarrhea and its cousin dysentery were the two biggest killers of the war: a man with dysentery, which was acute, bloody diarrhea, would often discharge more than a liter of liquid every hour.[7]

The first goal of the medical corps was to get these men away from the ghoulish field hospitals as quickly as possible. On the morning of May 7, the day after the last fighting in the Wilderness, General Meade ordered seven thousand wounded men transported west to Rappahannock Station, located on the Orange and Alexandria Railroad.[8] There they would be taken in trains seventy miles to Washington and placed in hospitals.[9] They would be swimming upstream along Grant's main supply line: guns and men and food and medical supplies moved south to the 120,000-man army, while the wounded, using the same train cars, would flow back north. Getting the men to Washington seemed like a reasonable plan.

But it was the beginning of a thousand nightmares.

The first problem — which would seem quite mild compared to what happened later — was that Meade's army had run out of ambulances. Though the medical service had been upgraded since the beginning of the war — at First Bull Run the army's medical department had, as one observer put it, "no plans, no organization, no enlisted personnel, no supplies, no ambulance corps" — the rate and volume of casualties in the Wilderness overwhelmed it.[10] The quartermaster did the only thing he could do: he rounded up empty ammunition and ration wagons and ordered them to transport the wounded.

This, too, seemed like a good idea, until it was put into practice. Civil War ambulances were four-wheeled covered wagons drawn by two horses. They had padded seats and padded platforms and heavy springs to help absorb shocks. But the stripped-down, springless army wagons had none of these features. The only cushion was evergreen boughs hastily thrown into their beds. A man on the bed of such a vehicle that was running over deeply rutted or wildly uneven roads experienced a jolting, yawing, bone-rattling ride. For severely injured men who bounced violently in the wagon bed and sometimes clung to extemporized straps, each jolt brought cries of pain that could be heard long before the wagons came into sight.[11] Wounds were reopened, dressings and bandages torn away. Many men died in the wagons *because of* the wagons.[12] When a man died, the driver would stop the wagon and the body would be hauled into the woods and buried in a shallow grave or sometimes left for others to bury.[13] Standard ambulances were no bargain either — they, too, caused men to suffer terribly on the rough roads — but they were models of comfort and luxury compared to the army wagons. And even the additional army wagons were not enough for all the wounded, many of whom would remain in field hospitals with minimal care.[14]

As bad as all that was for the men, however, it was about to get much worse. While Meade's seven-mile-long wagon train and its groaning cargo was pushing on through billowing dust clouds toward Rappahannock Station — toward the salvation of the railroad — it received new orders that would change every assumption about the disposition of the wounded in the campaign.[15] The move from the Wilderness to Spotsylvania Court House had been wildly popular, but it had also raised a serious problem: as the Army of the Potomac sprinted around Lee's right flank, it got farther and farther away from its original base at Brandy Station. Forty miles away. That was too far. It meant that the army's lifeline was more vulnerable than ever to raiding Confederate cavalry. So that line would have to shift to the east — and quickly.

And shift it did: with a stroke of his pen Grant changed the route and destination of every supply he received, from crackers and cartridges to mules, cannonballs, dried vegetables, and raw recruits, while simultaneously dictating a new path for the wounded. The new base, Grant decreed, would be an obscure steamboat landing on a nondescript bend in the Potomac River known as Belle Plain, which was neither beautiful nor a plain, just a couple of hundred yards of muddy red clay that backed up to a scrubby, drab-looking bluff. Steamships would bring supplies down the Potomac to Belle Plain, where they would be off-loaded and taken by wagon to Spotsylvania Court House.

On the evening of May 7 the entire train of wounded were ordered to turn around.[16] They were told, to their gape-mouthed disbelief, to head back east and to follow the army, away from dreams of comfort and relief in a Washington hospital and back into the smoldering thickets of the Wilderness that smelled of rotting flesh. By the morning of May 8 the high command had decided that the medical train should proceed to the Union-held city of Fredericksburg, Virginia, which was ten miles southwest of Belle Plain. So the wagons rumbled on. Between them were the walking wounded, who begged for water from passing cavalry.[17] For the severely injured, the dithering and indecision at Union headquarters had meant a harrowing extra twenty-four hours in the wagons. Many of them died because of it.

By 1864, Fredericksburg had become a landmark in the war. This drowsy eighteenth-century redbrick city had been the site of one of Robert E. Lee's greatest victories, which had prompted a disconsolate Abraham Lincoln to say, "If there is a worse place than hell, I am in it." The Battle of Fredericksburg, fought in December 1862, also marked the first time in the war that an army had shelled

a major civilian target. The Union's bombard-
ment on December 11, 1862, which at its
peak delivered a hundred shells a minute,
had reduced whole sections of the city to
rubble.[18] Witnesses on both sides had been
shocked by the barbarity of the assault. What
was not destroyed outright was riddled with
jagged holes. Parts of the city burned. When
the shelling stopped, federal troops looted
whatever the artillery had left standing.

Into this miserable, half-destroyed city the
first of the medical wagons rolled, in pitch-
darkness, at 1:00 a.m. on May 9. The scene
was eerie, unreal. No advance party had been
sent to let the residents know that seven
thousand injured men were about to descend
on them. No army supplies or doctors or
tents or medical equipment had preceded
them. And the city itself had no stockpiles of
medical or any other supplies. The only
sounds to alert anyone that a change was
coming were the creaking of the wagons, the
nickering of horses in their traces, and the
moans of the men. The wounded in the
wagons, meanwhile, were dying at an acceler-
ated rate; many of them had had nothing to
eat or drink for two or three days.[19]

While the miles-long caravan continued to
pile into the sleeping city, the few doctors on
hand commandeered whatever buildings they
could find. The wounded men were off-
loaded into churches, warehouses, mills, and

larger houses.[20] Many were simply dumped in the streets. Some wounded officers were lodged in private homes, but these residences remained off-limits to common soldiers — a policy that would soon prove bitterly controversial. The city's residents kept their doors shut. Many of the empty buildings were full of water from a recent rain. So men were laid out in puddles, their blood mixing with the pools of stagnant water, and in one of the warehouses the blood and water mixed with spilled molasses, which covered the floor.[21] Because the town didn't have enough room for all the men, large numbers of them stayed in the wagons and many died there. For more than twenty-four hours no more than thirty doctors attended seven thousand wounded.[22] In the warehouses men lay in pools of cold, bloody water for days without food or care while maggots and gangrene consumed what remained of their arms or legs. A nurse who observed the scene wrote that the makeshift hospitals were "shocking in filth and neglect."[23]

But the medical disaster was just beginning. Even before all of the Wilderness wounded had been evacuated, long trains of injured men from Spotsylvania Court House began arriving in the city. Soon there were more than fourteen thousand wounded in Fredericksburg. This was the meaning of nonstop battle: disaster layered upon disaster. The medical corps had been forced to cover the two battlefields, which meant that, while the wounded poured into Fredericksburg in ever greater numbers, doctors and medical supplies were still tied up in field hospitals. This meant not enough of anything for anybody. Veteran nurse Jane Stuart Woolsey offered this chilling description:

No words can express the horrible confusion of this place. The wounded arrive one train a day, but the trains are miles long; blocked by all sorts of accidents, bad roads, broken bridges; two, three days on the way, plunged in quagmires, jolted over corduroy; without food, fainting, starving, filthy; frightfully wounded, arms gone to the shoulder, horrible wounds in the face and head. I would rather a thousand times have a friend killed on the field than suffer in this way. . . . Many die on the way.[24]

Not until May 10, fully five days after the start of the combat at the Wilderness, did the first boats with medical supplies arrive in the docks at Belle Plain.

Adding to the chaos was the unsettling presence of five thousand Union men who simply did not want to fight. They had drifted in with the medical trains. Some were lightly wounded, some had self-inflicted wounds, some had appropriated bloody bandages from dead soldiers. They were mostly cowards on the hustle, trying to arrange a plausible escape, trying to get themselves away from flying bullets and random death and to convince the doctors that they really were wounded. They competed for food, lodging, and transport with injured men. There were so many that no one knew quite what to do with them. Like the severely wounded, they were products of the horrors of war.[25] They were its spiritual casualties, men who could not bear the idea of fighting anymore, men who preferred public disgrace to dismemberment or death.

But hauling the wounded to "depot hospitals" in Fredericksburg had been merely an interim solution. The larger plan was to take them ten miles to Belle Plain by wagon and thence by steamship up the Potomac River to Washington. (A train track had run from Fredericksburg to the Potomac port at Aquia Creek, but it had been wrecked in 1863 and never rebuilt; the other way out, the Rappahannock River, was mined and guerrilla infested.)[26]

Unfortunately, Belle Plain, too, had intractable problems. With fifteen hundred wounded men coming north each day and large quantities of army supplies moving south, the mudflats at Belle Plain became a giant logistical bottleneck, which caused yet more untold suffering. Men continued to die in the wagons. According to one observer, an average of six corpses per mile lay beside the road to Fredericksburg, where the drivers had dumped them.[27] Some of the corpses simply remained in the wagons where they had died. "We found thirty-five dead in ambulances today," wrote Woolsey, "and six more died on the stretchers while being put on board the boats. . . . Mules, stretchers, army wagons, prisoners, dead men and officials . . . are tumbled and jumbled on the wretched dock, which falls in every once in a while and keeps the trains waiting for hours."[28]

Thus the suffering and dying persisted, as the army and its medical department struggled to adapt to Grant's tactical whims. Among the horrors were some small moments of sweetness and hope. Walking by a church one night, a reporter for *Harper's Weekly* heard organ music. He entered the building, and in the ghostly light from a dozen lanterns he saw wounded men crowding into every aisle and pew while, above them, in the organ loft a man with a bandaged arm played "Home Sweet Home" on the keyboard. Soldiers sang and wept, and when the song was over, a voice piped up from the far corner of the church: "Now give us 'Yankee Doodle'!"[29]

CHAPTER SEVEN:
BATTLEFIELD ANGEL

CLARA BARTON: One of the war's most unlikely heroes, she helped reinvent wartime medicine.

On the morning of May 13, eight days after the start of the Battle of the Wilderness, an attractive, diminutive, dark-haired woman in a bonnet with a red bow, plain blouse, and plain dark skirt stepped off a shuttle barge and onto the temporary pier at Belle Plain.[1] Because women in general were not welcome in such places, she had obtained a special pass to come down the Potomac on a steamship. While almost everyone else in the world with a choice wanted to get far away from the horrors of the Virginia campaign, she had gone to great trouble to get in. To call her a wartime nurse would be profoundly insufficient. The newspapers called her "the angel of the battlefield," and she had invented an entirely new role for women on the male-dominated killing fields of the Civil War.[2] She was quite famous now, both in America and abroad. As she strode forward into the bloody chaos of Belle Plain, it is likely that someone pointed to her and said, "Look, there goes Clara Barton."

Even Barton was amazed by what she saw, writing: "I shall never forget the scene which met my eye as I stepped from the boat to the top of the ridge. Standing in its plain of mortar-mud were at least two hundred six-mule army wagons, crowded full of wounded men waiting to be taken on the boats for Washington." None of the wagons were moving. All were mired in knee-deep muck. They had nowhere to go anyway in that monstrous traffic jam. Barton quickly saw that these suffering men, who had come up from Fredericksburg, would not be getting to Washington anytime soon. Since she could not put them on the boats, and since no one was paying any attention to them, she decided to feed them. She dragooned an idle clergyman, gathered kindling and built a fire, hung a pot on crotched sticks, and soon had "a dozen camp-kettles of steaming coffee." She found some cracker barrels, then waded through the deep mud to serve the coffee and hardtack to the men in the wagons.[3]

But this was not why Barton had come. Belle Plain was just a point of transit. Her destination was Fredericksburg, the great unfolding medical catastrophe she had heard rumors of in Washington. She had been there before, nursing soldiers during the great battle in 1862, the only woman at the front. She had nursed them under fire in a burning city; she had had parts of her skirt ripped away by artillery shells. When she arrived in Fredericksburg from Belle Plain the next day, May 14, she saw a version of the nightmare that had followed the Battle of the Wilderness, now complicated and compounded by the arrival of the Spotsylvania wounded. Wagons full of hurt and dying men stood in lines that snaked off and disappeared beyond the hills. Beneath many of them, she recalled, "The dark spot in the mud . . . told only too plainly where some poor fellow's life had dripped out in those dreadful hours."[4] In an old hotel, she found "lying helpless on its bare, wet, bloody floors, five hundred fainting men" who "beg[ged] me in Heaven's name for a cracker to keep them from starving (and I had none); or to give them a cup that they might have something to drink water from, if they could get it."[5]

What caught her attention, though, even more than this burgeoning misery, was something she heard from one of the Union officers in charge of the Fredericksburg depot:

A little dapper captain, quartered with the owners of one of the finest mansions in the town, boasted that he had changed his opinion since entering the city the day before; that it was in fact a pretty hard thing for refined people like the people of Fredericksburg to be compelled to open their homes and admit these "dirty, lousy, common soldiers," and that he was not going to compel it.[6]

So that was it. The men were lying in the streets and in bloody pools of water because the city's inhabitants — Confederate traitors — had refused to allow them into their homes and had been supported in their selfishness and self-regard by the Union's own commanders. Their doors remained shut tight, "the haughty occupants holding barricade

146

within," wrote Barton in her diary. They had locked up the grocery stores, too. Barton, with the sort of cold fury that many people in power had learned to respect, decided that she was going to fix the problem and fix it now, that very day, even though she held no rank and knew almost no one in the city. Within the hour, she had commandeered a light army wagon with four horses, which took her to Belle Plain. From there she boarded a steam tug for Washington, more than forty miles upriver. By dusk she was in the city and had "sent for" her close friend Massachusetts senator Henry Wilson, chairman of the Military Committee of the Senate and one of the country's most powerful politicians. By eight o'clock that same evening Wilson had arrived at her apartment to hear what had made the redoubtable Clara Barton so upset.[7]

Her road to that moment was long and uneven — perhaps because no woman had ever traveled it before. She grew up in North Oxford, Massachusetts, near Worcester, the shy, sensitive, intelligent daughter of a successful businessman. She was pretty, prim, and ladylike; she was also a superb rider and a crack shot with a revolver. She was handy with tools. She was prodigiously capable. She idolized her father and loved hearing his stories of his days in the army with General

Mad Anthony Wayne in the Michigan territory. She loved war stories. She loved everything about war.

Barton became a schoolteacher and by all accounts a phenomenal one. She was the opposite of the strict schoolmarm. She was warm, friendly, and interested in the students. She founded a school in Massachusetts at the age of twenty-four that quickly became oversubscribed. When she was twenty-nine, she founded another in Bordentown, New Jersey — one of the state's first public schools — which also became wildly popular. Its numbers grew so quickly that after Barton's first year the town commissioned a brand-new building to accommodate six hundred children. She had single-handedly redefined the idea of education in the town.[8]

She had also pushed the limits of what a professional woman could expect to accomplish in the 1850s. When the new school building was finished, town officials did what probably seemed predictable to everyone but Clara Barton: they hired a man for the top job and paid him twice what they had paid her. Her new title was the same as that of the other women there: "female assistant." She was bitterly disappointed. She had a keen sense of fairness, and this was terribly unfair.

She resigned and moved to Washington, where she became one of the first female clerks in the US Patent Office. Here, too, her intelligence, charm, and obvious ability won her quick success. She was soon making $1,400 a year, an extraordinarily high salary for a woman and comparable to what her male counterparts made. (By comparison, a female bookkeeper made $500, a teacher $250.) The men did not take this easily or graciously. Women were not supposed to be ambitious. They were supposed to be sitting demurely at home taking care of the children. Barton was aggressive, handsome, forthright, and, though she had many suitors, unmarried, which made her even more deeply suspect. So the men spread rumors. They said she was promiscuous. They said she had given birth to illegitimate children, some of them with "negroid" features. In the morning when she walked to her desk, she was sometimes greeted with catcalls and whistles. Some of the men even spat at her.[9] Though she persisted and performed well, she lost that job, too, when the election of 1856 brought in a new administration. She retreated to her family in Massachusetts, applied for and was turned down for a number of jobs, mostly because of her sex, fell into the life of a domestic spinster, and became thoroughly depressed.

Like so many others whom the war made influential and famous, Clara Barton began the decade of the 1860s as a failure. Certainly in her own eyes she was. In June 1860, at the age of thirty-eight, she felt so useless, hopeless, and alone that she suffered a physical and emotional breakdown. While she convalesced with friends, she contemplated suicide, writing in her diary that her death "must be the sweetest hour of my whole existence."[10] When a Republican administration swept into office with Lincoln in 1860, she got another job at the US Patent Office, but in a lesser position, working for a fraction of her former salary. By now many more women worked for the Patent Office. Which meant that, when the war started in April 1861, she was just like everybody else, a situation she found "mortifying."

But the war changed everything for Clara Barton, just as it did for failures such as Ulysses S. Grant, William Tecumseh Sherman, and Thomas Jonathan "Stonewall" Jackson.[11] She had wanted from the beginning to do something to help the Union war effort. She would have preferred to enlist — she desperately wanted to be a soldier — but that was impossible. The logical next move would have been to join the brand-new Army Nursing Corps under Dorothea L. Dix, a righteous, humorless crusader who had made her name caring for the mentally ill, the destitute, and the imprisoned. Thousands of women traveled to Washington to join up. (Until then, all army nurses had been male.) Unfortunately, the formidable Miss Dix did not want most of the women, especially not those young, attractive, and unmarried. She wanted old, plain ones, preferably with unengaging personalities. She wanted no one under thirty. She detested "wasp" waists. She had a frank horror of the idea of slender, personable young women tending to injured or sick young men. One observer remarked that to be hired an applicant had to be "plain almost to repulsion in dress."[12] Though Clara Barton was nearing forty, she looked ten years younger, and she indeed had a wasp waist, sparkling eyes, and a charming nature. She was almost everything Dix did not want.

Besides, Barton had her own ideas. In her spare time from the Patent Office, she began to solicit food, clothing, and medical supplies from her home state to distribute to Massachusetts regiments. These included everything from pies and cakes and jellies and pickled vegetables to whiskey and tobacco, shirts, and bandages. She bought supplies with her own money. She cooked food. She rented a warehouse. Then she distributed it all to the volunteer regiments from Massachusetts, which were part of the seventy-five thousand troops who had answered Abraham Lincoln's call to put down the rebellion. People on their way to church on Sunday might see her familiar small figure, mounted on a wagonload of supplies, making her way through the streets of Washington.[13]

(On these trips she was always in the company of a man, often her nephew; ladies who went alone into army camps gained reputations as slatterns or concubines.) She became her own relief operation. She pursued this with single-minded intensity in the first year and a half of the war.

Still, Barton wanted more. She wanted to fight, but since she could not do that, she wanted at least to be where the battles were taking place, or as close as she could possibly get. She knew there was an enormous unfilled need. Army medical services were still sorely lacking, and food and other supplies for the sick and wounded were intermittent at best. Civilian relief agencies called sanitary commissions had arisen to try to fill this need; but the closer one got to the front lines, the spottier the service became. The Dix nurses were still mostly found in cities, far from the battlefields.

In the summer of 1862 Barton used her sparkling conversational abilities and powers of persuasion to convince the head of the army's quartermaster depot in Washington to give her six wagons with horses along with passes to army camps in "non-engaged" areas, far from the front. She distributed the food and other goods from three full warehouses. She then fudged the passes and headed straight for the front, or as near to it as she could get. The little town of Culpeper

Court House was a few miles from the battlefield at Cedar Mountain, where a Confederate army under Stonewall Jackson had just beaten a Union army under Nathaniel Banks. Wounded men were flooding in, and as usual the medical department was not prepared to deal with them. Barton arrived with a wagon and four-horse team at a field hospital at midnight, where doctors covered in blood had run out of every type of wound dressing. She replenished their supplies. She found herself inside a world of human suffering she had never imagined: men with body parts blown or hacked off, their intestines trailing from their bodies, surgeons brandishing bone saws in hospitals whose floors were smeared with blood and feces.[14] She pitched in, working for two nights without sleep or food, scrubbing floors and passing out bandages.

Three weeks later, she talked her way into yet another medical disaster in the wake of a major Union defeat, this time at the Second Battle of Bull Run. She and her traveling companions were the only volunteers there.[15] She again brought food and bandages and cooked for the men, but now for the first time she worked as a nurse, too, tending wounds, making compresses and slings, applying tourniquets, replacing bandages. She worked sixty hours without sleep in the hospitals at Fairfax, Virginia, and when she did sleep, it was in a tent full of water.[16] She got out just ahead of the vanguard of Stonewall Jackson's troops.

But the soldier in Barton was still not satisfied. She wanted to be where the bullets were actually flying, on the very margins of the battlefield — as utterly irrational as that desire appeared to be. This was not just glory seeking, though Barton did have a well-developed ego. She had observed at close hand the failure of the army's medical services. She knew how overwhelmed and undersupplied the field hospitals were. That no women were in those places, and that there was no precedent for a woman's presence there, did not matter to her. She believed she could help. She was about to be proven spectacularly right.

In September 1862, Robert E. Lee and the Army of Northern Virginia crossed the Potomac River into Maryland, where they would soon engage the Army of the Potomac under Major General George McClellan. Though no one knew yet where the fighting would take place, Barton took off anyway, accompanied by a six-mule quartermaster's wagon full of food, bandages, and dressings. She left Washington on September 14, a petite, primly dressed woman sitting next to a teamster and a male companion (her friend the Reverend Cornelius Welles) in an over-stuffed covered wagon, clattering through the streets of the capital.

Barton had a pass to go only as far as Harpers Ferry. But she ignored its restrictions. Following McClellan's eighty-five-thousand-man army, she camped in open fields at night and rose early in the morning to try to fight her way forward through the army's own ten-mile-long tangle of supply wagons.[17] She managed to get around them, using narrow, rough back roads, passing thousands of Union camps and campfires. (In her diary she noted the "noxious" stink of the huge army.)[18] She landed on the flank of Ambrose Burnside's 9th Corps in the vicinity of the town of Sharpsburg, Maryland, near a narrow stream called Antietam Creek. She was on the Union left. When the fighting began the next morning on the Union right, several miles to the north, she took off toward the sounds of the booming artillery. She made a loop around McClellan's army, then followed an infantry column under General Joseph Hooker to where the fighting was. It is a wonder no one stopped her. She positioned herself near what history would come to know as "the cornfield," where Joe Hooker and Stonewall Jackson were engaged in the bloodiest part of the bloodiest day in American history. Artillery roared around her. She had gotten her wish: she was virtually on the battlefield.

While she was making her way toward the

gunfire, surgeons working at the Poffenberger farmhouse north of the cornfield were being overwhelmed by the numbers of wounded. No one had seen killing at this rate before. The ambulance service had been much improved and now delivered many more wounded men much faster to the hospital. Which meant that the hospital had already run out of nearly everything. Barton quickly found the hospital, where one of the surgeons, Dr. James Dunn, who knew and admired her from the battles of Second Bull Run and Cedar Mountain, told her that they had "torn up the last sheets we could find in this house, [we] have not a bandage, rag, lint or string, and all these shell-wounded men are bleeding to death."[19] Soldiers were being bandaged with corn husks. Barton was loaded with hospital supplies, which she quickly unpacked. She also went to work, cooking up and ladling out vats of gruel, rounding up idle soldiers to help bring in the wounded, tending and comforting patients. Men obeyed her as they would a senior officer. When night fell, to the amazement of the surgeons she produced candle lanterns so they could continue to operate.

She did all of this under fire. While Barton was giving a man water, she felt a sudden tug on the sleeve of her blouse, then saw the soldier fall away. The bullet that had just missed her killed him instantly. Later a soldier asked her to remove a bullet that had become painfully lodged in his cheek. When she protested that she could not bring herself to cause him so much pain, he replied, "You cannot hurt me, dear lady. I can endure any pain that your hands can create." While another man held the soldier's head, she used her pocketknife to cut out the bullet, then washed and bandaged his wound and sent him on his way.[20] During all this time, Barton was likely also ill with typhoid fever.

When the smoke cleared from the battlefield, everyone at the Poffenberger farm knew that Clara Barton had done something extraordinary and without precedent in the war. She had single-handedly supplied a Union army field hospital that treated as many as fifteen hundred men and performed brilliantly as both nurse and manager. Her achievement caused people to expand their definitions of heroism. Here a small, determined woman, covered in dirt and blood, had nursed men while guns boomed and bullets and shot and shell whizzed around her. The cannonading became so fierce at one point that the male nurses and assistants all fled and took cover. Only Barton and the chief surgeon stayed in place.

Clara Barton fought the Civil War on her own terms, as a one-woman relief and nursing agency. She redefined the limits of what women were allowed to do, of how people of the age thought about what women *could* do. But by the spring of 1864 the rest of the world had begun to catch up with her. Stories about her wartime nursing had appeared in newspapers and magazines across the North. The United States Sanitary Commission and the Christian Commission had become large, institutionalized versions of Barton's solo supply mission. Both gathered and distributed supplies from thousands of local affiliates. The Dix nurses had moved beyond the cities and into the divisional field hospitals. The army's own medical services, from stretchers to ambulances and hospitals, had greatly improved. The day of the independent battlefield nurse was over. There hadn't been many of them anyway. Barton was famous but oddly unnecessary. She had spent a year away from Washington with the army on the Carolina coast, and when she returned, she found that times had changed. Her arrangement with the Patent Office, which in effect subsidized her war work, was terminated. For the first time she had been unable to secure passes to the war zones. Secretary of War Edwin Stanton had turned her down flat. The army's medical department would not help, either. In April 1864, as the armies were readying for the Wilderness, she hit one of her hopeless, depressive lows. "This was one of the most downspirited days that ever came to me," she wrote in her diary. "All the world

appeared selfish and treacherous. . . . I have
scanned over and over the whole moral
horizon and it is all so dark . . . so dead, so
selfish, so calculating."[21]

But Grant's Virginia campaign had excited
her. She had been in the crowd at the White
House that evening in March when Ulysses S.
Grant had walked in and electrified the room,
and she came away full of hope, and wanting
more than ever to be near the action. When
the fighting began in the Wilderness, she had
pulled in all of her favors — and spent more
than a week pleading, coaxing, and cajoling
in the corridors of Washington — until she
had finally gotten an official pass to Belle
Plain and Fredericksburg, where she had seen
the appalling conditions and headed to
Washington to report them.

When she reached her small apartment in
the capital on the night of May 14, she had
summoned Senator Henry Wilson, who had
dropped everything and hustled over to see
her. How could a woman without an official
position peremptorily "send for" one of the
most powerful men in Washington? The
answer is that Barton and Wilson had a
special relationship. They had met shortly
after Lincoln's inauguration. He was from
her home state; she saw him as someone who
could help her. When he became chairman of
the Military Committee of the Senate, he was
even better positioned to assist. So she

cultivated him, and he probably fell in love with her. At least he behaved in such a way that people could conclude that. No evidence suggests the relationship was sexual, but people certainly talked about that, and Barton was not above having an affair with a married man, as she had done with an army lieutenant colonel in 1863 in Hilton Head, South Carolina. The talk arose because the lively, stout, gray-haired senator from a poor background called on her constantly for years. She called on him, too. Sometimes he called on her daily. She was, as always, a brilliant, engaging conversationalist. He was enthralled with her talk and her easy informality, and he was deeply impressed by what she had done in the field. She became as famous as he was. He helped her navigate the US army and its labyrinthine regulations.

That night in her Washington apartment she told him in detail of the grim conditions in Fredericksburg, and of the Union policy that kept common soldiers out of local houses. He was shocked at what he heard. By ten o'clock that same night he was at the War Department, relaying Barton's news. They, too, had heard nothing about a medical disaster. No reports of unusual suffering had reached them. So they chose not to believe it. Senator Wilson then informed the federal officials that one of two things was going to happen. Either the War Department would send someone that night to investigate the abuses of the wounded at Fredericksburg, or the Senate would send someone the following day. The War Department chose the former. At 2:00 a.m. the army's quartermaster, Montgomery Meigs, and his staff were galloping to Washington's Sixth Street wharf. At 10:00 a.m. they were in Fredericksburg, and by noon, in Barton's own words, "the wounded men were fed from the food of the city and the houses were opened to the *'dirty, lousy soldiers'* of the Union army."[22]

Three days later, Barton was back in Fredericksburg with three wagons of supplies. Five days after that, the improvised military installation at Belle Plain was abandoned, and it disappeared from the face of the earth as quickly as it had arisen. Its pontoon docks and floating wharves were dismantled, the flotilla of supply ships and barges and tugs and the long lines of wagons simply vanished as the army's supply depot suffered again. By the end of the month Belle Plain was once more an ugly, muddy little shallow-water steamboat landing in a place civilization had passed by, its horrors forever frozen in the memories of the 26,191 sick and wounded men who came from the Fredericksburg hospitals and passed through it over a nearly two-week period.[23] By the last week in May — three weeks after the start of the fighting — 131 wounded men still languished in field hospitals in the Wilderness. The last of them would not leave that place of death until June 8, by which time the armies were many miles to the south, across the James River, and the war had changed again.[24]

THE DEFENSE OF WASHINGTON: In the winter of 1864, Washington, DC, was the most heavily defended city on earth, with 37 miles of trenches and 60 forts manned by 50,000 soldiers. Fort Totten, shown here, was located about three miles north of the Capitol, on the road to Silver Spring, Maryland.

ROBERT E. LEE'S HOME IN ARLINGTON, VIRGINIA: Known as Arlington House, this magnificent Greek Revival mansion was based on the temple of Hephaestus. Because of its location across the Potomac River from Washington, Union forces occupied it early in the war and eventually used it as a cemetery. It would later become the site of Arlington National Cemetery.

Willard's hotel was one of the social and political centers of Washington, DC, during the Civil War. The arrival of General Ulysses S. Grant there in March 1864 sparked a minor riot in the hotel's dining room and presaged large and bloody changes in the war.

FREDERICK DOUGLASS: A leader of the anti-slavery movement and one of the nineteenth century's most remarkable men, he pushed Lincoln hard to emancipate slaves and transform the conflict into a war of black liberation.

By the war's final year, Abraham Lincoln was perhaps the most hated man in America. He was hated widely and democratically, by Republicans and Democrats alike. The South collectively saw him as the devil incarnate.

THE MASSACRE AT FORT PILLOW: An obscure fort on the Mississippi River in western Tennessee became the site of the brutal killing of black Union troops by Confederate soldiers. The atrocity—the war's worst—was a stark and brutal sign of the revolutionary change that had swept through the war.

DEAD REBEL SOLDIERS AT SPOTSYLVANIA: Though no battle had turned primarily on fieldworks before Spotsylvania, every major battle that followed it, well into the twentieth century, would look like a version of that battle, with honeycombed trenches running to the horizon.

UNION SECRETARY OF WAR EDWIN STANTON: One of Lincoln's closest advisers, he helped marshal the Union's enormous military assets to win the war. He was also uncompromising, overly cautious, and meddlesome. One of Grant's most important achievements was neutralizing Stanton's power.

UNION GENERAL GEORGE B. McCLELLAN: Lincoln removed him for being too timid on the battlefield. Two years later the vainglorious Little Mac ran against Lincoln as the Democratic Party's presidential nominee in the most important election in American history.

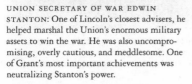

HENRY WAGER HALLECK: He was general-in-chief of Union armies until Ulysses S. Grant came to power, when he was demoted to army chief of staff. Though a soldier, he had the soul of a bureaucrat: petty, micromanaging, overly cautious, and, like his boss Stanton, intensely meddlesome. Halleck was one of the reasons the Union couldn't win the war.

CONFEDERATE GENERAL JOSEPH E. JOHNSTON: One of the top rebel commanders of the war, he feuded incessantly with Confederate president Jefferson Davis and made a treaty with Union general William Tecumseh Sherman that rocked the Northern political establishment.

CONFEDERATE GENERAL JUBAL EARLY:
Robert E. Lee's profane, tobacco-spewing,
prophet-bearded subordinate who, to everyone's
astonishment, marched unhindered with 16,000
men to the very gates of Washington in the
summer of 1864.

CONFEDERATE GENERAL JOHN BELL
HOOD: His reckless bravery served him well
in the early war. Later, when he faced William
Tecumseh Sherman in Georgia, his aggressiveness
became a liability. His defeat at Atlanta on
September 2, 1864, was the most significant
event of the war.

HORACE GREELEY: The flighty, impulsive,
and prodigiously influential editor of the *New-
York Tribune* tried to broker a peace conference
between Lincoln and Confederate officials.
But he made a fatally wrong assumption: that
Lincoln would agree to anything short of the
abolition of slavery and the full restoration of
the Union.

ROBERT E. LEE: This rare, unposed shot shows
Lee alone on his horse, Traveller, while inspect-
ing fortifications at Petersburg. While he was
tying the North in political and military knots,
Lee was experiencing his own deep sense of loss,
frustration, and failure.

WHARVES AT CITY POINT,
VIRGINIA: The site of the
Union command center and
supply depot for the Petersburg campaign. The camp,
located at the confluence of the
James and Appomattox Rivers,
provisioned more than 100,000
soldiers and 65,000 animals.

BLACK UNION PICKETS AT
DUTCH GAP, VIRGINIA: By
the end of the war 180,000
blacks had served, transforming
the war and providing a clear
path to emancipation and new
identities as American citizens.

ULYSSES S. GRANT'S FIELD
HEADQUARTERS AT CITY
POINT: While the rest of his
country brooded about its dim
prospects, Grant's message of
hope began to pulse outward
from this place, moving
through thousands of miles
of telegraph wire and into the
nation's human circuitry.

BREASTWORKS OUTSIDE PETERSBURG: The land was something out of a nightmare, stripped of its trees and grasses, refashioned into a wasteland of raw dirt and sharpened timber. In a war that had seen its share of digging in, there was really nothing to compare to the fortifications in front of the city of Petersburg.

SOLDIERS OF THE 114TH PENNSYLVANIA REGIMENT: You may think you know what a Union soldier looked like, but look again. These men are wearing popular Zouave uniforms, modeled on ones worn by French North African troops and featuring baggy trousers, short jackets, colorful sashes, and turbans or fezzes.

21

THE CONFEDERATE ROLLING MILL IN ATLANTA, GEORGIA, EARLY WAR: The South's second-largest metal rolling mill, it produced railroad rails, cannons, and iron cladding for ships. The mill was a large and visible symbol of Atlanta's manufacturing prowess.

22

THE RUINS OF THE CONFEDERATE ROLLING MILL: Before he and his rebel army fled Atlanta in September 1864, Confederate general John Bell Hood and his men set fire to eighty-one railroad cars loaded with ammunition. The resulting blasts shook the country for miles around and utterly destroyed the mill. Though Union general Sherman was infamous for burning Atlanta, Hood's men destroyed a large part of the city before they left.

23

UNION STATION IN ATLANTA: Built in 1853, this splendid facility served four railroads and was the center of the antebellum Southern rail system. It was a prime example of Atlanta's critical role in Southern commerce and transportation.

24

THE RUINS OF ATLANTA'S UNION STATION: In November 1864, Union general William Tecumseh Sherman departed Atlanta on his march to the sea. Before he left, he destroyed the railroad depot and many other buildings that could be of use to the Confederate army.

CAMPAIGN POSTER FOR THE ELECTION OF 1864: Lincoln and vice presidential candidate Andrew Johnson faced a fierce fight for reelection—first from his own party and then from Democrats determined to oust him from power. If Sherman had not taken Atlanta in September, Lincoln would likely have lost.

LINCOLN'S SECOND INAUGURATION, MARCH 4, 1865: In what was arguably his greatest speech in a career full of brilliant public oration (including the Gettysburg Address), Lincoln asserted that slavery, the sin of which the North was every bit as guilty as the South, would be atoned by blood in quantities commensurate with blood shed by slaves over two and a half centuries of bondage.

THE McLEAN HOUSE IN APPOMATTOX COURT HOUSE, WHERE ROBERT E. LEE
SURRENDERED: Four years earlier, Wilmer McLean had lived near Manassas Junction, where his
house had served as Confederate headquarters during the First Battle of Bull Run until an artillery
shell had wrecked it. So McLean had moved 150 miles south to this somnolent crossroads where,
surely, the war would not find him.

INTERIOR OF THE McLEAN HOUSE (RE-CREATED): No photo of the surrender exists. Grant
sat at the oval table on the right, Lee at the square, marble-topped table on the left. The two men
chatted amicably about their time together in Mexico before getting down to business.

Head Quarters Army of N. Va.
10 April 1865

General Orders
No 9

After four years of arduous service marked with by unsurpassed courage and fortitude the Army of Northern Virginia has been compelled to yield to overwhelming numbers and resources

I need not tell the brave survivors of so many hard fought battles who have remained steadfast to the last, that I have consented to this result from no distrust of them

But feeling that valor and devotion could accomplish nothing that could compensate for the loss that must have attended the continuance of the contest I determined to avoid the useless sacrifice of those whose past services have endeared them to their Countrymen

By the terms of the agreement, officers and men can return to their homes and remain until exchanged You will take with you the satisfaction that proceeds from the consciousness of duty faithfully performed, and I earnestly pray that a Merciful God will extend to you his blessing and protection

With an increasing admiration of your constancy and devotion to your country, and a grateful remembrance of your kind and generous consideration for myself I bid you an affectionate farewell

R E Lee
Genl

LEE'S GENERAL ORDER NO. 9 TO THE SOLDIERS OF THE ARMY OF NORTHERN VIRGINIA, TELLING THEM HE HAD SURRENDERED AND THAT THEY COULD GO HOME: "After four years of arduous service marked by unsurpassed courage and fortitude, the Army of Northern Virginia has been compelled to yield to overwhelming numbers and resources. I need not tell the brave survivors of so many hard fought battles who have remained steadfast to the last that I have consented to this result from no distrust of them; but feeling that valor and devotion could accomplish nothing that would compensate for the loss that would have attended the continuance of the contest, I determined to avoid the useless sacrifice of those whose past services have endeared them to their Countrymen. By the terms of the agreement, officers and men can return to their homes and remain there until exchanged. You will take with you the satisfaction that proceeds from the consciousness of duty faithfully performed, and I earnestly pray that a Merciful God will extend to you his blessing and protection. With an unceasing admiration of your constancy and devotion to your country and a grateful remembrance of your kind and generous consideration for myself, I bid you all an affectionate farewell."

THE JOY OF RICHMOND'S FALL: No one was happier to see the surrender of Richmond than the city's former slaves and freedmen. They were even more thrilled when the first Union infantry regiment to enter the city was black.

ABRAHAM LINCOLN IN RICHMOND: He risked his life to visit the city, under a light armed guard, in the days after its fall. Black residents of Richmond came out by the thousands to greet him.

NEWSPAPER CORRESPONDENT T. M. CHESTER: He wrote some of the most insightful dispatches of the war, none more so than the one he composed sitting at the Speaker's desk in the Confederate House of Representatives after the fall of Richmond.

RICHMOND IN RUINS: The destruction was done entirely by Confederates in an attempt to prevent items of military value from falling into the hands of the enemy. Blowing up the arsenal made sense. Setting fire to tobacco warehouses, which ended up destroying a large part of the city, did not.

CAPTURED CONFEDERATE LOCOMOTIVE IN RICHMOND: The rebels burned or blew up everything they thought might be useful to the Union army. That included this Philadelphia-built locomotive, which was found in the Richmond and Petersburg railroad depot, also destroyed by departing Confederates.

FUNERAL PROCESSION
FOR ABRAHAM LINCOLN
IN WASHINGTON, DC: It was
led by black soldiers, followed
by 40,000 newly freed blacks,
holding hands, and witnessed
by 100,000 people. The silence,
according to observers, was
profound.

ABRAHAM LINCOLN LYING
IN STATE IN NEW YORK
CITY: His funeral procession in
New York lasted four hours and
included 120,000 marchers.
The city's commerce came to a
virtual halt for a full two weeks.

ABRAHAM LINCOLN'S HEARSE IN THE STREETS OF BUFFALO, NEW YORK: Lincoln's funeral train left Washington on April 21, bound for Springfield, Illinois, where he would be buried on May 4. At each stop, the president's coffin was carried in a horse-drawn hearse to a place of public viewing.

THE RAISING OF THE AMERICAN FLAG AT ANDERSONVILLE: Finding and naming the dead at Andersonville Prison, the South's most lethal prisoner-of-war camp, was one of Clara Barton's greatest accomplishments. She raised the flag herself. (Upper left shows cemetery layout.)

CHAPTER EIGHT:
A CIRCUS OF INEPTITUDE

UNION GENERAL BEN BUTLER, *perhaps the war's least competent general and one of its most nimble minds.*

Grant's war plan was driven by a single, elemental idea. He was going to kill a lot of

Southerners, he was going to kill them so quickly they could not be replaced, and he was willing to do that at the expense of comparable numbers of Northern lives. If he could win outright on a battlefield, he would do that. If he could not, he would simply pound away at the dwindling resources — human and material — of an adversary whose white population was only a quarter of the North's and whose industries and communications were collapsing.[1] The war had always been about death and injury, but now it was mostly about death and injury. How much, how fast. Confederate general Porter Alexander called it a "campaign of extermination."[2] If the strategy had any elegance, it lay in the nation-spanning management of Grant's staggeringly complex war machine, in the plans to keep the machine killing so the rebels could not do the very thing Lee wanted: concentrate their armies to deliver a blow that would tilt the November elections.

In the first week of May, Grant had put in motion some 270,000 men on five separate fronts spanning more than a thousand miles. Nothing on this scale had ever been done in the war. No such concerted effort to defeat the Confederacy had ever been attempted. President Lincoln had been thrilled when Grant had described the plan to him and later told his private secretary John Hay that he was "powerfully reminded" of his own "old suggestion so constantly made and as constantly neglected . . . to move at once upon the enemy's whole line so as to bring into action our great superiority in numbers."[3] Lincoln's efforts to make his generals move in concert had failed again and again, to his amazement and bitter frustration, and neither threats nor blandishments seemed to work. The generals did not go where they did not want to go.

But all that was changing, or so it seemed.

The core of Grant's strategy, the thing around which everything else revolved, was the destruction of Robert E. Lee in central Virginia, where 122,000 Union soldiers were engaged. But elsewhere in the state another 49,000 federal troops were on the move, too, in what amounted to a grand-scale encirclement of the Army of Northern Virginia. While Grant fought Lee in the Wilderness and at Spotsylvania, Major General Benjamin Butler, with 30,000 federal troops, was ascending the James River to threaten Richmond in Lee's rear. In the Shenandoah Valley, on Lee's far-western flank, Major General Franz Sigel was marching south with 9,000 men to seize the strategically critical railhead at Staunton, which fed Lee's army. Another 10,000 would move against railroads, lead mines, and salt works in western Virginia, and then on to the rail depots and warehouses in Lynchburg, which also supplied Lee's army. These three peripheral campaigns would also prevent reinforcements from reaching Lee. Grant was especially interested in the latter. Attrition did not work if the enemy was constantly supplied with fresh troops.

Grant had men on the move in the western theater, too. That same week he dispatched his favorite subordinate, William Tecumseh Sherman, from Tennessee into Georgia with 100,000 men. Sherman's objective was the destruction of Confederate general Joseph E. Johnston's 60,000-man Army of the Tennessee, the last great Confederate force in the west.*

But Grant's immediate focus was the state of Virginia, where 165,000 Union troops faced 90,000 Confederates, and where he and his bosses believed they had an excellent chance to end the war. This was not some gauzy theory. The numerical odds in their favor were so lopsided, their adversaries spread so thinly across the state, the rebel supply lines so tantalizingly fragile, that it had seemed almost impossible that the campaign could fail to destroy or at least cripple

---

* In the other piece of Grant's western strategy, Major General Nathaniel Banks was dispatched to Mobile, Alabama, with thirty thousand soldiers. Banks was, however, tied up in an ill-conceived campaign in Louisiana.

the Confederate war effort in Virginia.

What happened instead was a military disaster that would go down in history as the last great spasm of Union ineptitude and timidity in a war that had seen full measures of both. The campaign quickly became an object lesson in why the Union, with its vastly superior resources, had not been able to win the war.

Franz Sigel was in many ways everything that was wrong with the Northern army. He owed his job to politics, not fighting skill. He was the worst sort of petty empire builder, fiercely protective of his turf, jealous of his rival generals, pathologically sensitive to perceived unfairness, and uncooperative nearly to the point of treason when his hegemony was threatened. Except for one unaccountably solid performance as a division commander at the Battle of Pea Ridge in 1862, on the battlefield the thirty-nine-year-old Union general tended to behave like a frightened rabbit: he saw threats everywhere, and when he saw threats, he ran from them.

Sigel had been born and raised in Germany, had fought in the failed 1848 revolution, and had afterward moved to the United States — part of the prodigious wave of German immigration that had begun in 1820. He soon became a leading figure in the German American community, first in New York, then in St. Louis, and eventually became a steadfast supporter of Abraham Lincoln and the Republican Party. He helped suppress the secessionist movement in the volatile border state of Missouri.

For this support he extracted a price, becoming one of the first "political generals" in the war, men whom Lincoln promoted more for their vote-wrangling abilities than their prowess on the battlefield, and who ended up doing enormous damage to the Union war effort. Sigel had, indeed, performed poorly in the early war. But like other political generals he could not easily be brushed aside. When he was passed over for command, his German supporters organized mass protests and flooded Lincoln with petitions, and their noisy complaints set the tone for the rest of Sigel's war career. Whenever he felt slighted, as he often did in the largely anglophone army, he went to Lincoln to air his grievances, supported by his clamorous Germans and their congressional representatives. When a younger officer was promoted over him in 1862, he sent a personal emissary to Lincoln to protest his mistreatment. Lincoln admonished him "not to keep up this constant complaining," which made it seem, in Lincoln's eyes, that Sigel was "only anxious about himself." When another Sigel envoy appeared at the White House a few months later to retail a new set of injustices, Lincoln cried, "Don't talk to me any longer about *that man!*"[4] In 1863 Sigel had made the mistake of demanding to be relieved of duty and had been immediately and cheerfully obliged. He was reinstated a year later only because Lincoln desperately needed him to draw votes away from John C. Frémont, Lincoln's main rival for the 1864 Republican nomination.[5] To win the war, Lincoln had to win the election. One more incompetent general, more or less, wasn't going to make much difference.

Or so the president's thinking went. But Sigel had done more than just pull political strings to secure his command in the Shenandoah Valley. He had also refused outright to cooperate with Grant's original plan, which would have sent Grant's chosen officer, Major General Edward Ord, on a single, sweeping campaign from West Virginia through Virginia. Sigel, who commanded the Department of West Virginia and did not like interlopers, simply shut Ord out. He gave Ord half the troops Grant had promised and then refused to provide him with supplies. So Ord withdrew, and a new plan emerged with three campaigns instead of one. Sigel, predictably, would command one of them.[6] Grant and Halleck were apparently helpless against Lincoln's electoral needs.

The Shenandoah Valley was one of the strategic jewels of the war's eastern theater, a slanting 150-mile-long corridor of rich agricultural land between two mountain ranges that served as the breadbasket of the northern Confederacy. Food was gathered in the city of Staunton in the southern end of the valley, taken by the Virginia Central Railroad to Richmond, and distributed as rations to Lee's army. The valley also offered a tailor-made invasion route to Richmond. Thus Staunton — a prize of enormous and even war-changing value — became Sigel's target, and he took off with hopes and regimental banners held high, heading south on the macadamized Valley Turnpike.

What followed demonstrated with singular clarity the effect political generals had on the war. Sigel's jauntiness quickly evaporated. His once confident army of nine thousand now crept warily through the valley, frightened first by a small detachment of Confederate cavalry, then by rumors that the rebel force held as many as twenty thousand soldiers. (It was one-quarter that size.) Sigel stalled for days in the tiny hamlet of Woodstock trying to understand just how vast and lethal his enemy was. The hallmark of many hypercautious Union army generals, dating from the days of George McClellan, was to grossly overestimate enemy strength. General McClellan had employed his intelligence chief, Allan Pinkerton, for this specific purpose. If your opponent had twice your force, then it made no sense to attack, did it? Better to withdraw and ask for reinforcements. Better to wait. Sigel, like McClellan, saw phantoms everywhere.

There were more complex reasons why Union generals — especially in the Army of the Potomac and its adjuncts — quailed at critical moments.* On the march in the exotic Confederate wilderness, in a land full of hostile citizens and miles from a supply base, the world was indeed a dangerous place. The terrain alone was frightening: vast stretches of unknown or poorly mapped lands containing precipitous mountains, unfordable rivers and swamps, tangled forests. Every crook in a river could conceal a trap, every swamp a dead end where an army could be cornered and destroyed. If a commander made a mistake, many of his men and officers could die or be wounded. Generals in the war died at a much higher rate than men in the ranks. If a general retreated or surrendered, his reputation and career could be ruined, which might actually be worse than death. He could spend the rest of his life — as many Civil War generals did — trying to defend the actions of a single day, or even a

* The North had no monopoly on executive incompetence, but Union generals, fighting in a hostile country, were subject to more of these influences than their Southern counterparts.

171

single hour. As a result, the more timid generals could easily be persuaded that to risk anything was to risk everything. Only the rare commander could make a decision involving large stretches of unfamiliar land and enemies of unknown size and whereabouts and stick resolutely to it. In war, every moment brought the opportunity for second thoughts.

In the town of New Market, in the middle of the Shenandoah Valley, Sigel finally encountered the dreaded foe: a motley gang of 5,335 hastily assembled Confederates that included nearly 1,000 aging reservists equipped mostly with shotguns and hunting rifles, cadets from the Virginia Military Institute, and other irregulars along with the veterans, all under the command of perhaps the ultimate political general, John C. Breckinridge, vice president of the United States from 1857 to 1861.[7] Breckinridge, an extreme pro-slavery candidate in the 1860 election, had finished second to Lincoln in electoral votes. Unlike Sigel, Breckinridge for some reason knew how to fight. Like most Confederate generals, he was accustomed to being outnumbered.

The battle, which took place on open, cultivated farmland, was Napoleonic in its scale and simplicity and should have favored Sigel. But in spite of his nearly two-to-one advantage in troops — not to mention the boys and old men fighting in his opponent's ranks — Sigel mismanaged it from the start. He neutralized his own battle lines by deploying them in front of each other. He was maneuvered into using a small force to attack a much larger one.[8] His charges failed, his troops' morale collapsed, and his lines disintegrated. "The enemy fled in confusion," wrote a Confederate officer, "leaving killed, wounded, artillery, and prisoners in our hands."[9] The cadets alone took one hundred prisoners, while suffering fifty-five casualties of their own.

Sigel's troops retreated north. Although they still greatly outnumbered the rebels and had burned a bridge that effectively halted pursuit, they kept on running anyway until they reached the town of Strasburg, thirty-two miles away. There the campaign ended. Sigel would not mount another operation. He would no longer be a threat to Breckinridge, to Staunton, to the Virginia Central Railroad, or to Lee's supply lines. His victorious opponent was soon sending reinforcements to the Army of Northern Virginia.

Grant was furious. Halleck, who had feuded with Sigel for years, told Grant bluntly, "If you expect anything from Sigel, you will be mistaken. He will do nothing but run. He never did anything else."[10] (Rebel soldiers called him, derisively, the Flying Dutchman.)[11] Two weeks later, Sigel was removed from command in the Shenandoah Valley.

Two months after that, following another embarrassing performance, he exhausted Lincoln's patience and was relieved entirely of command in the army. That may have made people in the War Department feel better. But it did nothing to end Confederate dominance in the valley. Though excuses were made and battle reports filed with the usual rationalizations, what had defeated Franz Sigel at the Battle of New Market was mostly abject fear: of Robert E. Lee and his terrifying prowess; of the horrific possibilities that lay just over the next ridge; of the prospect of Sigel's own failure. Nothing else could explain his behavior.[12]

The other wing of the campaign in Sigel's department failed in different ways, but for the same reasons. Brigadier General George R. Crook's expedition against the Virginia and Tennessee Railroad had started well with a victory at the Battle of Cloyd's Mountain and the destruction of a railroad bridge, but had stalled when Crook saw rebel dispatches saying that Grant was losing to Lee.[13] Frightened of the specter of rebel reinforcements headed his way — even though he was 230 miles from the fighting — Crook retreated as fast as he could back to safety, pushing his men on a brutally hard, eight-day, 150-mile march in bad weather into the mountains of West Virginia.[14] His subordinate William Averell lost a minor engagement, tore up a few sections of track, then joined Crook in the weird, hasty retreat into the safety of Union-held West Virginia, ignoring all orders to do otherwise.[15]

The result of these failures was that Confederate general John Breckinridge was able to report to Lee that Sigel, Crook, and Averell were all falling back and no longer posed any threat. Soon twenty-five hundred rebel troops — precious commodities in the collapsing world of the Confederacy — were on their way to join Lee's army. Three years into the war, after countless engagements and many army shake-ups, the strange truth was that, in an organization that nominally valued obedience and discipline, Union generals would still not go where they did not want to go.

But the sins of Sigel, Crook, and Averell were minor compared to the mortal transgressions of Major General Benjamin Butler. In early May 1864, as Grant was engaging Lee in the Wilderness, Butler was given the sort of opportunity that no general in the war had ever been given and that no one had even believed possible: a cakewalk with thirty thousand men straight into the undefended heart of the Confederacy — Richmond — and a chance to cut Lee's supply lines and destroy his army right there.

Just how Butler failed to accomplish that is

one of the most remarkable stories of the Civil War.

Benjamin Franklin Butler was a brilliant man. Few people who ever met him would have disagreed with that. He was one of the most exceptional officers on either side in the Civil War, and perhaps, if one was measuring sheer brainpower, the smartest. What he was good at, however, was not fighting battles. He was abysmally suited to that. It was, in fact, the collision of his coruscating genius and his appalling tactical incompetence that made him one of the most colorful and compelling figures in the American Civil War.

He grew up in the industrial boomtown of Lowell, Massachusetts, a precocious and irreverent child who was smarter than everyone else and not shy about letting them know it. He had a way with words, an exceptional command of facts, a willingness to bend rules, and a talent for winning. He became one of the richest lawyers in the country. At the age of twenty-seven he became the youngest attorney ever admitted to practice before the US Supreme Court.

He also rubbed people the wrong way. Portly, bald, and cross-eyed, with a sagging mustache and a permanent squint (and, implausibly, a beautiful, intelligent actress wife who doted on him), he was seen by his many enemies as the worst sort of influence peddler and backroom fixer. As a member of the Massachusetts state legislature, he was called "a notorious demagogue and political scoundrel" and a "putrid carcass" by local papers.[16] Not that criticism bothered him. Butler was Butler, a force to be reckoned with whether you liked him or not. As a delegate at the 1860 Democratic Party convention, he voted fifty-seven times to nominate Mississippi senator Jefferson Davis for president, which caused a crowd of six thousand people in his home state to burn him in effigy.[17] When the war came, he transformed himself within a year from a South-sympathizing Democrat into a Lincoln-supporting abolitionist Republican.

He became one of the war's first heroes. When Fort Sumter fell on April 13, 1861, Butler, who had no military experience other than with local militias, outmaneuvered rivals to lead two regiments of Massachusetts militia to Washington, which had been isolated by the destruction of telegraph lines and railroad bridges in Maryland.[18] One of his regiments fought the war's first battle against an armed mob in Baltimore. He took the other regiment on a wild ride through secessionist Maryland that included capturing the hostile state capital of Annapolis. He later seized a key junction on the Baltimore and Ohio Railroad and, acting without orders, marched on and occupied the city of Baltimore. He was credited with helping to

177

keep the volatile, slaveholding state of Maryland in the Union at a critical moment. The news was greeted in the North by celebrations and fireworks.[19] He was promoted to the rank of major general.

A few months later he became famous again, but for an entirely different reason.

After his adventure in Maryland, Butler had taken a new assignment at Fort Monroe in coastal Virginia. There he encountered a problem that many other Union commanders would soon face: what to do with thousands of slaves who sought refuge with the Union army. The war was not yet about freeing them. Lincoln's Emancipation Proclamation was seventeen months away, and Lincoln himself still believed that freeing slaves would be unfair to their owners.[20] In the absence of any other plan, most Union commanders obeyed the Fugitive Slave Act, which required them to return runaway slaves to their owners. They thus avoided the more practical problem of how to feed and house them.

Butler saw the issue as a purely legal problem and therefore one his agile mind could solve. When three slaves belonging to a Confederate colonel sought refuge in his fort, he decided that he had a good reason for not returning them. His conversation with an astonished Confederate major named M. B. Carey is worth repeating:

"I am informed that three negroes belonging to Colonel Mallory have escaped within your line," said Major Carey. ". . . What do you mean to do with these negroes?"

"I intend to hold them," replied Butler.

"Do you mean, then, to set aside your constitutional obligation to return them?"

"I mean to take Virginia at her word, as declared in the ordinance of secession passed yesterday. I am under no constitutional obligations to a foreign country, which Virginia now claims to be."

"But you say we cannot secede, and so you cannot consistently detain those negroes."

"But you say you have seceded, so you cannot consistently claim them. I shall hold these negroes as contraband of war, since they were engaged in construction of your battery and are claimed as your property."[21]

Contraband of war. With these three words Butler not only turned the South's own legalistic arguments against it, but offered a new way to think about the war and the question of slavery. Word of his action spread quickly, and soon most people in the North and especially abolitionists were exulting at the simple elegance of his solution.[22] Not everyone in Washington thought this was a good idea — Lincoln, for example, refused to recognize the Confederacy as a foreign country and did not agree to officially free the escapees — but its relentless, practical logic was impossible to miss. The War Department approved Butler's action, and hundreds of fugitive slaves soon showed up at his camp, wanting to claim their new status not as escaped slaves but as "contrabands of war." He fed them and housed them and put them to work for the army. He had thus provided a path to freedom for thousands of slaves that anticipated the Emancipation Proclamation by a year and a half.

For this, the South despised him. It grew to hate him even more during his draconian rule as commander in occupied New Orleans. There he arrested dissidents, censored newspapers, executed a man for tearing up the Union flag, and took aim at Confederate women with his bitterly controversial General Order no. 28. To stop the women from insulting, spitting on, emptying chamber pots on, and generally antagonizing Union officers, Butler issued an order stating, "Hereafter when any female shall by word, gesture, or movement insult or show contempt for any officer or soldier of the United States she shall be regarded and held liable to be treated as a woman of the town plying her avocation." He would, in other words, treat the ladies of New Orleans as prostitutes. Butler's outraged critics wrote that he was advocating rape, that he was proof of the immoral, godless, and tyrannical Northern character. The Confederate Congress called him a war criminal and vowed that he would be executed if captured. Throughout the South he was referred to simply as the Beast.

All of which made him quite popular in the North. By early 1864 he was so popular that he had been mentioned as a candidate for the presidency, the vice presidency, or a cabinet position. He was a large-scale and more powerful version of Franz Sigel. He was too powerful to be dismissed, as Grant learned on several occasions. Butler's presence in the army was a political calculation by Abraham Lincoln that Butler would do less harm there than unleashed into the arena of national politics.

On May 5, the Beast found himself on Richmond's doorstep. He and his Army of the James had steamed up the James River that day in an armada of fifty-nine ships and fetched up at a place called Bermuda Hundred, about fifteen miles south of Richmond and eight miles north of Petersburg. That a large Union army could so casually get close to the Confederate capital seems astounding. It seemed astounding even then. The approach was made possible by federal control of the James River, which runs from the Appalachian Mountains through Richmond and down to Chesapeake Bay. But that control ended abruptly just north of Bermuda Hundred. There the river narrowed dramatically and became decidedly more hostile: mines had been laid, rams and ironclads deployed. At ninety-foot-high Drewry's Bluff, the big guns of Fort Darling controlled the river. No one was getting to Richmond by water. Butler's orders were therefore to put ashore as close to the city as he could and to move against the city by land, either by attacking it directly, or by joining forces with Grant's army and then attacking.

Butler was only a few hours march from the rebel capital. He was also in possession of perhaps the war's most significant piece of intelligence.[23] After he landed, he had been approached by a member of the Richmond spy ring operated by an eccentric, socially prominent abolitionist named Elizabeth Van Lew. Van Lew was one of the war's best spies, with sources inside the Confederate War Department and even in the household of President Jefferson Davis. She used ciphers, invisible ink, courier systems, and messages smuggled in hollow eggs. Her material was so consistently good that the intelligence officer of the Army of the Potomac credited with her "the greater portion [of our intelligence] from Richmond in 1864 and 1865."[24] Butler had worked with her before and trusted her.

The operative gave Butler the breathtaking news that "all the troops had gone from

Richmond to Lee's army" and that their replacements from North Carolina had not yet arrived.[25] Which meant that the Army of the James could march virtually unopposed into the capital. This turned out to be only a slight overstatement. Confederate general George Pickett actually had 750 men in Richmond awaiting assignment, and perhaps a few thousand defenders were strung out around the city. Petersburg was held by less than a thousand soldiers.[26] Van Lew was right: Richmond and Petersburg were there for the taking, and along with them the entirety of Lee's supply lines. Butler had stumbled into one of the great opportunities of the war. With the two cities in Union hands, all of Lee's supplies would be cut off, the rebel government decapitated, and its leaders in captivity. The war would be as good as over.* The beating heart of the Confederacy lay open before Benjamin Butler and his thirty thousand men. To his credit, he did not doubt it.

To his eternal discredit, he failed to act on

---

* If the Union commander at Bermuda Hundred had been, say, Philip Sheridan or Ulysses Grant, instead of Benjamin Butler, both Richmond and Petersburg would likely have fallen on May 6 and 7, placing thirty thousand Union troops directly in Lee's rear and in possession of his supply lines as he fought the second day in the Wilderness.

it. Butler's first instinct was the logical and correct one: move now, quickly, before the enemy could reinforce. He went to his corps commanders, Major General Quincy Gillmore and Major General William F. "Baldy" Smith, with a proposal to march that very night on Richmond. The soldiers were restless from twenty-four hours on the boats, Butler said, and would enjoy the march. Richmond was sixteen miles away, the weather balmy, the road clear, and the moon full.

Gillmore and Smith were experienced fighters and West Point graduates, and Grant had placed them precisely there, in proximity to Butler, because Grant did not trust Butler. Grant thought highly of Smith, in particular, and Grant believed he was saving Butler from his own mistakes. As Grant would soon realize, he had actually given Butler a pair of fearful, small-minded, and self-advancing incompetents who made everything worse.

Neither general wanted anything to do with an attack on Richmond. They were scared of the unknown and of everything that might go wrong and were horrified that Butler would even suggest it. Gillmore stated flatly that if he received such an order, he would feel it his duty not to obey it.[27] Butler, unpersuaded, sought counsel from his friend the former West Point professor General Godfrey Weitzel, who, in keeping with long-standing

Army of the Potomac tradition, transformed a military problem into a political one. He pointed out that if Butler failed, after such strenuous opposition from his own corps commanders, "it would entirely ruin you." Not only that, Weitzel added helpfully, but Gillmore and Smith would do everything they could to make the mission fail, thus helping to fulfill their own prophecies.[28] Butler would, in short, be risking his career and reputation by marching north. Instead of asserting himself, Butler quietly backed down. There would be no march against an undefended Richmond. Butler would satisfy himself with lesser objectives.

What followed in the next ten days was by any standard a remarkable display of incompetence. Instead of moving toward enemy-held positions, Butler's men spent their time digging fortifications that spanned the Bermuda Hundred peninsula. The thinking was entirely defensive: establish a strong, unassailable base from which to operate. Many troops would be doing nothing but digging in the coming days, instead of marching and fighting. While they built their fieldworks, their enemies, who had panicked when they realized how close Butler's force was to their capital, were rushing reinforcements to the scene. Richmond was left untouched.

Instead Butler moved first against the railroad, then against Petersburg. But his attacks were half-hearted, fragmentary, and delayed. In spite of his three-to-one advantage, his force was repulsed.[29] When he proposed a larger attack against Petersburg, he argued bitterly with Gillmore and Smith, who disagreed with Butler and this time put their objections in writing. So nothing happened. To read the traffic between Gillmore, Smith, and Butler is to observe men lost in minor details, pettifoggery, and self-protection.[30] Petersburg, one of the most important tactical prizes in the Confederacy, too remained unharmed. Meanwhile tempers flared, frustrations mounted, everybody blamed everyone else, and still nothing got done. And the number of rebel troops steadily grew. (By May 10, five days after Butler landed, 12,500 of them would be entrenched in front of Richmond.)[31]

Now the War Department in Washington added to the confusion. On May 9, as Butler was trying to make up his mind about attacking Petersburg, he received a remarkable set of dispatches from Secretary of War Edwin Stanton. The first claimed, "On Friday night [May 6] Lee's army were in full retreat for Richmond. Grant pursuing with his army." The second, written a few hours later but equally breathless, read, "A dispatch from General Grant has just been received. He is on the march with his whole army to form a junction with you, but has not determined his route."[32]

This information was false in all of its particulars: that Grant had won, that Lee was retreating to Richmond, that Grant was on his way to join Butler. It was pure uncorroborated War Department nonsense. At the time Butler received the message, Grant was assaulting Lee's trenches at Spotsylvania and would not leave that battlefield for eleven more days. But Butler didn't know that, and the news finally emboldened him to move north toward Richmond. Grant was on his way, after all. So Butler marched north with a vague idea that he wasn't going to really attack but simply "demonstrate" for a while, marking time until Grant got there. Instead of attacking he dug in again, then sat inertly in place for several days until Confederate general Pierre Gustave Toutant Beauregard — now with eighteen thousand troops — attacked him. The resulting Battle of Proctor's Creek (also known as the Battle of Drewry's Bluff) did not amount to much. Beauregard inflicted fifteen hundred casualties on Butler and captured fifteen hundred men but could not dislodge him. Butler, who finally received news that Grant was not coming after all, retreated immediately back to the safety of his deep trenches across the Bermuda Hundred peninsula. When his men got there, they took shelter along a five-mile line of fortifications that stretched from the James River to the Appomattox River. They were secure and happy behind their works. All of that digging had apparently paid off.

Then something happened that Butler and his corps commanders had not quite thought of. Beauregard's men — the eighteen thousand who were chasing the thirty thousand — did exactly the same thing the Army of the James had. They advanced right up to the waist of the peninsula and dug their own trenches, just as impregnable as Butler's. As anyone can see from a map of Bermuda Hundred, this meant that Butler's brilliant defensive position had suddenly become a perfect trap, with water on three sides and Beauregard's fortifications on the fourth. Butler was now securely contained in his own base. Not only that, but Beauregard figured out that Butler's army could be held there by a small force. As a disgusted Ulysses S. Grant put it, Butler's army "was as completely shut off from further operations against Richmond as if it had been in a bottle strongly corked." Soon seven thousand more reinforcements were on their way to Robert E. Lee. These, added to the troops released by Sigel's retreat, amounted to 19 percent of Lee's army after Spotsylvania.[33]

Butler, helpless in place, was soon stripped of twenty thousand men, who were sent to join Grant. In spite of the fiasco at Bermuda Hundred, his political support was still too strong for him to be fired. He had at least two more large blunders left in him before he would be removed from command.[34] He did, however, acquire a new nickname to place alongside the Beast, one that caught on quickly in the North: Bottled-Up Butler. His campaign was both a disaster and an omen of Union disasters still to come.

CHAPTER NINE:
THE PERSUASIVE LOGIC
OF GUNPOWDER

BLACK UNION TROOPS IN THE FIELD: In the war's last year, fully 10 percent of the Northern army was black, more than half of whom were escaped slaves.

The land was something out of a nightmare, stripped of its trees and grasses and anything remotely green, refashioned into a bulging, pockmarked wasteland of raw dirt and sharpened timber. In a campaign that had seen its share of digging in, nothing compared to the fortifications in front of the city of Petersburg,

Virginia, in July 1864. The armies had entrenched within rifle range of each other, and their lines mirrored each other as far as the eye could see — clear to Richmond, twenty-six miles away. Inside these realms of packed earth lay, fully concealed, enormous numbers of men. Unlike Spotsylvania, where the trenches had been constructed quickly, here both Yankee and rebel engineers had been given plenty of time to perfect their defenses.[1] The ugliness of the dirt mounds — which looked more like the work of prairie dogs than men — concealed the brilliance of their construction.

The entrenchments had gotten stronger and deeper. They were now fronted by twelve feet of earth reinforced by ingeniously stacked and interlocked timber.[2] Traverses ran perpendicular to battle lines, with rifle pits in front of the main works, sleeping holes, alleyways, and various rear-running and connecting trenches, many of them covered by timber roofs and wide enough to accommodate supply wagons.[3] At intervals in this immense honeycomb were armored forts that housed mortars and artillery with embrasures for shooting — forty-one of them in the federal lines alone.[4] There were bombproofs, too, deeper pits the men called gopher holes. In front of the main fortifications yet more trenches had been dug, fifteen feet wide by eight feet deep. Athwart them lay a variety of unpleasant obstacles: felled trees that had been piled up and pointed toward the enemy (abatis); sharpened rows of stakes jammed into the ground (fraises); and eight- to ten-foot-long spikes held in place by drilled logs (chevaux-de-frise).

Thus had the soldiers rebuilt the world to their own specifications. Unfortunately, their excavations did not guarantee that they would not die. Sharpshooters on both sides still managed to hit, with diabolical accuracy, any piece of human flesh or clothing that flashed in front of them. Heads that popped above the works, even for a moment, often became explosions of blood, skin, hair, teeth, and bone.[5] Men in the advance rifle pits were especially vulnerable. Worst of all were the persistent mortar shells. Both sides lobbed them over the trenches in lofty arcs. They hung motionless in the air for a moment before tumbling gently forward, their fuses hissing audibly, then detonating and raining hot chunks of jagged iron down into the soft flesh in the entrenchments.[6] The largest of the mortars was a 17,120-pound Union gun known as the Dictator, which fired a thirteen-inch-wide, 220-pound exploding shell that could destroy a bombproof.

But such killing was almost incidental. Mounting a general assault on the war's strongest fieldworks amounted to suicide, and by now everyone knew it. In mid-June Grant and Meade had missed several chances to break through at Petersburg before most of Lee's soldiers had gotten there, which meant that their enemies had had time to reinforce and fortify and that, as a general proposition, the rebel position was now unassailable. Even Ulysses S. Grant, the hammerer, understood that. The glorious war-ending schemes of early May had ended with a dreary fizzle two months later in the doomsday trenches of Petersburg.

Which was why the proposal made by Lieutenant Colonel Henry Pleasants — though it sounded radical and possibly crazy — was exactly what his army needed to hear. Pleasants was a mining engineer in civilian life and now commanded a Pennsylvania regiment that contained a number of coal miners. He had noticed a section of the Petersburg lines where only 135 yards separated Union and Confederate trenches.[7] Because he and his men dug holes and blew things up for a living, he suggested to his commanding general, Ambrose Burnside, that they build a tunnel across the no-man's-land of felled trees and sharpened sticks and under the Confederate works. His miners would pack in twelve thousand pounds of gunpowder and blow the whole thing to kingdom come — fortifications, men, artillery, everything — creating a wide gap in the enemy's defenses. Burnside, a poor general but a technically clever man who had invented a breech-loading carbine that was in wide use in the war, saw no reason why the technology would not work. He thought it was a splendid idea. Meade hated it. He thought it was "all claptrap and nonsense," said Pleasants later, and "that such a length of mine had never been excavated in military operations."[8] Grant, to whom Burnside reported directly, loved the plan, especially the notion that Grant had nothing in particular to lose by trying it. He dismissed Meade's objections.

So on June 25 the Pennsylvanians took up their picks and shovels and began to dig. From the start, the prickly, jealous Meade worked diligently to sabotage the project, denying Burnside soldiers, equipment, tools, and assistance.[9] When Meade refused to give them wheelbarrows, Pleasants's men fashioned them from cracker boxes and hickory sticks.[10] Nor would Meade allow Pleasants the full measure of gunpowder he had requested. He would get only eight thousand pounds of it, in spite of his protest that the lesser amount would create a narrower, deeper bomb crater that would be hard for attacking Union soldiers to pass through.[11] The consequences of that piece of petty, spiteful politics would soon shake the entire army.

The battle plan was straightforward: the

bomb would go off, then soldiers from Burnside's 9th Corps would pour into the theoretical hole in the Confederate lines, deploying this way and that to shore it up and hold it open so that more troops could follow. What was not straightforward at all, and actually without precedent, was Burnside's choice of troops to lead the attack. His freshest troops were in his 4th Division, which consisted of forty-three hundred black soldiers and white officers. They were fresh because they had done almost no fighting. That was because they were black and Meade thought they were best used for guard and fatigue duty. But Burnside had confidence in them, and because he reported to Grant and not Meade, it would be black men who would spearhead what could prove to be the war's definitive attack.

Though Burnside was in a minority of Union generals who thought that blacks should fight, the United States Colored Troops (USCT) as a whole had done well in combat. They had not been perfect. Their willingness to stand and fight resembled closely the behavior of their white counterparts: sometimes they were brave, sometimes they were not. Soldiers were soldiers, and many people were surprised to learn that. Meanwhile their brilliant and courageous exploits in the doomed assault on Fort Wagner near Charleston in the summer of 1863 were by now common knowledge in the army. One of their greatest successes had taken place just a few weeks before, when the Union army had first arrived at Petersburg. On June 15, twenty-two hundred black soldiers in Ben Butler's Army of the James had advanced under fire across four hundred yards of open ground to attack entrenched rebels. They had withstood fire and taken heavy casualties and had stormed the rebel works, capturing one hundred prisoners and sixteen cannons. They could barely contain their joy and embraced the captured cannons as though they were alive.[12] Unfortunately — for themselves and for the fate of the Union — they were under the command of the stupefyingly incompetent Baldy Smith, who, with yet another clear shot into the heart of the Confederacy — another war-changing moonlight walk in good weather with few rebel defenders in place — decided it would be better to wait. More Union bungling had followed, and the chance had been missed. But that took nothing away from what the African American troops had done.

And now Burnside was sending his 4th Division in. In early July he had told the division's commander, Brigadier General Edward Ferrero, a Spanish-born dancing teacher and choreographer from New York City, that his men would lead the charge.[13] Ferrero inspected the terrain as best he could, formulated a plan of assault, and gave his troops the necessary tactical training. They all understood the significance of the assignment. At 3:30 a.m. on July 30 the gates of hell were going to open inside the Confederate lines, and the forces of freedom were going to surge through to victory. This was going to be the most important moment of the war. And black men were going in first.

White people on both sides saw simply black men in uniform. They called them coloreds or Negroes or niggers and had an idea that to be a black person was to be just this one thing, a personality type and a racial type, the thing denoted by the blackness alone. But anyone looking hard — and no one was — at the actual composition of the 4th Division of the 9th Corps of the Army of the Potomac would have been astounded by its variety. The men came from Connecticut, Illinois, Ohio, Indiana, Pennsylvania, Maryland, and Virginia. They came from cities and farms. Roughly half had been slaves in the border states.* The 20th Connecticut regiment contained, along with its New Englanders, former slaves from Virginia. Literate blacks

* Of the black soldiers in the Union army, 57 percent came from the eleven Confederate states; 24 percent from border states; 19 percent from eighteen Northern states.

from Northern cities sat around campfires with illiterate slaves, and if they felt superior to their Southern brethren, they were also happy to learn the slaves' spirituals and bring them back home to their Northern churches.[14] Among the free blacks were farmers, waiters, cooks, teamsters, sailors, masons, plasterers, hostlers, laborers, butchers, and shoemakers. Some men had seen combat and some had not even been near it.[15] The skin of some soldiers was very black and others were Anglo-Saxon white, with every shade in between. As in the white army, the division had plenty of good, hardworking men — many officers said they picked up basic drills faster than white soldiers — and also slackers, drunks, and thieves. If their ranks had any consistency at all, it lay in their religiousness, their love of music, and in the dates of their recruitment: the majority of the men in the 4th Division USCT had mustered in during the winter and spring of 1864.

But all of them would have agreed that life was very hard for black soldiers in an army that did not want them. Though the war was on some level supposed to be about equality among men, black recruits found themselves in a terribly unequal world in which prejudices against them — as soldiers and as human beings — often seemed to run as deep as they did in the South.

This began with unequal pay, which was by

far their biggest grievance. The differences, which persisted until late in the war, were large and deliberate. On May 1, 1864, the *Chicago Tribune* published an editorial with the headline "Read and Blush" condemning the stark differences between black and white monthly paychecks and showing how wide the gap was.[16]

Rank	White Pay	Black Pay
Private	$13	$7
Corporal	$13	$7
Sergeant	$17	$7
First Sergeant	$20	$7

The USCT were denied more than an equal salary. They did not receive the $100 enlistment bounty — more than a year's pay — that white soldiers had gotten since the early days of the war. Nor did the families of dead black soldiers receive federal pensions, as white families did. The men of the 54th Massachusetts regiment, heroes of Fort Wagner, had been so bitterly upset about these double standards that they had refused to accept their pay and had gone without it for eighteen months.[17] Other units stacked their rifles and staged what amounted to salary strikes.

Such federal policies were rooted in pure politics: full equality of any sort was abhorrent to many Northern whites. The idea of comparable pay challenged carefully nurtured stereotypes: that blacks were intellectually inferior, closer to animals than to whites; that they were childlike, irresponsible, lacking discipline and self-control. In short, that they were not worth, in economic terms, what white people were. Many whites hated the idea that they were fighting and dying to liberate African Americans from slavery and the notion that they somehow needed black soldiers to help them do this. They hated the notion that free blacks would flood the market with cheap labor and take their jobs. In 1862 in a Chicago packinghouse, workers had gone so far as to take a pledge "not to work for any packer, under any consideration, who will, in any manner, bring negro labor into competition with our labor." The workers saw the hiring of blacks as a deliberate attempt to lower white wages. Marches in New York City in the summer of 1863 that had begun as draft protests had exploded into race riots, driven by anger among poor whites, including many Irish immigrants, who shared the same bleak, racially colored vision of their economic future.

Thus the politics of war became politics of race, and Lincoln was as vulnerable to these shifting winds as anyone else. In the summer of 1863 — the summer of Fort Wagner — Lincoln had told Frederick Douglass that, since blacks "had larger motives for being soldiers than white men . . . they ought to be willing to enter the services upon any condition," and that the lower pay "seemed a necessary concession to smooth the way to their employment at all as soldiers."[18] Lincoln was simply voicing what appeared to be the will of the majority.

He soon changed his mind. But not until August 1864, after spirited congressional debate, were black soldiers' salaries finally brought up to parity with their white counterparts'. And not until March 1865, a month before the end of the war, did most of them receive retroactive compensation from the date of their enlistment. So there was bad faith all around. The harm that such policies did to the morale of black recruits, or to their sense of what they were supposed to be fighting for, is incalculable.

Salary was only one of their troubles. The army's most basic form of racism came in the form of "fatigue" duty, noncombat labor that soldiers performed as part of their jobs. In other words, the scut work: kitchen duty, digging and covering latrines, digging trenches, building fortifications, loading and hauling supplies and equipment, gathering wood and water. In principle, such work was distributed evenly among the ranks. In fact, it fell disproportionately on the USCT. This was not just because they were not trusted to

201

fight. The main reason, articulated by any number of Northern officers, was their belief that blacks were lesser beings best suited to hard labor, particularly in hot Southern climates.

Which meant that, in spite of promises of equal treatment, blacks' white officers often played the roles of slaveholders. Some thought of themselves as "nigger drivers," forcing black soldiers into heavy work details in hellish summer climates in mosquito-infested places such as Morganza, Louisiana. One black soldier wrote to Secretary Stanton to complain that he had been placed under the command of "slave drivers" who put him to work "cleaning up farms and cutting up stumps." Another said he and his comrades were worked "like horses or mules."[19] In Louisiana in 1863, excessive fatigue duty contributed to rising death rates among blacks. Such practices soon led to public outcry, especially among abolitionists. The *Chicago Tribune,* among other papers, published crusading editorials in protest. On June 14, 1864, the US secretary of war finally issued an order forbidding them. But efforts to stop them were usually half-hearted. Discriminatory fatigue duty persisted until the end of the war.

Black soldiers were frequently and harshly punished. In several documented cases, they were whipped and tied up for long periods.

Bondage, in particular, reminded escaped slaves of their former lives, and they hated it with a special passion. In one celebrated instance, a white officer staked out a black man and covered him in molasses, struck another, and whipped two others. When it seemed likely that the officer would not be punished, the soldiers rioted. Though a court-martial found the officer guilty and dismissed him from service, two of the soldiers were executed and six others were imprisoned for mutiny.[20] Mutinies among black soldiers were common in the war, and African Americans accounted for 80 percent of all soldiers executed for mutiny in the Civil War.[21]

Black soldiers suffered in almost all areas of army service. They were often equipped with obsolete weapons. As late as 1864 they were given superannuated .54- and .69-caliber Austrian and Prussian muskets.[22] When they were wounded or sick, they received care inferior to that of whites and died at higher rates. "Very few surgeons will do precisely the same for blacks as they would for whites," said a Massachusetts surgeon assigned to a USCT regiment, admitting what everyone knew to be true.[23] Even apparently friendly officers abused blacks. Many cases were documented of white officers stealing or embezzling their charges' money, which had been given to them for safekeeping.[24]

Nor were the soldiers' relatives spared. Mistreatment of the families of slaves who had enlisted in the Union army from border states was also widespread and well-documented. In one typical case, a Union private's wife was beaten with a leather strap from a horse harness because of her husband's enlistment. "They abuse me because you went & say they will not take care of our children," she wrote to her husband. "[They] do nothing but quarrel with me all the time and beat me scandalously the day before yesterday." Women and children were routinely beaten and sometimes driven away for the sin of their husbands' and fathers' enlistments.[25]

Such pervasive mistreatment — along with the Southern refusal to give blacks rights as soldiers — ought to have crushed black enthusiasm for enlistment. Somehow it did not. By October 1864, 135,089 African American troops had been recorded in military service since the first enlistments — more than double the number from a year before.[26] And new recruits continued to pour in, filling out new units such as the 4th Division. For many the war offered answers to questions about their own identities. Who, exactly, were they? The refrain in a popular camp song called the "Negro Battle Hymn" suggested one answer:

They look like men, they look like men
They look like men of war.
All arm'd and dressed in uniform,
They look like men of war.[27]

A man of war was not a slave, or a person of no account. He was an American and a soldier, with a decent job and a clear sense of purpose.

The army also supplied a real, palpable idea of a future that had never before existed. One former slave, who had arrived in a Union camp after a brutal nine-day escape through Carolina swamps, told a Rhode Island soldier that he had been able to endure the hardship because "I seed de lamp of life ahead and de lamp of death behind." Another man who had escaped said, "When I seed dat flag, it lift me right up."[28]

The men of the 4th Division had crossed the Rapidan River with Ulysses S. Grant a full two months before they were chosen to lead the attack against Petersburg. All were new recruits back in those days. None had seen combat.[29] They weren't going to see any frontline fighting, either, if the commanding generals could help it. Lincoln and the abolitionist cohort may have believed in the viability of black soldiers in combat, but most of Lincoln's generals still did not. Thus as Grant's army plunged into the dark thickets of the Wilderness in early May, the forty-three hundred soldiers of the 4th stayed behind to guard the wagons. This was not fighting, but neither was it dishonorable work. It was not digging latrines. And though they were posted primarily as a deterrent, they did fight in two minor engagements. Confederate cavalry attacked their sector twice. Both times black regiments repulsed them easily, suffering few casualties.

But mainly they were just sentries. As Grant moved south and east against Lee, the 4th moved in his army's wake as wagon guards. The men were thus spared the multiplying horrors of that campaign. After the stalemate at Spotsylvania, Grant had shuffled south again, this time to the North Anna River. After some inconclusive fighting, he had realized that Lee's position was too strong to attack, so Grant had moved yet again, pushing his army along in the now-familiar crabwise movement in the direction of Richmond. This time his army landed at a nondescript crossroads in the middle of a nondescript forest in a place that held harrowing memories from fighting there two years before: Cold Harbor.

On June 3, while the 4th stood diligently on guard in the rear, Grant threw his entire army against Lee's heavily armored, seven-mile-long line of fortifications, blindly hoping that one of his divisions, somewhere, somehow, was going to break through.[30] That was the only plan, if you could call it that. In effect, Grant was repeating at Cold Harbor the mistakes he had made at Spotsylvania. He had ordered the attack because he felt that, whatever he did, he could not do nothing. He could not back down again from the challenge of Lee's works. Staying put would have ceded the initiative to the enemy and made Grant look timid and outgeneraled as the national Republican convention opened in Baltimore.[31] So he ordered his men forward.

He knew better and his generals knew better and he regretted his decision for the rest of his life. Many of the men went into the fight believing they were going to die. Just as everyone expected, they were slaughtered, as one soldier put it, like hogs in a pen. In slightly less than an hour, Union troops suffered seven thousand casualties. They accomplished nothing. "We felt it was murder, not war," said a New York soldier, "or at best a very serious mistake had been made."[32]

The mistake was to believe, and to expect others to believe, that the Confederate fieldworks were vulnerable, that the solution was to simply keep throwing men at them. The rebels were not vulnerable. Not at Spotsylvania, not at the North Anna River, and not at Cold Harbor. Somewhere in the middle of this horribly bloody campaign, warfare itself had changed. It would just take time before everyone was absolutely certain that this was true, that the generals and the engineers had not noticed some weakness in the emerging theory of fortification. Other engagements were fought at Cold Harbor in the first two weeks of June. But they, too, failed to dislodge Lee's army. So Grant, having failed again to do anything except pile up more bodies on both sides, made yet another sweeping run around Lee's army. This time he pulled it off in secret, moving his 115,000-man army by water and by land, through swollen rivers and swampy bottomlands and dense brush and across the wide James River, while his cavalry brilliantly screened his move from rebel scouts. Lee soon caught on, racing south at full speed to close the gap. Grant had pulled off one of the great tactical maneuvers of the war, a move that took him clear past Richmond, swinging in a wide arc that brought his army up on the eastern outskirts of Petersburg. Unfortunately his maneuver wasn't quite brilliant enough to take the city, where, once again, he found himself confronted with impenetrable rebel fortifications.

This was where the 4th Division found itself on July 29, preparing for its momentous assault the next morning.

CHAPTER TEN:
AN ELABORATE SLAUGHTER

THE AFTERMATH OF THE CRATER EXPLOSION: *A year and considerable weathering after the great detonation, the blast area was still a lonely, haunted place of death and destruction.*

What really annoyed Major General George Gordon Meade that spring was that, in the Army of the Potomac, of which he was nominally commander, Grant treated him like an errand boy. This was obvious to everyone. Even before the campaign started, Meade had complained to his wife that "the whole public press . . . has ever since Grant's arrival here been so uniform & consistent in endeavoring to make him out to be the actual commander of this army."[1] The press was right, and Meade's ability to make anything like a significant decision had only grown more tenuous. He was, in fact, an errand boy, and he knew it.

Meade, an imperious, bug-eyed Philadelphia aristocrat who was openly contemptuous of common people, was acutely sensitive to real or perceived slights. He had been the victor at Gettysburg over Robert E. Lee but had been widely criticized for letting Lee escape. The title *lieutenant general,* meanwhile, which might have been his, had been bestowed upon his rival from the west, the man who had won at Vicksburg and Chattanooga against generals who were not remotely in Lee's class.[2] Grant humored Meade, showered him with paternalistic kindness, and paid little attention to his advice. To make matters worse, rumors were sweeping the army that Meade was on his way out. His response was to make himself intolerable to everyone. He had a terrible temper anyway, and now it just got worse. "I do not think he has a friend in the whole army," wrote Assistant Secretary of War Charles Anderson Dana to Secretary of War Edwin Stanton. "No man, no matter what his business or his service, approaches him without being insulted in one way or another, and his own staff-officers do not dare to speak to him unless first spoken to for fear of either sneers or curses."[3]

By the latter part of July, the most prominent sign of Meade's powerlessness was the Grant-approved plan to blow up the rebel trenches. From the beginning Meade had opposed it, at least in part because it was not his idea. He also disliked the idea of using black troops to lead the charge. He had no confidence in them.[4] He believed that if the attack failed, abolitionists would howl that the men had been used as cannon fodder. He had therefore done all he could to impede the project. He had prevented Pleasants from getting the scientific instruments he needed to calculate the length of the tunnel. Meade had not intervened when the 4th Division was swamped with fatigue duty — digging trenches and doing heavy labor in the searing summer heat — that prevented it from training for the assault. But the project went ahead anyway. And if something went wrong, naturally Meade would be blamed for it. It was the same old story: Grant got what he wanted, while Meade fumed in his tent.

By July 26 Meade could contain himself no

longer. He summoned Ambrose Burnside and demanded a full recitation of the plan. Two days later, Meade told Burnside that he would not, under any circumstances, allow the 4th to lead the attack. Burnside persuaded Meade to put the question to Grant. At noon on July 29 — sixteen hours before the attack — the persistent Meade showed up again, this time brandishing an order from Grant forbidding the 4th from attacking.[5]

Burnside then did something that, even in a war career replete with missteps and blunders, stood out for its sheer stupidity. Instead of personally choosing another division to lead the attack, he had his commanders draw lots. The man who drew the short straw, Brigadier General James Ledlie, was a drunk and a coward who would soon leave the army in disgrace. On May 24, at the North Anna River, he had been found sleeping on the ground and was so drunk he had to be kicked awake.[6] Still, his 1st Division would lead the attack. They would be followed by two other divisions. Only then would the black soldiers of the 4th go forward. They were crushed by this news. It seemed terribly unfair. But they were going to be part of the fight, which on the steamy night of July 29 still seemed like the best opportunity of the war to prove themselves.

At three thirty in the morning of July 30, the

Pennsylvania miners lit the fuse.

Nothing happened.

So two very brave men went back into the tunnel and, at 4:44, reignited it. This time it worked. Considering that four tons of explosives had just been detonated, the noise was minimal, just a low-pitched rumble. The earth rocked and shook and an enormous tongue of flame in the shape of a sheaf of wheat shot two hundred feet into the sky.[7] Behind it came a mass of red earth that, according to one witness, lifted up "slowly and majestically, as if a volcano had just opened, followed by an immense volume of smoke rolling out in every direction."[8] Along with the rising earth came men and guns and timbers and planks and every sort of debris; then it all came crashing down with "a great concussion," said a Michigan soldier.[9] Into this mayhem of smoke and bodies and upended earth, 110 Union cannon and 54 mortars unloaded with everything they had.[10]

After the cannonade the Union men rose up out of their trenches and walked across no-man's-land and into the enveloping swirl of dust and smoke. Ledlie's division went in first, and behind them came the 3rd and 2nd Divisions. None of them were prepared for the horror and wreckage they found, and none knew exactly what to do when they found it. That was in part because, in the broad devastation before them, they had at

213

first nothing to shoot at. The explosion had created a hole in the ground that was 170 feet long, 100 feet wide, and 30 feet deep. In it were dead rebel soldiers and pieces of rebel soldiers and rebels turned upside down in the dirt and rebels struggling to dig themselves free. Debris from the exploded fortifications littered the ground. On either side the honeycomb of works and trenches and bombproofs had been sliced open and were now visible in cross section. Thousands of Union men surged into this narrow, steep, blasted-out piece of land. They either went down into the crater or skirted it by heading obliquely toward the opened trenches. Then they came to a complete stop and gazed about them as though experiencing an entirely new world.

This behavior had several causes. The first and main one was that the crater's walls were so steep that movement in any direction was difficult. "The men could find no footing except by facing inward," one soldier recalled, "digging their heels into the earth, and throwing their backs against the side of the crater."[11] The second was that no one seemed to understand the plan of battle. Certainly Ledlie's men did not because he had not bothered to share it with them. Soon men from all three divisions had piled into a cramped area in and around the bomb crater. They clogged the approaches to the blast areas and the Confederate fortifications and stared blankly at their regimental officers as they screamed contradictory orders. James Ledlie himself was nowhere to be found. He was safely tucked away with a supply of liquor in a nearby bombproof that was being used for surgery. From the safety of this sanctuary he issued orders for troop movements, one of which was "The general wishes you to move your troops forward to the crest of the hill and hold it."[12] One can only imagine his astonished officers, standing at the bottom of the crater hip deep in dirt and debris and dismembered rebels, reading orders from a man who had no idea what was going on, or what the place even looked like. The central idea, in the original plans, had been to move forward to seize the high ground of Cemetery Hill, five hundred yards behind the lines. But for the moment the idea got lost, along with everything else, in the strange new world of the bomb hole. As the bluecoats moved about in confusion and tried to untangle themselves, the dazed and shell-shocked rebels came to their senses and began to return fire.

Ferrero's 4th Division, meanwhile, waited impatiently in the Union trenches for orders to advance. An hour passed, then another. They were waiting because their commander, Brigadier General Edward Ferrero, was relaxing in the same bombproof as the inebriated James Ledlie, chatting with the surgeons, who shared their rum, responding to orders to advance with blandly worded protests that he could not do so because too many men were in the way. This went on for a while. Finally Burnside issued an order Ferrero could not sidestep: you will attack now.

Though attacking was very much what the African Americans wanted to do, at least some officers in the vicinity saw clearly that sending forty-three hundred more troops — untested ones, no less — into such burgeoning chaos was a horrible mistake. The idea was so absurdly bad that one of Burnside's aides immediately countermanded it and went to Burnside to talk him out of it. Burnside, who was being leaned on by Meade to make something happen, merely repeated the order. The men of the 4th would go in, even though it looked very much as though they were indeed being used as cannon fodder.

Around 7:30 a.m. Ferrero's men finally advanced on the crater, where they plunged into the shapeless mass of soldiers. Their precise battle lines instantly fell apart. Suddenly they were just individual soldiers trying to follow regimental flags. Still, they somehow pushed right through the middle of the crater and beyond it. They did it quite handsomely and courageously, as all witnesses later agreed. But having pushed forward, they soon found themselves in an impossible position, taking the brunt of the Confederate counter-attack. Worse still, many of their white officers had fallen. Ferrero was absent from the field. So the soldiers retreated, most of them in panic and disorder, and most ended up in the crater.[13]

By eight thirty, almost four hours after the blast, the rebels began to methodically take back what they had lost. Though it is difficult to imagine, the crater was so jammed with Union soldiers that many could not even lift their arms. Rebels had by now pushed their way back to the crater's edge. Their mortars had found the range and were doing their terrible work. The slaughter, of a sort no one had quite seen before even in a war full of battlefield butchery, went on for hour after hour. The crater had become a death trap. "When the enemy would rush for our lines, we would give them such a volley as would force them back within the pit," recalled one rebel officer.[14] Orders to withdraw went out from Meade's office at 9:00 a.m., but those orders took an astonishing three hours to travel a few hundred yards into the crater. Grant, who had gone to the launch point of the attack, had quickly concluded, as he told Burnside, "These troops must be immediately withdrawn. It is slaughter to leave them there." So it was.

The hapless troops of the 4th, who had been sent too late into that maelstrom of blood and death, and who were now trapped there with everyone else, got the worst of it. Rebels hated them anyway, but rumors of black soldiers yelling "No quarter" had spread through the Confederate ranks, and blacks were singled out for killing, and much of the killing was performed at close range with bayonets and rifle butts. Blacks died at rates far greater than their white counterparts. The five hundred black casualties were grotesquely disproportionate to the numbers in other divisions. Once again blacks had been targeted, and their offers of surrender had been refused. One white officer had taken refuge along with a black soldier in a bombproof, where they were forced to surrender. When they emerged from the shelter, "the negro was touching my side," recalled the officer. "The rebels were about eight feet from me. They yelled out, 'Shoot the nigger, but don't kill the white man,' and the negro was promptly shot down by my side." When the same officer was taken to the rear, he "saw the rebs run up and shoot negro prisoners in front of me. One was shot four times."[15] Wrote Confederate colonel William Pegram in a letter home, "I think over two hundred negroes got into our lines, by surrendering & running in, along with the whites. . . . I don't believe that much over half of these reached the rear."[16] One Union officer saw a rebel officer shoot five wounded blacks in the head with his pistol.[17]

Many accounts of USCT's bravery have survived, too. One Pennsylvania captain recalled seeing a black soldier "climb atop a pile of twenty bodies to fire. [While] hurriedly reloading, [he] was shot in the face; still loading he was shot again in the back of the head, yet loading when a third shot laid him prostrate like those beneath him; all done within the space of a few seconds."[18] In later testimony Burnside, while acknowledging that the black troops "ran to the rear in considerable of a panic," also noted that they "moved forward gallantly under the first fire and until their ranks were as broken as any I ever saw in action. . . . They were subjected to probably the hottest fire that any troops had been subjected to that day."[19] Union officer Charles Francis Adams Jr. probably summed up their performance best when he said, "They seem to have behaved just as well and just as badly as the rest and to have suffered more severely."[20]

That did not change the outcome of the battle, which lasted until midafternoon, when the last of the bloodied and bedraggled Union soldiers in the crater finally surrendered. The assault had failed miserably. Union forces had suffered 3,798 casualties compared to the rebels' 1,491. From Meade's meddling to Burnside's drawing of lots to the pathetic cowardice of Ledlie and Ferrero, the

Army of the Potomac had blundered its way to shame and disgrace and defeat once again. Grant, who could almost always salvage good news from bad, was heartsick. According to one of his aides, he stayed in his bed, overcome by grief.[21] He wrote to Henry Halleck on August 1 that the battle "was the saddest affair I have witnessed in the war. Such opportunity for carrying fortifications I have never seen and do not expect again to have." Burnside predictably came in for much of the blame, as did his 9th Corps. "All who dislike black troops shoulder the blame onto them," wrote one observer.[22] Congress launched a lengthy inquiry.

Oddly, though, the unusually large number of black casualties did not receive much publicity in the North. In the congressional investigation no questions were asked about it. Newspapers largely ignored it, in part because the battle was so confusing, and because white and black soldiers had been intermixed in the combat.[23] People in the South, on the other hand, openly gloated about the bloodbath and the deaths of black soldiers.[24] To them the Battle of the Crater was a signal victory, proof again of the failure of the Union's black enlistment policy, and of the inferiority of blacks. Their feelings were apparent when captured federal soldiers were paraded through the streets of Petersburg the day after the battle, arranged deliberately in alternating rows of black and white. "See the white and nigger equality soldiers," yelled one man in the crowd. Said another, "Yanks and niggers sleep in the same bed."

Soon the fortifications were repaired and Petersburg was safe again and everything was as it had been before the explosion. Grant was never again given such an opportunity to break Lee's defenses.* But in all of the sadness and death and failure and destruction were shards of glory, too, bits and pieces of history that could not be erased. For their bravery in the Battle of the Crater, four soldiers in Ferrero's 4th Division received the Congressional Medal of Honor. Of these, three were white officers. The fourth was a twenty-five-year-old corporal in the 39th Regiment, United States Colored Infantry, named Decatur Dorsey. He had been born a slave in Maryland and had enlisted in the Union army in Baltimore four months before. As the 39th's color-bearer, he had ventured out ahead of the rest of his men, under heavy fire, and had planted the regimental flag on Confederate fortifications. When his regiment was thrown back, still under heavy fire, he had retrieved the colors and rallied his comrades for another attack, during which they captured two hundred rebel soldiers.

* Neither Burnside nor Ledlie would ever be recalled to duty. Ferrero was later promoted.

Dorsey's remarkable courage under fire by a man carrying a flag instead of a gun was in a small way — even amid the grim news of the crater disaster — a sign of the change that was sweeping through the Civil War.

CHAPTER ELEVEN:
THE MAN WHO
LOST EVERYTHING

ROBERT E. LEE IN YOUNGER DAYS: Men and women alike once considered him the handsomest officer in the army.

To people in the North, Grant's campaign had been a crushing disappointment, made all the worse because expectations had been so high. He had arrived in Washington four months earlier and with him had come a hopeful, almost joyful feeling that the war might soon be over. Now that was all gone. In its place was simply a new form of defeat, a grinding failure to win that took the form of stalemate in the armored wastelands of Petersburg. Those trenches became symbols of the war itself, its ugliness and brutality, its want of meaning, its impossibility of resolution.

They were emblems of death, too. Since the first of Grant's troops had splashed across the Rapidan River on May 4, sixty-five thousand Union soldiers had been killed or wounded — more than 60 percent of the total casualties in the Army of the Potomac in the entire war to that point.[1] For these sacrifices the Union had achieved virtually nothing. Robert E. Lee roosted in front of his national capital, unbroken and lethal as ever, daring his opponents to assault his unbreachable fortifications. His forces elsewhere in Virginia had easily brushed off the Yankee threat. Sigel, Crook, and Averell had been chased from the field. Ben Butler's army had been trapped and caged on a bend of the James River. The ease with which rebel forces had done this was baffling and made the prospects for victory seem more remote than ever.

Then came bad news from Georgia, too. On June 27 at Kennesaw Mountain, just north of Atlanta, in the largest battle of Sherman's mostly successful campaign, a Confederate army under Joseph E. Johnston won a tactical victory. Sherman, who had far more soldiers than Johnston, was unable to break the rebel lines and had suffered three times their casualties. He had not lost anything in particular and had not even lost that many men. But he had not won, either, and with the fall election looming, not winning was beginning to look very much like losing.

Then, in high summer, seemingly from out of nowhere — or perhaps out of Abraham Lincoln's worst nightmare — came an attack on Washington, DC. Though he could do nothing against Grant in the Petersburg trenches, Lee had collected troops and sent them north under the command of his profane, tobacco-spewing, prophet-bearded subordinate Jubal Early. Early had thrashed Franz Sigel's successor David Hunter at Lynchburg, and then, to everyone's astonishment, North and South, had marched unhindered with sixteen thousand men straight down the Shenandoah Valley, across the Potomac River, and into the United States of America. He defeated a small Union force under General Lew Wallace near Frederick, Maryland, then turned his attention to Washington, DC.*

* Wallace had around six thousand men to defend

225

At that moment not a single Union soldier was deployed between Early and the city's battlements. The city had hardly any defenders, either, beyond a motley assemblage of clerks, convalescents from military hospitals, staffers from various military departments, militia irregulars, and quartermaster employees who had been hastily scraped together. On July 10 an anxious Abraham Lincoln wired Grant to tell him that the national capital was in danger and virtually undefended. "We have absolutely no force here fit to go to the field," Lincoln wrote. And he knew the reason, too, though he may have been too polite to mention it. Grant had stripped eighteen thousand men from the city's defenses a few months before to fight Lee in Virginia. And now troops that Lee had taken from his Richmond and Petersburg ranks were gunning for the defensive gap that Grant had created.[2] Lee, apparently frozen in his trenches, had managed to outmaneuver the Army of the Potomac yet again.

With no one to stop him, Early marched on the city. A day later his army was camped six miles from the White House, staring into the hazy distance at the newly finished

the national capital. While he had mixed success in the war, he would go on to write the bestselling book *Ben-Hur*.

Capitol dome. Washington panicked. Rumors spread — carried by terrified refugees from nearby towns who fled into the city "in wild disorder," according to one observer — that Lee was invading the North again with his entire army.[3] The city came alive with rushing couriers, quick-stepping regiments, and rumbling supply wagons. Desperate calls went out to local militias.[4] US treasurer Francis E. Spinner gathered the money in the Treasury Department's vaults and prepared to load it onto a tugboat.[5] "We understood that the city was cut off from the north and east," wrote *Sacramento Daily Union* correspondent Noah Brooks, "and that the famine of market-stuff, New York newspapers, and other necessities of life, was due to the cutting of railway lines leading northward. For two or three days we had no mail, no telegraphic messages, and no railway travel. . . . Washington was in a ferment."[6]

An edgy Abraham Lincoln wired Grant, asking that he "make a vigorous effort to destroy the enemie's force in this vicinity," meaning that Grant should bring his army north.[7] But Grant wanted nothing to do with this. He wasn't about to dismantle his siege to deal with what he regarded as an inferior Confederate general with a small force. He stayed where he was and dispatched most of his crack 6th Corps — more than twenty thousand men — who steamed up the Potomac River and arrived at the Washington docks at the last possible minute.

Early was aggressive, but he wasn't suicidal. After briefly engaging Union forces in front of Washington, he noticed the banners of a full army corps fluttering behind the earthworks. He understood that his enemy's position was now too strong and soon withdrew.[8] For Washington it had been the narrowest of escapes. A day before, Early might literally have walked into the halls of Congress. That a small rebel army could do that in the fourth year of the war was astounding. So was the curious fact that Early had come closer to capturing Washington than Grant had come to taking Richmond. As though to underscore this unaccountable Union weakness, two weeks later Early's cavalry burned most of the town of Chambersburg, Pennsylvania, which had refused his demand to pay $500,000 in reparations for buildings burned by Yankee soldiers in the Shenandoah Valley.[9] He left three hundred families homeless.[10] For Lincoln, Early's relatively easy escape was one of the most exasperating events of a consistently exasperating war.[11]

In the North, the shift from hope to despair had been agonizingly abrupt. "The earlier years of the war, it is true, had been full of grief, despondency, and even agony," wrote Brooks. "But the darkness that settled upon us in the summer of 1864 was the more difficult to be endured because of its unexpectedness. The hopes so buoyantly entertained by our people when Grant opened his campaign in Virginia had been dashed. No joyful tiding came from the army now; a deadly calm prevailed where had so lately resounded the shouts of victory."[12]

The rest of the world seemed to feel the same way. The US dollar dropped to its lowest level of the war on foreign exchanges, while the *London Times* declared flatly, "The Confederacy is more formidable than ever." Yankee diarist George Templeton Strong summarized this feeling of deep discouragement: "I see no bright spot anywhere," he wrote. "The blood and treasure spent on this summer's campaign have done little for the country." He added that even the war's supporters seemed "discouraged, weary, and faint-hearted. They ask plaintively, 'Why don't Grant and Sherman do something?' "[13] Popular songs of the moment were "When This Cruel War Is Over," with its despairing catchphrase "weeping, sad, and lonely," and "Tenting Tonight on the Old Campground," written by a New Hampshire conscript, which declared, "We are tired of war on the old camp ground / Many are dead and gone."[14] If all of this wasn't bad enough, the bitterly hated draft was back, too. President Lincoln issued a new call for half a million more men to feed into Grant's chopping machines in Virginia and Georgia.

All of that had taken place *before* the Battle of the Crater. The other military setbacks in Virginia had rattled citizens of the North, but the crater catastrophe made them turn their eyes away. By midsummer, spirits in the Union were even lower than they had been in the dark days of 1862 after the South's victories at the Seven Days, Cedar Mountain, and Second Battle of Bull Run. Antiwar Democrats were in full cry, proclaiming, as one newspaper did, "Each hour is but sinking us deeper into bankruptcy and desolation."[15]

Abraham Lincoln felt all of this acutely. He was beginning to believe, along with many others, that he would not be reelected in November. In a mood of deepening gloom, he told his friend General Andrew Hamilton, "You think I don't know I am going to be beaten, but I do, and unless some great change takes place *badly beaten. . . .* The people promised themselves when Gen. Grant started out that he would take Richmond in June — he didn't take it, and they blame me, but I promised them no such thing, & yet they hold me responsible."[16]

Robert E. Lee did not, alone, account for the feelings of despondency that swept through the North that summer. The war was a big place, with many theaters, and many players.

But the grizzled fifty-seven-year-old general was undoubtedly the single overriding reason the North could not beat the South. For two years he had tied the Union in knots, politically as well as militarily. He had made fools of its generals. As he had stacked up victories, an elaborate personal mythology had grown up around him. His opponents not only had to contend with the physical fact of his armies. They also had to contend with the *idea* of Lee — the legendary, indomitable, not-quite-real genius — and the idea often frightened people more than the armies did. Joe Hooker at Chancellorsville had fled, ultimately, from the idea. When John Pope's large Union army had beaten a hasty retreat into Washington after the Second Battle of Bull Run the reason was not because it was outnumbered or outgunned.

This phenomenon was in full bloom in the summer of 1864. Lee's Army of Northern Virginia was buried in its fortifications, going nowhere and worried about its supply lines. But the North — its politicians, generals, newspaper editors, and ordinary citizens — could never see it that way. Lee, at least the mythological Lee, looked to them as dangerous as ever. Sixty-five thousand Union casualties in a little over two months testified to that. Early's raid testified to that. Though Sigel, Crook, and Averell did not admit to this in their battle reports, the phantom of Lee had likely caused them to run, too. Robert E. Lee still terrified everyone.

Ironically Lee himself — the man, the hero, the legend, the scourge of the Union — was that summer sunk in sadness, frustration, unhappiness, and loss. He did not show this except in small ways that the rest of the world could not see. His feelings were hidden behind his legendary reserve, his self-control, and his abiding sense of honor and duty. But the great general, who could sometimes seem almost too perfect — his West Point classmates nicknamed him "the marble model" for his exceptional good looks, his flawless character, his brilliant grades, and his perfect disciplinary record — was a troubled man. His troubles were not solely the products of war. Long before that, he had seen himself as a failure, both in the temporal world and in the eyes of God.

By the middle of 1864, most of the world Robert E. Lee had known before the war was already in ruins around him, if not vanished altogether. The collapsing Confederacy was steadily taking everything and everyone down with it, starting in the places that had seen the most fighting. Two-thirds of all Southern wealth had vanished, along with 40 percent of its livestock, half of its farm machinery, and 25 percent of all white men between the ages of twenty and forty. Large expanses of Lee's home state of Virginia, where so many armies had laid waste to the land, had been rendered unrecognizable. Thus the Lee paradox: *the more he won, the faster his world, and the world of the American South, disappeared.*

His personal losses were breathtaking. The most visible were his family's homes and estates. Though he was from one of Virginia's most prominent families — his father, "Light-Horse Harry" Lee, was a legendary Revolutionary War cavalry officer and later governor of Virginia, and Robert E. Lee's mother was one of the Tidewater Carters, once thought to be the wealthiest family in America — Lee himself had not grown up wealthy. But he married rich. His wife, Mary Anna Randolph Custis, was the great-granddaughter of George Washington's wife, Martha. Mary's father, George Washington Parke Custis, had been raised by the Washingtons — one of the richest families in the country — and had inherited land and houses. When he died in 1857, Mary became sole owner of three splendid estates in Virginia that included houses, five thousand acres of farmland, and 150 slaves. By far the most splendid of these was the Lees' principal residence, Arlington House, a Greek Revival mansion with a sixty-foot-wide, Doric-columned portico, part of an eleven-hundred-acre estate overlooking the Potomac across the river from the national capital. Though Robert pursued an army career in different places, Mary often stayed home in Arlington, and their seven children were largely raised there. For them Arlington House was more than a lavish knockoff of the Greek Temple of Hephaestus: it was the distilled essence of who they were, as Virginians, as Southerners, and as Americans.

But Arlington House was unfortunately located inside the District of Columbia — a mere stretch of river from the offices of the US government — and the coming of war meant that the Lees had to leave. In May 1861, a month after the fall of Fort Sumter, Mary Lee boxed up the family silver, crated George Washington's papers, and fled Arlington House, never to see it again.[17] Within weeks it had been transformed into a rough Union army camp, its gardens and woodlands denuded, its contents ransacked for souvenirs, its grounds turned into a Freedmen's Village for former slaves. In the days following the Battle of the Wilderness, the federal government began to bury Union soldiers there, which was yet another ironic turn: the soldiers Lee was killing were being laid to rest in his front yard, and the more he killed, the more his beloved old estate was engulfed by the graves of those very men. While Lee wintered with his troops in Virginia, the government was auctioning off Arlington House because of tax delinquency.[18] Soon the remaining Lee estates, White House and Romancoke, were behind enemy lines, too, and thus all of the family's lovely antebellum estates were effectively lost. Mary Lee and daughters Annie and Mildred were briefly captives of George McClellan's army during the Seven Days, until the Union general arranged safe passage for them through Union lines.

For Lee these were crippling losses — of identity, selfhood, heritage. He had invested enormous amounts of his time in the three properties as well. When his father-in-law died in 1857, he left Lee almost nothing except the thankless task of executing the estate, which was badly run and deeply in debt and now carried the many stipulations of the Custis will. It was an irresponsible man's last act of irresponsibility. Lee, shuttling between his army career at various postings and his home obligations, struggled for years to rehabilitate the properties.

Much of this work had been difficult and unpleasant. Debtors had to be paid. Money had to be found to fulfill overgenerous bequests to family members. Sundry parcels of land had to be sold. The Custis slaves had immediately rebelled against Lee. The will required that they be freed within five years of his father-in-law's death. Lee eventually complied with this, but he wanted to keep the slaves long enough to improve the economic performance of the estates' farmlands, which would in turn enable him to satisfy his father-in-law's demanding will.* Meanwhile his slaves, who understood that the will had freed them, were bitterly upset. They refused to work. They ran away. Lee had them arrested, punished some of them, rented some of them out, and sold off a number of them, thus breaking up families.[19] Though Lee once wrote that slavery was "a moral and political evil," he nonetheless believed in the institution, as he wrote in an 1856 letter to his wife:

I think it however a greater evil to the white man than to the black race, & while my feelings are strongly enlisted on behalf of the latter, my sympathies are more strong for the former. The blacks are immeasurably better off here than in Africa, morally, socially, & physically. The painful discipline they are undergoing is necessary for their instruction as a race, & I hope will prepare and lead them to better things. How long their subjugation may be necessary is known & ordered by a wise Merciful Providence.[20]

So Lee, who believed that only God could

* When Lee did finally free his slaves, many of them, including all the ones at Arlington House, were out of his control or behind Union lines.

ultimately free the slaves — in spite of Lee's legal obligations to do so — became a planter, using them as his principal labor. By 1859 all three of the farms were making money, most of it the product of slave labor, and Lee had paid off the whopping Custis debt. In a sense he had been mired in the legacy of George Washington himself, some of whose riches Custis had inherited. Lee was acutely aware of these connections.

But Lee's diligence only increased the magnitude of his family's loss, which left them not only landless but feeling desperately sad. "Your old home, if not destroyed by our enemies," Lee wrote Mary, "has been so desecrated I cannot bear to think of it. I should have preferred it to be wiped from the face of the earth, its beautiful hill sunk, and its sacred trees buried."[21] He later told her, "As to our old home, if not destroyed it will be difficult ever to be recognized. . . . It is better to make up our minds to a general loss. They cannot take away the remembrances of the spot, and the memories of those that to us rendered it sacred."[22]

Lee's personal wealth was also as good as gone by the summer of 1864. By his own reckoning, most of what he had left was denominated in increasingly worthless Confederate bonds. In August 1863 he told his oldest son, Custis:

237

I have nothing now not in the hands of the enemy, except $5,000 in Confederate States' bonds . . . and $5,000 or $8,000 in N. C. [North Carolina] bonds, I forget which. . . . I own three horses, a watch, my apparel and camp equipment. You know the condition of the estates of your grandfather. They are either in the hands of the enemy or beyond my reach. The negroes have been liberated, everything swept off them [the estates], houses, fences, etc., all gone. The land alone remains a waste.[23]

Lee still had his army income. But those Confederate dollars were fast losing their value and would soon lose all of their value.

A glimpse of the Lee family in their rented house in Richmond in the Christmas season of 1863, on the eve of Lee's great fight with Grant, shows how dramatically their lives had changed. They were all refugees now. They were scattered, without permanent homes, lodged with friends or in temporary dwellings in parts of Virginia or North Carolina that Union troops had not yet occupied. They would never again assemble as a complete family. His three sons were in the army, which just underscored the extent and precariousness of the exile. Like Lee himself, they had no other real home. His wife, Mary, the spoiled, self-centered only child of a doting father, had never been healthy. She suffered from frequent illnesses and at the age of forty began to suffer from rheumatoid arthritis, which became worse as she got older. By the war's second year she was confined to a wheelchair and needed constant care. She had aged far beyond her years. Lee himself was in poor health, often in pain due to a form of heart disease we now know as angina pectoris. His eyesight was failing. His once ruddy countenance had turned a pasty white. He had gained considerable weight, and his hair had turned a bristly gray-white. This was the immaculately turned-out officer who was once considered by men and women alike the handsomest man in the army. He was acutely aware of this transformation and referred to it frequently in letters. He told his wife to tailor his uniform jackets "to fit a big old man & cut them large."

The Lee family was haunted by death, too. Lee's daughter Annie had died of typhoid at the age of twenty-three in North Carolina in 1862. His granddaughter Mary Custis Lee had died that same year. And her mother, Lee's much-loved daughter-in-law Charlotte Wickham "Chass" Lee, who had been gravely ill, died during the Christmas holidays in 1863. Her husband, Lee's son William Henry Fitzhugh "Rooney" Lee, had been unable to care for her because he was languishing in a

Union prisoner-of-war camp in New York.* Rooney and Chass had lived at the Custis estate called White House, east of Richmond, from which they, too, had been exiled. "God knows how I loved your dear dear wife," Lee wrote Rooney later, "how Sweet her memory is to me, and how I mourn her loss. My grief could not be greater if you had been taken from me." That season Lee's daughter Agnes was sick with neuralgia.

Adding to this growing inventory of unhappiness and tragedy was Lee's own feeling of alienation. By that Christmas in Richmond he felt that he no longer quite fit in his family setting. He had shown evidence of such feelings as early as 1860, when he wrote his daughter Annie from Texas, "If you wish to see me you will have to come here, for I do not know when I will be able to go in there [Arlington]." He explained that by telling her, "You know I was much in the way of everybody and my tastes and pursuits did not coincide with the rest of the household." Now he was leaning this way again. He was burdened and distracted by the many demands being made on him, both by his family members and others. He had never gotten along well with his wife, and their bickering

* Rooney Lee was later part of a prisoner exchange that sent him back to the South and to the rebel army in March 1864.

240

was perhaps worse now than it had been. He chose, entirely of his own accord, to cut short his Christmas vacation. Though no military action on the Rapidan called him away, he left Richmond on December 21 to return to the army and his cold tent. Thus he was absent for the death of his beloved daughter-in-law on December 26.

Had he brought this all on himself by choosing to leave the US army to side with the Confederates, a decision initially opposed by much of his family, including his wife and all but one of his children?[24] Fighting for the North — which had offered him the command of all of its armies — might have allowed him and Mary to keep Arlington House. But none of them could have foreseen that, and Lee never regretted or second-guessed his decision.

That did not keep him from feeling personally responsible for the loss of his family's home. To understand those feelings one must grasp Lee's relationship with God. He was convinced, as many people on both sides were, that God was on his side and on the side of his country. He prayed every day and read the Bible and invoked God in his letters and speech quite as often as any Northern preacher did. His was the warlike God of the Old Testament, the jealous and avenging God who did not like to be ignored. Lee's God had led three hundred Israelites under Gideon, armed with only trumpets, to slaughter 135,000 Midianites, as recounted in the Book of Judges. God, not man, was the arbiter of war. God decided who won and who lost. A divine hand, not Robert E. Lee and his generals, guided the Army of Northern Virginia. Slaughtering Yankees was God's work, and the rebel victories were God's victories.[25]

The corollary of this belief was that God rewarded the righteous and punished the wicked. Thus losses in battle, especially repeated losses in battle — say, Vicksburg, Gettysburg, Chattanooga in later 1863, and the blood-drenched war of attrition in the spring and summer of 1864 — were a result of a fall from grace. No other interpretation was reasonable. When Lee won, he thanked God for blessing his army with victory. When he lost, as in an early failed campaign in West Virginia, he saw the same divine force at work: "I had taken every precaution to insure success . . . but the Ruler of the Universe willed otherwise, and sent a storm to disconcert the well-laid plan."[26] In 1862, after a disastrous run of rebel defeats, he wrote his daughter Annie:

It is plain we have not suffered enough, labored enough, repented enough, to deserve success. But they will brighten after awhile, and I trust that a merciful God will

242

arouse us to a sense of our danger, bless our honest efforts, and drive back our enemies to their homes. Our people have not been earnest enough, have thought too much of themselves and their ease.[27]

Which meant, by extension, that both Lee himself and the Confederate nation were in some way estranged from God. He felt this deeply and mentioned it frequently in letters. (His subordinate Stonewall Jackson had precisely the same feelings and mentioned them as often.) Failure in battle meant that his soldiers had been selfish and vainglorious and taken credit for their victories instead of giving it to God. It was therefore "necessary that we should be humbled and taught to be less boastful, less selfish, and more devoted to right."[28] After Gettysburg he had articulated the same sentiment, this time even more precisely.

Soldiers! We have sinned against Almighty God, we have forgotten his signal mercies and have cultivated a vengeful, haughty, and boastful spirit. We have not remembered that the defenders of a just cause should be pure in His eyes; that our lives are in His hand and we have relied too much on our own arms for the achievement of our independence.[29]

His wife, Mary, saw this turn of the war in

more apocalyptic terms. She wrote her husband:

> I think the thousand years must be commencing when Satan is to be let loose upon earth, to blacken & mar its fair surface & while we must feel that our sins both personal & national merit the chastisement of the Almighty we may still implore him to spare us & with mercy in wrath not to visit us.[30]

Robert and Mary had similar feelings about the loss of Arlington House. Lee was convinced that it was the result of his own sins against God. Defeat on the battlefield may have been caused by his countrymen's transgressions, but the sins that lost his homestead were his own. He said this so many times and so succinctly, mostly in letters to his family, that his sincerity cannot be doubted. As he wrote Mary soon after she left the house for the last time:

> I fear we have not been grateful enough for the happiness there within our reach, and our Heavenly Father has found it necessary to deprive us of what he has given us. I acknowledge my ingratitude, my transgressions, my unworthiness, & submit with resignation to what he thinks proper to inflict on me.[31]

244

To read such language is surprising, particularly from one of the war's most prominent figures and one of the most famous men of his day, a man whose brilliant success — whether he was loved or hated — was undeniable. But Robert E. Lee had been afflicted with feelings of failure and frustration for a long time, from far back into his life and army career. They were just of a different, more earthly sort, rooted in his early childhood.

His father, the celebrated Harry, led a double life. The first part was often magnificent and occasionally legendary. The second was an ascending sequence of failure, leading to disgrace, debtors' prison, and exile. By the time his son Robert was two, Harry's once-sterling reputation had vanished. He was on the run from his creditors and from the prospect of more time in jail. So he abandoned the family for the West Indies and never came back. Robert's half brother "Black-Horse" Henry Lee IV, had his own moral shortcomings. He had an affair with his wife's younger sister, misappropriated trust funds, then tried to conceal the misappropriation by marrying the sister off. In the ensuing scandal, he was forced to sell off the family's ancestral home — and his brother Robert's birthplace — Stratford Hall.

Robert was painfully aware of these prominent black marks against the Lee name. His immaculate military record and his strict personal discipline were in reaction to all of that. The "marble model" was atoning for his family's sins. His record in the Mexican-American War, as a member of General Winfield Scott's staff, was exemplary, and he returned home from that war a hero.

But the rest of his army career was, though nominally successful, oddly unexceptional, and far from the mythic exploits of his father. Lee spent thirty-two years in the army, almost all of that time as an engineer, building projects. He was reserved, smart, diligent, hardworking, and moderate in all things. He did not womanize (though he always flirted), did not use tobacco, and only drank a small amount of wine. A typical stint was five years at Fort Hamilton in New York rebuilding aging fortifications. Nothing about it was particularly exciting. This was engineer work. Most of that time he was away from his family. He often found his life boring, mired in bureaucracy and political favoritism, and marked by dull post assignments and extended absences from his family. During his brief assignment to fight Indians with the 2nd Cavalry in Texas, he was never in combat.

Worst of all, promotion came with excruciating slowness. By 1846 he had been in the army seventeen years and was still only a captain, making a captain's modest wages. Though he had been brevetted a full colonel in Mexico, it took him until the eve of the

Civil War to attain that actual rank and pay. Even though he had been superintendent of West Point from 1852 to 1855 — which showed how respected he was inside the army — his West Point classmate Joseph E. Johnston had been promoted over him in 1860 to the rank of brigadier general.

In the decade before the war Lee's correspondence begins to reflect this disappointment. In place of the bright, confident jauntiness of his earlier communications, he makes more and more frequent references to his imperfections. When he was posted to a distant barracks, which meant he would see his family less and less, he wrote that he saw this as "a just punishment for my sins" and that "I may truly repent of the many errors of my life, that my sins may be forgiven." In a letter to one of his favorite cousins, he wrote, "I am conscious of my faults . . . and make many resolutions and attempts to do better, but fail. . . . You who know my weakness will I fear have little confidence in my success." As he repeated so often, he was "thankless and sinful." These were not the words of a happy man.

Along with his sense of his sin came feelings of unworthiness. In spite of his brief, brilliant career in Mexico, he had left no particular mark on the earth, as his father had, no hard evidence that he had ever lived. He owned nothing of any note: the estates were all Mary's. He spent the majority of his time away from his family. Perhaps worst of all, he had done nothing to improve his family's name, nothing to erase the stains left by his father and half brother. This led him to make the startling assertion, in a letter congratulating his son Rooney on the birth of Lee's grandson, that "I wish I could offer him a more worthy name and a better example. He must elevate the first, and make use of the latter to avoid the errors I have committed."[32] It had not helped, perhaps, that he had performed poorly at the start of the Civil War, had been called Evacuating Lee and Granny Lee, and had little support from the rebel officer corps when he was made commander of the Army of the Potomac in June 1862. After that, of course, everything had changed. But Lee had only been the Lee of legend, the stalwart, invincible Lee, for a scant two years in a long life.

One of his most revealing comments came in a letter to his wife on the eve of the Battle of the Crater and on the occasion of their anniversary:

Do you recollect what a happy day thirty years ago this was? God has been very merciful & kind to us & how thankless & sinful I have been. I pray that he may continue his mercies & blessings to us & give us a little peace and rest together in this world &

248

finally gather us & all he has given us around his throne in the world to come!

Those words sound very much like a death wish, another repeating theme of his later years. Those who favor that theory can also point to Lee's attempts, on four separate occasions in the Wilderness and at Spotsylvania, to lead his men into battle. He had to be forcibly restrained while his men chanted, "Lee to the rear." He tried it twice at the Mule Shoe salient, which would have amounted to suicide.[33]

In the trenches of Petersburg the legendary Lee was a sick, corpulent old man who had lost his dashing good looks and his former cheerful optimism. He was brutally demanding of his staff, who came to fear the angry glare that looked to one of them as though "it might penetrate a two-inch plank." Though he continued to have the confidence of his country and of the country's president, Jefferson Davis, what any of that added up to was less and less clear. As he put it in a letter to Confederate war secretary James Seddon that summer, "Unless some measures can be devised to replace our losses, the consequences may be disastrous. . . . Without some increase of our strength, I cannot see how we are to escape the natural military consequences of the enemy's numerical superiority." Though the language was moderate, the sentiment was bitterly pessimistic. Lee knew as well as anyone else that the South had no significant untapped source of manpower other than the most obvious one — slaves. Any increase in his force would be small and marginal. Though he wielded great power in the Confederacy, he was still — unlike Grant — in command of a single army. When President Davis wanted to replace Joseph E. Johnston in Georgia that summer, Lee advised Davis not to appoint John Bell Hood. Davis ignored Lee and promoted Hood anyway.

Considering the immense burdens that Lee shouldered, the bleak and inexorable mathematics of the war, and his virtual imprisonment in the fortifications of Richmond and Petersburg, perhaps the most remarkable thing about him was his stubborn resiliency. He did not mope in his tent. He did not exhibit discouragement in front of officers or men. He had not lost hope, even when most of the evidence in front of him suggested that he should have. He had not forsaken God, nor did he believe that God had forsaken him, and since God was the final arbiter of the war, anything was possible. Though Lee was uncomfortable on a horse, he rode his lines, sometimes up to thirty miles in a day, sometimes giving detailed directions for shoring up fortifications. He traveled to and from Richmond to lobby for more food and supplies for his men. He went to church on Sundays. He attended to the infinite details of running his army. And he did all this as the world was crumbling around him. But it had not quite fallen, yet.

CHAPTER TWELVE:
THE MIND OF
ULYSSES S. GRANT

Lieutenant General Ulysses S. Grant and staff at Petersburg, perhaps pondering why they could not win the war.

Grant was drinking. Or he wasn't drinking. Or he was drinking some of the time, or all of the time, or only at moments when the fate of the Union was at stake. Rumors flew. They always did, and the higher he rose, the nastier and more persistent they became, the more the jealousy and spitefulness of the officer corps were expressed in that sweeping condemnation: General Grant is a drunk. It would have been better for Grant if he did not drink at all, but he did drink sometimes, and when he did, it was always too much, and these occasions seemed to prove the worst of what everyone was saying about him.

Grant was a binge drinker, as opposed to a drinker who required a steady stream of alcohol. His imbibing episodes were brief, generally out of the public eye, and no evidence suggests that they impaired his ability to command. Though much has been made of his weakness — alcoholism in the nineteenth century was seen not as a disease but as a sign of moral degeneracy and feckless self-indulgence — Grant did a remarkable job of managing his addiction. He kept it mostly under control during a long career, often under the sort of pressure most people cannot imagine. He did not drink during the desperate years following his departure from the army. He did not drink while he was, later, president of the United States and did not drink in retirement. He took pains to keep people near him — his wife, Julia, and his loyal aide John Rawlins — who would not allow him to consume liquor.

And he only drank on a few occasions during the Civil War. In spite of the number of stories about Grant's boozing and the sheer volume of innuendo, supposition, and outright lies spread by respected and influential generals such as Henry Halleck, Grant had only three demonstrably true drinking incidents during the war. The first came during the Vicksburg campaign in June 1863, when his self-appointed minder Rawlins was away and Grant got hold of some medicinal wine. The second was in New Orleans three months later, when he slipped the Rawlins leash again and this time fell off his horse.*

* The elaborate and oft-repeated story told by newspaper reporter Sylvanus Cadwallader about Grant's extended Yazoo River "bender" is mostly just that — an elaborate story. But Grant did indeed get drunk in early June 1863, and the proof is the extraordinary letter John Rawlins wrote to Grant after the incident, saying, "I find you where the wine bottle has just been emptied, in company with those who drink and urge you to do likewise. . . . You have the *full* control of your appetite and can let drinking alone." Though the sources of the New Orleans story were generals hostile to Grant — Nathaniel Banks and William B. Franklin — the measure of the truth of the incident is that Rawlins himself believed it. The famous story about Grant's drunkenness at Shiloh in early 1862 — like most of the Grant drinking stories — is false. See James H. Wilson, *The Life of John A. Rawlins,* 91ff. Similarly, the story of Grant drinking heavily at Chattanooga is apocryphal. He may have had a glass of wine during that time, but he was not drunk. The hypercritical,

The final incident occurred in late June 1864 in Petersburg and fit the general pattern of his relapses: they happened when he was bored or inactive — Petersburg and Vicksburg were both dreary sieges — and when he was away from the moral supervision of either his wife or John Rawlins. In this case there may have been another cause: a kind of failure he had never before experienced. His spring campaign against Lee had been bitterly frustrating, closing with the senseless slaughter of his men at Cold Harbor and the stalemate at Petersburg. His relapse fit another familiar pattern, too: how stories of Grant's drinking became commingled with lies and exaggerations and were then used against him and in the service of others' political agendas.

The trouble, initially, had nothing to do with drinking. It all started with Grant's attempt to remove Ben Butler from battlefield command. Though Grant had always admired Butler's administrative abilities, Grant believed — along with the rest of the army and anyone who knew anything about war — that

---

straitlaced Rawlins, who was never shy about protesting Grant's drinking, withheld a harshly critical letter he had prepared to send the general about the alleged Chattanooga incident. That was because Rawlins learned that nothing had happened.

Butler had no talent for fighting. Grant had first tried to solve the problem by assigning William F. "Baldy" Smith, a general Grant admired, to serve under Butler at Bermuda Hundred. This had been a disaster, though Grant was not yet sure why. His new plan was to gently kick Butler upstairs, leaving him in charge of his department but moving him eighty miles south and east to Fort Monroe, Virginia. Baldy Smith would assume command of Butler's troops at Bermuda Hundred. This all seemed quite reasonable, and Lincoln approved the order.

But the treacherous political tides of the Army of the Potomac began almost immediately to set against it. Grant met with the brusque, outspoken Smith, an unpleasant man under the best of conditions, who portrayed his senior officers, including Meade and Butler, as idiots and incompetents and disparaged the management of the entire Virginia campaign. Smith had something bad to say about almost everyone and managed to convince Grant that, instead of being promoted, Smith should be removed from command.

Butler had by this time concluded, after thinking about it, that he did not want to be stuck in an empty administrative command at the tip of the York-James peninsula.[1] Once he had decided that, his nimble legal mind quickly determined how to thwart the clumsy

Lincoln/Halleck/Grant plan to get rid of him. As head of the Department of Virginia and North Carolina, he not only commanded all the troops in it but could dictate the location of his headquarters. He decided that his headquarters would stay right where they were, in Bermuda Hundred. Butler, who still wielded substantial political power and influence, wasn't going anywhere. After his meeting with Grant on July 9, the order transferring Butler was rescinded. Meanwhile Baldy Smith, through his mean-spirited diatribe, had just bought himself a one-way ticket out of the war. On July 19 Grant formally relieved him of command, sent him to New York to "await orders," and explained why: "You talk too much."

Smith was furious. In a little over two weeks he had gone from a prestigious appointment as commander of the 18th Corps to ignominious exile in the remote North, while his nemesis, the incompetent Benjamin Butler, was restored to his old command. Smith thought he knew exactly why. In a letter to Vermont senator Solomon Foot — for sheer malice and invention one of the more remarkable documents of the war — Smith explained in detail how all of this disgraceful political chicanery was really the by-product of a drinking binge by General Grant.

Baldy Smith's story went like this: Several weeks earlier Grant had gone to Burnside's headquarters, where he requested a drink to relieve a headache. Later, at Smith's headquarters, in the company of both Smith and Butler, Grant had a second drink. In the letter, Smith wrote, "After the lapse of an hour, the general asked for another drink, which he took. Shortly after, his voice showed plainly that the liquor had affected him, and after a little time he left."

But Grant's being drunk was not the critical part of the story. What mattered most — and the axis of Smith's theory — was *who* had witnessed the event. "As soon as I returned to my tent," Smith added, "I said to a staff officer who had witnessed his departure, 'General Grant has gone away drunk. Gen. Butler has seen it, and he will not fail to use the weapon which has been put into his hands.' "[2]

Smith's prediction had then come wondrously true. He wrote, "I have heard from two different sources that Gen. Butler went to Gen. Grant and threatened to expose his intoxications." And Grant, feeling vulnerable after his failure to vanquish Lee's army, had in Smith's version acquiesced to Butler's demand. Smith closed the letter with a leering suggestion that he knew a lot more about Grant's bad habits: "I have not referred to the state of things existing at headquarters when I left, and to the fact that General Grant was then in the habit of getting liquor in a surreptitious manner."

Most or all of what Smith said was probably not true. He may have seen Grant take a drink, but the idea that Butler blackmailed Grant is almost certainly false. Butler emphatically denied that he had ever seen Grant drink and also denied Smith's allegation that he had encouraged Grant. If he had done that, Butler said, "I should have expected Grant to dismiss me from the service, as he ought to have done." Moreover the idea that Grant had been drinking wasn't exactly news in the army. Such charges had been made many times in the past with no effect and could not have been expected to have any effect now. Then, too, Grant successfully removed Butler from command a few months later, without a whimper. If Butler's blackmail had worked so well in the summer, as Smith suggested, why wouldn't it have worked later on, too?[3]

Nor did Grant's moral monitor John Rawlins — Grant's most influential staff officer and probably his closest friend and always the most reliable bellwether of the general's tippling — believe the story. He dismissed it out of hand. What is interesting — and also confusing — is that Rawlins *did* believe Grant had taken a drink, or several drinks, within days of the events described by Smith. Rawlins was so upset about this that he had referred to it in a letter dated June 28:

I find the general in my absence digressed from his true path. The God of heaven only knows how long I am to serve my country as the guardian of the habits of him whom it has honored. . . . Owing to this faltering of his, I shall not be able to leave here til the rebel movement in Maryland is settled and also the fate of Atlanta.[4]

Whatever Grant had done was enough to make Rawlins vow never to leave him again.

In the end, Baldy Smith was dispatched to New York and Grant made sure his irascible general never received new orders. But his story, and his active promotion of it, wound its way deep into the army's culture. It was an example of how rumors haunted Grant and also illustrated how he contributed to them. Though he had not been drunk in the way Smith said, Grant had been drunk around that time. Thus truth and lies got all jumbled together, and many people came to the same old conclusion: the general-in-chief of the Union armies was a drunk.

If any moment in the war fit Grant's drinking model, the early summer of 1864 would have been it. He had sacrificed thousands of lives for little or no gain. His army was stuck in its muddy fortifications, going nowhere. In the North the popularity of the war was in free fall. And Grant was the one most responsible for the Union's failures. Even his own army was beginning to distrust him. As Congressman James Ashley of Ohio put it to John Rawlins, there was "a good deal of discontent and mutinous spirit among staff officers of the Army of the Potomac."[5] Grant should have been depressed. Everyone else was.

But he did not see it that way. He was always at his best when things were desperate, and at this fragile, fateful moment he saw the opposite of what the world saw. Whatever had caused him to briefly hit the bottle in late June, he was more hopeful now than he had ever been about the prospects for victory, and as the weeks passed, this feeling would grow. There were no more drinking episodes. As his actions over the next two months would clearly demonstrate, he saw the whole war in focus. He saw it with great clarity across a thousand-mile front and believed he knew precisely how to win it. While Abraham Lincoln was preparing for a loss in the November election and the Democrats were already toasting their imminent victory, Grant was arrogating to himself the full powers of his command in what amounted to the private takeover of the war by a single man. That change took place from the middle of July to the middle of September and was largely invisible to the outside world. While the rest of his country brooded about its dim prospects, Grant's dissonant message of courage and hope began to pulse outward from his camp at City Point, slowly at first, then, as weeks passed, with ever-greater speed and momentum, moving out through thousands of miles of telegraph wire and into the nation's human circuitry. In retrospect, it is possible to see several important turning points in the Civil War. Grant's quiet assumption of complete and unchallenged power that summer was one of them.

The first sign that something elemental had shifted inside the Army of the Potomac came when Jubal Early had arrived at the gates of Washington, DC. Lee had fully understood the potential of such a raid. The Union War Department and its generals had always been easily stampeded, easily convinced that they were in greater peril than they were. Lee had made a wartime career out of preying upon those instincts. In the past a raid such as Early's would have sent large numbers of federal troops flying northward to save the beleaguered capital, which would have shifted the tactical war in Virginia. This was what Lee wanted.*

But Grant refused to panic. He would not

---

* Stonewall Jackson's Shenandoah Valley campaign in 1862, in which his small force diverted enormous resources from the Union army's move against Richmond, was an excellent example of this phenomenon.

be bullied. It had not bothered him to take troops from the defenses of Washington to fight in Virginia, and it did not bother him much that Lee, later on, tried to capitalize on it. He saw a far simpler truth, which was that Jubal Early could not, ultimately, do much damage. Grant understood his own strength, which, curiously, the Union's other generals had never seemed able to do. "The movement was looked upon by Gen. Grant as a mere foray which could have no decisive issue," wrote one Union general.[6] So while all hell seemed to be breaking loose in the suburbs of Washington, Grant calmly detached his 6th Corps and sent it north, and the problem was solved and the calculus of the siege did not change for Robert E. Lee. As Grant saw it, the war was turning. He had his boot on Lee's neck, and Sherman was moving steadily south. In a country increasingly convinced that the sky was falling, Grant was that rarest of things: an optimist.

He was not the only one. Though Abraham Lincoln despaired of winning the election, his confidence in Grant remained unshaken. He believed in the optimist. The two men from Illinois had gotten along well from their first meeting. In succeeding months they had grown even closer. They were unlike so many people in the Eastern political and military establishments. They were plainer, more direct, more sensible, less encumbered by jealousy and petty intrigues. Less burdened by fear. They fit nobody's physical prototype for greatness. Both men were convinced, moreover, that in spite of the South's nearly incredible resilience, the war must be pursued to complete victory, with no compromise, no terms of peace except unconditional surrender. Lincoln had always admired Grant's toughness and his willingness to work with what he was given rather than complaining, as most generals did, about lack of troops and support. Grant, meanwhile, had come to feel affection and admiration for Lincoln and was grateful that the president had left him largely alone to run the war. (Lincoln suggested ideas to Grant, but never imposed them.) Grant, too, had been a diligent student of Lincoln's evolutionary politics. Lincoln had persuaded Grant not only that slavery was a great evil, but that emancipation was a powerful weapon of war in its own right.[7] In the summer of 1864, both men were confident the war could be won. And both were deeply worried about what might happen at the polls in November.

On July 31, Lincoln and Grant met at Fort Monroe on the Virginia coast. The meeting is noteworthy for several reasons. First, because there is no record of what they talked about. Grant failed to even mention it in his memoirs. And second, because it likely changed the course of the war. The timing was momentous, in the most negative sense of the word. The meeting took place two weeks after Grant's bungled first assault on Petersburg, two weeks after Early's raid on Washington, and a day after both the disaster of the Crater and Early's burning of Chambersburg. Happiness with the war effort was not the theme of the meeting. But one can guess that its guiding idea was that Lincoln, against the evidence of all contemporaneous events, and against a strong tide of opinion in both the nation and in the army, *had decided to sustain Grant.* Lincoln would not be bowing to public opinion or political opinion or editorial opinion or any opinion at all. Lincoln would not be changing horses. He would not be curtailing Grant's power. Lincoln believed in Grant and told him so.

Proof of this was the dramatic sequence of events that followed. One of the subjects the two men talked about, of necessity, was Jubal Early, whose army still drifted with impunity through northern Virginia, Maryland, and Pennsylvania. The day following the meeting, Grant sent a simple but unusual telegram — with Lincoln's concurrence — to Henry Halleck, the army's chief of staff. "I want Sheridan put in command of all the troops in the field [Shenandoah Valley]," Grant wrote, "with instructions to put himself south of the enemy and to follow him to the death."[8]

Grant's reference was to Philip H. Sheridan, at thirty-three one of the most junior major generals in the army, a brash cavalry officer who had not even seen combat until the second year of the war. Grant was bypassing all sorts of nominally more qualified officers. He was going dead against the wishes of both Halleck and Secretary of War Edwin Stanton. Grant was turning the army's seniority system on its head. And he was not only trusting Sheridan with the de facto defense of Washington, but giving him three infantry corps and two full divisions of cavalry — forty-eight thousand men — with which to do it. Lincoln, too, had opposed the appointment of Sheridan — at least until Grant had talked him out of it during their meeting.[9]

Two days later, on August 3, 1864, Lincoln sent his own remarkable telegram to Grant:

I have seen your dispatch in which you say, "I want Sheridan put in command of all troops in the field, with instructions to put himself south of the enemy, and follow him to the death. Wherever the enemy goes, let our troops go also." This, I think, is exactly right, as to how our forces should move. But please look over the despatches [sic] you may have received from here, even since you made that order, and discover, if you can, that there is any idea in the head of any one here, of "putting our army south of the enemy," or of "following him to the *death"* in any direction. I repeat to you it will neither be done nor attempted unless you watch it every day, and hour, and enforce it.[10]

In this way Lincoln both encouraged Grant and alerted him that the War Department would try to undercut his plans. (Two weeks before, the constantly maneuvering Halleck had confided to Sherman, in a typical piece of poison-laced gossip, *"Entre nous.* I fear Grant has made a fatal mistake in placing himself south of the James River. He can not now reach Richmond without taking Petersburg, which is strongly fortified, crossing the Appomattox and re-crossing the James."[11] Though the reference point here was the James River, this was the sort of sub-rosa lobbying Lincoln was talking about.) Grant was proposing a radical thing: not only giving a large army to a young, relatively untested general, but also leaving Washington uncovered while Grant's protégé trailed the dangerous Early through the hinterlands of the national capital. Both set off alarms in capital meeting rooms where the cautious men who ran the war had grown accustomed to having things their way. War Department meddling had recently taken the form of orders whose purpose was nominally to protect Washington but had kept the Army of the Shenandoah semiparalyzed, marching and countermarch-

267

ing and not certain whether it was supposed to defend the capital or attack the enemy. Lincoln was telling Grant that more of the same could be expected.*

What was most important about Lincoln's wire was how Grant read it. He interpreted it not simply as the helpful suggestion it was, but as a personal call to arms. As he saw it, Lincoln was telling him that he needed to assert full control over the army's command structure — including the labyrinthine bureaucracy of the War Department — and he needed to do it right now, and if he did, he would have the full authority of the presidency behind him. It is unlikely that another Union general could possibly have read Lincoln's note this way.

Grant wasted no time. Two hours after he received the wire, he was on a boat, steaming up the Potomac River. But Washington was not his destination. He did not stop there and saw no one. Instead he quietly boarded a

* In Grant's *Memoirs* (p. 614), he notes that the trouble in the Shenandoah Valley was "chiefly because of interference from Washington. It seemed to be the policy of General Halleck and Secretary Stanton to keep any force sent there . . . moving right and left so as to keep between the enemy and our capital; and generally speaking they pursued this policy until all knowledge of the whereabouts of the enemy was lost."

train for a Union army camp on the Monocacy River, near Frederick, Maryland, about forty miles northwest of the capital. Grant was once described by Meade's aide Theodore Lyman as wearing "an expression as if he had determined to drive his head through a brick wall, and was about to do it."[12] One can imagine just such a look on his face as his train swayed through the Maryland countryside.

At the Union camp he met with the commanding general of the Army of the Shenandoah, Major General David Hunter, who had been badly beaten by Early at Lynchburg seven weeks before and had fled into West Virginia, opening Early's invasion route to the north. Grant made short work of Hunter. He began by asking his subordinate where the enemy was. Hunter said he did not know. If Grant was startled by the answer, he did not record it. Instead, as he put it, "I told the general I would find out where the enemy was."[13] Grant immediately ordered trains and supply wagons prepared for departure, then sent the bulk of Hunter's army rolling southward to Hallstown, near Harpers Ferry. He would find Early — whose infantry and cavalry were scattered and marauding at leisure in the countryside — by pointing more than thirty thousand blue-uniformed men directly at the heart of the Confederacy's breadbasket. Sure enough, Early's entire force soon appeared in front of them. Grant again met with Hunter, who, seeing the writing on the wall, volunteered to be relieved of duty. "Very well then" came Grant's unadorned reply to one of the army's most senior generals.

The next day Grant met with Sheridan, giving him orders that reflected Grant's rapidly shifting priorities. That spring when Grant had ordered Hunter to advance to Lynchburg, he had told Hunter to destroy railroads and canals and factories along the way. While Hunter had extended this idea to include some private residences, those acts had been outside his orders. Now the federal warfighting policy would officially change. The Shenandoah Valley, with its rich agricultural lands, was enormously important to Robert E. Lee. As Grant later noted, the valley "was the principal store-house they had for feeding the armies about Richmond. It was known that they would make a desperate struggle to maintain it."[14]

Grant now told Sheridan that he wanted him not only to defeat Early but to turn one of the loveliest parts of Virginia into a wasteland that would not be worth defending. "In pushing up the Shenandoah Valley," Grant told Sheridan, "it is desirable that nothing should be left to invite the enemy to return. Take all provisions, forage and stock wanted for the use of your command. Such as cannot be consumed, destroy." Grant had mentioned a version of this idea in a letter to Halleck two weeks before, suggesting that the Union army in the valley "eat out Virginia clear and clean . . . so that crows flying over it . . . will have to carry their provender with them." Either way, the strategy was quite clear, and if Southern civilians starved to death, that was the price of their rebellion. Sheridan, moreover, would report directly to Grant, which meant that no one in the War Department or anywhere else in the military could countermand Grant's orders. Their meeting did not last long. Within two hours Sheridan was hurrying to the front and to the hard and implacable new war — Grant's war — that awaited him.

Grant went directly to the War Department in Washington, where he met, successively, with chief of staff and former general-in-chief of the Union army Henry Halleck and Secretary of War Edwin Stanton. Though no record exists of what was said at these meetings, they were landmarks in the management of the war and in Grant's rise to power. He had tried mightily in previous months to resolve the organizational mess in the Union army on the Upper Potomac, but his proposals had all been rejected.[15] This was business as usual. The War Department, as always, had its own ideas, often supported by the president, and even Grant's exalted rank had not been enough to overcome them.

Now all that would change. Grant, with Lincoln's hortatory language sounding in his head, asserted full control over military affairs. The Union commands on the Upper Potomac would be consolidated as Grant had wanted them to be. Objections to Sheridan were brushed away. Grant was giving the orders now, and there would be no interference with him. Though Stanton ran the War Department, without Lincoln's backing he would have a much more difficult time meddling in Grant's affairs. Now Grant had broken Halleck's power. The measure of this achievement — breathtaking when viewed against the historical backdrop of the war — was taken by Grant's adjutant Theodore Bowers, who described what had happened in a letter to Grant's aide John Rawlins: "He has settled Halleck down to a mere staff officer for Stanton. Halleck has no control over troops except as Grant delegates it. He can give no orders and exercise no discretion. Grant now runs the whole machine independent of the Washington directory."[16]

Halleck, a brilliant political infighter and the essence of bureaucratic power in Washington, almost immediately tested the new order. Within the week he was lobbying hard for large transfers of troops from Virginia to Northern cities to deal with potential draft riots. This was typical War Department thinking: almost paranoically cautious, logical in a small way but strategically unwise, unable to assess actual risk, and always willing to overestimate a threat. Grant shut him down, flatly refusing to do it and responding tersely, "My withdrawal now from the James would insure the defeat of Sherman" (by allowing Lee to release troops to the Georgia theater).

Once again Lincoln weighed in with a ringing endorsement, writing Grant, "I have seen your dispatch expressing your unwillingness to break your hold where you are. Neither am I willing. Hold on with a bulldog grip, and chew and choke as much as possible." When Grant read the wire, he laughed aloud, something he rarely did. When his aides asked him what he found so funny, he replied, "The president has more nerve than any of his advisers."[17]

Thus did City Point, Virginia, the giant Union supply base and makeshift harbor on the Potomac River east of Petersburg, become the military capital of the United States of America.[18] The "directory" in Washington, as Bowers had put it, was now a subsidiary enterprise. From a tent and later from a small cabin, Ulysses S. Grant guided the war as it unfolded across a wide front. Politicians and foreign emissaries visited him there. Eventually the president did, too. Streams of telegraphed orders went out from Grant's headquarters, shaping every corner of the war, from fighting to personnel, logistics, and supply. Grant's output was prodigious but not feverish. He quietly composed his missives and smoked his cigars, and the world about him shifted. Charles Francis Adams Jr., grandson of President John Quincy Adams and a captain in the Union army, who visited Grant that summer, remarked on Grant's "calm, open, cheerful but dignified way" and described him as "a very approachable man with easy, unaffected manners, neither stern nor vulgar, he talked to me as he would had he been another captain of cavalry whom I was visiting on business."[19]

Grant was seeing the war as a single, unified theater, in which everything from Arkansas to Washington was interlinked and troop movements were a zero-sum game. In this larger world, the Army of the Potomac's stalemate in front of Petersburg and Richmond took on a new meaning. Grant's role, as he now saw it, was to hold Lee firmly in place, to chew and choke and make it impossible for the Army of Northern Virginia to release troops to Georgia or the Shenandoah Valley. To accomplish this Grant mounted a series of offensives against Lee around Richmond and Petersburg. On August 14, acting on news that Lee had sent three divisions to Early, Grant ordered a force under Winfield Scott Hancock to cross the James River and attack the extreme Confederate left at Richmond. Lee had in reality diverted no divisions to Early, and several days of skirmishing in the Second Battle of Deep Bottom produced no results for the Union.

But the fighting did force Lee to weaken his right flank south of Petersburg, and Grant took immediate advantage of it, driving straight for his opponent's greatest vulnerability: his fragile supply lines. On the morning of August 18, Grant sent four divisions under Gouverneur Warren to seize the critical Weldon Railroad, five miles south of Petersburg. At the Battle of Globe Tavern, Warren captured a large chunk of track. After the rebels built a parallel supply line to replace it, Grant hit that, too. Though he failed to break it, he again stretched Lee's thin resources and, as always, killed and wounded more Confederates. Grant's forces attacked Lee twice more, at New Market Heights and Peebles Farm. Though neither ended the siege of Richmond and Petersburg, both battles forced Lee to stretch to protect himself. "The enemy's position enables him to move his troops to right or left without our knowledge," Lee complained in a letter to Jefferson Davis. "We are then compelled to hurry our men to meet him, incurring the risk of being too late to check his progress and the additional risk of the advantage he may derive from their absence." Grant was driving Lee crazy.

Grant also tackled perhaps the greatest issue of the later war: manpower. Both sides desperately needed more of it. The Union had more men than the Confederacy but was spread far more thinly. Its armies of occupation had ever-lengthening supply lines to defend and ever-larger land areas to police. Sherman, for example, had an extremely long supply line that had to be defended against Confederate raiders such as Nathan Bedford Forrest. Even Grant, whose detached forces had to guard an area that encompassed Washington, DC, coastal Virginia, and Harpers Ferry, West Virginia, no longer enjoyed his old crushing numerical advantage at Petersburg.

But it was Sherman — whose large army had been moving south from Tennessee into Georgia, thus far with many casualties and no results — who needed the most help, and Grant pushed hard to get him every possible soldier. Grant refused prisoner exchanges, arguing, in spite of their popularity, that they "simply reinforce the enemy." When he heard that one of his generals was trading prisoners with the enemy, Grant wired Stanton to make him stop.[20] In a war of attrition, exchanges favored the South. So prisoners on both sides would stay where they were, languishing in often atrocious prison conditions. Grant ordered all escaped slaves shipped to Nashville, where their care and supervision would no longer be an impediment to fighting troops. He sent a regiment composed of Confederate deserters west in exchange for reliably loyal Northern men, had surgeons clean out Northern hospitals of men who could possibly fight, and ordered Halleck to cull a thousand men from existing forces in the towns of Cairo, Columbus, and Paducah. He even lobbied against allowing Massachusetts to fulfill its troop quotas by recruiting freed slaves. None of this, as one might imagine, was popular.

Sherman needed support and protection in other ways, too. Having prevented Halleck and the War Department from siphoning off Sherman's troops, Grant now went even further to shield Sherman's hundred-thousand-man army from rebel threats in the South. Grant readied a Union army expedition to hold Confederate general Kirby Smith, commander of the South's Trans-Mississippi Department, in place and to intercept him if he moved east against Sherman. Grant ordered all new recruits, then training in the Midwest, to be sent immediately to Sherman.

What worried Grant most were Northern attitudes about the war. To help solve that problem he went outside normal channels of command to conduct his own extraordinary public relations campaign, whose purpose was to convince the citizens of the North to be patient and to give them hope. He did this by way of letters to Northern politicians that he knew would be widely published. He preached steadfastness and resolve, as in this August 16, 1864, letter to his longtime ally Illinois congressman Elihu Washburne, which found a large newspaper audience:

All we want now to insure an early restoration of the Union is a determined unity of sentiment [in the] North. The rebels now have in their ranks their last man. . . . A man lost by them cannot be replaced. They have robbed the cradle and the grave equally to get their present force. Besides what they lose in frequent skirmishes and battles they are now losing from desertions and other causes at least one regiment per day. With this drain upon them the end is visible if we will but be true to ourselves. Their only hope now is in a divided North."[21]

Grant was right. This was the rebels' only hope. But in many ways that hope had already been fulfilled. In the summer of 1864 the North was bitterly divided, heartily sick of the war, and headed into an election that would give full voice to all of that smoldering dissent. On August 23, in a desolate mood, Lincoln had written himself a memo:

This morning, as for some days past, it

seems exceedingly probable that this administration will not be re-elected. Then it will be my duty to so co-operate with the president elect as to save the union between the election and the inauguration; as he will have secured his election on such ground that he cannot possibly save it afterwards.

Lincoln sealed this little note and then, for some strange reason, asked his cabinet to sign the envelope, without telling them what was in it. Lincoln's secret correspondence was a bit of sympathetic magic, a way to summon a different future from the one that seemed to wait, inevitably, just ahead.

CHAPTER THIRTEEN:
THE WAR AGAINST LINCOLN

SECRETARY OF THE TREASURY SALMON P. CHASE: Fiercely ambitious, he became the spearhead of the political movement to get rid of Abraham Lincoln.

Salmon P. Chase wanted desperately to be president of the United States. He dreamed of it and prayed on it. He believed he was destined to have the job and, believing that, could not stop himself from wanting it. He had served Ohio as a US senator and then as governor. But he craved more. He had twice sought the Republican nomination for president, in 1856 and 1860. Both times he had been disappointed. His failure in 1860, especially, had amazed and mystified him. He did not see how it was possible that his rivals, particularly the ribald, yarn-spinning primitive from the western frontier who had actually won the nomination and then the general election in 1860 could have beaten him.*

Certainly Chase, who was Lincoln's secretary of the treasury, looked and acted the part of the great statesman. He was handsome and broad shouldered. He stood a full six feet two in a country where the average man was five feet seven. In Washington meeting rooms he often towered over everyone except Lincoln. Chase had a large head, a square, clean-shaven jaw, an unflinching eye, and an air of great and austere dignity. To make sure that no one missed these attributes, Chase had seen to it that his own image, wearing a

* Chase finished a distant third in the balloting at the party's convention behind Abraham Lincoln and William Seward, receiving only two votes on the final ballot.

281

starched collar and looking years younger and far less bald than he actually was, appeared on every one-dollar bill. He spoke earnestly in sentences strewn with provisos and caveats; his slight lisp seemed to add depth and character to whatever he was saying. To his supporters in the antislavery community he was known as a man of conviction, too, a lawyer who had once defended fugitive slaves and later became an uncompromising abolitionist.[1]

On a personal level he was a far meaner and more calculating piece of work. He was described by contemporaries as inaccessible and remote, simultaneously ice-cold and feverishly ambitious. He was utterly humorless. He was appalled by Lincoln's jokes and barnyard stories and did not understand why anyone would find them funny. He had little patience for his intellectual inferiors, held grudges, and plotted against anyone who crossed him.

But mainly he just thought he was better than everyone else. "[Chase] held so poor an opinion of Lincoln's character," wrote the president's personal secretaries, John Hay and John G. Nicolay, "that he could not believe people so blind as to deliberately prefer the president to himself. . . . He regarded himself all the while as the serious candidate, and the opposition to him knavish and insincere."[2] One of Lincoln's supporters told the president, "He [Chase] thinks he is a great deal bigger than you are."[3] Even Chase's friends found his ambition a trifle overweening. "Chase is a good man, but his theology is unsound," said fellow Radical Republican Ben Wade, senator from Ohio, who did have a sense of humor. "He thinks there is a fourth person in the Trinity."[4] As one of the leading politicians of his era, Chase wielded enormous power and patronage at one of the most politically charged moments in American history. His cherished illusions were not simply flaws. They made him what he was.

In the service of his elevated ambitions Chase became Abraham Lincoln's first great obstacle on the road to reelection. When Lincoln appointed him treasury secretary, Lincoln had also filled his cabinet with other political rivals and adversaries. This had proven, by and large, to be a wise choice, and the cabinet members who had sought the Republican nomination in 1860 — William Seward, Edward Bates, Simon Cameron, and Chase — were less dangerous on the leash than off. Of this group only Salmon Chase continued to burn for the presidency. Having failed twice to win the nomination, a less obdurate man might have given up. But three years of war had only made him more ardent. In the fall of 1863 and winter of 1864, the man who was nominally Lincoln's colleague, friend, and ally secretly laid the groundwork for a run against his weakened and vulnerable boss. For a brief, starlit moment, he became the face of the Radical challenge to Lincoln's presidency, the symbol of the great change Chase believed was going to sweep through the Republican Party.

It was impossible, in the year 1864, to look into the mind of the American voter. Scientific opinion polling did not exist. Ordinary citizens, from New York to California, could not be sampled to find out which candidates they preferred. Public soundings consisted of straw polls taken by political parties in town halls, streetcars, riverboats, bars, or wherever people gathered.[5] They were informal, unapologetically local, and often wildly biased.

Which meant that the only valid surveys of the presidential campaign were *other elections,* especially congressional and state races. These had been terribly erratic. For Abraham Lincoln and his Republican Party, 1862 had been an outright disaster. In an election widely seen as a referendum on the president's conduct of the war and his Emancipation Proclamation, five of the key states he had carried in 1860 — New York, Pennsylvania, Ohio, Indiana, and Illinois — had gone against him, sending Democratic majorities to Congress. In the fall of 1863, after Union victories at Vicksburg and Gettysburg, momentum had again swung to the Republicans, who won decisive victories in all sixteen states. In the most closely watched of those contests, the Ohio governor's race, the flamboyant Copperhead Democrat Clement Vallandigham — who advocated immediate peace and letting the South keep its slaves — had been thumpingly defeated.

But those elections had taken place before the blood-drowned failure of Grant's Virginia campaigns, before Sherman's inconclusive march into Georgia, before Jubal Early's raid on Washington, and before the free fall of the dollar and financial markets. How would the Northern electorate — with its seemingly hair-trigger emotions — react to those events?

Without knowing what 4 million voters really thought, the country had to depend on its public talkers — editors, reporters, writers, politicians, and preachers — to take its political pulse. If you listened to the speechifiers and editorializers, the most despised man in America that year would certainly, and by a large margin, have been Abraham Lincoln. He was widely and democratically hated, by members of his own party and by the opposition. It was fashionable to hate him. The reasons were often colliding and contradictory: he had either done too much or too little; had moved too slowly or too fast; had been too harsh or not harsh enough; had been too tyrannical or too kind. He inspired a circus of name-calling, nearly exhausting the English language's stock of pejorative epithets. He was, to take a small sample of descriptions of him in the Northern media, a tyrant, fiend, buffoon, braggart, perjurer, robber, swindler, ignoramus, monster, usurper, dictator, ape, coward, scoundrel, ghoul, imbecile, nigger lover, weakling, traitor, butcher, fanatic, fool, gorilla, trampler of civil liberties, scourge of the Constitution, etc., etc.[6]

As time went by, such talk became ever more shrill, ever more insistent. Though Lincoln still had many supporters, by the summer of 1864 it was difficult to find people of influence in the North who thought he was going to be reelected. How could such a man, derided by large segments of his own party — who could neither win the war nor make peace — possibly be given a second term? Sensible people understood that he could not. His friends in the Republican Party thought he could not. He himself doubted it. No president since Andrew Jackson, thirty-two years before, had been reelected. None since 1840 had even been renominated. Why should Lincoln be different? This feeling is captured in the mocking prose of James Gordon Bennett, editor of the powerful *New York Herald,* which had the largest circulation of any American newspaper:

President Lincoln is a joke incarnated. His election was a very sorry joke. The idea that such a man as he should be the President of such a country as this is a very ridiculous joke. . . . His emancipation proclamation was a very solemn joke. . . . His intrigues to secure a renomination and the hopes he appears to entertain of a re-election are, however, the most laughable jokes of all.[7]

The largest and fiercest predators who came sniffing around the apparently faltering president were from his own party. Republicans in those years were split into warring camps: conservative and Radical. Conservatives were defined by the policies of Lincoln and his administration. Radicals, a once-marginal group made powerful by the war, shared certain fundamental beliefs with conservatives. They opposed slavery and wanted a vigorous prosecution of the war. But they also saw an administration that was inefficient, disorganized, and inept, run by a weak and vacillating president. Lincoln, as they saw it, had mismanaged the two biggest issues of his office: the war and emancipation. Evidence of his failure at war arrived daily on the wharves of the Potomac River: wounded and dead soldiers. His war-fighting blunders had begun with his appointment of the inexplicably timid, South-sympathizing general George McClellan as head of the armies in 1861 and continued with Grant's paralysis in the Petersburg trenches. On the question of slavery, the president had waited too long to issue his Emancipation Proclamation and had then delivered half-baked goods: the proclamation only applied to the seceded states, not to slaves in Missouri, Kentucky, Maryland, or Delaware. The Radicals advocated immediate abolition of slavery everywhere. In their minds Lincoln had been tardy, too, in enlisting black soldiers in the Union army. Even Frederick Douglass, who presumably had a great deal at stake in Lincoln's political success, later told an editor friend, "When there was any shadow of a hope that a man of a more decided antislavery conviction and policy could be elected, I was not for Mr. Lincoln."[8]

But the most critical difference between the two camps concerned what had come to be called reconstruction — the notion of what to do with the South once the Union had won the war. The word had come into currency starting in the summer of 1863, after Union victories at Vicksburg and Gettysburg, when it suddenly looked as though the Union might win the war soon. Lincoln, always a kindhearted and forgiving man, favored gentle treatment of the conquered South, lenient rules for its reentry into the republic. The Radicals, led by such politicians as Thaddeus Stevens of Pennsylvania, Ben Wade of

Ohio, and Charles Sumner of Massachusetts, wanted no such thing. They wanted vengeance. They wanted the South and its leadership punished. They wanted, as Secretary of the Navy Gideon Welles put it, "to kill them, to exile them, to subjugate them, to confiscate their property [and] deprive them of their legal and constitutional rights."[9] By removing Southern Democrats from Congress, secession and war had given Republicans a majority for the first time. Now the Radicals wanted to use that power to annihilate slavery, crush the slaveholding classes, and re-create the South as a protectorate of the Republican Party. They saw an opportunity to shift the balance of political power to Republicans for generations to come.

The darling of these powerful, ambitious, and rancorous men was Salmon P. Chase. The *New York Herald* called him "the Moses of the radicals." Their goal was to make sure that Chase, not Lincoln, won the Republican nomination at the party's convention in Baltimore in June. (The Republican Party temporarily changed its name that year to the National Union Party, in an attempt to attract War Democrats and other groups. The state parties did not change their names.) The Radicals' plan was risky. They would have to move quietly and discreetly, building strength and adding supporters and waiting for the

289

right moment to emerge into the open. To move too soon was to risk everything. This was party-shattering disloyalty. For the moment all was stealth and secrecy. The conspirators had started their campaign the year before, and by early 1864 they had organized national, state, and local committees "to make SP Chase President" and could count twenty-seven US senators in their silent, secret mutiny.

Lincoln knew exactly what was going on. In spite of the subterfuge and dissembling, he knew precisely who was moving against him and why. He had been warned of this over and over. Even his wife, Mary, had told him, "Mr. Lincoln, you are either blind or will not see. I am not the only one who has warned you against [Chase]. . . . If he thought he could make anything of it, he would betray you tomorrow."[10] It was typical of Lincoln's forgiving and conciliatory nature that he left Chase and his mischief alone. In John Hay's account the president found Chase's maneuvering in "very bad taste" but "had determined to shut his eyes to all these performances." Lincoln said that "Chase made a good secretary and he would keep him where he is. . . . If he becomes president, all right. I hope we may never have a worse man. . . . I am entirely indifferent as to his success or failure in these schemes, so long as he does his duty as the head of the Treasury Department."[11]

Chase refused to acknowledge that any such scheme was afoot. Even if his friends were bruiting such ideas about, he said, he himself had nothing to do with it. He presented himself as a model of selflessness and Olympian detachment, a man who, while he understood that other people might want him to be president, could never want such a thing for himself. His correspondence was thus a textbook example of false modesty and political doublespeak. "Some friends are saying that my name will receive favorable consideration from the people in connection with the presidency," he wrote an Ohio friend on January 26, 1864. "I tell them that I can take no part in anything they may propose to do, except by trying to merit confidence where I am." On January 28, he wrote another friend, "So far as the presidency is concerned, I leave that wholly to the people. [They] are fully competent, and far more competent than I am, to bring the matter before the public generally; and the people will dispose of the case according to their own judgment."[12]

While he was issuing these baroque denials, Chase was busy building a political machine inside his Treasury Department, whose eleven thousand workers made it the largest patronage network in the federal government. Workers with conservative leanings were purged; Radicals were hired; political contributions were extracted. His supporters organized Chase Clubs with the goal of dominating delegate elections to the party convention. "Mr. Chase's head is turned by his eagerness in pursuit of the presidency," wrote Attorney General Edward Bates. "For a long time back he has been filling all the offices in his own vast patronage with extreme partisans."[13] One tax collector in Indiana who worked for Treasury told Lincoln that he "understood that Secretary Chase would remove all who did not actively take the field for him and against you."[14]

Chase's underground campaign became public in February 1864 with the publication of two broadsides, prepared and distributed by his supporters. The first was a six-page paper entitled "The Next Presidential Election." Its anonymous authors argued that Lincoln's weakness and indecisiveness were "the real cause why our well-appointed armies have not succeeded in the destruction of the rebellion." They asserted that Lincoln was not fit to be president and that a replacement had to be found but did not mention any other politician by name. One hundred thousand copies were sent out under the franks of different senators, including John Sherman of Ohio, brother of William Tecumseh Sherman. The paper was widely covered in the press and caused a minor stir in political circles. But what, exactly, did it mean?

The answer arrived in the form of a supposedly "strictly private" document, signed by Kansas senator Samuel C. Pomeroy, that nonetheless found its way into print in a Washington newspaper. The arguments in it were similar to those in the first document: Lincoln was both unfit for the office and unelectable. But now it named the talented and able man who could solve these problems: Salmon P. Chase. And it delivered the happy news that a national organization to support Chase's candidacy already existed.

The Pomeroy Circular, as it came to be known, was one of those apparently incisive political ideas that became an instantaneous disaster. The backlash was immediate and ferocious. Pomeroy and his minions had moved too soon, too naively. They had not built sufficient support. Chase himself was horrified. While he had welcomed the backroom politicking on his behalf, he had not known when or how his friends were going public. He immediately sent Lincoln a note disavowing any knowledge of the circular or its contents and offered his resignation.

Lincoln's response, amid a rising public storm, was both deliberately mild and a pointed reminder that he knew more about the circular and its origins than, apparently, Chase did. Lincoln's note was a masterpiece of controlled understatement:

I find there is really very little to say. . . . My knowledge of Mr. Pomeroy's letter having been made *public* came to me only the day before you wrote; but I had, in spite of myself, known of its *existence* several days before. I have not yet read it, and I think I shall not. . . . . I have known just as little of these things as my own friends have allowed me to know. They bring the documents to me, but I do not read them — they tell me what they think fit to tell me, but I do not inquire for more. I fully concur with you that neither of us can be justly held responsible for what our respective friends do without our instigation and countenance.

Lincoln flicked away Chase's offer of resignation as though it were a trifling concern:

Whether you shall remain at the head of the Treasury Department is a question which I do not allow myself to consider from any standpoint other than my judgment of the public service, and, in that view, I do not perceive occasion for a change.[15]

But that was far from the end of it. While Lincoln was writing to Chase in a spirit of mild forgiveness, elsewhere in the Lincoln-controlled party long knives were being sharpened. Chase had gone too far, or his friends had gone too far, and retribution was surely coming. The main blow was delivered by Frank Blair, the Princeton-educated scion of the celebrated Missouri Blairs, who were no strangers to political knife fights. On February 26, Blair, a congressman who was on leave as a corps commander in Sherman's army, rose on the floor of the House of Representatives and delivered a scorching condemnation of Chase's Treasury Department. The Mississippi valley, he said, was "rank and fetid with the fraud and corruptions practiced there by his agents. . . . The practice of taking bribes on the part of these Treasury agents . . . is so common that it has almost ceased to attract attention or excite comment. It is the most corrupting and demoralizing system that ever was invented and has become a public scandal."[16] Thus did Blair signal to the Radicals and everyone else in the party what lay ahead for a Chase candidacy. Lincoln denied that he had set Blair upon Chase, but Chase never believed it. The speech caused a sensation.

But what really doomed Chase's campaign was the backlash in the state party organizations, where Lincoln had also masterfully outflanked the radicals. Lincoln had shrewdly used his own patronage to shore up support among party leaders, and now this support came into play. Within a few days of the Pomeroy Circular's publication Republican state legislators had produced a wave of resolutions unanimously endorsing Lincoln's renomination. The most telling of these came from Ohio — sending the exquisitely clear message that Chase could not even carry his own state's delegation. His election committee's poorly timed and intemperate broadside had produced the reverse of its intended effect: it had prompted a rush to support Lincoln.[17] On March 5, a beaten and angry Chase sent a letter to his Ohio friends requesting that his name be withdrawn from consideration. His fall was abrupt, spectacular, and definitive. He would not rise again as a candidate for the National Union Party's nomination.

Chase's political decapitation meant that Abraham Lincoln and his running mate, Tennessee governor Andrew Johnson, handily won nomination at the National Union Party Convention in Baltimore in June. The Radicals seethed and said terrible things about the president, the Blairs, William Seward, and the cabinet in general. They told themselves that Ulysses S. Grant should be the nominee. But they could not stop Lincoln's nomination, even with the guns of Cold Harbor thundering in the background. In the end Lincolnian conciliation trumped Radical sedition. His operatives rallied the party on two points that almost all Republicans could agree on: a constitutional amendment to abolish slavery in the entire country, and a fast end to the war.[18] "The proper and wise thing for Republicans to do," wrote an Illinois delegate, "was to bring together all the elements of the Republican party — including the impracticables, the Pharisees, the better-than-thou declaimers, the long-haired men and the short-haired women — and continue to prosecute the war with vigor until the last enemy should lay down his arms."[19]

These were noble sentiments. In fact a large segment of the party thought that Lincoln had been rammed down their throats. A further measure of the unhappiness in the party was that, as of the first week in June, two Republicans were nominees for president. The week before, a group of disaffected party members had held their own convention in Cleveland. Under the banner of the Radical Democracy Party, they had nominated John C. Frémont, who had gained fame as a Western explorer, had been the 1856 Republican presidential candidate, and was one of the least competent of the Union's political generals. But the convention had been little more than a gathering of what the press called "soreheads and cranks." Henry Raymond of the *New York Times* saw it as "a precious piece of foolery" and "a mental hallucination." In spite of such dismissive language, one could not tell how strong a candidate Frémont might be. What happened on the battlefield could change everything in hours. Navigating a presidential campaign with a war raging and in the absence of reliable polling was like riding a horse blindfolded. You might tug on the reins, but you could not, ultimately, see where the horse was going to take you.

There was nothing nice about Henry Winter Davis, the ultra-Radical Republican congressman from Maryland. He was youthful, handsome, smart, and an orator of uncommon ability. But he was also vengeful, self-righteous, and mean. Reporter Noah Brooks thought him "hollow-hearted and cold-blooded." He hated many things, and the thing he hated above all else was Abraham Lincoln. This may have been due to Davis's extreme political beliefs, or to Lincoln's having overlooked him for a cabinet position, or to the president's having failed to take Davis's side against his enemies, the Blairs. Or to some combination of the three. Over the years Davis had expressed his displeasure in constant political attacks despite Lincoln's professed goodwill toward the man he had once considered a friend. "It appears to do him good," said Lincoln charitably of these ad hominem assaults. "And as it does me no injury (that is, I don't feel it does) what's the harm in letting him have his fling? If he did not pitch into me he would into some poor fellow whom he might hurt."[20]

Lincoln would soon change that assessment. In early August 1864 Davis launched his sharpest attack to date. The subject was reconstruction, the politically loaded idea that everyone suddenly had an opinion about. The attack had its roots in Lincoln's December 1863 "Proclamation of Amnesty and Reconstruction," in which he offered a rough outline for dealing with a conquered Confederacy.[21] All slaves in the South would be set free, he said. Southerners who took a solemn oath to support and defend the Constitution would be granted pardons and property rights (not including their slaves). Exceptions to this were members of Congress, judges, or army officers who had left their posts to fight for the South; officers and agents of the Confederate government; and anyone who had mistreated black prisoners of war or their white officers. When 10 percent of a state's voters had taken the oath and established a republican state government, they would be eligible, with congressional approval, to rejoin the United States. Beyond that, Lincoln offered few details. He was keeping his options open. He was also being nice. Ten percent was a low number. His requirements were not punitive. "I am for conciliation," he said. "There is, by my theory, much to forgive." Lincoln's leniency was part of his larger agenda, which was to move quickly to reconstruct the Union-occupied states of Louisiana, Arkansas, Tennessee, and Florida and push them back into the Union.[22]

Radicals saw disaster in such a plan. They believed that, with a requirement that only 10 percent of a state's voters take the oath and a fast track back to statehood, the planter class would quickly be returned to power. They would soon occupy their old seats of influence in Washington. Former slave owners would be deciding how to abolish slavery, how to educate and protect the rights of their black citizens. In the Radical view *a minimum of 50 percent* of a state's population should be required to sign the oath, a requirement that would automatically make reconstruction a postwar event. There would be no ramming through of state constitutions, no hurry-up reentry into the union, no restoration of planter power. Congress, not the president, would dictate how and on what terms each state was allowed back into the union. Radicals believed that, instead of letting the reconstructed states abolish slavery, as the Lincoln plan had it (in the absence of a constitutional amendment), slavery should immediately be terminated in all of them.*

The Radicals' rhetoric was imperial, unforgiv-

* Lincoln believed, as a point of constitutional law, that Congress had no power over slavery in the states. He maintained that the Emancipation Proclamation had been an exercise of his war pow-

ing, and unleavened by mercy. "A rebel has sacrificed all his rights," said Senator Zachariah Chandler of Michigan, an extreme Radical. "He has no right to life, liberty, property, or the pursuit of happiness. Everything you give him, even life itself, is a boon which he has forfeited."[23]

(The most extreme among the Radicals wanted to treat Southern states as mere territories, grant full black suffrage, seize plantations, and give them to former slaves.[24] The Radicals believed they would have these things eventually. For now the party's Jacobins would have to wait.)

Henry Winter Davis used the full force of his corrosive personality and ringing oratory to push through a bill in opposition to Lincoln's plan. It embodied many — but by no means all — of the Radicals' ideas. Its main feature was congressional control of reconstruction. Its intent was to stop Lincoln from proceeding with his own plan. On July 2, the Wade-Davis Bill, as it was known, passed both houses of Congress.[25] On July 8, to the general amazement of the political world, Lincoln simply let the bill die without signing it. Though he was not obligated to explain this "pocket veto," he did anyway, saying that

---

ers. To abolish slavery he favored a constitutional amendment.

he was "unprepared . . . to be inflexibly committed to any single plan of restoration," and that he was not "ready to declare that the free-state constitutions and governments, already adopted and installed in Arkansas and Louisiana, shall be set aside and held for nought."[26]

The Radicals were outraged. A furious Davis stood at his desk as the House of Representatives emptied at the end of its session, flailing his arms and hurling invective at the president. He was not as helpless as he looked. On August 5 he and Ben Wade retaliated, publishing a scathing denunciation of Lincoln and his veto. The language was remarkably intemperate, as though all of the Radical grievances against Lincoln were being aired at the same moment. Davis and Wade charged the president with "dictatorial usurpation." They argued that "this rash and fatal act" ignored Congress, disregarded the Supreme Court, and was "a blow at the . . . rights of humanity, and the principles of republican government. . . . A more studied outrage on the legislative authority of the people has never been perpetrated." At issue was who got to decide what would happen in the Southern states, particularly in Arkansas and Louisiana, which Lincoln was reorganizing. The manifesto's main argument — this was what the fight was really about — was that Lincoln "must confine himself to his

Executive duties — to obey and execute, not make the laws — to suppress by arms armed rebellion, and *leave political reorganization to Congress*" (italics added).[27]

The Wade-Davis Manifesto was seen immediately for what it was: a vicious and no-holds-barred assault against Lincoln. John Hay called it the strongest attack "ever directed against the President from his own party during his term."[28] Its purpose was not to bring Lincoln into line but to spur a "dump Lincoln" movement that would get rid of him, if possible before the Democratic convention at the end of August. Calls rang out for a new convention and a new nominee. "People regard Lincoln's candidacy as a misfortune," wrote Richard Smith, editor of the *Cincinnati Gazette* and a friend of Lincoln's, echoing sentiments shared by many moderate Republicans. "His apparent strength when nominated was fictitious, and now the fiction has disappeared, and instead of confidence there is distrust." This was from someone who liked Lincoln.

The president was surprised, hurt, and angry. He told Noah Brooks, "To be wounded in the house of one's friends is perhaps the most grievous affliction that can befall a man. I have tried my best to meet the wishes of this man [Davis], and to do my whole duty by the country."[29] Confederates were predictably jubilant. The message of the manifesto was everything they wanted to believe. "Abraham Lincoln is lost. . . . He will never be president again," crowed the *Richmond Examiner,* which had concluded that the manifesto was "a legal impeachment." "The obscene ape of Illinois is about to be deposed from the Washington purple, and the White House will echo to his little jokes no more."[30]

While many Republicans disagreed with the manifesto, few did not think or at least suspect that Lincoln had become a lost cause. Through the heats of August, the feeling only grew as more and more voices were added to the growing din inside the political echo chamber: Lincoln had to go. The war-driven crisis in Northern morale, which was splashed across headlines in the Democratic press, had collided with the civil war inside the Republican Party. By early August the veteran Republican fixer Thurlow Weed of New York no longer had any doubt that "Lincoln's reelection [is] an impossibility. . . . The people are wild for peace." Meetings were held by prominent Republicans to discuss a date for the new convention. Grant's name was often mentioned, especially in the pages of the *New York Herald,* as were the names of Ben Butler, celebrated Union Admiral David Farragut, William Tecumseh Sherman, Major General Winfield Scott Hancock (the man who had repelled Pickett's charge at Gettysburg), and even Salmon Chase.

The calls for Grant grew so strident that Lincoln sent a friend to ask Grant how he felt. "The question is not whether you wish to run," the president's emissary, John Eaton, told Grant, "but whether you could be compelled to run in answer to the demand of the people for a candidate who could save the Union." In reply, Grant brought his clenched fist down hard on the arm of his chair and exclaimed, "They can't do it! They can't compel me to do it!" He added, "I consider it as important for the cause that he should be elected as that the army should be successful in the field." That reassured Lincoln, but calls for Grant to run persisted.

Even Henry Raymond, the editor of the *New York Times* and a stalwart Lincoln supporter, had begun to believe that Lincoln was lost. "I am in active correspondence with your staunchest friends in every state and from them all I hear but one report," Raymond wrote Lincoln on August 22, which had to be the darkest moment of a dark summer. "The tide is setting strongly against us." Raymond then predicted that if the election were held that day, the Democrats would win. The main problem for large parts of the country, he said, was Lincoln's insistence on linking the abolition of slavery to any peace agreement. Why not, Raymond suggested, go to Jefferson Davis with an offer of peace contingent only on the South's rejoining the Union? The other issues, including slavery, could be settled later. This suggestion, coming from one of the most powerful editors in the country, was a measure of the desperation in the air. Lincoln would never agree to any such thing. (Nor, as it soon became apparent, would Davis.) To Lincoln it must have sounded like the abandonment of all hope. Lincoln told Raymond that doing as he suggested "would be worse than losing the Presidential contest — it would be ignominiously surrendering it in advance."[31]

CHAPTER FOURTEEN:
POLITICS OF THE
NOT QUITE REAL

OHIOAN CLEMENT VALLANDIGHAM: He was the leading voice of the powerful antiwar movement in the North.

On the spring morning of May 6, 1864 — two and a half months before the great political turmoils of August and Lincoln's descent into hopelessness — three Confederate agents boarded the steamship *Thistle* in Wilmington, North Carolina. They were on a top-secret mission with the objective of finishing the job the Radical Republicans had started: the political destruction of Abraham Lincoln. Their specific objective was to break the will of the people in the North to win the war. If this seemed wildly ambitious, so did their plan to accomplish it. They intended to launch a separatist insurrection, free thousands of Southern prisoners of war, sink Union steamships and destroy Union property, finance political candidates, suborn editors and newspapers, and influence elections. They understood that they could not win the war. But they believed they could make people in the North even more desperate for peace than they already were. If enough Yankees believed that the war had to end *now,* they would elect an antiwar candidate and Lincoln would be gone and the war would end on terms favorable to the South. That was the theory. The South would achieve by ballot what its armies could not. The agents were not a cabal of bug-eyed extremists. They were personal envoys of President Jefferson Davis. In secret session that spring the Confederate Congress had appropriated $5 million for their mission, a large sum in a nation that was nearly bankrupt. As he stood on the deck of the *Thistle,* Jacob Thompson, one of the agents and a former secretary of the interior in the Buchanan administration, was in possession of $1 million in Confederate bank drafts redeemable in gold.[1]

Thistle left the Wilmington docks and steamed south on the rebel-controlled Cape Fear River toward the open sea, twenty miles away. Wilmington was one of the last major unoccupied Southern ports, where rebel ships could bring in goods and war matériel and export cotton. But to do that they had to pass through the Union blockade. Thus *Thistle* was no ordinary vessel. Built and outfitted in Scotland as a blockade runner, the iron-hulled side-wheeler was long, narrow, and sleek, 204 feet at the waterline with a sylph-like 29-foot beam. She rode low in the water, burned smokeless anthracite coal, and was painted a dull gray to make her hard to spot. She was extremely fast. With her masts raked and smokestacks telescoped she presented a profile so slight that it was hard to see her even in daylight at a distance of a quarter mile.

In late afternoon *Thistle* set anchor, waited for nightfall — May 6 was moonless, chosen for that reason — then slipped silently across the shoal and into the open sea. That sea was dense with Union cruisers. Thirteen of them lay anchored just off the coast to prevent the passage of rebel ships. *Thistle* dashed ahead anyway, moving at flank speed in the darkness with her lights out and furnace hooded, running a gauntlet of ghostly hulls, smokestacks, and towering masts. Amazingly, the Union lookouts missed her. She was finally spotted just after dawn, but by then it was too late to catch her. After a five-hour chase she outran her pursuers, landing safely in Bermuda several days later. From there the rebel agents took a mail boat to Halifax, Nova Scotia, then found their way to Toronto, where they were joined by other Davis-appointed agents.[2] The main "commission" consisted of Thompson, Clement C. Clay, a former US senator from Alabama, and James P. Holcombe, a prominent legal scholar. With them was a small assemblage of what might be termed military adventurers, influence peddlers, opportunists, and spies.

Their great conspiracy would be launched from Canada.

In their quest to subvert Northern politics, Jefferson Davis and his agents looked for natural allies, people who saw the archenemy Lincoln as they did: as a tyrant, usurper, and destroyer of freedoms. This description perfectly fit the Democratic Party in the North. While that party did not promote itself as pro-Confederate — that would have meant acknowledging they were traitors, an accusation often leveled at them by Republicans — their bitter and increasingly strident criticisms of Lincoln gave the Confederates hope. The Democrats' political victories, especially in the elections of 1862, had shown how many Lincoln haters there were.[3] The caustic anti-Lincoln rants in Democrat-controlled newspapers reassured rebel officials that they were not alone in their loathing of his administration.

Northern Democrats in general could agree on four main areas of grievance. First, they believed — along with many Radical Republicans — that Lincoln and his cabinet had been so inept in their management of the war that they had crippled the Union's ability to fight. Second, they were convinced that Lincoln had turned a war for union into a misguided crusade to abolish slavery. They were appalled that white men were dying to save black people who would later take their jobs. They wanted the president to retract his "wicked, inhuman, and unholy" Emancipation Proclamation.[4] Third, they believed that his senseless war for black liberation was going to bankrupt the nation.[5]

Finally, they condemned the president's attacks on civil liberties. Lincoln had used his war powers to suppress freedom of speech and muzzle the press.* Dissenters, peace advocates, and newspaper editors had been

---

* The strongest argument against the oft-repeated charge that Lincoln had become a dictator was his

311

locked up. Hundreds of thousands of formerly free young men had been forcibly drafted to fight and die in Lincoln's war. In August 1862 he had suspended the writ of habeas corpus throughout the country.[6] Anyone who was disloyal to the United States, gave aid and comfort to the enemy, or resisted the draft and discouraged enlistment could be held indefinitely, without formal charges, in a military prison.[7] As a result, thirteen thousand US citizens were arrested under martial law during the war. Many were actual traitors, spies, and enemy operatives. But many were jailed on the flimsiest of charges. Because the War Department was not equal to the task of managing this new system of justice, the policy gave de facto license to an army of small-town constables and other petty functionaries to decide who was loyal and who was not.[8]

All of these policies and laws were deplored by the Democratic Party and its members.

But Democrats were hardly a united front. Like Republicans, they were split into two feuding factions. War Democrats wanted victory in the war followed by a restoration of union. Peace Democrats, also known as Copperheads, wanted peace now, peace above all,

decision to stand for reelection in 1864. A true despot would have suspended the election.

and peace at virtually any cost.* Though both factions wanted "the Constitution as it is, and the Union as it was" — meaning a union put back together with slavery intact — *immediate peace* was a radical notion, not only because it meant that a stronger country would surrender its advantages to a weaker one, but also because it meant that peace overrode all other issues. If only the bloodshed would cease, cease right this minute, the Copperheads believed, everything else would sort itself out.

That made them ideal allies of the Confederacy.

Soon after their arrival in Canada the rebel commissioners met with the Copperheads' leader, the handsome, mercurial forty-three-year-old Clement L. Vallandigham, a former Ohio congressman who had become the most celebrated example of Lincoln's assault on civil liberties. In 1863, following Vallandigham's deliberately provocative antiwar speech, army officers under the command of General Ambrose Burnside — living up to critics' charges of tyranny and suppression of

* Republicans used the term *Copperheads* derisively, comparing antiwar Democrats to venomous snakes. The Democrats embraced the term, seeing the copper "head" as the likeness of Lady Liberty on coins, which they sometimes cut out and wore as badges.

free speech — broke down Vallandigham's door in the middle of the night and hauled him away. A military commission convicted him of disloyalty, imprisoned him, then exiled him to the Confederacy. He eventually found his way to Canada, from which he ran a losing campaign for Ohio governor. To many war-weary Northerners he was a lonely voice of reason in an ocean of militarized fanaticism. He denounced "this wicked, cruel, and unnecessary war" that was being conducted "for the purpose of crushing out liberty and erecting a despotism . . . a war for the freedom of blacks and the enslavement of whites." He saw "more barbarism and sin, a thousand times, in the continuance of war" than in the institution of slavery.

Vallandigham and rebel agent Thompson had known each other before the war, and now they found much to talk about. What sounded like treason in the North (and was, in fact, treason) seemed, to Confederate ears, a prudent and reasonable course of action. Vallandigham told Thompson he was convinced that, with Grant stalled in Virginia and Sherman sputtering in Georgia, Lincoln could be beaten at the polls.[9] And Vallandigham had one big idea that the rebel agent found irresistible. The Confederate government had been receiving reports of a "northwest conspiracy" of antiwar Democrats who might be persuaded to break away from the

314

United States in a second confederacy. (The "northwest," circa 1864, included the states of Indiana, Illinois, Missouri, Wisconsin, Iowa, Minnesota, and Ohio.) This was not a new idea. But Vallandigham convinced Jacob Thompson that it was not just a crazy rebel fantasy, either. The Ohioan was supreme commander of a shadowy group with supposedly half a million members known alternately as the Sons of Liberty, the Order of American Knights, and the Knights of the Golden Circle. They were scattered through the Midwest, passionately opposed to the war, horrified by Lincoln's violations of civil liberties, and willing to use force to accomplish their goals. Though they were not necessarily pro-South, they were much interested in a "western confederacy."[10]

Thus did a large and militant group of Midwestern dissidents become entangled with agents of a hostile foreign government who had money to spend.

And thus did a dizzying variety of plots begin to hatch, some of which sounded just this side of insane. The first was a scheme to seize the state governments of Illinois, Indiana, Ohio, Kentucky, and Missouri. Confederate prisoners of war would rise up in their camps, according to the plan, join with escaped rebel prisoners from Canada and with the Sons of Liberty, liberate federal arsenals, and sweep into state capitals. Money for arms and transport — $500,000 — would come from the Confederate government.[11] The center of it all, and the touchstone, was Vallandigham. He was due to return from his Canadian exile in June. Lincoln would almost certainly have him arrested again, and the arrest would ignite the insurrection. The Sons of Liberty would rise up. But when Vallandigham returned to Ohio, flashing the same inflammatory rhetoric that had gotten him jailed the year before, Lincoln simply ignored him. No prisoners rose up. Nothing happened. There would be no glorious political martyrdom.[12]

But the conspirators were just getting started. Thompson and his crew met daily in Toronto and other cities with representatives of various disaffected groups, many of them courting treason. Thompson funded antiwar newspapers and peace rallies. He gave money to antiwar Democratic candidates for state office. He paid for the liberation of Confederate POWs in Ohio and Illinois. His operatives destroyed or damaged an army warehouse in Mattoon, Illinois, six military steamboats, and several hotels in New York City. Rebel agents distributed canisters of "Greek fire," a type of chemical-based incendiary weapon first used by the Byzantine Empire in 672. In one of their most daring — and tactically pointless — raids, they robbed banks in the tiny town of St. Albans,

Vermont, burning all of the money they took. Thompson reported back to Jefferson Davis that Copperheads and rebel agents in his service had destroyed "a great amount of property."[13] That may have been true in absolute terms, but in the geographically immense North such actions amounted to a minor nuisance, like a gnat's bite on the belly of a horse. The Confederates and their co-conspirators proceeded anyway. The long summer stretched out ahead, the election loomed, and they had plenty of money.

In the war-weary, peace-mad United States that summer, all sorts of odd alliances flourished. War Democrats held their noses and huddled with their peace-loving brethren. Confederate spies trafficked with shadowy Copperhead separatists. Radical Republicans cast their lots with the vainglorious and ambition-crazed incompetent John C. Frémont. But perhaps oddest of all was the peace conference that Horace Greeley, the august, impulsive, and unpredictable editor of the powerful *New-York Daily Tribune,* tried to arrange between Abraham Lincoln and the troublemaking Confederate "commissioners" in Canada.

Greeley believed that one of his most important duties in this life was to badger Abraham Lincoln. This he had done with great energy in letters and in *Tribune* columns on subjects ranging from the conduct of the war ("On to Richmond!") to the emancipation of slaves ("every hour of deference to Slavery is an hour of added and deepened peril to the Union!"). Greeley, who tended to change his mind often but was indiscriminately passionate about all of his idées fixes, drove Lincoln to distraction. "He makes me almost as much trouble as the whole Southern Confederacy," Lincoln told a friend. But Greeley could not be ignored. By the summer of 1864 the meddlesome editor had turned his attention to the idea of peace. He was desperate for it and did not understand why he could not have it.

Greeley had become aware of the presence of the Confederate commissioners in Canada and had learned that they were open to discussing peace. He seems not to have heard that they were also interested in blowing things up. He was told by an intermediary that these agents, as representatives of the Confederate government, were not only located near Niagara Falls, just across the border with Canada, but also that they had "full and complete powers of peace." The intermediary, William Cornell Jewett, was a former gold-mine tout who was described variously as "that dancing windbag of popinjay conceit" (*New York World*), a "crackbrained simpleton" (Attorney General Edward Bates), and a "very credulous" person of "fruitful imagination" (commissioner Clement Clay).

So Greeley came up with a brilliantly simple idea. Why not set up a peace conference with Lincoln himself?

Possessed by this idea, and by the conviction that unless Lincoln changed his ways, he would lose the election, Greeley sent the president an urgent, pleading letter: "Our bleeding, bankrupt, almost dying country longs for peace. [It] shudders at the prospect of fresh conscriptions, of further wholesale devastations, and of new rivers of human blood." Greeley told Lincoln that "the widespread conviction that the Government [is] not anxious for peace" would do him great harm at the polls. "I entreat you, in your own time and manner, to submit overtures for pacification to the Southern insurgents which the impartial must pronounce frank and generous." Greeley concluded with the original purpose of the note: "I beg you to invite those now at Niagara to exhibit their credentials and submit their ultimatum."[14]

Lincoln replied immediately. He gave the *Tribune*'s editor permission to bring to Washington "any person anywhere professing to have any proposition of Jefferson Davis in writing, for peace, embracing the restoration of the Union and abandonment of slavery."[15]

Then, suddenly, Lincoln was pushing Greeley. The president didn't believe that the rebel commissioners wanted peace or that they had been authorized by Jeff Davis to sign anything, least of all an agreement to abandon slavery and rejoin the union. Lincoln believed they were there to make trouble and stir up antiwar sentiment. But he wanted to expose the lie. And he needed to humor Greeley. So Lincoln sent his trusted secretary John Hay to New York with a letter that repeated his offer. Lincoln once again guaranteed the agents safe conduct. Greeley, meanwhile, was getting more and more nervous about the whole endeavor. He did not, personally, want the job of bringing the commissioners south. He anticipated all sorts of potential trouble. He feared he would be "blackguarded" in the press. Worse still, in his earnest desire to set a meeting, he had not actually informed the Confederates of Lincoln's twin conditions: reunion and abolition. Lincoln did not know that, but still sensed a chance to make Greeley eat his exhortations.

So a nervous and reluctant Greeley went to Niagara Falls, where he learned immediately by letter that the rebel "ambassadors" had no standing whatsoever. They could not commit the Confederacy to peace. Still, Greeley persisted, telling Lincoln that the men were close to Davis and that talks with them could lead to official peace talks.

Greeley hadn't yet mentioned Lincoln's conditions.

Lincoln, pushing harder, now sent John Hay to Niagara Falls with a longer and more explicit statement of terms. Lincoln said that he would entertain any proposal from authorized sources that accepted "the restoration of peace, the integrity of the whole Union, and the abandonment of slavery." Greeley, feeling cornered by his own deceptions, now complained to Hay that Lincoln was refusing to negotiate in good faith and without preconditions, to which Hay replied that those conditions perfectly reflected Lincoln's beliefs. Greeley tried to back out again. But Hay, under orders from Lincoln, insisted that they cross the river and meet with the rebels. Greeley would have to play out his endgame. In Canada they found only one of the "commissioners" — Holcombe — along with a disheveled associate with wild hair named Sanders. Hay noted that Holcombe was a "false-looking man with false teeth, false eyes, and false hair."[16]

Greeley's plan blew up almost immediately. The rebel commissioners, in a fit of stage-managed fury, complained to the Associated Press that Lincoln was setting terms that he knew would be unacceptable, deliberately scuttling any chance to end hostilities. "If there be any citizen of the Confederate States who has clung to the hope that peace is possible," they wrote, "[Lincoln's preconditions] will strip from their eyes the last film of such

321

delusion." Lincoln's letter and the rebels' sharp reply caused a sensation. The Democratic press denounced him for negotiating in bad faith. Even Republican newspapers lashed out at him for making full emancipation the precondition of any talks.[17] Lincoln's obsession with slavery had once again made him blind to everything else, they insisted. The *Cincinnati Daily Enquirer* called his letter "a *finality,* which . . . will preclude any conference for a settlement. Every soldier that is killed will lose his life not for Union, the Stars and Stripes, but for the negro."[18] Even Greeley, who had been badly outmaneuvered by Lincoln and made to look foolish and naive, chastised the president privately for creating the impression that though the Confederates "were anxious to negotiate . . . we repulse their advances."[19] For Lincoln it seemed to be just more bad news in a season of bad news, and it underscored the hopelessness of his position in the dreary and despairing month of August.

But what he had done was to uncover the gigantic untruth — nurtured by Northern Democrats and Confederates alike — that lay at the heart of the peace frenzy in the summer of 1864. The falsehood was rooted in the Democrats' belief that the South would agree to peace and reunion if only Lincoln would make *restoration of the union* his only prerequisite for talks. This idea was dutifully parroted by the rebel agents in Canada.

In fact the South had absolutely no interest in reuniting with the North. The South wanted independence, period — a relatively simple concept that so many people in the North seemed unable to grasp. To help clarify the Confederate position, Lincoln had approved an unofficial mission that summer by two Northerners, journalist James R. Gilmore and clergyman and Illinois colonel James Jaquess, to discuss peace with Jefferson Davis. Lincoln had no more expectations of success in Richmond than he had in Niagara Falls. His goal, however, was not to make peace but to smoke Jeff Davis out. And smoke him out he did. When the Yankee emissaries met with Davis and his secretary of state, Judah Benjamin, and repeated the terms Lincoln had proposed in his reconstruction proclamation, the emissaries were greeted with thinly disguised contempt.

"Amnesty, sir, applies to criminals," President Davis told them. "We have committed no crime. At your door lies all the misery and crime of this war. . . . We are fighting for independence — and that, or extermination, we will have. . . . You may emancipate every Negro in the Confederacy, but we will be free. We will govern ourselves . . . if we have to see every Southern plantation sacked, and every Southern city in flames." Davis added that the war "must go on till the last man of this generation falls in his tracks, and his children seize his musket and fight his battle, *unless you acknowledge our right to self-government.* We are not fighting for slavery." This was startling language. He was talking about the bloody deaths of millions of white people — he pointedly included children — in the South, all sacrificed to the idea of political independence.

Davis and his country were fighting for the one thing that the North, including the Democrats, could never grant them: self-determination. The rebel commissioners were lying. Peace was never going to happen. The fight, as Davis suggested, was to the death.[20] Copperheads and conservative Democrats in general had based their entire campaign on a disastrous misreading of Southern opinion.[21]

Both Davis and Lincoln saw their own interests quite clearly. They understood that there was no going back. Peace with slavery intact did nothing but reset the clock to the moment before the war started. All of the old problems would still exist, especially the biggest and least tractable one: what to do with slavery in the country's new territories and states. How could the South possibly preserve its influence in a nation where it was badly outnumbered at the ballot box? But to the old intractable problems were now added two more. The war had seen the rise to power of the formerly weak and marginal abolitionists.

In 1861 they were in no position to impose their will on anyone. Now they — and their antislavery agendas — controlled much of the politics in the North. Now they were in a position to impose their will. And they were now the representatives of a vastly more powerful country. The last four years had seen the rapid growth of a large, industrialized Northern nation, enhanced by war, fueled by Irish and German immigrants, and overseen by what had become a highly centralized federal government. Peace and reunion meant the South could not possibly win; it would be subsumed. Peace with reunion meant, at best, that a war would have to be refought. Peace with reunion meant that nothing had been resolved. Davis was right: the choice was liberty or death. With nothing to negotiate with, or for, neither side was giving an inch.

Because most of the Northern media did not understand the issue, most people did not either, which allowed the Democrats to cling mulishly to their old suppositions while the Confederate commissioners stuck falsely to theirs. "The stupid tyrant who now disgraces the Chair of Washington and Jackson could, any day, have peace and restoration of the Union," said Clement C. Clay in an address that summer, lying through his teeth, "and would have them, only that he persists in the war to merely free the slaves."[22]

It was difficult to kill such a big lie.

The conspirators' other subversive work that summer was an equally dismal failure. They continued to believe in Vallandigham's dreams of insurrection. They continued to throw money at the Sons of Liberty and other dissidents, who were all too happy to take it. If the money was flowing, who cared if all of these grand conspiracies amounted to Confederate opium dreams? Having failed to produce a June uprising, they tried again in July, this time scheduled to coincide with the July 4 Democratic convention. They were thwarted when the convention was postponed. They tried again on July 20, in the wake of Lincoln's unpopular call for half a million more soldiers. This time the dauntless Sons of Liberty were poised to sweep into Indianapolis and take the city. Nothing happened. The insurrectionists failed to show again on August 16. They were obviously losing their nerve. On August 29, a pathetically small band of rebel adventurers showed up in Chicago, where the Democratic convention was being held. Revolvers in hand, they looked for the throngs of Sons of Liberty who were supposed to rise up with them. But no one was there. Nothing happened. The Peace Democrats were starting to believe they could get what they wanted at the ballot box. Violent counterrevolution could get them killed or imprisoned. Why risk it?

The Democratic Party and the Confederacy as a whole shared one other piece of common ground. Northern Democrats held disturbingly similar views on race, an issue they had shamelessly exploited with great success in the recent past. The party's victories in the 1862 election — just weeks after Lincoln had issued his preliminary Emancipation Proclamation — had been fueled by scare stories about the horrors of racial equality and the mixing of races.[23] So in 1864 the party and its captive newspapers dusted off the rhetoric and once again mounted a shameless, vulgar, and remarkably persistent appeal to Northern racism. Its most pernicious element was a phony study of race relations written by two enterprising employees of the *New York World,* which supported George McClellan for the Democratic nomination.

The authors had come up with a brilliant concept. Instead of attacking Republicans for their policies on race, they wrote a seventy-two-page tract showing how noble, virtuous, scientifically sound, and socially practical the mixing of races was — how it was the ultimate solution to the race problem in America. The research was phony, as were all of their conclusions. They titled it "Miscegenation:

The Theory of the Blending of the Races."
(They invented the word *miscegenation,* a
combination of *miscere,* the Latin verb for
"to mix," with *genus,* "race." The neologism
sounded something like *amalgamation,* the
traditional term for the mixing of races.)

"If any fact is well established in history,"
they wrote, posing as thoughtful Republicans
and envisioning a happy time when everyone
was a single color, presumably mocha, "it is
that miscegenetic or mixed races are much
superior, mentally, physically, and morally, to
those pure or unmixed." The image conjured
was of white and black people marrying, having sex, raising children. The purpose of the
war, they said, was to make that happen. "It
is idle to maintain that this present war is not
a war for the negro . . . a war looking, as its
final fruit, to the blending of the white and
black." Chapter headings included "Superiority of Mixed Races," "The March of the Dark
Races Northward," and "Love of the Blonde
for the Black." The authors suggested such
mixing should start with the Irish — the
people at the core of the antiblack race riots
of the preceding summer in New York.

The tract was as incendiary as it was false.
But people believed it and many were predictably appalled. The nation was not ready for
any such thing. The word *miscegenation*
entered the language, and the Democrats
exploited it fully, starting with the *New York*

328

World. The Emancipation Proclamation became the "Miscegenation Proclamation."[24] A pamphlet called *Miscegenation Endorsed by the Republican Party* found wide circulation. One New York paper reported, "Filthy black niggers, greasy, sweaty, and disgusting . . . now jostle white people and even ladies everywhere, even at the president's levees." The *Detroit Free Press* and the *Ohio Statesman* both printed a story about the daughter of a wealthy farmer who ran off with a black laborer. The article called the elopement "an act of tender passion" and stated, "Her Fond Parents . . . will receive them with open arms."[25] One of the main goals of the tract was to get actual abolitionists and Republicans to endorse it. Which many did, including the *Anglo-African Review* and the *National Anti-Slavery Standard.*[26]

As tracts proliferated, so did Democratic resourcefulness. Cartoons circulated widely showing black men with devilish grins kissing girls with "snow-white bosoms." Another featured the "Miscegenation Ball," a dance at which Republican politicians cavorted with black women. "Ise 'quainted wid Missus Linkum, I is," says one of the black women in minstrel-show dialect, "washed for her 'fore de hebenly Miscegenation times was cum. Dont do nuffin now but gallevant 'round wid de white gemmen!"[27] Nor did Democratic

Racist political cartoon from the 1864 presidential electi
campaign: Democrats tried to scare

Mars
not cut

Oh! You dear crea-
ture, I am so agita-
ted! Go and ask Pa.

Lubly Julia Anna,
name de day when
Brodder Beecher
shall make us one!

Adolphus, now you'll
be sure to come to
my lecture to morrow
night wont you?

Ill be there, Honey,
on de front seat,
sure!

Ah! my dear Miss Snowball
we have at last reached
ur political and social Pa-
adise. Isn't it extatic?

Most hextwadinary!
Aw neva witnessed
the like in all me life,
if I did dem me!

And is it to drag na-
gur babies that I left
old Ireland? Bad luck
to me.

Mine Got, vat
a guntry, vat
a beebles!

red according to act of Congress in the year 1864 by Bromley & Co. New York in the Clerks office of the District Court of the United States for the Southern District of New York.

ATION

ABOLITIONISM.

26331

480

July 1 1864

hite voters by saying that Lincoln and the Republicans advocated
e full mixing of the races.

politicians miss the chance to exploit the issue. Ohio congressman Samuel S. Cox stood on the floor of the House of Representatives and howled that the Republican Party was "moving steadily forward to perfect social equality of black and white, and can only end in this detestable doctrine of — Miscegenation."[28]

While this was pure hogwash, Lincoln and Republicans were extremely vulnerable on race, and the Democrats knew it. So much so that such a social and political force as Frederick Douglass was not, by decree of the party's wise men, allowed to play any visible role in the election. "I am not doing much in this presidential canvass," he wrote, "for the reason that the Republican committees do not wish to expose themselves to being the 'N——r party.' The negro is the deformed child, which is put out of the room when company comes."[29]

The race-baiting campaign was in full flower as the Democrats rolled into Chicago at the end of August for their party's convention. They had every reason to be thrilled with the summer's events. Lincoln was assailed on every front, most especially by his own party. The failures of backdoor diplomacy had revealed him to be insincere and not in favor of peace. If, as Lincoln's secretary John G. Nicolay wrote, "Everything is darkness and doubt and discouragement" for the Republicans, the opposite was true for the Democrats. Their prospects had never been brighter. The war was going horribly, which was wonderful news for them. Lincoln's popularity was at the lowest point in his career.

The Democratic convention opened with a roar. A hundred thousand people jammed the city and filled its bars and restaurants. Liquor flowed, bands played, salutes were fired in the streets, cheers rolled through the great hall. The opening speeches were great sanctimonious rants against the politicians who had needlessly drenched the land in fraternal blood.

The loudest of the cheers were reserved for George Brinton McClellan, the man who was going to ride this great wave of national pessimism and war-weariness into the White House. McClellan, the most controversial general of the Civil War, was in many ways everything the Democratic Party might have wanted in a candidate. He was smart, charming, charismatic, and a gifted administrator. He had rebuilt the Army of the Potomac from the ragged corps it was after losing at First Bull Run into a trim fighting unit. Most of his troops loved him unconditionally. He was on paper the perfect anti-Lincoln, a soldier's soldier who nonetheless believed the South should be treated gently. He was famous, a household name in both countries.

He was also deeply flawed, though only some of his shortcomings were then visible to the general public. He simmered with ill will. He was egotistical to an almost shocking degree, vainglorious, disloyal, and sneeringly dismissive of rivals and superiors, including Abraham Lincoln, whom he called a "baboon." Because of his miserable performance as a general, Lincoln had relieved him of command in the fall of 1862 and had never invited him back. Little Mac spent the next year and a half on the sidelines.

But there was something unkillable about George McClellan, something that resisted objective analysis. In his leisure time he had written out his own thousand-page version of the war, portraying himself as a fighter and a winner who had been held back by petty and parochial politicians. In spite of his record, this was how many Americans saw him. Contrary to his nemesis Lincoln, McClellan thought that the purpose of winning the war should be to put the nation back together as gently as possible with slavery in place. "Neither confiscation of property, political executions of persons, or forcible abolition of slavery should be contemplated," he had written. ". . . All private property should be strictly protected."[30] He won the Democratic nomination for president on the first ballot.

The problem — a large problem — was that

McClellan, a War Democrat, did not agree with his own party, which had in essence been hijacked by Peace Democrats and their leader, Clement Vallandigham. The Democrats nominated as McClellan's running mate Congressman George Pendleton of Ohio, who disagreed with McClellan on all major points. Pendleton, a radical Copperhead, had spoken warmly and sympathetically about the South and had opposed the war from the beginning.

But the Copperheads' real coup was the party's platform. Most of it was acceptable to the general run of Democrats: resolutions complaining about martial law and violations of civil liberties and in favor of preserving "the rights of the states unimpaired" (code for slavery), and blandly supporting the Union and the Constitution.

The platform's second plank, however, crafted by Vallandigham, might have been written by Jefferson Davis himself. It declared:

After four years of failure to restore the Union by the experiment of war, during which, under the pretense of a military necessity of war-power higher than the Constitution, the Constitution itself has been disregarded in every part . . . immediate efforts [must] be made for a cessation of hostilities, with a view of an ultimate conven-

335

tion of the States, or other peaceable means, to the end that, at the earliest practicable moment, peace may be restored on the basis of the Federal Union of the States.[31]

The language was remarkable. First, it dismissed the war effort — including the deaths and woundings, the fighting and heroism, of a million Union soldiers — as an outright failure. Whether this was true was beside the point. Such blunt and dismissive language could not help but shock and offend and would continue to harm the Democratic Party for a generation.[32] But that was the least of it. Calling for "cessation of hostilities, with a view of an ultimate convention of the States," suggested a sort of backward version of unconditional surrender in which the victors gave up all of their advantages. The resolution's overwhelming priority was peace. Peace mattered more than slavery. Only then would the idea of Union come into play. Only then would it be left to a vague notion of what a "convention of the States" might ultimately decide. The resolution was both defeatist and submissionist, and precisely what the rebels wanted to hear. "The election of Gen. McClellan upon such a declaration of wrongs and platform," wrote the *Charleston (SC) Mercury*, "must lead to our peace and independence . . . [provided] that for the next two months we hold our own."[33]

When McClellan formally accepted the nomination a week later, he rejected the idea that the war had been a failure and refused to endorse, as the Copperheads wanted him to, an immediate armistice followed by negotiations. But in other ways the letter was pure McClellan: equivocal, vacillating. He spoke of the national longing for peace. He asserted that when any Southern state wanted to rejoin the Union, on any terms, he would negotiate. (Lincoln insisted that all states come back together and that all abandon slavery.)

In spite of these mixed messages, the Democrats emerged from the convention convinced they were going to win. "Four years of failure" was inarguable. They had a strong candidate. They could worry about exactly how peace might come later. For now, the priority was to get rid of Abraham Lincoln.

While the Democrats were giving their thunderous speeches in Chicago, Sherman was doing what he had been doing since mid-July: fighting inconclusive battles in the environs of Atlanta. He had been moving against Atlanta for four months now, and this was starting to seem a long time. "Capturing Atlanta" had the feel of "taking Petersburg" — something that just wasn't going to happen anytime soon. The breathless coverage of the campaign's early days in Northern newspapers and magazines had given way to a less patient and more skeptical tone. Summer passed and armies maneuvered and men continued to die, and still Atlanta stood, defiant and unbowed.

The one piece of good war news that summer was a Union victory at Mobile Bay, in Alabama, on August 5. The battle had been won when a fleet of ships under Admiral David Farragut ran a gauntlet of gunfire and seized control over one of the last great blockade-running ports. Over the next three weeks the Union army and navy had captured Mobile's key forts with much bravery and some wonderful theatrics. Farragut's cry, while lashed to the mast, of "Damn the torpedoes! Full speed ahead!" was one of the war's most memorable moments — but Mobile Bay was in no way conclusive. Its seizure was like everything else that summer: incremental, marginal, a tightening of the noose. No one believed that occupying coastal Alabama was going to end the war. The meaning of Farragut's victory would become clear only later.[34]

With Grant and Lee still locked in stalemate, the eyes of both nations were on William Tecumseh Sherman, a clever and articulate man whose skill as a commander was still in question. Since May his large army had maneuvered around his enemy's flanks as Grant had in his Virginia campaign, but without the apocalyptic battles. Sherman would advance, find his outnumbered opponent, Joseph E. Johnston, entrenched in front of him, and instead of assaulting the fortifications — as Grant had at Spotsylvania and Cold Harbor — Sherman would simply march around them, skirting the rebel left and heading for their rearward supply lines and thus forcing them back.

The one major exception, the Battle of Kennesaw Mountain in Georgia, about twenty-five miles northwest of Atlanta, was yet another lesson in the idiocy of attacking fortifications. Sherman feigned a flank march and instead hit the center of Johnston's lines, where the rebel fieldworks were nearly as strong as those at Petersburg. Many Union boys died and nothing was accomplished. This, and the dozens of other battles, skirmishes, and minor actions of the Atlanta Campaign, amounted to little more than a slow but steady Confederate retreat from the larger federal force. Nothing had been "won" by the Yankees except a rugged, rural part of Georgia no one cared about.

Grant, whose eyes were firmly fixed on the Democratic convention at the end of August and the national elections two months later, was acutely aware of this. He peppered Sherman daily with exhortations to move, to try to make something happen and soon. On August 18, ten days before the Democratic convention, Grant told Sherman that, even if Forrest cut Sherman's supply lines, which provisioned one hundred thousand soldiers and their horses, he was not to retreat. At most other times in the war, this would have been a shocking statement. Now time was running out and there was no choice. Retrograde movement of any kind meant defeat at the polls. "Richmond papers of the 17th give it as the opinion of military men that Atlanta can hold out one month yet," Grant wrote Sherman. "In the meantime, like Micawber, they expect something to turn up.★ If you can hold fast as you are now and prevent raids upon your rear you will destroy most of that army. *I never would advise going backward even if your roads are cut* so as to preclude the possibility of receiving supplies from the North" (italics added).[35]

So Sherman, understanding what was at stake, pushed ahead. Atlanta was a big prize, a major industrial hub with foundries, factories, supply depots, munitions plants, railroads, and a population of twenty thousand.

★ Grant's reference is to Wilkins Micawber, the recklessly optimistic character in Charles Dickens's *David Copperfield*, who was put in debtors' prison for failing to pay creditors. His misguided but cheerful motto was "Something will turn up."

Losing it, as Jeff Davis observed, would open the coasts to Union armies and "close up the rich granaries from which Lee's army is supplied." More than that, the city had become, like Richmond, a national symbol of resistance. Because Johnston had not been able to stop Sherman's advance, the testy general had become immensely unpopular. Where was the old rebel toughness? Had not Stonewall Jackson won victories with fractions of his enemy's force?

Desperate to do something other than retreat, Jefferson Davis relieved Johnston of command and in his place put the hyperaggressive John Bell Hood, who had made his name in a spectacular charge at the Battle of Gaines's Mill in 1862. Hood was not only an aggressive campaigner but also a fierce political infighter. He had lobbied hard against Johnston. In a stream of letters to Richmond that summer he had claimed that he had constantly urged Johnston to attack, but that Johnston had refused. This was not true. Hood had advocated retreat a number of times, and for fewer than sixty thousand men to constantly attack one hundred thousand in the open field was a bad bet. But Hood got the job anyway.

With it came an immediate imperative: attack. And Hood did. Between July 20 and July 28 his soldiers came out of their entrenchments and attacked three times at the

Battles of Peachtree Creek, Atlanta, and Ezra Church. Though the fighting was often fierce, Hood's assaults were strategic failures. They cost him a shocking twenty-three thousand men (twenty thousand killed and wounded and three thousand captured). At the Battle of Atlanta (a fight for the suburbs of Atlanta) on July 22, the rebels lost ten thousand alone, compared to thirty-seven hundred for the Union.

Grant had maintained, throughout the summer, that the Confederate armies were no longer able to come out of their trenches and fight on open ground. They had been forced, he argued, by their dwindling numbers and resources, to fight only defensive battles, behind thick fortifications. Otherwise they would quickly be defeated. These were radical notions, greeted with deep skepticism in most parts of the country. Grant was convinced that the game had, indeed, fundamentally changed. Most people — on both sides — required a good deal more evidence.

But Hood's triple disaster now proved Grant right. Johnston's decision to retreat and "look for advantage," as he had put it, had been the correct tactic. He could not win a stand-up fight any more than Lee could at Petersburg. Fighting as Hood did merely hastened the rebels' destruction. As a Union sergeant under Sherman wrote in a letter, after the Battle of Ezra Church, "We kill a great many rebs in the fights — now more than ever, because they come out from their works, and charge our men, which is useless for them. For they do not do any good, only get their men slaughtered."[36]

In the weeks after Hood's attacks Sherman extended his entrenched lines and tightened his stranglehold on the city. His goal was not to take it by assault. Sherman was not that sort of general. He placed immense value on the lives of his soldiers. Instead he would encircle Atlanta and cut off its railways, and while he was doing that, he would throw three thousand to four thousand artillery shells a day into the city. Frustrated in his repeated attempts to seize the last rail line supplying the city, in late August Sherman pulled most of his army out of its trenches and cut loose from his supply lines. From Hood's point of view, Sherman had simply disappeared, which led to celebrations in the city. Sherman was actually marching south, making what he called "a desolating circle" around the city. He broke Atlanta's last rail communications. While the Democrats were denouncing Lincoln's failed war, Sherman's men were making "Sherman neckties" out of the last railroad into Atlanta. Hood, who realized too late what was happening, made one last, desperate lunge at Sherman at the Battle of Jonesborough on August 31. But he was thrown back. His forces badly depleted, his lines of communication cut, he evacuated the city on September 1, burning everything he could not carry. Sherman's troops entered Atlanta on September 2 accompanied by band music, Union songs, and "wild hallooing and glorious laughter." Sherman's note to the War Department read simply, "Atlanta is ours, and fairly won."

It is impossible to overstate the importance of the Union capture of Atlanta. Sherman had proven, incontrovertibly, that the war was not a failure. He had proven that the Democrats, who had just days before been celebrating wildly in Chicago, were wrong. The one thing that could save Lincoln, the fall of Atlanta, had happened, and all of the arguments about the president's dismal failure to win the war seemed to run out of steam at precisely the same moment.[37] Farragut's victory at Mobile Bay now seemed part of a *trend.* The war was larger than the fate of a single city, but just now none of that mattered.

Grant, who understood that the capture of Atlanta was the most significant event of the war, said as much in a wire to Sherman in a rare outpouring of emotion: "I feel you have accomplished the most gigantic undertaking given to any general in this war, and with a skill and ability that will be acknowledged in history as not surpassed, if not unequalled. It gives me as much pleasure to record this in your favor as it would in favor of any living man, including myself." Grant celebrated by ordering a hundred-gun salute from shotted cannon aimed at the rebel works in Petersburg.

The North erupted into something like pure happiness. The gloom of late summer lifted, and a thousand editorials celebrated the genius of Sherman and the magnificence of his achievement. The victory "set the country all aglow," wrote Grant, who also saw it as "the first great political campaign for the Republicans in their canvass of 1864."[38] On September 3 bells rung in churches across the North, brass cannons boomed on every town square, and people greeted each other joyously. Meanwhile Southern diarist Mary Chesnut, always a good barometer of rebel sentiment, wrote despondently, "The end has come. No doubt of that fact. . . . We are going to be wiped off the face of the earth."[39]

CHAPTER FIFTEEN:
VALLEY OF FIRE

CONFEDERATE COMMANDER JOHN SINGLETON MOSBY: He was the war's greatest guerrilla fighter, whose swashbuckling exploits tapped into the South's longing for a lost, heroic past.

The election — the most important in American history — loomed just ahead. Though

Abraham Lincoln's political fortunes had undergone a seismic shift, enormous tasks still lay ahead. Lee was dug in at Petersburg and Richmond. Several other large Confederate forces were abroad on the land: sizable armies under Edmund Kirby Smith in the Trans-Mississippi and John Bell Hood in Alabama and Tennessee, as well as a small army under Sterling Price that threatened Missouri. The rogue candidacy of John C. Frémont was much alive, and the Republican Party was deeply riven from its own civil wars. The country was still mad for peace, exhausted by death and hardship. The war, everyone now knew, was a razor's edge. A single victory could change everything. Who knew what Lee might do?

The first and most urgent of these tasks — the defeat of rebels in the Shenandoah Valley — fell to Philip Sheridan, Grant's unpopular choice for command. Sheridan had distinguished himself at the Battle of Stones River as the man who had slowed a seemingly inexorable Confederate attack; at the Battle of Missionary Ridge (Chattanooga) as the only Union commander who had refused to stop chasing the fleeing Confederate army and who had captured most of the rebel prisoners; and at the Battle of Yellow Tavern, as the cavalry officer who had finally beaten — and killed — Jeb Stuart. The five-foot-five-in-shoes Sheridan was an odd-looking fellow. Lincoln, who was also odd looking, described him as "a brown, chunky little chap, with a long body, short legs, not enough neck to hang him, and such long arms that if his ankles itch he can scratch them without stooping."[1] Lincoln might have added that Sheridan, with his chin beard, curling mustache, and piercing, Asiatic eyes, closely resembled a Mongolian horse soldier. Either way, he was not anyone's idea of what a major general of cavalry ought to look like. But he was the sort of officer Grant was looking for.

Grant had gone to great lengths to secure Sheridan's position, then had ordered him to destroy Jubal Early. Now, as September rolled in and the Northern nation turned its hopeful eyes to the accursed Shenandoah Valley, the peppery little general was doing . . . virtually nothing. Or so it seemed to increasing numbers of impatient politicians and newspaper editors in the North.

They had good reason to think so. Sheridan had been poised to attack and had maneuvered himself in position to do so. But then Early had been reinforced with two divisions, and suddenly the old Union-army reflex — an exaggerated fear of the unknown — had kicked in. Sheridan believed he was outnumbered (he wasn't) and was reminded by the ever-vigilant Halleck and Stanton that a defeat would have disastrous political consequences. Even Grant had urged caution in some of his wires.[2] As a result Sheridan could see no clear course of action. Nothing in his behavior, either before or after these events, suggested timidity. Quite the opposite. But for some reason — perhaps the notion that the outcome of the presidential election, less than two months away, depended on his performance — he hesitated. Then he withdrew a few miles to the north. His men wrecked some farms in the valley, skirmished with Early's troops in the shadow of the Blue Ridge Mountains, but accomplished little else.

A month after Sheridan's dramatic meeting with Grant, Early's force was exactly where it had been, intact and unharmed, about six miles south of the federal army in the northern part of the Shenandoah Valley. The Confederates saw Sheridan as part of a long tradition of weak valley commanders that included Nathaniel Banks, James Shields, John C. Frémont, Franz Sigel, and David Hunter. "The commander opposed to me was without enterprise," Early wrote dismissively, "and possessed an excessive caution which amounted to timidity."[3] This was acceptable to War Department officials, who rather liked stasis, which suggested to them the absence of immediate peril.

But Grant had not hired Little Phil to do nothing. Grant had told him in September that he was to push Early "with all vigor. Give

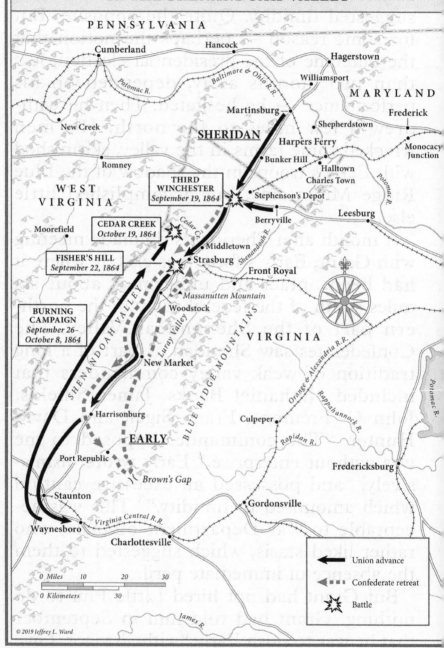

SHERIDAN'S FALL 1864 CAMPAIGN IN THE SHENANDOAH VALLEY

PENNSYLVANIA

Cumberland
Hancock
Hagerstown

Potomac R.
Baltimore & Ohio R.R.
Williamsport

MARYLAND

New Creek

Martinsburg
Shepherdstown
Frederick

SHERIDAN

Harpers Ferry
Monocacy
Junction

Romney
Bunker Hill
Halltown
Charles Town

WEST
VIRGINIA

**THIRD
WINCHESTER**
September 19, 1864

Stephenson's Depot

Berryville
Leesburg

Moorefield

CEDAR CREEK
October 19, 1864

Cedar Cr.

Middletown

Strasburg

Shenandoah R.

FISHER'S HILL
September 22, 1864

Front Royal

Massanutten Mountain

**BURNING
CAMPAIGN**
*September 26–
October 8, 1864*

Woodstock

SHENANDOAH VALLEY

Luray Valley

VIRGINIA

New Market

BLUE RIDGE MOUNTAINS

Orange & Alexandria R.R.

Rappahannock R.

Harrisonburg

Culpeper

Rapidan R.

EARLY

Port Republic

Brown's Gap

Fredericksburg

Staunton

Gordonsville

Waynesboro

Virginia Central R.R.

Charlottesville

Potomac R.

0 Miles   10   20   30
0 Kilometers   30

→ Union advance
▶ ▶ ▶ Confederate retreat
✸ Battle

© 2019 Jeffrey L. Ward

James R.

the enemy no rest." Nothing like that was happening. Lincoln was getting edgy, too, asking Grant on September 12 if they "could not pick up a regiment here and there, to the number of, say, ten thousand, and quietly but suddenly concentrate them at Sheridan's camp and allow him to make a quick strike?"[4]

Something had to be done. Because this was Grant's war now, and because Sheridan was his man, and because great events were in the wind, Grant would be the one to do it. On September 15 he traveled north again to see Sheridan, once more bypassing the White House and the War Department. He wanted to meet Sheridan face-to-face. Grant also wanted to neutralize the wire traffic coming out of Halleck's office in Washington, whose message was, Grant worried, "contradictory to mine."[5] He did not trust the War Department.

This time there would be no theoretical discussions of how Sheridan might proceed. Grant had taken the extraordinary step of writing out a specific "plan of campaign," as he later phrased it, ordering Sheridan to attack and telling him exactly how to do it. Early would either be destroyed or driven from the valley.[6] Those were the two options. There would be no argument, no more hesitation, no undercutting of Grant's plans by Washington. Grant had this document in his pocket when he met Sheridan at Charles-

351

town, ten miles southwest of Harpers Ferry. But because Grant liked and trusted Sheridan, Grant decided he would wait to see what the young general had to say. Grant started by asking Sheridan if he had a map indicating the positions of the two armies.

To Grant's surprise and delight, Sheridan had just such a map, a detailed one showing roads and streams and the exact positions of the two military camps. Sheridan wasn't stupid; he understood that a visit from the general-in-chief of the Union armies was not a casual affair. Sheridan said he had received reliable intelligence that a division of Confederate troops was headed back to Lee, and as Grant and Sheridan walked and talked in an open field near Sheridan's camp, he traced the troop movements that would defeat the remaining rebel forces. Grant liked Sheridan's plan, his enthusiasm, and his energy so much that he kept his own plan in his pocket and never mentioned it. Still, he wanted to make sure there would be no more delay. Would Sheridan's army be able to move within four days? Sheridan said he could move in three. Grant told him to do it and departed. Such was Grant's confidence in Sheridan that the lieutenant general took a detour on his way home to visit his wife in Burlington, New Jersey, 150 miles from Washington.[7]

On September 19, at Opequon Creek, Union forces under Philip Sheridan engaged and defeated the Confederate army of Jubal Early.* In midafternoon the battle turned into a rout as the bluecoats drove the gray-backs through the streets of Winchester, Virginia, capturing twenty-five hundred of them. Though the numbers of men involved were small compared to the fighting near Richmond, or Atlanta, the battle was one of the most politically important of the war and was seen that way immediately by the press and general public on both sides. Lincoln's personal secretaries, John G. Nicolay and John Hay, later described its meaning and impact on the United States:

> This brilliant victory of Sheridan, unprom-ised and unheralded, prepared with infinite prudence and pains, and then carried through with such dash and valor, was greeted with an outburst of patriotic joy. Sheridan's dispatch, with its trooper-like phrase, "We have just sent them whirling through Winchester, and we are after them tomorrow," became a household word in a few hours after it was written.[8]

Sheridan was indeed after them. Three days later he routed them again at the Battle of Fisher's Hill and sent them on a high-speed retreat south along the Valley Pike. Grant was

* Also known as the Third Battle of Winchester.

353

ecstatic. He promoted Sheridan to permanent command of the army's Middle Division and sent him a telegram: "Have just heard of your great victory. God bless you all, officers and men. Strongly inclined to come up and see you." A month later, Sheridan extinguished the final Confederate spark in the valley, routing a risen-from-the-dead Early in spectacular fashion at the Battle of Cedar Creek. Sheridan, mounted on his great black stallion, waving his cap, crying out in his great bellowing voice and riding at furious speed, personally led the final counterattack while his men cheered and rallied to him. Little Phil's star had been rising since the bloody spring in the Wilderness. At Cedar Creek he outdid his own legend, proving once and forever that Grant had made the right choice. The bloody and bitter battle for the Shenandoah Valley was over. The rebels would never take it back.

The Shenandoah Valley had witnessed not only the military conquest of a Confederate army. After his victories over Early at Opequon Creek and Fisher's Hill, Sheridan had begun a deliberate campaign of destruction against the valley's residents. Or, more specifically, their property. Nothing on this scale had ever before been done in the war. While he was doing that, Sheridan waged another sort of radically unconventional war: a desperately violent fight against rebel guerrillas. The two nontraditional wars often merged and overlapped. War by an army against civilians was countered by civilian war against the army.

Sheridan's nemesis, in his campaign of destruction, was a rebel commander who, like Sheridan, had swiftly risen to national prominence and whose name filled the pages of newspapers everywhere: John Singleton Mosby. He was the greatest guerrilla fighter of the war and one of the most gifted officers America has ever produced. Among Northerners he was perhaps the most hated rebel of all, the symbol of the informal resistance and the unconquerability of the Confederacy. Unlike the infamous guerrillas Bloody Bill Anderson and William C. Quantrill in Missouri, who were little more than outlaws, Mosby was an actual soldier with an actual commission. He reported to Lee and mostly played by the accepted rules of war, except when he didn't.

On paper, the fight between Sheridan and Mosby was an absurd mismatch, a caricature of the disadvantages the South faced in the larger war. More than thirty-five thousand men were pitted against three hundred to four hundred who often attacked in groups of less than fifty. An army with city-size camps and miles-long supply trains was matched against a gang of riders with no apparent base of operations and no known whereabouts. The Union's state-of-the-art killing machine against an older — and, as the South saw it, more noble and chivalric — style of war.

Grant never ordered Sheridan to burn anything. He never used the word, perhaps because of the way it might have sounded to the supposedly civilized people of his country and down through all history. Though he had ordered Sheridan quite specifically to "destroy all forage and subsistence," to annihilate all stores of wheat and grain, to reduce the lush Shenandoah Valley to a "barren waste" so denuded of anything like food that a crow flying over it could find nothing to eat, Grant made not a single reference to firing or torching or burning, or any suggestion that uniformed men should take firebrands from hot fires and apply them to barns full of grain and fields owned by ordinary citizens, destroying their wealth and their means of survival.[9]

But that is what he meant. And that is what Phil Sheridan did. He destroyed property on a scale hitherto unseen in the war and in a way that would change its fundamental nature. This was entirely Grant's fight now and would be waged according to his rules, and that meant hard and unforgiving war against civilians.

After Sheridan's army had thrashed the irksome Jubal Early in mid-September, Early had escaped by heading south, fleeing along the macadamized Valley Turnpike and then ducking off into the tiny river town of Port Republic, near one of those backdoor, escape-hatch routes through the Blue Ridge Mountains that Stonewall Jackson, two years before, had so brilliantly exploited. Sheridan pursued Early for a while, then paused at the town of Harrisonburg and considered what to do next. He thought about this for a while, exchanged telegraphs with Grant, then made up his mind. Instead of pursuing Early's ragged, outnumbered army, Sheridan would turn north and "carry out my original instructions," which meant following to the letter the orders Grant had given him in early August.

So his army swung round. His infantry and trains retraced their steps north through the valley while his cavalry, more than ten thousand strong, fanned out behind them. As Sheridan later wrote, the horsemen were "stretched across the country from the Blue Ridge to the eastern slope of the Alleghenies," a distance, on average, of twenty-five miles.[10] For the first time in the war, no Confederate army was left in the valley to confront these soldiers, whose orders were to destroy everything except homes and to kill or drive off all horses, cattle, pigs, sheep, chickens, and goats. They were to seize slaves, too, and ship them back through Union lines and into new

lives in camps in Virginia and Washington —
places of freedom, yes, but also misery and
destitution that would change all of their lives
forever.

Though some Union soldiers recoiled in
horror from this sort of duty, Sheridan's army
had endured so many guerrilla attacks — so
many cold-blooded murders, as the Yankees
believed — that most of them needed no
incentive to carry out their orders. Indeed,
while the primary goal of such destruction
was to remove a major food source from
Lee's army, it achieved another strategic
objective as well: burned-out land could not
support guerrilla bands, either. They and
their corn-fed horses had to eat, too.

So the burning began. Though a full inventory of the destruction cannot be taken, a
report from Sheridan to Grant on October 7
suggests its scope:

> I have destroyed over two thousand barns
> filled with wheat, hay & farming implements,
> over seventy mills filled with flour & wheat,
> have driven in front of the army over 4,000
> head of stock and have killed & issued to
> the troops not less than 3,000 sheep. . . .
> Tomorrow I will continue the destruction of
> wheat, forage, Etc., down to Fisher's Hill.
> When this is completed the valley from
> Winchester up to Staunton, 92 miles, will
> have but little in it for man or beast.[11]

The sheer malevolent thoroughness of the devastation astounded everyone who saw it. Black smoke swirled up from thousands of fires and rose in columns and filled the valley as far as the eye could see in every direction. It hung on the ridges of mountains. At night the bright flames that shot skyward from once-picturesque farms reminded some people of hell itself. Though the orders said not to burn homes — as opposed to barns, chicken coops, and other outbuildings — Sheridan's men did plenty of that, too, often in reprisal for partisan attacks.[12] On August 18, for example, Brigadier General Colonel George Armstrong Custer, one of Sheridan's division commanders, ordered the burning of five houses in retaliation for the killing, by guerrillas, of one of his soldiers.[13] Many more than that would be burned to the ground.

But even if people kept their homes, everything else they owned was consigned to the flames. As one resident put it, "There was nothing left for man or beast from the horse down to the chicken."[14] Often the soldiers were kind enough to leave destitute families some food in their larders. Sometimes they were not. Most of the valley's wealth literally went up in smoke. That included, in addition to the smoldering mounds of charcoal that had once been buildings, every fence rail, shovel, plow, milk bucket, egg, barrel, chicken, mule, cow, horse, and grain of corn and wheat. The residents were shocked, and panicked. They had witnessed omnivorous, locustlike Union armies tramping up and down the valley since 1862, but had never experienced anything like this.[15] Many began discussing their prospects for starvation, which were suddenly quite real.[16]

The burning raid had an immediate effect on the Confederate army. On October 9, while Sheridan's horsemen were still setting fires, Confederate general Jubal Early was already complaining to Robert E. Lee that, because everything in his normal supply area had been burned or driven off, "I will have to rely on Augusta [Georgia] for my supplies, and they are not abundant there."[17] Augusta was far away, in a country that was fast collapsing. Some of Early's men were reduced to picking green corn in the countryside and trading labor for food.

Sheridan liked what he saw. He had not invented this style of war, but now he undertook it with the zeal of the newly converted.[18] While Southerners were condemning him as the spawn of Satan, Little Phil was embracing what he believed to be the pure and inexorable logic of his position. "There is more mercy in destroying supplies than in killing young men," he told an army friend. "If I had a barn full of wheat and a son, I would much sooner lose the barn and wheat than my son."[19] Such a choice was highly theoretical since many valley residents had now lost *both* their sons and their farms. But Sheridan believed what he was saying and was convinced that burning the valley would hasten the end of the war and ultimately spare lives. "Death is popularly considered the maximum punishment of the war, but it is not," he wrote. "Reduction to poverty brings prayers for peace more surely and more quickly than does the destruction of human life, as the selfishness of man has demonstrated in more than one great conflict."[20]

Grant was convinced of this, too, but what may have seemed practical to him was pure horror for civilians, many of whom saw this as the conflict's final turn into pure hatred, bitterness, and revenge. "The war has now assumed that phase in which no mercy can be shown to the enemy," wrote Confederate chief of ordnance Josiah Gorgas. "He burns, robs, murders, ravishes, and is to be met only by killing all."[21] The *Richmond Whig* suggested that the Confederacy retaliate by burning a Northern city to the ground. "They chose to substitute the torch for the sword," wrote one columnist. "It is a game at which we can beat them. New York is worth twenty Richmonds."[22] In the fight to the death between cultures, this suddenly seemed like a good idea.

In the summer of 1862 Confederate scout John S. Mosby came up with a radical proposal for fighting the war. The idea was so implausible on its face, so lacking in precedent, and so inherently dangerous that scarcely anyone else believed it possible. Even Mosby's boss, friend, and protector, General James Ewell Brown "Jeb" Stuart, himself one of the most daring and innovative officers in the war, thought it sounded a bit crazy. Mosby proposed to take a unit of Confederate cavalry and operate entirely behind Union lines. He would provide the rebel army with intelligence of Union troop deployments. He would disrupt communications. That meant moving by stealth around enemy camps, attacking supply wagons, cutting telegraph wires, raiding the railroads, picking off Union patrols. He would fight deliberately unfairly, lurking in darkness and shadow, avoiding large-scale confrontations, forcing the Union army to divert troops to deal with him. That was the main idea. He wanted the enemy to hunt him. The more men chasing him, or guarding trains and wagons against his attacks, the fewer would be available to fight on the front lines against Robert E. Lee.

But the most radical part of Mosby's idea was that, when his raids were completed, he and his men would not retreat to the safety of areas controlled by rebel armies. This differentiated his scheme from the methods of such rebel partisans as John Hunt Morgan, who had become famous for two lengthy raids into Kentucky, Ohio, and Indiana (the second of which was ultimately a disaster), but whose idea was always to raid and then return to the safety of his home base in Tennessee. Mosby's partisans would, instead, remain permanently in Union-occupied northern Virginia, where the Union army controlled all the roads, rails, waterways, and towns, and where captured guerrillas were often summarily shot or hanged. There would be no safe haven.* Mosby chose to operate,

* Most rebel bushwhackers operated in small groups and raided Confederate loyalists as well as Unionists. They were often little more than outlaws, out for their own gain. Robert E. Lee came to hate them and in 1864 officially disbanded all but two of the units that had been organized under the Partisan Ranger Act. Mosby, by contrast, was part of the Confederate States army. Though he had an independent command, he reported to superiors, including Lee himself. While Bloody Bill Anderson and William C. Quantrill sometimes commanded large groups of men, they were essentially outlaws and beyond the control of the regular Confederate army or the Missouri State militia. Mosby was mostly about attacking Union-army supply lines. He took

moreover, just west of Washington, DC, which put him squarely between the most heavily defended city on earth and the Union's largest army.[23] Whole sections of it were crawling with bluecoats. The crowning — and, to Jeb Stuart, least rational — feature of Mosby's plan was that he and his men would require no supplies of any kind from rebel forces: no food, no horses or saddles, no weapons or ammunition. They would reside in ordinary homes — sometimes their own, sometimes those of others, moving constantly to avoid capture — and live entirely off the largesse of the enemy.[24]

Though Mosby had proved himself dazzlingly capable as a scout, Stuart resisted his idea for six months.[†] In November 1862 Stuart finally agreed to let his ambitious subordi-

---

several thousand prisoners during the war and treated most of them well. Anderson and Quantrill were about killing people, looting, and creating mayhem. Mosby operated in the shadow of Washington, DC, and in the immediate presence of large Union armies. Missouri and Kansas were in many ways lawless states.

† Mosby had advance-scouted Stuart's legendary ride around the entire Union army to collect intelligence before the Seven Days Battles — a feat that had made Stuart a household name in the North and the South.

nate conduct a reconnaissance behind Union lines to gather information but also to see if Mosby's unusual plan could work. Stuart detailed nine men to accompany him on the mission, which took them thirty-five miles in the enemy's rear. Mosby performed brilliantly, moving undetected around the enemy's camps and patrols and predicting exactly where its troops were going.

He also dramatically demonstrated his theory that the enemy was most vulnerable behind its own lines. Near the old Bull Run battlefield, just west of Washington, Mosby and his unit encountered a full regiment of Union cavalry — more than a thousand men. The federals were taking a break, with ten men on picket duty. Instead of quietly slipping away, as any prudent commander would have done, Mosby's vastly outnumbered men dismounted, spread out over a hundred yards, then attacked, firing their guns and yelling, while Mosby himself galloped back and forth shouting out orders to bodies of men that did not exist. The Union pickets panicked and ran for the rear, which stampeded the rest of the regiment. When the "battle" was over, Mosby and his small unit had routed an entire Union regiment.[25] This almost casual demonstration of what he could do was a preview of a thousand headaches to come for Union commanders. On December 30, 1862, shortly after Mosby's twenty-ninth birthday, Stuart gave him fifteen men and the highly unusual, nonspecific assignment to pierce Union lines, remain there isolated and alone and without reinforcements or resupply, and wreak havoc. Mosby thus, finally, had his dream job and began a spectacular new career.

Mosby grew up in a family of middling Virginia gentry, prosperous and slave owning but not rich. A small, delicate child, he was ill-suited to athletics. He preferred reading books. Like many undersized boys he was bullied, too, and developed a finely calibrated sense of justice. He attended the University of Virginia in Charlottesville, where he excelled in the classics and spent much of his time reading Greek literature. He might have had a normal and perhaps even distinguished college career (in the classics, certainly — he was less adept at math) except for a strange, wild, and violent streak in his otherwise temperate personality.

The streak took various forms, such as his fondness for riding his horse at breakneck speed through the streets of Charlottesville in defiance of the town's laws. Mosby was a brilliant rider, as good as any his classmates had ever seen. He also tended, despite his size — five feet eight inches tall, 128 pounds — to settle problems with violence. During his first year at the University of Virginia, he was at a boisterous student party known as a callithump when a local policeman threw one of the students to the ground and began beating him. Mosby considered the attack unjust, intervened, kicked and punched the policeman, then broke a gunstock over his head. Mosby was tried, found guilty of assault, and fined.[26]

Toward the end of his second year at the University of Virginia he was in a far more violent altercation with the school's resident bully, a student named George R. Turpin, who had slashed one student with a knife and severely beaten another with a rock. Mosby drew Turpin's ire by engaging a musician for a party on a night when Turpin wanted that same musician. Turpin made insulting remarks about Mosby. Mosby, following the rules of the ancient code duello, sent a letter asking Turpin to explain himself. Turpin responded by saying he would "see the damn rascal and eat him up, blood raw, on sight." When the two encountered each other at a boardinghouse, Mosby approached Turpin and said, "I understand you have been making some assertions." Turpin responded by charging him. Mosby drew a pistol and shot him in the jaw. Turpin bled a good deal but lived and recovered. Mosby, on the other hand, would never again be quite the same.

The nineteen-year-old was arrested, tried, convicted of "unlawful shooting," fined $500, and sentenced to one year in the county jail.

He and his family were horrified. None of them thought he would serve time for defending himself against a violent bully. His parents made a number of unsuccessful efforts — including an appeal to the governor — to nullify the verdict. Mosby still served nine months.

But his jail time changed his life. While he was in prison his literary interests impressed his prosecutor, William J. Robertson. Seeing Mosby reading Milton's *Paradise Lost* in his cell, Robertson offered the young man access to his legal library. So Mosby started reading law and eventually read a great deal of it. Robertson became his teacher. When Mosby was released, he continued to study law and two years later, in September 1855, he passed the bar and opened what would become a successful law practice. He married and had two children. Like fellow Virginians Robert E. Lee, Stonewall Jackson, and Jubal Early, he opposed the state's secession.

When the war came, he joined Jeb Stuart's First Virginia cavalry, and everything changed again.

In the months that followed his commission from Stuart, Mosby and his 43rd Battalion Virginia Cavalry made all of his wild promises come true. He became instantly famous. Operating in a multicounty area west of Washington, DC, which soon came to be known as Mosby's Confederacy, his detachments burned trains, tore up tracks, captured supply wagons, and fought and won countless engagements against Union troops.[27] He attacked in snowstorms. He made a specialty of defeating and capturing the cavalry patrols sent to destroy him. On a single night he successfully ambushed the 6th Michigan Cavalry *twice,* taking prisoners both times. He captured a Union camp of three hundred men with only one hundred of his own.[28] He took 167 men into battle against 160 Yankees at Dranesville and inflicted 107 casualties while suffering only 6.[29] He lost some fights, too, but not many.

He seemed to toy with his enemies, riding into and out of large Union camps by night, undetected and often in disguise. He promoted the myth of his ubiquity, letting his enemies know on every raid that he was there, even if not — and indeed the Yankees believed him to be everywhere. His men fought at close range with .44-caliber Colt six-shooters, and Union commanders took far longer than they should have to understand that sabers were no match for the Colts in that sort of combat. ("My men were as little impressed by a body of cavalry charging them with sabres as though they had been armed with cornstalks," Mosby wrote later.)[30] Nor were the federals' fancy repeating carbines effective at such intimate range.

Most unnerving to Mosby's opponents was his ability to appear and disappear seemingly at will, which accounted for his nickname, the Gray Ghost. This was not accidental. Mosby worked hard at it. Mounted cavalry made a distinctive noise, a whirring, humming sound produced by clanking sabers, scabbards, canteens, and tack that could be heard several hundred yards away. Mosby stripped away most of the noisemakers. When his men attacked dismounted, they removed their spurs. He used snow or dirt from farm fields to muffle hoofbeats. One of his rangers' specialties was the "skedaddle," which happened when they decided they were outnumbered or overmatched. They seemed to know instinctively when that moment arrived. Instead of retreating together in a group, they scattered like chaff in a wind — on horses that were faster and fresher than their opponents' — each in his own direction, to meet up later at a prearranged location.

As he had promised Stuart, Mosby got everything he needed from the Union army. This included the Union's finest weapons, food, uniforms, operating cash, whiskey, and best thoroughbreds. Mosby's men each had several good horses, most of them jumpers, and he made sure that the horses were both fast and rested when he went on a raid. He forbade the killing of unarmed Unionists, distributed booty from raids liberally among his soldiers — which was legal under his commission from the Confederate government — and sent the vast majority of stolen supplies by wagon train to Lee. In person Mosby could be casual, intimate, funny, and erudite. He loved to quote Lord Byron. He could also be cantankerous, mean, intolerant, and belligerent, a man never to be crossed. Everyone agreed he had two sides.

Mosby's signature raid — the one that made him an instant legend, North and South — took place two months after Stuart had dispatched him on his new mission. On the night of March 8, 1863, Mosby and twenty-nine men penetrated Union lines in the town of Fairfax Court House, just outside Washington. They took down Union pickets in hand-to-hand combat, then rode undetected into the camp of a Vermont brigade. They captured several Union staff officers — some of whom were so shocked at the implausibility of what was happening that they laughed out loud — and cut the telegraph wires.[31] Mosby and five men rode to the headquarters of the commanding officer, Brigadier General Edwin H. Stoughton, roused him roughly from his bed, and told him he was a prisoner.

By the time they emerged onto the public square with the indignant Stoughton, Mosby's men were waiting with thirty Union prisoners and fifty-eight captured horses. All of this had taken place in proximity to thousands of Union troops. Not a shot had been fired. Not a ranger had been lost. Mosby and his men then made their silent escape, prisoners in tow, dodging Union patrols and swimming in a swollen, icy river with their horses, arriving safely beyond Union lines just after daybreak. In the town of Warrenton, the entire population turned out in the streets to give them an ovation.[32] That morning Mosby delivered the general and other prisoners to the Confederate cavalry.

Mosby's dark-of-night raid in Fairfax made him the new hero of the Southern people and offered yet another opportunity for Northerners to marvel at the failure of their large and colossally expensive armies. Northern newspapers called the event "utterly disgraceful" and suggested, "There is a screw loose somewhere," while the *Richmond Enquirer* published a glowing commendation from Jeb Stuart calling Mosby's raid "a brilliant act" and stating that praise for the young partisan leader "was on every lip."[33] Robert E. Lee promoted him to major and expanded his command to a full battalion (he would soon command more than three hundred men). Mosby did not break stride. Eight days later he and forty men pierced the Union screen again, this time capturing twenty-five prisoners and twenty-six horses. "Still Gobbling Them Up," read the headline in the *Washington Star*. Suddenly everyone in America was talking about the Gray Ghost.

Mosby's success carried a larger meaning, too, one that was impossible to miss. His success had proven to many Southerners, as well as some people in the North, that extended guerrilla war was a viable choice for the Confederacy. Even if rebel armies were defeated, this sort of thinking went, Confederate government could simply shift to Mosby's unconventional style of war. And if they did that, how could the South ever be fully and truly conquered?

This was a legitimate question. Though the unconquered Confederacy was far smaller in 1864 than it had been in 1862, the still-enormous expanse of land contained relatively few blue-uniformed soldiers. How could something so big be truly beaten and held? Even now, Southerners pointed out, Sherman's supply line, which stretched from Atlanta to Chattanooga, with several major tributaries, was being constantly raided by guerrillas. In such a hostile land, filled with armed partisans, how could Sherman even continue to feed his army, let alone roost as a colonizing force in Georgia? In Macon, President Jefferson Davis probed this idea in a fiery speech, saying, "Our cause is not lost. Sherman cannot keep his long line of communications; retreat sooner or later he must. . . . When that day comes, the fate that befell the army of the French in its retreat from Moscow will be reenacted."[34] Many Southerners believed this woolly logic. An unconventional war, on the other hand, was not theoretical at all, as Mosby had proven.

The Mosby legend also tapped into a deep longing among Southerners for a lost, heroic past, one that could somehow replace the miserable reality they were increasingly forced to confront. That longing was rooted in the Revolutionary War, a time when out-gunned and outnumbered partisans — starting with the highly mobile "minutemen" of Massachusetts — waged successful guerrilla war against the tightly regimented redcoats of the British army. Though George Washington's Continental Army mostly won the war, the image of ponytailed American irregulars in breeches, leather stockings, and three-cornered hats, shouldering varmint guns and attacking from behind trees, was indelible. With their bravery, resourcefulness, and native cunning, these revolutionary partisans seemed to exemplify the best attributes of the American character. Mosby was the latest commander in this tradition, which included such dashing cavaliers as Turner Ashby, Jeb Stuart, and John Hunt Morgan — all of whom were dead by the fall of 1864.

The most famous Revolutionary War guerrilla was Mosby's childhood hero, Francis Marion, who had become known to generations of Americans through two popular biographies.[35] From 1780 to 1782, the "Swamp Fox" waged a brutally effective partisan war against British and Loyalist troops in the lowlands of South Carolina.[36] Like Mosby, he was slight in stature, an unprepossessing, frail-looking, slave-owning Southerner who staged ambushes with men who scattered like quail into the forest when threatened. Perhaps predictably, the beleaguered Confederacy, in its hour of greatest need, looked to such a model for salvation. The comparison was obvious, and Southern newspapers could not resist making it: Mosby was the new Marion, the new indomitable underdog, the new reason the Union could never win the war.

But Mosby's legend suggested even deeper connections to the idea of a lost romantic past. One of the most successful authors in antebellum America was Sir Walter Scott, who in many novels glamorized and popularized the Middle Ages, refashioning them as a grand narrative of the age of chivalry, replete with castles, gallant knights, bright pavilions with streaming banners, and fair damsels.[37] His most famous work was *Ivanhoe* (1820), the story of the knight Wilfred of Ivanhoe. The novel, set in twelfth-century England, featured, among other attractions, the Crusades, a jousting tournament, Richard the

Lionheart, and Robin Hood. Scott was wildly popular in America, selling more than half a million books between 1814 and 1823. Americans, North and South, adored the pageantry and lofty sentiments.

But while Northerners simply enjoyed the marvelous suspension of disbelief, many Southerners took the romantic myth to heart. They named their estates and children after Scott's characters. They wrote poems comparing the contemporary South to Scott's gauzy version of the past. A typical example was a poem published in 1861 by prominent Southern writer Francis Orray Ticknor, which described Virginians thus:

The knightliest of the knightly race,
Who, since the days of old,
Have kept the lamp of chivalry
Alight in hearts of gold[38]

Southerners, particularly the planter class, liked to see themselves as a noble, chivalric aristocracy — knights and beaux sabreurs — and the most dashing, swashbuckling, plume-hatted cavalier in the war was John S. Mosby.[39] Everyone knew that his ranks included the cream of Virginia's antebellum aristocracy, as well as graduates of West Point and the Virginia Military Institute — Christian gentlemen all.[40] Again, the comparisons to Scott's golden age were impossible for

376

Southern writers to resist.[41]

Many Northerners found this fixation contemptible. The most famous of them was Mark Twain, who believed that the "Walter Scott disease" the South had contracted was in some ways responsible for the war itself. He wrote:

> Then comes Sir Walter Scott with his enchantments, and . . . sets the world in love with dreams and phantoms; with decayed and swinish forms of religion; with decayed and degraded systems of government; with sillinesses and emptinesses, sham grandeurs, sham gauds, and sham chivalries of a brainless and long-vanished society. He did measureless harm; more real, perhaps, than any other individual that ever wrote.[42]

Mosby disliked being compared to romantic legends and even addressed the issue directly in a postwar letter. He wrote that he viewed war not as a "tournament or pastime but as one of the most practical undertakings. I learned the maxims on which I conducted it from Napoleon and not from Walter Scott."[43]

Despite the romance of a figure such as Mosby, darker currents were at play. "Black flag" war meant death by execution of all enemy prisoners, wounded or not, surrendered or not. It encouraged murder and massacre conspicuously in violation of conventional rules of war. In the early days of the fighting both sides toyed with the idea. In Ohio one legislator proposed appropriating $1 million to pay for "rebel scalps." His bill failed. Stonewall Jackson briefly advocated a black-flag policy to scare the Yankees into suing for peace. He backed off. In 1862, rebel general P. G. T. Beauregard predicted, "We will yet . . . come to proclaiming this a war to the knife, when no quarter will be asked or granted."[44] Both sides were always ready to assert that, if the other side refused to give quarter, they would be more than happy to do the same. Better yet, they said, we'll kill two of your men for every one of our prisoners killed.

With one large exception — the Confederate treatment of black Union prisoners — both sides largely behaved themselves until the summer of 1864. Despite a few "no quarter" incidents, as a general rule white men respected the traditional wartime rights of other white men.[45] This applied principally to soldiers fighting in uniform as part of official armies. Bushwhackers and thugs such as Quantrill and Anderson neither expected nor were granted rights as soldiers.

But with the burning of the Shenandoah Valley first by Hunter and then by Sheridan, all that changed, and the war took yet another turn into hard, retributive violence. Yankees who burned property were seen as lawless brigands, undeserving of any of the normal rights given to soldiers in civilized warfare, and the response to their actions took the immediate form of no-quarter guerrilla war. Union soldiers were waylaid and ambushed and shot and hanged and nailed to trees with placards on them warning others of what would happen if they stole or destroyed property.[46] Prisoners were rarely taken, and when they were, it was usually so they could be hanged later. The federals responded in kind, executing scores of guerrillas. Many of the rebel groups were highly informal; some, such as those under partisan leaders John Hanson McNeill, Elijah V. White, and Harry Gilmor, were more disciplined and organized.[47] Mosby's partisans were by far the most numerous, effective, and deadly guerrillas Sheridan faced.[48] In his words, they were "the most redoubtable"; they were the most troublesome, and the most in need of extermination.[49]

What happened that summer and fall was one of the ugliest parts of the civil conflict, a brutally destructive pattern of retaliation and prisoner execution that resulted in some of the war's most inhumane actions. At times a black flag seemed to be flying over the entire Shenandoah Valley, though no such policy was ever officially declared. The two most prominent players in this bloody drama, which played out on the front pages of news-papers across the country, were Sheridan and Mosby. Their fight took place from August to November in the shadow of Sheridan's skirmishes and battles with Jubal Early, and of his campaign of destruction.

The cycle of retribution began on August 13, a week after Sheridan had assumed com-mand in the valley, when Mosby struck a wagon train near the town of Winchester, in the northern part of the valley. This was no typical raid. Mosby had spotted a major weakness in the Union supply line and was at battalion strength — 250 men. He and his rangers attacked in their familiar "horse race" style, at full gallop, revolvers blazing. They simply blew through the Union defenders, killing six, wounding nine, and taking two hundred prisoners. Mosby's force suffered only two men killed and three wounded. They attained their objective, capturing 40 fully loaded wagons, 200 head of cattle, 420 mules, and 36 horses.

Grant was furious when he heard the news. Mosby had embarrassed his splendid new commander. Grant immediately issued a shockingly intemperate order for the taking of *civilian* prisoners, potentially thousands of them, and hauling them off to jail in another state. "The families of most of Mosby's men are known and can be collected," Grant wrote to Sheridan, as though it were the most normal thing in the world. "I think they should be taken and kept at Fort McHenry, or some secure place, as hostages for the good conduct of Mosby and his men." Grant quickly realized that he had gone too far and amended his orders to require the arrest of all males between seventeen and fifty in the areas where Mosby operated, on the theory that anyone of that age who was not already in the army must be a guerrilla.[50] It still amounted to preemptively locking up unarmed civilians.[51]

Then Grant ordered Sheridan to destroy farms in Loudoun County, known to be one of Mosby's main bases. Though the burning in Loudoun was minor compared to what happened in the Shenandoah Valley later — fifty fires versus thousands — the idea was the same: clean out guerrillas and shut down food production. Sheridan had already begun to address the Mosby problem on his own by executing captured guerrillas. He had been humiliated by Mosby's exploits, and it didn't help that the Northern press constantly mocked Little Phil for his inability to stop the guerrillas.* On August 17 Sheridan wrote

* When the *New York Times* asserted that fear of Mosby was one of the reasons for Sheridan's withdrawal down the valley in August, Sheridan erupted in anger and ordered all war correspondents out of his military department. He relented, but the

to Grant, "We hung one and shot six of [Mosby's] men yesterday." Two days later Sheridan wrote again: "Guerrillas give me great annoyance, but I am quietly disposing of numbers of them."[52] "Quietly" meant that no reports were made. The killings had not officially taken place.

On August 18 George Armstrong Custer ordered the homes of five prominent citizens burned in retaliation for the "murder" by Mosby's partisans of one of Custer's men. His soldiers were doing just that when they were discovered by Mosby's lieutenant William Chapman and seventy-five partisans. Mosby had directed that "house burners" were to be executed. Chapman followed his orders. His rangers quickly cornered Custer's men, who surrendered, then shot twenty-five of them to death and left them on the ground. Killing helpless, unarmed prisoners was the precise meaning of *black flag*. Such executions had been carried out by Confederates before, including at Fort Pillow, but these were white men. The definition of what was acceptable in war had evidently changed.

The executions shocked people in the North. One *New York Times* headline read, "Massacre by Mosby — Rebel Treachery —

---

incident showed how sensitive he was to Mosby-related slights.

Cowardly Cruelty." Another headline read, "Mosby Hanging Union Soldiers." The *Times* suggested that Mosby was flying the black flag. Sheridan retaliated immediately, rounding up twenty wagonloads of men, aged sixteen to sixty, from areas of guerrilla activity and shipping them off to Charleston, West Virginia. One of his cavalry regiments was sent on a mission with specific orders "to bring in no prisoners." He dispatched the Union army's foremost guerrilla specialist, Captain Richard Blazer, with a team of one hundred "hunter-killers" and a single mission: destroy Mosby.

As the summer passed, the retaliations on both sides only got worse. On September 23, a detachment of Mosby's men under Chapman wounded and then trampled Union lieutenant Charles McMaster. Though Mosby's men insisted that they had obeyed the rules of war and that the trampling was accidental, McMaster told his comrades that he had been shot while trying to surrender. (He later died of his wounds.) The Union soldiers retaliated with a fury. In the town of Front Royal, they hanged two of Mosby's men and shot four others. The last to die was seventeen-year-old Henry C. Rhodes. He was dragged by horses through the streets of Front Royal and into an open field, where Custer's brigade band mocked him by playing "Love Not, the One You Love May Die."

Then he was shot to death. He was placed in a wheelbarrow and delivered to his mother, who stood nearby.[53]

The reprisals continued through the early fall. As time passed, people on both sides began to wonder why Mosby had not retaliated for the brutal killings of his men at Front Royal. He had a specific reason for holding off. He believed that Custer had ordered the executions (he had not) and was thus quietly collecting prisoners from Custer's brigade. On October 29, Mosby wrote to Robert E. Lee with an unusual request: "It is my purpose to hang an equal number of Custer's men." Mosby's motive had nothing to do with retribution, he said. He simply wanted to protect his men, to stop the cycle of revenge by showing the Union army that he was fully prepared to retaliate. Lee and Confederate secretary of war James Seddon agreed to the executions.[54] By then the federals had executed another ranger, which made seven. Mosby had his number.

On November 6 Mosby assembled the prisoners in Rectortown, Virginia, about fifty miles due west of Washington, DC, and lined up twenty-seven prisoners in front a corncrib. Seven of them were then selected by lottery to be executed in retaliation for the killings of Mosby's men. Mosby's men were extremely reluctant to carry out the executions. Of the seven chosen, two escaped, three were hanged, and two were shot and left for dead, though they survived and managed to escape. Still, Mosby believed he had made his point. "I was really glad they got away," he wrote later of the escapees, "as they carried the story to Sheridan's army which was the best way to stop the business."

Then Mosby sent Sheridan a letter, a copy of which he sent to the newspapers in Richmond:

Since the murder of my men, not less than seven hundred prisoners, including many officers of high rank, captured from your army by this command have been forwarded to Richmond; but the execution of my purpose of retaliation was deferred, in order, as far as possible, to confine its operation to the men of Custer and Powell. Accordingly, on the 6th instant, seven of your men were, by my order, executed on the Valley Pike — your highway of travel.

Hereafter, any prisoners falling into my hands will be treated with the kindness due their condition, unless some new act of barbarity shall compel me, reluctantly, to adopt a line of policy repugnant to humanity.[55]

Mosby said later that he never regretted what he did. "If I had not retaliated," he wrote later, "the war in the Valley would have degenerated into a massacre."[56] Though Sheridan never replied to Mosby's letter, after the Rectortown "lottery" the reprisals rapidly dwindled and eventually stopped altogether.

But Sheridan's pursuit of Mosby continued. Sheridan's designated force of hunter-killers under Captain Richard Blazer, which had been chasing Mosby since mid-August, had experienced mixed luck. While they had failed to capture him or stop his raids, in early September they had handed Mosby's men their worst defeat of the war, killing thirteen, wounding six, and capturing five. Blazer won another small skirmish in early November. By then Mosby had had enough. On November 17, he detailed 210 men in two groups to destroy the hunter-killers. Hunter became prey. Mosby's raiders made short work of it. His lieutenant Adolphus "Dolly" Richards set an ambush and quickly destroyed Blazer's force, killing or wounding twenty-three and capturing twenty-two — a stunning casualty rate of 73 percent. And they captured Blazer himself, who languished in Southern prisons for the remainder of the war, where he developed a kidney disease that left him disabled.

Ten days after Blazer's defeat a highly irritated Phil Sheridan sent five thousand men on a four-day burning raid into Mosby's Confederacy. Nothing in particular came of it except more destruction and more impoverishment of Southern citizens.

And Sheridan never would catch the Gray Ghost.

In the end the Sheridan-Mosby fights were little more than a grim sideshow, another sign of how desperate and formless the war had become. The real meaning of Sheridan's campaign lay in his conclusive victories over Early and his cruel demonstration that Northern armies in Virginia could now go where they wanted and do what they wanted. Guerrillas could annoy the federals — even in spectacular and headline-grabbing ways — but they could not stop them. The real meaning of Sheridan's valley campaign — layered on top of what Sherman had done in Atlanta — was that the North was winning the war.

In the two months leading up to the presidential election, the war had turned, as though by a miracle, in Lincoln's favor. The timing of the Union victories, in the context of the larger war, was astounding, and it was the clear and direct product of Grant's arrogation of war powers in the late summer. Grant had been right to see through the national gloom, and now the rest of his country had come to see things his way. The war could, and would, be won.

Northern politics swung hard to Lincoln, too. The Republican press had stopped its endless carping and now brought forth hosannas to the brilliance of the president and his three-star general. The avalanche of war headlines ("Another Glorious Triumph in the Shenandoah Valley!") cast other news to the back pages. Everyone wanted to read about the war now, and all of the war news was good. Lincoln's rival among Radicals, John C. Frémont, withdrew in September. In state elections in September and October in Maine, Vermont, Ohio, Indiana, and Pennsylvania, National Union Party (Republican) candidates won decisive majorities. Lincoln pressed his advantage. Surrogates were dispatched, fence sitters and Democrats in government cut off from patronage and promotion, federal employees dunned for contributions, unfriendly newspapers denied advertising. Even army promotions were contingent on party affiliation.[57] Lincoln was a decent and generous man. He was also a consummate politician.

The first election returns on November 8 came in from Indiana at 6:30 p.m. Lincoln walked over to the War Department at around 7:00 p.m. — a place he had haunted for years — and read the telegrams as they came in. By 9:00 p.m. the first of the good news rolled in, and by 1:00 a.m. Lincoln knew that victory was his. He won the election by a margin of 411,428 votes, 2,213,665 (55 percent) to 1,802,237 (45 percent). He completely dominated the electoral vote, 212 to 21.

McClellan carried only Delaware, New Jersey, and Kentucky. The only real surprise, in Lincoln's landslide victory, was the desertion of McClellan by his own adoring troops. Of 150,635 soldiers' votes tallied, Lincoln won 116,887 to Little Mac's 33,748.

The Republican victory had another meaning, too, with immediate consequences for the nation. The election had created a three-quarters antislavery majority in Congress, which was powerful enough to abolish slavery by constitutional amendment. Lincoln saw this as a moment of national political clarity. "It is the voice of the people now," he said, "for the first time, heard upon the question."[58]

The citizens of the Confederacy were predictably disconsolate. While Jefferson Davis stood on the floor of the Congress in Richmond extolling the "indomitable valor" and "unquenchable spirit" of his people, a wave of mass desertions swept through the rebel armies in the field.

CHAPTER SIXTEEN:
BACK ROADS TO FAME

MAJOR GENERAL WILLIAM TECUMSEH
SHERMAN: One of the war's most
brilliant men, he became the ideologue of the anti-civilian war that
was waged against the South in
1864.

The most celebrated — and vilified — character of the war's final year was neither

Abraham Lincoln nor Ulysses S. Grant. That honor belongs to William Tecumseh Sherman, the baffling, wildly verbal theorist of mayhem and destruction whose capture of Atlanta made him instantly one of the most famous people in the world. His very name seemed to suggest an elaborate destiny. He captivated people then, as he does now. Over a long life, he was probably the most widely publicized American of his era, producing not only millions of words himself but occasioning millions more. His fame, and infamy, were rooted in his actions as a general in the Union army, most of which occurred in the final year of the Civil War.

The historical colossus that is General William T. Sherman has many interesting pieces. Perhaps the most surprising is that he was not a very good field commander at all, not in any conventional sense and certainly not as measured by the same standards used to rate other Civil War generals.[1] Nor was he a success in the antebellum world. Like Grant, he had an undistinguished career in the army. Like Grant, he failed repeatedly in business, hitting bottom not long before the war started. Grant redeemed himself early in the war by showing considerable tactical and managerial brilliance. Sherman's battle-fighting record fell somewhere between mediocrity and outright disaster.

How, then, did he become the William Tecumseh Sherman of legend? The Man Who Marched to the Sea? It's a mystery worth probing, because in spite of his failures and his flaws he deserves every bit of his fame and notoriety. He was indeed brilliant, perhaps the most brilliant man in all of the war. But his particular immortality was not the same as, say, Stonewall Jackson's. Part of Sherman's genius was to invent an entirely new category of genius, one that would have been unimaginable even a few years before.

William Tecumseh Sherman was exceptionally smart. No one who knew him ever doubted that. At West Point, the nation's leading engineering school, he was one of the best students in his class. Of the 119 students who entered with him in 1836, seventy-seven washed out and only forty-two finished. Sherman ranked sixth in his class and would have ranked fourth but for the demerits he had accumulated. He was rambunctious, high-spirited, mischief-prone, relentlessly talkative, and popular with his peers. He did not have to work hard to get high grades. Among his other talents, he was the finest artist in his class, a brilliant draftsman who could easily have drawn or painted professionally. While in school, he walked in the company of a glittering who's who of future Civil War celebrities. They included Henry Halleck, Joseph Hooker, Braxton Bragg, Jubal

Early, and the rumpled, somewhat sad-looking young man three classes below him known as Sam Grant. Sherman was smarter than most of them.[2]

Like many bright and ambitious West Point graduates, Sherman soon found himself mired in that dreariest and most stultifying of careers: the peacetime army. He spent monotonous time in the Florida swamps scouting Seminole Indians. He passed nearly five years in Charleston, South Carolina, logging in his hours at work but also hunting, fishing, and partying with the devoutly secessionist sons of planters — whose ideas of slavery he generally shared and endorsed. Still, he was bored and restless. He wrote hundreds of letters — the start of a lifelong habit that would eventually have a profound effect on American history. Many were written to Ellen Ewing, his intelligent, difficult, fussy, spoiled, hypochondriac, rabidly Catholic, home-clinging fiancée, who refused to leave Lancaster, Ohio, and join him in the army.

Then came the Mexican-American War in 1846, which should have rescued him from his dead-end career. Nothing of the sort happened. While many of his fellow West Pointers went on to adventure and glory and promotion at Veracruz and Mexico City and other exotic places south of the border, Sherman was ordered to California. He spent six months on a boat, then landed in a place where — though it was part of Mexico and technically a war zone — virtually no fighting was to be done. He had missed the war, or it had missed him. Instead of glory, there was only a dull emptiness. He soon grew bored and restless again and sank into depression. "I am so completely banished that I feel I have lost all hope," he wrote his balky fiancée.[3]

His suffering was briefly alleviated when he finally married her in 1850. How that happened is an important part of the Sherman story. His father had died when Sherman was nine, leaving the family destitute. Young Cump, as he was known, was sent to live with the family of Thomas Ewing, a man destined to become a major force in American politics as a US senator (from Ohio), secretary of the interior, and secretary of the treasury. Ellen Ewing was his daughter, which meant that Sherman's foster sister became his wife and his foster father became his father-in-law. It also meant that Sherman would have political connections as potent as those of any general in American history.[4] His wedding was one of the major events of Washington's social season. Attendees included President Zachary Taylor and his entire cabinet, the justices of the Supreme Court, Daniel Webster, and Henry Clay.

In 1852 Sherman left the army for a job managing a bank in San Francisco, trading an undistinguished military career for nearly a decade of consistent failure in the private sector. He did not fail all the time, and his life involved more than simply business — he and Ellen eventually had six children — but failures were its hallmarks. After several bad years, Sherman was forced to shut the bank down. He then moved to New York to open a new bank and ran headlong into the Panic of 1857 — the first worldwide economic crisis — which forced him to shut that bank as well. He landed back in San Francisco trying to salvage the plummeting real estate and delinquent loans of the original bank — plus moneys that had unfortunately been entrusted to him by his friends in the army. The affair was messy, difficult, and for Sherman bitterly disheartening.

His luck got progressively worse. Though he had determinedly avoided the patronage of his wealthy, influential foster father, Sherman now lugged himself back to Lancaster to take a job in Thomas Ewing's saltworks. Nearing forty and, in his own words, "poor as a church mouse," he wrote a friend, "I am utterly disqualified for business, my experience [in San Francisco] . . . has completely destroyed all confidence in myself, and everybody else."[5]

But there was still room to fall. Desperate for something new, Sherman took a job with his brother-in-law (and foster brother)

Thomas Ewing Jr. in a real estate and law office in Leavenworth, Kansas. The firm did poorly. Sherman appeared as a lawyer in court twice, argued unconvincingly, and lost both cases. He supplemented his meager income by running mule and horse auctions, surveying, and working as a notary. His income had plummeted from $5,000 a year in San Francisco to $650. In 1859 — less than two years from the guns of Fort Sumter — he finally hit rock bottom, unable to even find a low-level job in the army and reduced to fixing up properties for his in-laws. He described himself as "a dead cock in a pit." That year he tried to speculate by buying corn to sell to people going West for the Colorado gold rush. He miscalculated once again and lost his investment.

In the depths of discouragement, he landed a job as superintendent of a brand-new institution: the Louisiana State Seminary of Learning and Military Academy.* The job was decent. The pay was several multiples of what he had been making. He did well enough, though the students, faculty, and regents often seemed as unwieldy as the school's name. He thus spent the weeks and

* This institution eventually moved to Baton Rouge and became Louisiana State University, making Sherman, who was and is bitterly hated in that state, in effect the founding superintendent of LSU.

months leading up to the start of the war instructing the often spoiled and unruly sons of secessionist planters — roughly sixty of them — in a state that was about to secede. After Lincoln won the presidential election in November 1860, one Southern state after another left the Union. Finally, on January 26, 1861, Louisiana, too, went out. This meant that Sherman, an Ohioan and a Unionist, could not stay.

As a final humiliation, he was forced by the governor of Louisiana to store arms that rebel Louisianans had seized from federal facilities. To make room for a case of rifles, he had to vacate his own office. He wrote his final letters as superintendent on the tops of packing crates. On February 19 he traveled to New Orleans, where he said goodbye to his friend Braxton Bragg — destined to become a leading Confederate general — and witnessed what he called "glorious rejoicing at the downfall of our country."[6] He was already bitter that his failures had been caused by events out of his control: the boom-bust climate of San Francisco, the financial crash of 1857. Now he had failed again, and this time the cause was the coming of war. Thus did William Tecumseh Sherman, like Ulysses S. Grant, emerge into the war-haunted spring of 1861 as a middle-aged washout with nothing much to recommend him. At least Sherman did not have a drinking problem.

The vast majority of generals, North and South, performed badly in the early part of the Civil War. They did not know how to handle large bodies of men in maneuver or in battle. They were, as a whole, keenly afraid of the unknown in a war with almost nothing but the unknown. They routinely underestimated their own strength and overestimated the enemy's. They were terrified of running out of food and forage. They feared the land itself, especially the Northern generals who had to operate in the South's alien topographies. West Point–educated generals for the most part did better than non–West Pointers, and everyone did better than the political appointees. But most were not good fighters, at least in the early going. One of the best examples was Robert E. Lee, USMA class of 1829, whose campaigns in western Virginia in 1861 were minor disasters. The few exceptions to this rule became quickly famous. They included Stonewall Jackson, Ulysses S. Grant, and Jeb Stuart.[7]

In this sense Sherman was not unusual. He, too, misunderstood the new warfare. He, too, had much to learn about managing armies. The difference was that his early blunders — two in particular — were so staggeringly public, with such public consequences.

He entered the war in Washington, DC, as

a colonel in charge of a brigade of volunteers. In the spring of 1861, he was forty-one years old. Though he was not handsome in any conventional sense, his looks were striking. He was a slender five foot eleven with a posture one contemporary called "not very erect." The riveting part was the face: well-proportioned, with a long, bladelike nose offset by thatchy reddish-brown hair and a sparse rust-colored beard. His prematurely aging skin had already left deep furrows around his bright, darting eyes. The overall effect was: red. He wore his clothes with casual negligence. They were of good material — Brooks Brothers — but the coat flapped open and needed washing. The vest was secured by its bottom button only. He was restless, nervous, fidgety, kinetic. A pacer. In the words of one observer, he "jerked himself along."[8]

His first battle — Bull Run, fought just west of Washington, DC, on July 21, 1861 — was an outright catastrophe, though certainly not all his fault. Sherman's men participated in the Union's early success that day and, like all of the other federal soldiers, fled in panic when the fighting turned against them. The battle was one of the Union's most humiliating defeats. "It was disgraceful as words can portray," Sherman wrote Ellen. In another letter he told her, "Well, I am sufficiently disgraced now. I suppose I can sneak into some quiet corner." His miseries did not end with the battle. In the next two weeks he became the target of a near mutiny by his own soldiers followed by a strike in which they refused to perform their duties. He arrested sixty-five of them.

Though Sherman had been unable to stop his soldiers from running at Bull Run, he had done a better job than most other commanders of bringing them to heel. In the midst of welling chaos, as the terrified men crowded and pressed toward the safety of Washington, he had ordered the ferries to stop transporting them across the Potomac if they were not with their units. In this way he had brought some order to the disorder. Somehow his superiors had noticed. So, in a deeply humiliated army with crashing morale and a ruinous absence of leadership, he was unexpectedly promoted to brigadier general. He was rewarded for not being as incompetent as his peers. He was immediately sent west to be deputy commander of the Union's Department of the Cumberland, which included Kentucky and Tennessee. Sherman's main job was to look after Kentucky. Shortly after Sherman arrived at his new post, his new boss, Robert Anderson, the hero of Fort Sumter, resigned. Sherman got the job.

The promotion ought to have been a great stroke of luck. In fact it was a setup for another disaster, this time entirely his fault and entirely personal. From the first moment he assumed command, he was convinced that Kentucky — a border slave state that had not seceded — was a seething caldron of rebellion and disunion. He quickly concluded that he had nowhere near enough troops to resist the onslaught that was coming, both from regular and irregular Confederate forces. He expected to be quickly overwhelmed. He saw spies everywhere. "Our enemies have a terrible advantage in the fact that in our midst, in our camps, and along our venues of travel, they have active partisans who are in fact spies," he wrote the War Department. "Do not conclude . . . that I exaggerate the facts," he wrote to a civilian friend. "The future looks as dark as possible."[9]

Startled by this talk, Lincoln sent his secretary of war, Simon Cameron, to Louisville to see for himself how bad the situation was. Cameron was amazed by what he found. Sherman seemed to be in the grip of full-blown paranoia. He was convinced he needed two hundred thousand troops to hold back the tide of rebel violence that was about to be loosed against him. Cameron replied that no such numbers existed anywhere in the war. Sherman was seeing phantoms.[10] Other Union generals in Kentucky believed that Confederate forces were relatively sparse and poorly organized. Those in the meeting between Cameron and Sherman were struck by the general's highly agitated state. He seemed almost frantic. Back in Washington, Lincoln had begun to receive notes from people in the army and politics wondering about Sherman's "extreme depression of spirits and physical exhaustion."[11]

In the following weeks Sherman's delusions grew while his mental health deteriorated. He was drinking too much, eating too little.* He suffered from headaches and asthma. He chattered incessantly but seemed unable to listen to anyone else. He chain-smoked cigars and paced the floor. He sat rigidly at his desk obsessively writing notes and letters explaining how bad things were, including one to his brother insisting — preposterously — that he was outnumbered five to one. He stayed up at the telegraph office until 3:00 a.m. looking for the bad news he was certain was coming, then returned to his hotel and paced the corridor until dawn.[12] His behavior was so odd that "it was generally noticed and remarked upon by the guests and employees of the hotel," wrote Henry Villard of the *New York Herald*. "His strange ways led to gossip, and it was soon whispered about that he was suffering from mental depression."[13]

* Sherman did not have a chronic drinking problem, as Grant had. This period in his life, in which he drank more than his usual moderate amounts, would have been the exception to the rule.

The high command had noticed, too. Assistant Secretary of War Thomas A. Scott decided "Sherman's gone in the head. He's luny." General Henry Halleck, a senior commander in western theater, told George McClellan, now in command of all Union armies, that Sherman's "physical and mental system is so completely broken by labor and care as to render him for the present entirely unfit for duty."[14] Sherman was relieved of command on November 8, 1861, and shuffled off to a minor posting in St. Louis.* He was certain that his behavior — which sounds a lot like bipolar disorder — had ruined his army career. He later told his wife that he thought of killing himself. He took a three-week leave at home at Lancaster, where Ellen — so often difficult, selfish, and intractable — showed herself to be caring, compassionate, supportive, and sympathetic.[15]

Which was a good thing because in some ways the worst was yet to come. Just as Sherman was beginning to calm down, stories began to appear in the press about the "disorders" that had caused him to be re-

* McClellan too would soon prove to be extremely adept at inventing legions of enemy troops that did not exist. Within a few months he would be whining about his shocking lack of troops to combat these imaginary adversaries. But these aspects of his character were not yet known.

moved from command. Then came a December 11 headline in the *Cincinnati Commercial:* "General William T. Sherman Insane." The story described him as "stark mad," then gave examples that included his wildly exaggerating the size of the Confederate army; telegraphing the War Department three times in a single day for permission to abandon Kentucky altogether and retreat into Indiana; and giving orders so patently ridiculous that his officers refused to obey them.[16] Other papers smelled blood and followed. Soon everyone in the country was talking about Sherman's sanity, or lack of it. His friends came to his defense. The powerful Ewing family threatened lawsuits and financed a public relations campaign to discredit the newspapers. Ellen and her father, Thomas Ewing, met privately with President Lincoln and tried to convince him that Sherman was the victim of an army conspiracy. Henry Halleck, who was no one's idea of a loyal ally, actually supported and defended his old West Point friend. But he could not undo the damage to Sherman's reputation.

Under Ellen's care, Sherman quickly recovered. Some seven weeks after his demotion Halleck gave him a new assignment: running logistics for rising star Ulysses S. Grant. Sherman, though deeply hurt by the negative publicity, was indeed his old jaunty self again. Still, he should by rights have either been cashiered or sent offstage to await orders that never came — the eventual fate of many inept Union generals. Not only did Halleck sustain him, but Grant, who liked Sherman's forthright style and was inclined not to believe the rumor mill that had so often savaged Grant, soon put Sherman in charge of a division. Grant's generous act marked both the rebirth of Sherman's career and the beginning of a long friendship between two men whom large numbers of Americans considered to be, respectively, a drunk and a lunatic.

From that moment on Sherman's career was yoked to Grant's. The more Grant got to know Sherman, the more Grant liked and trusted him, and Sherman was caught in the great upsweep of Grant's war career. Grant put him in the public eye, promoted him, and made him famous. Sherman responded with affection and loyalty. He saw in Grant a confident, determined, and purposeful man who conceived of the war strategically and thought he knew how to win it — the qualities Sherman himself had been lacking in Kentucky.

But this apparently simple tale of success and redemption has some noteworthy flaws: Sherman, as a division and corps commander under Grant, committed major mistakes in several of the most important battles of the war. Though Sherman clearly had some ability as a field commander, he was terribly inconsistent, and his blunders took place when his army could least afford them. These missteps did not prevent his rocketlike rise to the upper echelon of the army. How could that happen? The simple answer is that Grant's sweeping vision of victory included his protégé William Tecumseh Sherman, and everyone else's calculations did not matter.

Sherman's first failure — at Shiloh in 1862 — nearly resulted in the defeat of a large Union army in one of the most important battles of the war. On April 5 a rebel army of some forty thousand men moved, unnoticed, to within two miles of a Union force in southwestern Tennessee. The Union army was commanded by Ulysses S. Grant. On its most exposed flank was a division commanded by William T. Sherman. That an army the size of a small city, with miles-long supply trains, could creep up on an even larger army seems virtually impossible, but that is exactly what happened. Sherman had failed to post defensive pickets or to send out probing patrols. He had ignored his own cavalry's multiple hostile encounters with the enemy a few miles from his lines. He had dismissed a number of reports from his own officers of rebel activity in his front as the woods thickened with rebel cavalry and rebel pickets. To one officer, whose cavalry had seen many rebels and believed them to be part of a larger army, Sherman tsk-tsked, "My dear sir, it is impossible that they should think of attacking us here, at our base of operations — [a] mere skirmish, sir." Though the Union was ultimately victorious at the Battle of Shiloh, and though Sherman performed well once the battle began, he and Grant both deserve blame for this startling failure of reconnaissance. Grant was later savaged in the press for it, while Sherman was miraculously spared. Grant could not criticize Sherman for making the same mistakes Grant had, so Sherman was promoted again, this time to major general.

His second failure was more strictly tactical. In the Vicksburg campaign, which was Grant's masterpiece, Sherman, one of Grant's three corps commanders, ordered a misguided frontal assault against a much smaller force of Union soldiers. His men were cut down and his force repulsed. Sherman was devastated by his defeat. He was certain that reporters would attack him again.

They did not disappoint. They dredged up all the old Kentucky stories. The *Cincinnati Gazette* even reprinted an article with the false report that Sherman "was confined to his stateroom perfectly insane."[17] Sherman groped in vain for a way to salvage the disaster. He ordered new assaults, only to cancel the orders. He soon gave up. He never got a chance to redeem himself in the Vicksburg campaign, in which his corps was oddly absent from its main battles. As one of the main commanders in one of the most successful and consequential Union campaigns in the war, Sherman's record fetches up somewhere between poor and undistinguished.

Sherman's worst tactical failure occurred at yet another glorious Grant victory: the Battles for Chattanooga.* To attack the rebel position along an elevation known as Missionary Ridge, Grant sent three full army corps: Sherman on the left, George H. Thomas in the center, and Joseph Hooker on the right. The plan was for Thomas to feint at the Confederate center, while Sherman's Army of the Tennessee smashed the Confederate right on the northern end of the ridge. Sherman, at Grant's directive, was going to be the main actor in the drama, the one who was going to roll up the rebel flank and drive on to victory. Everything would depend on him and his seventeen thousand troops.

Sherman's performance was dismal, on all levels of command. He missed golden opportunities to attack, committed yet more errors of reconnaissance — including one that put his army disastrously out of position —

* The battles of Lookout Mountain, Orchard Knob, and Missionary Ridge comprised the Battles for Chattanooga.

moved his corps with inexplicable sluggishness, and ordered his troops to fortify to defend an irrelevant position, which a contemporary historian and participant in the fight called "an astonishing error . . . which caused utter failure to the whole movement against Bragg's right."

The following day his delayed and terribly coordinated attack failed to accomplish anything except to pile up several thousand Union casualties. The general historical consensus is that Sherman's failure at Missionary Ridge ranks among the worst battle performances of the war. He had virtually nothing to do with the spectacular uphill attack by Union troops under George H. Thomas that won the battle.

The country never heard about Sherman's failure, which was, as one contemporaneous observer put it, "covered over in thick official reports and misleading histories."[18] Grant simply lied about it, saying in his official report that rebel desperation to stop Sherman had weakened their center and allowed Thomas's success. This was complete nonsense. Sherman played along with his boss's flawed analysis, consistently misrepresenting the plan of battle for the rest of his life. He later said that Missionary Ridge "was a great victory — the neatest and cleanest battle I was ever in."[19] It was indeed a great victory. He was at least right about that.

CHAPTER SEVENTEEN:
THE MORALIST FROM HELL

SHERMAN AND HIS CORPS COMMANDERS: Their capture of Atlanta was one of the war's most important events. What they did next shocked the world.

William Tecumseh Sherman's contribution to human history had less to do with his ability to fight than his ability to think, which was paired with a remarkable ability to write. What he thought about was what it meant to be at war. Though this might seem simple enough, it was not at all. The nation's experience of the conflict had fundamentally changed. A hard and destructive war was now being waged against the citizens of the South. Prisoner exchanges, one of the few civilized conventions of the war, had been suspended since the summer of 1863. Men on both sides now suffered and died in enemy prison camps. In Missouri and elsewhere, Union militias ran roughshod over the populace while rebel guerrillas roved freely through the lawless countryside. As life and war turned more desperate and more vengeful, people on both sides sought an answer to the most basic question of all: Who bore moral responsibility for all the bloodshed and devastation, for the hardening of the war?

As his military career progressed, Sherman had considered this problem. His thoughts — combined with his intimate experience of the army — led him to a theory of the war: who caused it, why it was being fought, who was fighting it, and how it might be stopped. Then he wrote out that theory in a years-long avalanche of letters, memorandums, and official papers that put forth principles, advice, anecdotes, and historical analysis. He taught his moral vision of the war to everybody, North and South. He talked his beliefs out, too. You could not shut him up. While he was evolving his theories, Sherman simultaneously transformed himself into the destructive war's most notorious proponent.[1]

But what made him so indelible, and so unlike anyone else, was less his scorched-earth campaigns than his unquenchable need to explain and justify his actions.[2] No one else in power in the North felt anything like this need. Sherman took pains to explain his ideas to everyone, from elderly Southern widows to small-town Southern mayors, local citizens groups, congressmen and senators, cabinet secretaries, and even Abraham Lincoln. To anyone who asked, and many who did not.

If Sherman had a counterpart at all on the Confederate side, it was President Jefferson Davis, the states'-rights zealot who offered his people a countermyth. Davis believed in a simple, central truth: that his Northern enemy was barbaric, ungodly, dishonest, cruel, and power mad. In a word, evil, in the biblical sense of the word. Thus the war was a crusade against evil. Against "barbarous enemies" from the North who wantonly ravaged the country while they themselves were held in thrall to a dictatorship. These were people, Davis said in a speech in Jackson, Mississippi, "who have determined to divide out the South among their Yankee troops."[3] They were pillagers, no better than Goths. He later reminded the Confederate Congress that "the recurring atrocities of the invader" included:

plunder and devastation of the property of noncombatants, destruction of private dwellings and even of edifices devoted to the worship of God, expeditions organized for the sole purpose of sacking cities, consigning them to the flames, killing the unarmed inhabitants and inflicting horrible outrages on women and children.[4]

Davis's message was easy to grasp: to vanquish the onrushing godless horror, the South must be prepared to sacrifice everything. "We will have extermination or independence," he bravely asserted, offering to let all of his countrymen die in defense of his beliefs.[5] If his vision was grim, single-minded, and wildly self-righteous, it offered at least the benefit of exquisite clarity.

Sherman had completely different ideas. The South, he argued, was entirely responsible for its own suffering. The North was full of benevolent, forgiving, and magnanimous people and was prepared at any moment to start acting that way.

Sherman's ideas grew directly out of his experience of the war. One of the most important of those experiences took place in Memphis, Tennessee, where he was appointed military governor in July 1862. His job was to pacify the region and get the city and its twenty-three thousand residents, which had fallen to the Union in June, up

413

and running again. He was almost immediately successful. Issuing a nonstop flood of orders, rules, and regulations — he was an extraordinary producer of words — he restored its commerce, cleaned up the city's legal and accounting systems, dealt with large numbers of escaped slaves, and curbed smuggling. He had been a failure in civilian life, but he was a talented administrator of civilian affairs.[6]

But he had far less success with partisans outside the city. The region was full of bushwhackers who conducted nonstop hit-and-run warfare against Union army patrols, local Unionists, and Union boats on the Mississippi River. The rebels burned bridges and disrupted trade. When Sherman's troops tried to find them, they did what guerrillas everywhere in the South did — they melted away into the countryside, returning to their homes and their apparently normal lives. Sherman, who had not dealt with this sort of warfare before, was both angry and exasperated. The entire countryside seemed to be against him. He was amazed, too, in his dealings with people in Memphis, at how many people were actively supporting the Southern war effort.

This led him to change his thinking.

When the fighting started, people in the North had widely assumed that Southerners were divided on the war, that many of them, particularly in the northernmost Southern states, had been dragged into it by fire-eating politicians. Thus in the early days Northern commanders tried to protect them. After the First Battle of Bull Run Sherman had been horrified by the predatory behavior of his troops and had subsequently given strict orders for them to leave Southern civilians and their property alone. Like most other commanders he drew a strict line between military and civilian worlds.

But now in Memphis Sherman decided that such a line existed only in his mind. Shortly after his arrival, guerrillas had attacked one of his supply trains. Since he could not catch them, he ordered the arrest of "twenty-five of the most prominent [men] of the vicinity." They were rounded up in the town of La Grange and shipped off to a prison in Columbia, Tennessee. To Sherman it did not matter if any of the twenty-five were guilty. He would hold the community responsible. He forcefully expressed this new thinking in a letter to Treasury Secretary Salmon P. Chase:

The war in which we are now engaged has been complicated with the belief on the one hand that all on the other side are *not* enemies. It would have been better if, at the outset, this mistake had not been made. And it is wrong longer to be misled by it. The government of the U.S. may now safely proceed on the proper rule that all in the

415

south *are* enemies of all in the north; and not only are they unfriendly, but all who can procure arms now bear them as organized regiments, or as guerrillas. There is not a garrison in Tennessee where a man can go beyond the sight of a flag-staff without being shot or captured.[7]

This line of thinking appeared in much of Sherman's correspondence from Memphis. "All the people are now guerrillas," he told Grant. He told Henry Halleck that there was "no other remedy to this ambush than to hold the neighborhood fully responsible."[8] To his brother, Ohio senator John Sherman, he wrote, "All their people are now armed and at war. You hear of vast armies at Richmond or Chattanooga . . . whilst the whole country is full of guerrilla bands, [each] numbering in the hundreds."[9]

To Sherman, the constant attacks on Union shipping on the Mississippi River were the best evidence of this. In September 1862 guerrillas fired on a Union packet boat containing civilian passengers and goods near the town of Randolph, Tennessee. Sherman, in nearby Memphis, made no attempt to investigate the attack or to assign blame. Instead he ordered the destruction of the town. After Randolph was burned — leaving one building as a monument to Sherman's draconian policy — he ordered the expulsion of ten families for every boat attacked. Sherman liked depopulation as punishment. By October 1862 more than forty people had been thus evicted, forced to leave their lands and their livelihoods, carrying whatever they could take with them in wagons.[10] No such orders had ever before been given by a military commander.

The destruction of Randolph shocked Memphis and the entire South. Northerners, too, had trouble understanding why such treatment of ordinary citizens was necessary. Sherman received many letters, from citizens as well as indignant Confederate officers, protesting his action and lecturing him on military ethics. When a Miss A. P. Fraser of Memphis wrote him to tell him his policy was "inhuman," he wrote her back:

When the time comes to settle the account we will see which is most cruel — for your partisans to fire cannon and musket balls through steamboats with women and children on board, set them afire with women and children sleeping . . . or for us to say the families of men engaged in such hellish deeds shall not live in peace where the flag of the United States floats.[11]

He was not only convinced that his actions at Randolph had been correct, but that the same model could successfully be applied to "every city, town, and hamlet in the South" where guerrillas interfered with the navigation of the Mississippi.[12] Old-style war did not work anymore, he insisted. He extended this harsh new regime to encourage "official" foraging — forcibly taking food, pigs, horses, wood, lumber, and other items from local citizens for the use of the Union army. No one in Washington was attempting to countermand Sherman's orders.

Still, he took pains to clarify to the residents of Memphis that he was willing to work with them — to be kind, generous, and forgiving — if they would acknowledge that they had been beaten, accept the rule of his military government, and prepare to lead lives as sensible American citizens again. He restored the jurisdiction of local courts, leaving them alone to arbitrate contracts and punish crimes. In a letter to the mayor of Memphis he also noted — this must have come as a shock to the citizenry, too — that "all persons in Memphis residing within our military lines are presumed to be loyal, good citizens, and may at any moment be called on to service on juries, posses comitatus, or other civil service."[13]

He sought always to remind his charges that the same army that could burn their towns and exile them forever could be decent, helpful, and even protective of them. In a long open letter to the editor of the *Memphis Bul-*

letin, he explained his opposition to pillaging by individual soldiers. He "felt mortified that our soldiers should do acts which are nothing more or less than stealing" and vowed "to punish them to the full extent of the law and orders." As always, however, the bludgeon was waiting just behind the offer of kindness. If the good citizens of Memphis wanted to taunt or insult "our country or our cause" or "speak contemptuously of the flag which is the silent emblem of [the] country, *I will not go out of my way to protect them or their property*" (italics added).[14]

His thinking shifted again in the wake of the Union victory at Vicksburg. On July 9, 1863, Sherman's troops arrived in Jackson, Mississippi, shelled the city, and drove off a Confederate army under Joseph E. Johnston. Victory in the Vicksburg campaign was virtually complete, a large rebel army captured, the state capital in Union hands. But now something else happened — something quite different from what had earlier that year happened in a raid against Jackson that had preceded the attack on Vicksburg. Sherman now divided his soldiers into working parties and ordered them to fan out in a fifteen-mile-wide circumference around the city. Their orders: destroy everything of economic or military value to the Confederacy, from cotton gins to hogs and corn. The men were extremely thorough and did not always adhere to Sherman's instructions not to burn residences or large buildings without orders and not to pillage for themselves.[15]

Again people were shocked, and again Sherman defended himself. His actions had a practical effect, but they held a deliberate lesson, too, for the arrogant Southern planters who had sought to rid themselves of the government they disliked. Sherman would show them what the world looked like without the normal protections of government, a judicial system, and the rule of law. By the act of rebellion, he reasoned, the South had elected to take its chances in a world of unrestrained violence and power.[16] When Southerners protested the destruction of their property, he answered with a stern lecture about the origins of property rights. "You must first make a government before you can have property," he wrote in a long and painstakingly detailed letter to the chairman of a citizens' group in Warren County, Mississippi. "There is no such thing as property without a government." He said the South needed to understand that "the Government of the United States is the only power on earth which can insure protection to life, property, and fame."[17]

In February and March of 1864, in a monthlong military campaign that amounted to a dress rehearsal for his march to the sea, Sherman finally put into practice everything he had been thinking about. He had sought and was given Grant's approval for a 130-mile west-to-east march clear across the state of Mississippi, from Vicksburg to the railroad center of Meridian. The march was unlike anything that had ever been done. A Union army would, for the first time, move completely independent of any supply lines. Sherman had learned this lesson during the Vicksburg campaign, when Grant's army had had its lines cut for two weeks.[18] Sherman's army of twenty thousand, flanked by seven thousand cavalry, would travel light and live entirely off the land. For the first time, Union troops were under specific orders to wage a campaign of destruction, tearing up railroads and burning crops. Soldiers were instructed to leave civilians only enough for survival. Their path of destruction, as they crossed the state, was fifty miles wide.

Prior to Sherman's Meridian campaign, Grant and his staff had regarded foraging or destruction as an extension of the battlefield, a way to directly hurt the opposing army — for example, denying the enemy supplies at Vicksburg. But this march was by design punitive, not only aimed at guerrillas but the people who harbored them. It also had the purpose of so denuding the land that it could not support either guerrillas or an army. Cavalry raiders such as Nathan Bedford Forrest would find nothing to eat. The new threat to hostile citizens was to "eat out" their country so thoroughly that no food or forage remained. Just as disruptive to the local economy was the mass emancipation of slaves that accompanied the march, as many as eight thousand of them, young and old, on foot, in oxcarts, or riding horses and mules.[19] The ultimate goal: destroy the enemy's ability and will to keep fighting. Break their spirit. As Sherman had written his brother before the campaign started, "It is about time the North understood the truth; that the entire South, man, woman, and child are against us, armed and determined."

When the Union army got to Meridian, the soldiers deconstructed or destroyed everything they could get their hands on. One of the campaign's hallmarks was the heating of railroad rails over fires, then twisting them into loops around trees. These, eventually scattered over Mississippi, Georgia, and the Carolinas, became known as "Sherman's neckties." They were emblems of a new type of military victory that did not involve two armies fighting on a battlefield — a type that Sherman, who hated wasting men in battle, clearly preferred.

Sherman had been fully aware that his Meridian march would change the nature of the war. He had expected to catch a good deal of heat for it, so in typical fashion he had gone to great lengths to justify what he was doing. On the eve of the march, he wrote a lengthy letter to a staff officer in Huntsville, Alabama, which he intended to be a major statement of war policy as well as a hard-war manual for his subordinates. It would soon become the de facto war policy of his country. He wrote it, as he did many of his letters, with the idea that it would be published in Northern newspapers. The *New York Times* printed it with the comment that "our readers, after perusing it, will know more of the temper and character of the commander of the Grand Military Division of the Mississippi than they have known heretofore."[20] They would indeed. The letter is often quoted as the archetypal anti-Southern pronouncement. But Sherman's purpose was more complex than that.

His precisely designed rhetoric deserves close attention. He began by citing a harsh historical precedent for the practice he had begun of driving hostile Southern property owners off their lands and deporting them. During the reign of British monarchs William and Mary in the seventeenth century, he wrote, "the English army occupied Ireland, then in a state of revolt, [and] the inhabitants were actually driven into foreign lands, dispossessed of their property, and a new population introduced." This vast and horrific repopulation seemed like a perfectly practical idea to Sherman. "No man will deny that the United States would be benefited by dispossessing a single, prejudiced, hardheaded and disloyal planter, and substitute in his place a dozen or more patient, industrious, good families, even if they be of foreign birth. . . . If [Southerners] want eternal war, well and good — we will accept the issue and dispossess them and put our friends in possession."[21] That Sherman thought such a solution was reasonable was astounding; its harshness was, in traditional American terms, unimaginable.

But he was just getting started. By their rebellion, he asserted, Southerners had forfeited all rights and expectations to be treated decently. "Three years ago, by a little reflection and patience, they could have had a hundred years of peace and prosperity, but they preferred war; very well, last year they could have saved their slaves, but now it is too late — all the powers of earth cannot restore to them their slaves any more than their dead grandfathers. Next year their lands will be taken, for in war we can take them, and rightfully, too, and in another year they may beg in vain for their lives."

No one else in the North had articulated anything like this. No one had ever heard this sort of cruel, clear, moralistic language. Sherman was in high dudgeon, at his hortatory best. He had emerged, virtually alone, as the Northern ideologue of war.

424

Though these were dire threats, the purpose of the letter was to extend an offer of federal *forbearance, forgiveness, and help.* He set strict rules for the seizure of homes. While he asserted his right to take storehouses, hospitals, provisions, horses, mills, forage, and wagons, as well as "all houses left vacant by an inimical people," he also promised safety for any houses owned by noncombatants, women and children and people who kept to their "accustomed business." Decent people — he was insisting on their existence, as he had in Memphis — would be decently treated.

He then asked a victor's question: "Should we treat as absolute enemies all in the South who differ from us in opinion or prejudice, kill or banish them; or, should we give them time to think and gradually change their conduct so as to conform to the new order of things . . . ?"

The answer was the latter, emphatically. Sherman would be patient. He would not — yet — offer Southerners the stark choice of loyalty oath or banishment. "In this belief, whilst I assert for our Government the highest military prerogatives, I am willing to bear in patience the political nonsense of slave rights, State rights, freedom of conscience, freedom of press, and other such trash, as have deluded Southern people into war, anarchy, bloodshed, and the foulest crimes that have disgraced any time or any people."

Sherman closed the letter with some biblical fire and brimstone, along with another suggestion of biblical leniency:

> To those who submit to the rightful law and authority, all gentleness and forbearance, but to the petulant and persistent Secessionists, why, death is mercy, and the quicker he or she is disposed of, the better. Satan, and the rebellious saints of heaven were allowed a continuance of existence in hell merely to swell their just punishment. To such as would rebel against a Government so mild and just as ours was in peace, a punishment equal would not be unjust.

This was an entirely new way of thinking.

CHAPTER EIGHTEEN:
UNCLE BILLY'S
BOOK OF MOMENTS

COLUMBIA, SOUTH CAROLINA, DECEMBER 1864: Sherman's army had been relatively restrained in its march to the sea in Georgia, but in South Carolina it demonstrated what a large military force could do when it was bent on pure destruction.

By the time he captured Atlanta on September 2, 1864, William Tecumseh Sherman had emerged into the full light of history. The failures and ill luck of his previous lives had dropped away. If his performance in the Atlanta campaign had been less than perfect

— he had missed several opportunities to destroy the rebel army and had launched a costly and misguided frontal assault at Kennesaw Mountain — his strategic victory was clear and unambiguous. He had taken one of the greatest prizes of the Confederacy and now stood as the dominant military power in the Deep South. People who might have seen him before, as one contemporary did, as "a splendid piece of machinery with all of the screws a little loose" now saw unalloyed genius.[1] He was so famous he needed the help of aides to sort through fan mail and requests for autographs.

He appears in sharp focus in the description of Lieutenant Colonel Horace Porter, an officer sent by Grant to Atlanta to help Sherman plan the next phase of the war. Porter arrived at Sherman's headquarters on September 20 full of curiosity to meet the man his boss had told him so much about — the general whose adoring troops called him Uncle Billy. When Porter encountered the forty-four-year-old "captor of Atlanta," the general was on his porch, settled back in an armchair and reading a newspaper. He was shabbily dressed: coat unbuttoned, black felt hat pulled down over his forehead, ratty-looking slippers on his feet. Still, Porter was impressed. Sherman, he recalled, "was in the prime of life and in the perfection of physical health. . . . With his large frame, tall, gaunt form, restless hazel eyes, aquiline nose, bronzed face, and crisp beard, he looked the picture of 'grimvisaged war.' "[2]

Then the general started talking, and the grimness vanished. His conversation as usual bounced manically from subject to subject: from an animated discussion of the larger war to his belief that Grant's leftward move in the Wilderness had been "the grandest act of his life," to his gratitude to Lincoln and Grant for their letters to him after the fall of Atlanta. All the while Sherman was moving. As Porter described it:

He twice rose from his chair, and sat down again, twisted the newspaper into every conceivable shape, and from time to time drew first one foot and then the other out of its slipper and followed up the movement by shoving out his leg so that the foot could recapture the slipper, and there was a peculiar energy of manner in uttering the crisp words and epigrammatic phrases which fell from his lips as rapidly as shots from a machine gun. I soon realized that he was one of the most dramatic and picturesque characters of the war.[3]

The harshness of Sherman's actions in Jackson and Memphis and on the march to Meridian had surprised and appalled the people of the South. Now came another shock from a commander who specialized in not doing what everyone expected him to do. On September 8 he ordered the expulsion of all civilians from the city of Atlanta. He did not want to have to feed them and did not want to have to worry about them as he destroyed buildings and constructed new defenses for the city.

He also wanted to make an example of them. "I knew that the people of the South would read in this measure two important conclusions," he wrote later. "One, that we were in earnest; and the other, if they were sincere in their common and popular clamor 'to die in the last ditch,' that opportunity would soon come." Residents had to leave within five days. Sherman arranged for trains to help take them out of town. Though most of the city's 22,000 people had already fled, 705 adults, 860 children, and 79 slaves were soon evacuated. (The expulsion meant that none of those who had already left could return to their homes.)

His order brought immediate howls of protest across the Confederacy. General John Bell Hood, who had relinquished the city to Sherman, wrote in a published letter that Sherman's order "transcends, in studious and ingenious cruelty, all acts ever before brought to my attention in the dark history of war." Sherman sniped back that Hood and other rebel leaders had brought on the war in the

SHERMAN'S MARCHES
MAY 7, 1864, TO APRIL 13, 1865

KENTUCKY

VIRGINIA

NORTH CAROLINA

Raleigh

TENNESSEE

APPALACHIAN MOUNTAINS

BATTLE OF BENTONVILLE
(Sherman victory)
March 19–21, 1865

Chattanooga

Fayetteville

SOUTH CAROLINA

Wilmington

ATLANTA
(surrender)
Sept. 2

Columbia (surrender)
February 17, 1865

Milledgeville

ALABAMA

Macon

Atlantic Ocean

GEORGIA

SAVANNAH
(surrender)
December 8–21

0 Miles   50   100   150

0 Kilometers   150

© 2019 Jeffrey L. Ward

first place, and that Hood himself "had burned dwelling houses because they stood in the way of your forts and men."[4]

Sherman also received a sharply worded petition from the mayor of Atlanta and two city councilmen. They pointed out that such an inhumane order had never before been given in the country's history. "What has this helpless people done," they asked, "that they should be driven from their homes to wander strangers and outcasts and exiles, and to subsist on charity?"[5]

431

Sherman's answer in a letter to the mayor became one of the most famous public statements of the war. He began by arguing the military necessity of what he was doing. He then moved on to a more deterministic line of reasoning: "You cannot qualify war in harsher terms than I will. War is cruelty and you cannot refine it. . . . You might as well appeal against the thunderstorm as against these terrible hardships of war. They are inevitable." Inevitable, in his view, because the South had made the catastrophic mistake of bringing on the war in the first place:

> The only way the people of Atlanta can hope once again to live in peace and quiet at home is to stop the war, which can only be done by admitting that it began in error and is perpetuated in pride. We don't want your negroes, or your horses, or your houses, or your lands, or anything you have, but we do want and will have a just obedience to the laws of the United States. That we will have, and if it involves the destruction of your improvements, we cannot help it.[6]

But this terrifying assertion of federal power was accompanied by an olive branch. As Sherman had told the citizens of Memphis, kindness and gentleness were waiting for Southerners who came around to the proper way of thinking:

I want peace, and I believe it can now only
be reached through union and war, and I
will ever conduct war with a view to perfect
an early success. But, my dear sirs, when
that peace does come, you may call on me
for anything. *Then I will share with you the
last cracker and watch with you to shield
your homes and families against danger
from every quarter* [italics added].[7]

He was undoubtedly sincere. He had previously offered Georgia governor Joe Brown,
who was famously independent of Richmond,
a free pass for the state if its inhabitants
would agree to stop fighting. Sherman closed
his letter with a Whitmanesque stretch of
prose that in spite of its poetic cadence
sounded monstrous to a large part of the
population. He was speaking directly to the
people he was deporting:

Now, you must go, and take with you the
old and the feeble; feed and nurse them,
and build for them in more quiet places
proper habitations to shield them against
the weather, until the mad passions of men
cool down, and allow the Union and peace
once more to settle on your old homes at
Atlanta.[8]

Sherman's surprises did not end with the
depopulation of a large industrial city. In

September Hood's beaten rebel army slipped away from the environs of Atlanta and headed north and west. Sherman, fearing for his supply lines and believing that a Confederate army simply could not be allowed to bang freely about the South, pursued him. He could not catch him. Rebel forces, including those under the brilliant Nathan Bedford Forrest, attacked railroads and wagon trains with ruthless efficiency. Sherman could not stop them. He had nothing but trouble and worry, with no particular end in sight. Even worse, his army, with its retrograde movement, was now "fighting twice for the same real estate."

By the middle of October he had been lured a hundred miles rearward from Atlanta, and he had had quite enough. So he came up with an entirely new plan, one so radical and unprecedented and seemingly impractical that virtually everyone who mattered in the Union military hierarchy, including Grant, army chief of staff Henry Halleck, and Sherman's own subordinate George H. Thomas opposed it. They all believed that Sherman's next move had to be *west,* in pursuit of Hood and in search of cavalry raiders and guerrillas who continued to disrupt the movement of Union supplies. Hood's army was still fully functional. Forrest's cavalry was as lethal as ever. They all had to be dealt with, didn't they?

Sherman's astonishing answer was no. Not by him, anyway. As he put it to Grant, "I regard the pursuit of Hood as useless." Hood and his army did not matter, Sherman said. So he would simply stop chasing them. This was the first time in the war that any general had ever said anything like this, the first time a victorious commander of a large army had proposed a willful disengagement from a beaten enemy. To appease the worrywarts in the Union brain trust, Sherman agreed to provide additional troops to George Thomas in Tennessee. *They* could worry about John Bell Hood.

Second, Sherman would abandon the thing that everyone in the high command, including Sherman, had been so persistently worried about: his supply line, which stretched from Atlanta into Tennessee. Not only would he abandon it, he would destroy it, tear it up so thoroughly that it could not be rebuilt. He would deliberately cut his army off from all of its usual sources of sustenance. Forrest could wreck all the train tracks he wanted to.

Then — this was the third and most revolutionary part of his plan — he would abandon Atlanta, too. He would leave no significant garrison there. Because holding Atlanta didn't matter, either.

What he cared about was showing the South what unconstrained military power looked like. He believed that the most important factor in the war in late 1864 was the South's unyielding will, and he intended to break it. He wanted, as he put it, *"to make its inhabitants feel that war and individual ruin are synonymous terms."*[9] This, perhaps the clearest single statement of Sherman's vision, is the best summary of how the Civil War had changed.

To do that he proposed marching 250 miles in a southeasterly direction from Atlanta to the coastal city of Savannah, living off the land and destroying everything in his path that had any military value, from factories to chickens, just as he had done in his Meridian campaign. "If we can march a well-appointed army right through [the enemy's] territory," he wrote to Grant,

it is a demonstration to the world, foreign and domestic, that we have a power which Davis cannot resist. This may not be war, but rather statesmanship, nevertheless it is overwhelming to my mind that there are thousands of people abroad and in the South who will reason thus: If the North can march an army right through the South, it is proof positive that the North can prevail in this contest.

He wanted to prove that beneath the hard shell of the Confederacy was only emptiness, hollowness: depleted armies stretched thinly

436

over a vast landscape; farms run by women and old men and populated by slaves. Hood had made Sherman worry about Hood's every move.[10] In Sherman's formulation, the entire Confederacy would now have to worry about *Sherman.* Where would *he* strike next? Macon? Augusta? Savannah? Cities in Alabama? What did he intend to do with an unopposed army of sixty thousand men in rural Georgia?

With some reluctance, Grant finally approved Sherman's plan. You can almost hear the sigh of resignation in his November 2 letter to his precocious protégé: "I do not see that you can withdraw from where you are to follow Hood, without giving up all we have gained in the territory. I say, then, go on as you propose." The idea was purely Sherman's, but credit goes to Grant for understanding and embracing its full, war-changing implications.

As Sherman prepared to roll toward the sea, he burned Atlanta to the ground.

Or, at least, generations of South-tilting historians would have you believe that. Anyone who has seen *Gone with the Wind* is familiar with the myth. In fact Sherman did no such thing. He did methodically destroy the city's considerable war-making potential: warehouses, machine shops, depots, factories, and foundries. Sherman knew all about

Atlanta's industrial prowess. Since the start of the war, Union forces had been capturing guns, wagons, and all sorts of military equipment that carried ATLANTA origin markings. Sherman felt this as a personal affront. His army, as he wrote later, "had been fighting Atlanta all the time."[11]

But contrary to the traditional Southern view that Sherman had burned all of the houses, he left most of them and most public buildings standing — more than four hundred by one count.[12] Much of the damage to the city's residential areas had already been done by General Hood's troops, first during his defense of the city, and then when they exploded eighty boxcars during their retreat. Probably half the city was ultimately destroyed. But much of that, and particularly the residential part, was not done by Sherman's army.

But Sherman's main intent emphatically *was* destruction, particularly of the South's means to wage war. The question is one of degree. The stated purpose of his march to Savannah was to annihilate everything in his path but private homes, their inhabitants, and whatever food and stores they would need to survive. He wanted quite specifically, as he had put it to Grant, to "make Georgia howl." He rode out of Atlanta with a force of sixty-two thousand hardened veterans that had largely been culled of poor and undisciplined soldiers. They were the finest Union army ever to take the field, and ironically they would barely be asked to fight at all. In front of them were a mere eight thousand Confederate cavalry, militia, and other assorted troops. They might harass Sherman's army. They would not stand a chance against it in battle.

Sherman split his force into two wings. He deployed them across four different roads in a stacked formation that stretched anywhere from twenty to sixty miles in width. Their orders — Sherman's Special Field Orders no. 120 — were remarkably brief. The army would "forage liberally" and live off the wealth of the land. Soldiers were forbidden to enter the homes of civilians, though they could help themselves to the inhabitants' food, livestock, horses, mules, and wagons. They were instructed to "leave with each family a reasonable portion [of food] for their maintenance." Only corps commanders could order the destruction of mills, warehouses, and cotton gins, or the deliberate burning of houses.[13]

The reality was nowhere near as tidy. Many homes were burned in violation of the order, particularly those of wealthy slaveholders. Private residences were sometimes entered and stripped of food and personal property. Soldiers often took more food than the army could consume and left the residents less than they needed to survive. Women and children watched in terror as soldiers swarmed through their property "like famished wolves." With winter approaching, many of the residents were left on the verge of starvation. The presence of so many irregulars and unsavory types along with the official foragers (known as bummers) and the regular columns made everything worse. Union and Confederate deserters and stragglers, escaped slaves, and opportunistic civilians, all did their own looting. Confederate cavalry units, notably under Major General Joseph Wheeler, were some of the worst plunderers of all.[14]

Sherman also had a vengeful side. On the march near the town of Milledgeville his troops came upon the plantation of Howell Cobb, a former Georgia governor, Speaker of the US House, and US secretary of the treasury, who had become an ardent secessionist. The troops began by confiscating Cobb's crops and food stores, including large quantities of corn, beans, peanuts, and sorghum molasses. The Union incursion might have stopped there but for the story an elderly black slave told Sherman of rebel troops disguised as Yankees who had severely beaten some of the plantation's slaves. Sherman was furious. He allowed the slaves and his soldiers to strip the Cobb plantation of anything they wanted. Then he ordered the entire place — from fence rails to the main house and its outbuildings — burned to the ground. He spared only the slave quarters.[15]

His retribution took harsher forms, too. When several of his soldiers were killed by mines buried by retreating rebels, Sherman's reaction was immediate and categorical: "This was not war, but murder, and it made me very angry." He approved orders for Confederate prisoners of war to clear the roads of mines. He had employed the same principle in his decision to burn Randolph, Tennessee, to the ground: the Confederacy would collectively be held responsible for its actions. Though the prisoners begged Sherman not to go through with it, he would not relent. He told them that "their people had put these things there to assassinate our men . . . and they must remove them," wrote one of Sherman's staff in his diary, "and if *they* got blown up he didn't care."[16] Such orders were considered cruel and inhumane by people in the South. They were enormously popular in the North.

But, like "the burning of Atlanta," Sherman's march to the sea was not as rigorously cruel as it has often been described. Historians sympathetic to the Confederacy claimed that large numbers of homes had been burned, but no hard evidence exists for this. Studies in the 1930s and 1950s concluded that most of the private antebellum homes along the route of march were still standing after the war. Southerners also complained loudly of the murders of white men and the rape and abuse of white women, though no proof exists of the former and only sketchy evidence for the latter.[17]

Black people, on the other hand, were abused by both sides, and most of the racial violence, as usual, went unreported. Perhaps the worst example took place on December 9, 1864. A Union corps under Major General Jefferson C. Davis had marched on pontoons across a rain-swollen creek, then had pulled up the pontoons, deliberately stranding hundreds of fugitive slaves who had been following them and who were being chased by Confederate cavalry. In their panic to escape the rebels, hundreds tried to swim to safety and many drowned.[18] The tragedy shocked many of Sherman's own troops. One Indiana surgeon wrote that if he had the power, he would hang General Davis "as high as Haman."*

Nor was Sherman happy about the ever-increasing numbers of African Americans who followed his army. They were a nuisance. They encumbered him. They had to be taken care of. They were victims of racial violence by both Union and Confederate troops and

* Haman was the principal antagonist in the biblical Book of Esther.

thus had to be accommodated. Though he fought for a country that had staked everything on the abolition of slavery, Sherman was far from enlightened on the subject. He believed in the superiority of the white race. Blacks were simply inferior to whites, he felt, and that was the "natural order of things." Before the war he had spent many years in the South and had adopted some of the South's conventional views. In those days he had vocally supported the institution of human bondage — "the mildest and best regulated system of slavery in the world" — and opposed emancipation, believing that it would lead to chaos and economic disorder. He had picked up the Southern habit of using the word *nigger,* which he never abandoned. His beliefs were tempered by some liberalism: he opposed separating black families and favored teaching them to read and write.

His views did not change. In a letter to an army recruiter in July 1864 that became public, he had opposed equating whites and blacks in the draft because he felt the blacks were useless as soldiers: "It is an insult to our Race to count them as part of the [draft] quota. A nigger is not a white man, and all the Psalm singing on earth won't make him so." Toward the end of the war he wrote a friend, "A nigger as such is a most excellent fellow, but he is not fit to marry, to associate,

443

or to vote with me and mine."[19] Such attitudes, it must be said, were common among people in the North.

More tellingly, he refused outright, in spite of Union army policy, to use black soldiers in combat. He defied the high command on this subject, and he defied Abraham Lincoln, virtually to the point of insubordination.[20] In this he was out of step with almost everyone else in the military. By the fall of 1864 more than one hundred thousand black troops were in the field. Many had had the chance to fight. But not in Sherman's army. There they performed manual labor so that the white soldiers could win the war.

All of which was completely irrelevant to the tens of thousands of slaves and former slaves in Georgia who regarded Sherman as a hero, a savior, and an all-around wonderful man. Many saw him in biblical terms, as an instrument of deliverance. To them Sherman's march was nothing less than the working out of God's will on earth. "I have wanted to preach the gospel to my people for a long time," said one young black man at a church service in December, "but the law would not let me, but Sherman and his army, as instruments in the hands of God, had divided the Red Sea of slavery, and the people were passing over."[21] The blacks were on the whole happy to see their masters punished and were extremely helpful to the Union army in locating roads, bridges, plantations, and the whereabouts of Confederate troops.

Sherman may have seen blacks as inferior, but in person with them he was generous, attentive, courteous, and even charming. They swarmed about him in public, shouted hosannas, and pressed to shake his hand. When it became known that he would receive individual black visitors at his headquarters, a long line soon formed. He conversed with them individually and often at length. He seemed perfectly happy to do this. He liked them and was interested in them. They repaid him with remarks such as "Been prayin' for you all long time, sir, prayin' day and night for you, and now, bless God, you is come."[22] In their faces and voices, Sherman had become something far larger than himself, a symbol of the destruction of the old institutional South. They understood that his name alone now inspired fear in their former masters. A whole new vocabulary had arisen to accommodate his power and influence. Charred chimneys left standing were *Sherman's monuments;* urban ruins were *Sherman's brickyard;* the thousands of African Americans who marched behind his army were *Sherman's freedmen;* and Sherman's neckties were ubiquitous.[23]

Still, Sherman's attitudes and statements about slavery made Union authorities nervous. Henry Halleck even warned him that some people in Washington thought he had "manifested an almost *criminal* dislike to the negro." Sherman was lectured and cautioned, though he did not understand what he had done wrong. "The negro should be a free man," he wrote, explaining his position to the abolitionist Salmon P. Chase, "but not put on any equality with the Whites. . . . Indeed it appears to me that the right of suffrage in our country should be rather abridged than enlarged." Such remarks didn't win him any friends in the administration, either. And Sherman's defense of his subordinate, General Jefferson C. Davis, over the pontoon affair had raised its own alarms.

Sherman's perceived antiblack attitudes — which some of his critics considered to be anti-Lincoln attitudes — led to a visit from Secretary of War Edwin Stanton, who insisted on a meeting with black leaders, one of the first times the US government had ever treated them with such respect.[24] The nominal reason was to poll them on their attitudes about slavery, emancipation, and the war. During the meeting Stanton, who also wanted to know what these former slaves thought of Sherman, asked him to leave. Sherman was shocked and insulted. But he needn't have worried. The leaders, mostly Methodist and Baptist preachers, gave him their highest praise. When asked, "What is the feeling of

446

the colored people toward General Sherman?," they replied that Sherman was

> a man, in the Providence of God, specially
> set apart to accomplish this work, and we
> unanimously felt inexpressible gratitude to
> him, looking upon him as a man who should
> be honored for the faithful performance of
> his duty. Some of us called upon him im-
> mediately upon his arrival, and it is prob-
> able he did not meet the Secretary with
> more courtesy than he did us. His conduct
> and deportment toward us characterized
> him as a friend and gentleman.
> We have confidence in General Sherman,
> and think what concerns us could not be in
> better hands.[25]

Stanton must have been astonished. He was certainly pleased. In another surprise at the meeting the black leaders told Sherman and Stanton, "The best way we can take care of ourselves is to have land, and turn and till it by our labor. . . . We want to be placed on land until we are able to buy it." So on January 16, 1865, four days after the meeting, Sherman, the man who supposedly had little time or use for black people, issued what is probably the war's single most radical order, confiscating property from wealthy slaveholders and designating it for settlement by former slaves. Special Field Orders no. 15

declared that the Sea Islands on the coast of South Carolina and Georgia — which included Hilton Head, Port Royal, and St. Helena — and other coastal areas would henceforth be reserved for freedmen. This was land distribution straight from the ultra-Radicals' playbook. Each family could have forty acres; Sherman would also give them army mules. They would be able to rent the land cheaply with options to buy. By June 1865 some forty thousand African Americans would be settled on the land, all administered by a new federal agency called the Freedmen's Bureau. The taking had been done under Sherman's "war powers." Though part of his motivation was clearly the welfare of black people, Special Field Orders no 15's main attraction was that it partly solved his own nagging administrative problem: What to do with all of those former slaves?*

Sherman took Savannah without a fight. The small Confederate force under General William J. Hardee abandoned the city on Decem-

* Sherman's plan, while it appeared to work for a while, ended badly through no fault of his own. Congress never passed a bill authorizing the permanent transfer of land, and by 1866 most of the land was returned to its original owners. Instead of owning land, the former slaves ended up as sharecroppers or contract laborers.

ber 21, a little more than a month after Sherman had left Atlanta. Once again, he saw no particular point in chasing the fleeing enemy, whom he could easily have bottled up and destroyed. Though Hardee and his men could never see themselves this way, they were nothing more than a minor nuisance in Sherman's grand vision. As he had made his way across the state, devastating the land at a rate of fifteen miles a day, his marching tactic — splitting his army into two parallel wings twenty or thirty miles apart — had made it impossible to predict his destination. So even the minimal rebel forces in the area could not be concentrated against him. No one knew where he was going. He deliberately bypassed well-defended cities, once again violating conventional wisdom.[26] Without a line of supply his army had to keep moving to eat. He could not afford even a brief siege. Simply grabbing and holding towns and cities — the goal of most tactics in the early war — was in his mind now trite and outdated. The sheer power of Sherman's army, with its ability to impose its will on a faltering Confederacy, was everything.

The residents of Savannah appeared properly humble and remorseful. They had no illusions about what happened to people who resisted the Union conquest. Sherman, true to his promises, treated the city well, inflicting minimal vandalism and destruction. His soldiers, generally on their best behavior, stepped in to prevent looting by locals. They actually paid for the same sorts of goods they had freely looted in the countryside. They celebrated Christmas and spent time sight-seeing in the old city.[27] Sherman, compulsively gregarious, charmed Savannah's women (its population was mostly women). He dandled their children on his knee. Having burned his way across the state, he was transfigured into the kind, gentle, and forgiving person he said he was ready to be. Sherman ordered a regimental band to play a concert for the city. He threw a party for officers and town leaders. He attended church. He governed Savannah not as the bloody tyrant of reputation, but — in a way reminiscent of his reign in Memphis — as a benevolent king who was eager to grant his subjects' wishes, provided they kissed his ring.

He was now wildly famous. Northern newspapers — once Sherman's worst enemy — celebrated his success. The New York Herald predicted that the fall of Savannah would lead to mass desertion in the Confederate ranks and the end of the war.[28] Fan mail poured in. Crowds clamored to see Sherman. After he had presented the city of Savannah to Abraham Lincoln as a Christmas gift, Lincoln wrote a note thanking him: "When you were about leaving Atlanta for the Atlantic coast, I was anxious, if not fearful. [But] I

450

did not interfere. Now, the undertaking being a success, the honor is all yours."

The occupation of Savannah was not the only good news in the North that Christmas season. On December 15 and 16, Sherman's subordinate generals George H. Thomas and John M. Schofield had dealt John Bell Hood's Army of the Tennessee a staggering blow at Nashville, which virtually ended Confederate power in the West and proved that Sherman had been right to divide his army.

Sherman won another concession from his boss, too. Grant had ordered him to take his army by sea to Virginia, but Sherman wanted nothing to do with a voyage on cramped ships that would debilitate his troops. He wanted very much to march them through South Carolina, the first state to secede and the leader in the secessionist movement. He was less interested in fighting Lee in Virginia than in renewing his psychological warfare on the South. He wanted less to kill than to change minds. Sherman wrote to Thomas:

It is nonsense to suppose that the people of the South are enraged or united by such movements. They reason very differently. They see in them the sure and irresistible destruction of all their property. They realize that the Confederate armies cannot protect them and they see in such raids the inevitable result of starvation and misery.[29]

451

From Savannah, Sherman sent Halleck an inventory of ruin: The army had torn up more than one hundred miles of railroad. It had "consumed the corn and fodder in the region of country thirty miles on either side of a line from Atlanta to Savannah, as also the sweet potatoes, cattle, hogs, sheep, and poultry, and [had] carried away more than 10,000 horses and mules, as well as a countless number of their slaves." He estimated that, of the $100 million in damage he thought he had done, only $20 million directly benefited the Union war effort.* The rest, he said breezily, as though human misery could be measured in these terms, "is simple waste and destruction."[30]

Sherman's march to the sea is one of the most famous events in American history, as much for its dramatic cruelty as for the crushing blow it dealt to Confederate hopes. But it paled in comparison to what his army did to South Carolina. Though his orders were not always followed, Sherman had tried hard in Georgia to set limits on what his men could and could not destroy. His army had been relatively restrained. No such rules applied in South Carolina, which quickly turned into a demonstration of what a highly moti-

* One hundred million dollars in 1864 is roughly $1.5 billion in 2018 dollars.

vated and mostly untrammeled sixty-thousand-man force could do when it really wanted to devastate everything in its path.

What happened to South Carolina was quite deliberate and done with the full blessing of the War Department. In the early days of that march Sherman told Major General Henry W. Slocum, who had commanded the left wing of the army in its March to the Sea, "You need not be so careful [in South Carolina] about property as we have been. The more of it you destroy the better it will be. The people of South Carolina should be made to feel the war, for they brought it on and are responsible more than anybody else for our presence here." This sentiment was fully shared by the War Department. Henry Halleck had written Sherman that, if he captured Charleston — the place where the first articles of secession had been passed — "I hope that by some accident the place may be destroyed, and if a little salt should be sown on its site it may prevent the growth of future crops of nullification and secession." Sherman replied, "I will bear in mind your hint as to Charleston, though I don't think salt will be necessary. . . . The truth is, the whole army is burning with an insatiable desire to wreak vengeance upon South Carolina. I almost tremble at her fate but feel that she deserves all that seems to be in store for her."[31] These were remarkably intemperate comments from buttoned-down army officers who had been taught at West Point to follow much stricter and more ethical rules of warfare.

The march saw the full realization of those vows. From the comforts of Savannah, the army now shouldered into the icy and rain-flooded swamplands of the South Carolina low country, finding unfordable rivers and countless streams. The Yankees built bridges and corduroyed roads — with the help of large numbers of freedmen — and moved determinedly forward.[32] As before, Sherman's soldiers cut a wide swath of ruin. But now entire towns were deliberately burned. What was once Robertsville became a charred ruin marked only by what one soldier called "one hundred 'monuments' (Chimnies) to Jefferson D." In the town of Barnwell only a few buildings survived. (The troops called it Burnwell.) In Blackville a few homes survived due to the work of fast-acting townspeople. The federals acted with purpose and with malice. One soldier wrote in his diary that he was shocked that his fellows "would have the heart to devastate and waste as we do. The living things are killed; even worn out horses are shot, and dogs, cows, and hogs are shot down and left."[33]

The most devastating, and infamous, violence happened in the state capital of Columbia on February 17, 1865. Sherman had ignored the defended cities of Augusta and Charleston — with ten thousand rebel soldiers each — and instead sliced between them and their communications, creating a brilliantly inverted situation where both cities were suddenly in the rear of his army.[34] After a brief but hopeless resistance from a pathetically small number of Confederate cavalry and artillery, Sherman's army entered Columbia to find chaos, disorder, and pillaging already well underway, having been started by rebel cavalry on its way out of town. Fires were burning here and there; the railroad depot and a large warehouse had already burned to the ground. Stacks of cotton bales had also caught on fire, so many that one of the first tasks of the Union conquerors was to try to put them out. Sherman was welcomed with cheers and shouts of joy by the city's black population. They danced and sang and clapped and thanked God for their deliverance.

Things quickly got out of hand. Liquor flowed abundantly, and soon large numbers of people, from Union soldiers to the city's white and black residents, were drunk and in the streets. A violent windstorm arose and sparks flew everywhere, which kindled or rekindled fires in the cotton bales. Fanned by those winds, the fires now defied all Union attempts to extinguish them. Suddenly everything seemed to be on fire. Buildings containing shot, powder, shells, and ammunition blew sky-high. Sherman, who had been napping in his headquarters, emerged to find a city in flames. Drunken men ran through the streets. Some of the federals tried to put out fires, while others, drunk on whiskey and vengeance, ran here and there setting new ones. By sunrise when the winds died down, large sections of Columbia lay in smoking ruins.

The residents immediately blamed Sherman. Many believed it had been done on his orders. The next day Sherman defended himself to a committee of local women. "Why then did you burn our town or allow your army to do so?" they asked. Sherman answered, "I did not burn your town, nor did my army. Your brothers, sons, husbands, and fathers set fire to every city, town, and village in the land when they fired on Fort Sumter. That fire kindled then and there by them has been burning ever since and reached your houses last night."[35] Virtually no one in the South bought this line of reasoning. Sherman would be denounced and cursed for the rest of his life for the destruction of Columbia. "Had I intended to burn Columbia," he said many years later, "I would have done it just as I would have done any act of war, and there would have been no concealment about it."

Sherman had indeed not ordered the entire

city burned. He had specifically exempted all private homes, libraries, hospitals, and asylums. He had even reassured citizens that, while they stood to lose some public buildings, their dwellings would be safe.[36] He meant what he said. He and a number of officers and soldiers tried to stop the fires from spreading. But many of his own men unfortunately worked against him as a by-product of the behavior he had encouraged on the march. Released Union prisoners joined in the burning and looting, too, as did a number of blacks. Most were drunk, and all were out of control. And the burning itself had been started by Confederate cavalry. Still, Sherman would spend the rest of his life trying to explain and justify what had happened.

In many ways Columbia was the bitterest moment in a bitter war. Blame abounded. Recriminations flew, and revenge was taken. Five days later, General Judson Kilpatrick, the Union cavalry commander, informed Sherman that eighteen of his men had been killed and mutilated after they had surrendered to Confederates, who hung a sign on them reading DEATH TO ALL FORAGERS. Later, another group of twenty-one Union soldiers were discovered naked and with their throats cut. Sherman ordered Kilpatrick to "retaliate man for man," then sent a note to Wade Hampton, the commander of the rebel cavalry, telling him that Sherman had ordered the executions of Confederate prisoners. An enraged Hampton replied that he would shoot two Union soldiers for every rebel soldier shot by Sherman's men.[37]

As always on these marches, African Americans gathered in large numbers to welcome Sherman's soldiers. When Charleston, South Carolina, was captured in February, a black regiment — the 21st United States Colored Troops — was the first to enter the city. They were received by the local black population with songs, dancing, prayers, and other expressions of pure joy. "I am sixty-nine years old," said one woman, "but I feel as if I wan't but sixteen!" She then started to chant, "Ye's long been a-comin', ye's long been a-comin', ye's long been a-comin', for to take the land."[38]

When Sherman's army crossed the border into North Carolina, one of the last states to secede and one that harbored large numbers of Unionists, the effusion of violence suddenly stopped. Soldiers still foraged, but there was nothing like the righteous violence that had been brought against South Carolina. Sherman let it be known that he now favored moderation, and moderation prevailed. Sherman's soldiers, if they were not quite angelic, became something much closer to what they had once been, and to what they aspired to be: decent, fair-minded, God-fearing Christians, who loved their families and held charity in their hearts for all.

459

CHAPTER NINETEEN:
DEATH AHEAD OF THEM,
DEATH BEHIND THEM

REBEL ENTRENCHMENTS AT PETERSBURG: Armored wastelands like these were the main reason Grant's great military campaign stalled in the last year of the war.

Fort Stedman was a "fort" only in the most primitive sense. Built by the Union army as part of the Petersburg siege lines in the summer of 1864, this square box with earthen walls reinforced by logs held big guns and the men who tended them. On three sides of the fort were the same nasty, antihuman entanglements that snaked for miles through the wastelands at the front: spiked and chained chevaux-de-frise, abatis strung with wire, embedded rows of sharpened stakes called fraises. The battlements stood a mere two hundred yards east of the rebel trenches. Like other works along Union and Confederate lines, Fort Stedman was a symbol of stasis — of nine months of armed standoff between Ulysses S. Grant and Robert E. Lee.

That equilibrium was about to be blown to pieces.

The first sign of that change was the movement of one hundred Confederate soldiers across no-man's-land at four o'clock in the frost-tinged and excessively dark morning of March 25, 1865. Their goal was to clear away the obstacles.[1] They did so, quickly and efficiently. But cutting and dragging heavy logs couldn't be done completely quietly, so the Yankee pickets — part of a regiment of heavy artillery from New York — inevitably heard them. But the pickets made a critical mistake. They assumed, because they had been seeing so many rebel deserters, that these men were deserters, too. (When Union soldiers heard firing on the battle lines, they often assumed

461

that the rebels were shooting at their own men, and they were often correct.)[2]

But this was no desertion. This was the opening act of Robert E. Lee's plan to concentrate 11,500 men — his entire 2nd Corps plus four brigades under John B. Gordon, his most aggressive general — hurl them forward against tiny, sleepy Fort Stedman, punch a hole in the Union line, and drive through to the supply depots in the Union rear, perhaps eventually as far as City Point, where Grant had his headquarters. Lee's goal: to create a gigantic distraction that would allow the rest of his army to escape from Petersburg and Richmond.

Why, after so many months in his trenches and fortifications, did Lee feel the sudden need to abandon his capital? Because destiny — in the form of a reinforced William Tecumseh Sherman and eighty thousand federal troops — now loomed from the Carolinas. Lee understood that he could not possibly fight and beat Grant and Sherman together. They would encircle Richmond and Petersburg and destroy him. His only chance was to break out, head to North Carolina, and unite with Joseph E. Johnston and his twenty-two thousand regulars, the last remaining Confederate army in the east. Their combined force would whip Sherman's army, then spin round and defeat Grant. That was the idea, as hopelessly far-fetched as it might have sounded to an impartial observer. In spite of the plan's improbability, Grant himself feared this strategy more than any other. He thought it might prolong the war for another year.[3]

On came the rebels in the inky darkness, up and over the earthworks, and before anyone on either side could quite grasp what had happened, Fort Stedman had fallen. The remaining obstructions were hacked away, the johnnies surged forward, and before dawn's first light they had not only occupied the fort but had seized several batteries, taken five hundred prisoners, and torn a thousand-foot hole in the Union line. Gordon was thrilled. Reinforcements were moving up. The plan was working perfectly. He had told Lee earlier that he envisioned "the disintegration of the whole left wing of the Union army, or at least the dealing of such a staggering blow upon it as would disable it temporarily, enabling us to withdraw from Petersburg in safety and join Johnston in North Carolina." Suddenly this bit of studied optimism looked quite possible. "Up to this point," Gordon wrote later, "the success had exceeded even my most sanguine expectations."[4]

Around this time, however, flush with their unexpectedly easy triumph, Gordon's men looked around them and began to realize that not quite everything was going their way. Soldiers who were supposed to follow them into the gap they had created were nowhere to be seen. As daylight broke, federal gunners from two nearby forts, who had a remarkably clear view of the interior of Fort Stedman, began to direct a deadly fire on the rebels with "spherical case," shells densely packed with dozens of lead or iron balls, which exploded into the enemy's troops. One newspaper reporter described it as "a rain of iron." Soon Gordon's men found themselves caught in a murderous cross fire, both from Union artillery and from some fifteen thousand infantry that were being rushed forward to plug the gap.

Worse still, there seemed to be no way out. Rebels who tried to leave found that the area outside the fort, including the path of retreat, was now raked by federal artillery. When Captain William H. Edwards, of the 17th South Carolina Regiment, led his men out in front of the fort, they got only a few yards before his unit was "mutilated by shot and shell," he wrote. "I did not go more than twenty yards before I was shot down."[5]

Soon the world inside sleepy old Fort Stedman was starting to look like a death trap.

These were hard times for the Confederate States of America. Or what was left of them. By early 1865 vast stretches of that country were under Union control in Tennessee, Virginia, Louisiana, Mississippi, and Georgia, along with every major coastal port and the entire Mississippi River. The only significant untouched areas left were in Alabama and the interior sections of North and South Carolina.[6] Just exactly what "the South" was now was hard to say. Perhaps the Southern nation consisted of nothing more than the embattled congressmen in Richmond who claimed to represent it. The commonwealth of Southern states had been an idea in the first place, a wild notion to rebel against the United States of America. Maybe it was a wild notion once again.

The South was in any case the victim of the Lee paradox: the more the Confederate army prolonged the war, the more the Confederacy was destroyed.[7] The marches of Sherman and Sheridan in Georgia, the Carolinas, and Virginia were intended to showcase that idea, but the war's economic devastation reached deep into places where armies never fought. Inflation raged out of control as the bankrupt rebel government kept printing money with nothing to back it. The value of Confederate currency was fast plunging toward zero. The Confederate War Department was compelled to pay one thousand paper dollars for a single pair of army boots; a month's pay for a soldier would not purchase a single ration.[8] Two-thirds of all Southern wealth and half of all of Southern farm machinery were already gone, as were the old markets for its main cash crops, cotton and tobacco. Many of its slaves — a major form of wealth — were gone, too. Farms fell out of production, impoverishing entire families. There were shortages everywhere. There were refugees everywhere. As early as 1863, one Mobile, Alabama, newspaper editor had put the number of displaced pro-Confederate Southerners at four hundred thousand — meaning nearly one in ten white Southerners.[9]

Anyone who thought that the Civil War was wrecking the Northern economy and bleeding its government dry — as both Confederate politicians and Northern Democrats had variously charged — simply wasn't paying attention. While the Confederacy was falling into an economic time warp, the United States of America was rising as a global commercial and industrial power. Coal and iron production and shipbuilding were all at record levels. Traffic on the North's railroads and canals had risen 50 percent during the war. Farmers in the Union alone produced more wheat in 1862–63 than the entire country had produced in 1859, and despite the enormous needs of the Union armies, the country had doubled its exports of wheat, corn, pork, and beef. Even manufacturing, which included the hard-hit textile business, was up 13 percent.[10]

The poverty of the South was fully visible in its principal army, where the frigid winter of 1864–65 became a nightmare of hardship, suffering, and want. In Petersburg and Richmond the men lived in filthy ratholes dug into the sides of their trenches. Their daily diet often consisted of little more than a few handfuls of musty, vermin-filled cornmeal and partial rations of "bacon" that was mostly rancid fat.[11] There was no coffee, no tea, no sugar. By one estimate six rebel soldiers got as much to eat as a single Yankee. Their clothes were worn thin, their blankets in tatters. Regiments of three hundred to four hundred men often had only fifty pairs of shoes.[12] There was no soap. Firewood was scant and green. The rebels' supplies of ammunition were so short they were reduced to digging enemy bullets out of the ground.[13]

In contrast to the squalor and near starvation behind Confederate lines, the Union camp at nearby Bermuda Hundred on the James River was populated by warm, dry, well-fed, and magnificently equipped soldiers. As the black newspaper correspondent T. M. Chester described it, the place constantly bustled with activity, both commercial and military, like a prosperous city:

> Schooners, tugboats, steamships, and seagoing craft are constantly going and coming. Here may be seen all classes and conditions of adventurers who follow in the wake of the army. Sutlers' establishments,

wholesale and retail, loom up. . . . Barbers are ready to shave you for fifteen, and cut your hair for thirty-five cents; ambrotypists are here to place your beautiful countenances in a town, while the embalmers . . . will undertake to forward to the North the honored dead, at the same time using the top of the coffin as a means for advertisement.[14]

Worst of all for the rebel soldiers, and more painful than any physical hardship, were the letters from home, where the privations of the wartime economy were often worse than at the front. Some of the messages from home were so dire they were censored. Wrote Lee's aide Colonel Walter H. Taylor, "Hundreds of letters addressed to soldiers were intercepted in which mothers, wives, & sisters told of their inability to respond to the appeals of the hungry children for bread, or to provide proper care & remedies for the sick . . . appealed to the men to come home."[15] Many letters simply begged the soldiers to walk away. "It is useless to conceal the truth any longer," wrote Confederate company commander Luther Rice Mills to his brother on March 2, 1865. "Many of our people at home have become so demoralized that they write to their husbands, sons, and brothers that desertion *now* is not dishonorable."[16] The rebel soldiers understood a basic truth: short of dying or being horribly maimed, getting out of the Confederate army was almost impossible. New draft laws kept in place veterans who had long since finished their enlistments. Large numbers had been wounded at least once. Many had recently been released from Northern prisons, only to be sent back to the lines. Going home, in the grim early spring of 1865, was no longer an official option.

The news from the war was almost uniformly bad. Confederate defeats at the Battles of Franklin and Nashville (November and December 1864) had meant the end of any significant rebel power in the west. At the Battle of Fort Fisher in North Carolina in January 1865, the Confederacy had lost access to its last major port — Wilmington. In March, Phil Sheridan had destroyed what was left of Jubal Early's ragged army in the Shenandoah Valley, and Sherman had defeated a badly outnumbered Joseph E. Johnston in North Carolina at the Battle of Bentonville. The dashing Union cavalier Harry Wilson, who had swept away Nathan Bedford Forrest's outgunned cavalry, had taken Montgomery and was on the verge of taking Selma. The sense, too, was that glory in the South had simply gone out-of-date. The signs were everywhere. In Richmond, the once-magnificent Lieutenant General John Bell Hood could now be seen hobbling to church on Sundays — a broken, heartsick shadow of the man who had carried the Union lines at Gaines Mill, and who had recently been welcomed as the hero of Chickamauga.[17] The limp-armed, one-legged general, who had been relieved of command in January at his own request after his bitter defeat at Nashville, and who now attracted little attention beyond pity, was simply another reminder that the myth of heroic Southern dominion was just that.

All attempts to negotiate peace had failed. The final attempt — a meeting on February 3, 1865, between Lincoln and Seward and three rebel commissioners aboard a steamship at Hampton Roads, Virginia — showed how far apart the two sides still were. Lincoln refused to talk about any solution short of restoration of the union and the abolition of slavery. Jefferson Davis's instruction to his commissioners was not to entertain any solution without "two countries." Though Southern politicians professed shock and outrage that Lincoln could show "so little care for the distress and suffering of the wounded party," he had never given them any reason to think he had changed his mind. Lincoln was steadfast.

Davis made much political hay from the failure of this démarche, which he blamed entirely on the North. The worst horror in the world, he argued — far worse than losing its slaves — was for the South to live under the bootheel of the Northern despot.[18] In a speech in Richmond, on February 6, the Confederate president thundered to wild applause that his country would never, ever submit to "the disgrace of surrender." He predicted that the hated Abraham Lincoln and William Seward would soon find that "they had been speaking to their masters" and predicted that the Confederacy's valiant armies would "compel the Yankees, in less than twelve months, to petition us for peace on our own terms."[19] This may have sounded utterly unmoored from reality, but many still believed it. They believed, above all, that as long as Robert E. Lee held the field they still had hope.

A leader of this school of thought was the Richmond journalist and historian Edward A. Pollard, who published a book in February 1865 that captured the feelings of this diehard patriotic South. He reassured his readers that there "was not the least occasion for us to despair. We still cover the vitals of the Confederacy with powerful armies." As for Sherman, his victories were ephemeral. "The march of Sherman may, by a defeat at any stage short of Richmond, be brought to thorough naught; the whole country which he has over-run be opened and recovered and nothing remain of his conquests but the narrow swath along the path of the invader."[20] Sherman's soldiers, who had just walked unhindered through a large section of the Deep South, would have been astonished to read it.

In Richmond and Petersburg, Grant had continued, in lesser engagements through the fall and winter, to test the strength of Lee's lines. Grant had attacked supply lines. He had inched closer, tightened his grips, seized a railroad. Lee, who was forced to defend a huge perimeter that included two major cities twenty-five miles apart, two wide, fast-moving rivers, and some thirty-seven miles of entrenchments, parried Grant's thrusts, moved soldiers around to fill gaps, and even launched a brief offensive of his own. But there had been no breakthroughs, no resolution. Lee knew that Grant would move against him when the roads dried, and Lee knew precisely what Grant was going to do. He would use his superior numbers to extend the Union lines to the west of Petersburg until Lee's own lines finally stretched and broke. Lee knew, too, that in time, perhaps only weeks, Sherman would arrive. Lee and his gaunt, depleted soldiers, advancing in the early darkness of March 25, were already out of time.

The south experienced one additional bit of unexpected agony. While Abraham Lincoln was ramming the Thirteenth Amendment through Congress in January 1865 — which abolished slavery in the United States — the Confederacy was tying itself in knots over a question no one would have thought to ask at the beginning of the war: Which was more crucial to the South, independence, or slavery? The two ideas had always been linked; each seemed necessary to the other. After Lincoln's Emancipation Proclamation in 1862, the connection if anything became stronger. But many Southerners had begun to ask, in terms that few of them would have dared breathe in 1861, why there had to be a link.

This revolutionary idea had been discussed informally for several years. Confederate major general Patrick Cleburne was the first to publicly express this, in a January 1864 letter to his immediate superior, Joseph E. Johnston, that was signed by fourteen officers, including four generals.[21] In a long and carefully reasoned argument, Cleburne made the case for arming slaves to fight for the South. He believed the South could not win the war without them. He believed that slavery had given the North a powerful cause to fight for as well as a rationale for the European powers to withhold support. He wrote:

The idea that it is [the North's] special mission to war against slavery has held growing sway over the Northern people for many years, and has at length ripened into an

473

armed and bloody crusade against it. This baleful superstition has so far supplied them with a courage and constancy not their own. It is the most powerful and honestly entertained plank in their war platform. Knock this away and what is left? A bloody ambition for more territory, a pretended veneration for the Union.[22]

Cleburne fully understood the implications of what he was saying. You could not ask hundreds of thousands of slaves to fight for the Confederate States of America without freeing them. Freedom would be the price of service. The cost of victory, Cleburne argued, was the end of slavery. Remove human bondage and you not only gave Confederate armies the wherewithal to win. You removed the very argument for war. "Let us recruit an army of slaves," he argued, and "guarantee freedom within a reasonable time to every slave in the South who shall remain true to the Confederacy."[23]

Though Jefferson Davis tried to suppress Cleburne's letter, the idea was afoot.[24] Like a number of other Southern newspapers, the *Jackson Mississippian* liked the idea, too. "Let not slavery prove a barrier to our independence," said an editorial. "Although slavery is one of the principles that we started to fight for . . . if it proves an insurmountable obstacle to achievement of our liberty and separate nationality, away with it!"

The idea could sound preposterous. Arm slaves in a nation that lived in mortal fear of a slave revolt? Davis himself had derided the Union's recruitment of slaves to the army as "the most execrable measure recorded in the history of guilty man." But in the wake of Confederate defeats at Vicksburg, Gettysburg, Chattanooga, and the Shenandoah Valley, of the man-wasting Virginia campaign in the spring and summer of 1864, and of the defection of a million slaves to the North, mathematics began to trump ideology. The South simply could not win a war of attrition without finding new soldiers, and the population of 4 million slaves was the only possible source. Slaves had already been employed in Southern armies as manual laborers, loading and unloading supplies, digging trenches, and helping to build everything from bridges to railroads and forts. They often did this while bullets and bombs flew around them. They also cooked, washed, mended, and generally served the needs of white officers. To do all these things, they were "impressed" from their owners for limited periods and then returned.

But they were never given weapons. To do so would have violated the logic of the system of slavery and the ideas on which it was based. To do so would have been to admit that what Southern politicians said they believed, and their reasons for believing it, were lies. There was no getting around this. If black men were something less than human, something undeserving of human rights, then they could not suddenly be something else. "If slaves will make good soldiers our whole theory of slavery is wrong," protested powerful Georgia politician Howell Cobb, who did not believe it was wrong. That the payment for military service would be freedom was also profoundly illogical, too — in the Southern way of thinking. "The idea of freeing slaves was based on the false assumption that the condition of freedom is so much better for the slave than servitude," wrote the *Richmond Whig,* "that it may be bestowed on him as a reward." In the Southern system of slavery, slaves were meant by God to live in bondage and were happier and better that way than as free men. One Alabama editor framed it in stark terms, as a straight philosophical sellout: "We are forced by necessity of condition to take a step *which is revolting to every sentiment of pride and every principle that governed our institutions before the war"* (italics added).[25]

Critics of such proposals held that, even if such an idea became law, white soldiers, considering the blacks deeply inferior and less than fully human, would never accept them into their ranks. "Victory itself would be robbed of its glory if shared with slaves," said a Mississippi congressman. But this, too, was not true. Letters in favor of arming blacks poured into the Richmond government from the trenches of Petersburg in early 1865. White soldiers thought that blacks were human enough to make good soldiers indeed. Anyone who had fought against them did not doubt it. Even Nathan Bedford Forrest, the former slave trader from Memphis, was in favor of it.

Though the Confederate Congress tore itself to pieces in debate over the issue, the most telling public support for the proposal came in February from none other than Robert E. Lee. He had lent his informal support to the idea for at least a year. Now he said it outright. On February 18, he wrote to Congressman Ethelbert Barksdale offering support to the "Negro soldier bill": "This measure was not only expedient but necessary. The negroes, under proper circumstances, will make efficient soldiers. I think we could at least do as well with them as the enemy. . . . They furnish a more promising material than many armies of which we read in history." Then the shocker, coming from Lee, anyway: "I think those who are employed should be freed."[26]

Reaction to Lee's letter was swift and sharp. Many people were simply astounded. The *Charleston Mercury,* a staunch defender of slavery and secession, disparaged the legendary general as "the author of this scheme of nigger soldiers and emancipation," calling him "an hereditary federalist and a disbeliever [in] slavery." The *Richmond Examiner,* edited by Edward A. Pollard, argued that Lee's view "suggests a doubt whether he is what used to be called a 'good southerner'; that is, whether he is thoroughly satisfied of the justice and beneficence of negro slavery as a sound, permanent basis of our national polity."

But Lee had given the legislation the push it needed. Less than a month later, on March 13, the Confederate Congress finally passed a bill allowing the enlistment of three hundred thousand black soldiers, more than twice the number of soldiers, black and white, in Grant's Army of the Potomac. Though Congress balked at offering emancipation, Jefferson Davis issued an executive order granting freedom in exchange for service, effectively settling the matter.

In spite of the bitter debate and months of legislative wrangling, nothing much came of it. Most slave owners, whose cooperation was necessary, hated the idea. Many considered it, as one Confederate War Department official wrote, "a colossal blunder" and simply did nothing. Recruiting proceeded fitfully, or not at all. Eventually a few black units were cobbled together. One of the most dislocating sights of the war was the spectacle, on

March 24, of two companies of newly recruited black troops, along with three companies of whites dredged up from hospital beds, marching up Main Street to Capitol Square in downtown Richmond, while a band played "Dixie." Thousands of spectators turned out, and the *Richmond Dispatch* even conceded that these slaves, looking sharp in their dress uniforms, showed "as much aptness and proficiency . . . as is usually shown by any white troops we have seen."[27] Perhaps they were human beings, after all.

Events of the next few weeks would make it clear that these actions were too little, too late. The Confederacy's new slave-soldiers would never make any difference in the war. But something more fundamental had taken place. Even if few Southerners admitted it, a moral threshold had been crossed. Slavery as an institution was as good as gone. As one rebel soldier put it, "Slavery has received its death blow."[28]

The sun was well up in the sky now, giving Union gunners clear targets. General Gordon's rebel divisions pushed forward anyway, beyond Fort Stedman and the two batteries they had seized and into the unarmored zones behind Union lines. They were advancing toward the Union supply depot. They might have gotten there, too, except for a quick-thinking Union brigadier general named John Hartranft, a soldier's soldier who had led a famous charge at Antietam in 1862.* Now, as he found his superior officer already packed and preparing to move to the rear, Hartranft took charge. He threw the 200th Pennsylvania Regiment at the oncoming rebels. The fight was unfair: a regiment against several divisions. The men of the 200th were badly shot up. They fell back, regrouped, tried again, were again swept by Confederate fire, then retreated again. But they had bought Hartranft time — which he used to build, in short order, a defensive battle line more than a mile long with several thousand more federal troops. By 7:30 a.m. he had effectively boxed in the entire rebel advance. Because their reinforcements never arrived, the Confederates never had enough men to bust through Hartranft's brilliantly organized secondary defenses. Just before 8:00 a.m. he launched his counterassault, and soon federal lines were closing on Fort Stedman from three sides. "The whole field was blue with them," recalled a Georgia captain.[29]

For many Confederate soldiers, the real horror began now. The no-man's-land between the lines — the way they had come — was swept by federal fire. The very air was lethal. Men who fled into it were cut down in large numbers. Which meant that thousands

* At Burnside's Bridge.

of rebels were now trapped. "My mind sickens at the memory of it," recalled one Union observer who had watched the slaughter. "For the victims had ceased fighting, and were now struggling between imprisonment and death."[30]

More than three thousand of Gordon's Confederates were killed or wounded — a staggering casualty rate. A thousand more surrendered. The Union suffered half those casualties. By eight thirty the Battle of Fort Stedman was over, and the battle lines were where they had been when the fight began. Lee received the news as a staggering blow. He had lost a large piece of his army. Worse, his great breakout attempt had rather easily been put down. Hartranft's scrappy Pennsylvanians had beaten back what would turn out to be the last great offensive by the Army of Northern Virginia. The Union high command, meanwhile, was barely ruffled by the morning's engagement. Abraham Lincoln, aboard the *River Queen* at City Point, had breakfasted with his son Robert while the battle was fought, then penned a quick wire to Edwin Stanton in Washington: "No war news. Robert just now tells me there was a little rumpus this morning up the line, ending about where it began." Lincoln's casual summary would have astonished the thirty-four hundred wounded or captured Confederates.

At Grant's suggestion, he and Lincoln now boarded a rickety military train that took them seven miles from City Point to the site of the battle. Lincoln was playing tourist. In spite of the many years of war and all of the combat he had authorized, he had never seen this much of war before.* He walked the battlefield, beheld a group of sixteen hundred wretched-looking rebel soldiers with matted hair and tangled beards, wounded men being taken in the cars, and dead men who had not yet been buried. He tried to comfort the wounded. He said that he "had seen enough of the horrors of war," that he hoped "this was the beginning of the end," and that he wished — this from a man who had overseen and approved the killing of hundreds of thousands of people and the burning of large patches of the South — "there would be no more bloodshed or ruin of homes."

---

* Lincoln had been near the fighting at Fort Stevens in Washington during the Jubal Early raid, where he came briefly under enemy fire; but he had seen nothing like the battlefield wreckage he observed at Fort Stedman.

CHAPTER TWENTY:
RICHMOND IS BURNING

Union major general Philip Sheridan, Grant's most aggressive fighter and a living symbol of the new hard war against the South.

It was April 1. All Fools' Day. What Robert E. Lee had believed would happen had happened. On March 27, two days after the fight at Fort Stedman, Ulysses S. Grant had set in motion an immense cascading movement of troops to the south and west of Petersburg — a ribbon of blue unspooling from the Appomattox River and out across the broken, river-and-stream-cut country of central Virginia. Grant had left a mere three divisions near Richmond. He did not care anymore about securing or holding or defending anything. He wanted to destroy Lee in place. Grant wanted to end the war here and now and without the help of Sherman's soldiers, the media's new darlings, who, rather annoyingly, had been getting all the attention. Grant knew that Lee had nowhere near enough men to defend such a sprawling perimeter. Only the rebel general's uncanny ability to conceptualize terrain and troop movements along his thirty-five-mile-long front had allowed him to hold out for so long. "If there ever was a general who was a past master in the art of stretching a thin line against a superior enemy in motion," wrote Porter Alexander, "it was Gen. Lee."[1] No one would have argued the point. But Lee was running out of tricks. Grant, with a greatly superior army, was going to force Lee to show his weakness. On March 29, Grant, with uncharacteristic impatience, told Phil Sheridan, "I feel like ending the matter."

Lee had no illusions about the meaning of

Grant's advance. The rebel general had been saying for months that his army might have to abandon Richmond, whose population had swelled from 40,000 at the war's outset to more than 130,000 in 1865.[2] He had also insisted that the end of Richmond was not the end of everything. In testimony before the Confederate Congress in January he had been asked, "Will the fall of Richmond end the war?" He had answered without hesitation:

> By no means, sir, by no means. [From] a military point of view I should be stronger after than before such an event, because it would enable me to make my plan of campaign and battle. From a moral and political point of view the abandonment or loss of Richmond would be a serious calamity, but when it has fallen I believe I can prolong the war for two years upon Virginia soil. Ever since the conflict began, I have been obliged to permit the enemy to make my plans for me, because [I was] compelled to defend the capital.[3]

The congressmen may not have been comforted to know that Lee, unchained from the dead weight of Richmond, would be a more effective campaigner. Many of them assumed that if captured they would be tried for treason and hanged by the neck in Capitol

Square. But the moment Lee had been talking about had now come. The roads were navigable. The Yankees were on the move, roughly 120,000 of them facing roughly 70,000 rebels.[4] Fort Stedman had been a disaster, a great and irreplaceable loss. All rebel losses were now irreplaceable. The question of the hour was, How long could Lee's lines hold?

Grant's plan was exactly what Lee had predicted. Grant would lengthen his battle lines westward, forcing Lee to do the same to avoid being flanked. That would cause Lee to run short of troops to man his fortifications. Then Grant's divisions would make a sharp right turn, head due north, and punch through Lee's overtaxed defenses. Thus Grant kept pushing, streaming his forces along back roads and through farm fields and alder thickets, four miles past the old rebel right toward obscure places called Dinwiddie Court House and Five Forks, about fifteen miles southwest of Petersburg. They were nothing in themselves. But they offered access to the Southside Railroad, the last rail route out of Petersburg and the city's main supply line. That was Grant's target, the thing he would make Lee defend. Losing it meant the probable end of Petersburg, which in turn meant that Richmond would be indefensible, which meant the surrender of Richmond.

Lee had few options. He could not extend

his line, man for man, to match Grant's legions. But he could do what he had been doing for the past nine months: shift troops, plug holes. So he ordered Major General George Pickett and two divisions along with cavalry under Lee's nephew Major General Fitzhugh Lee to confront Sheridan at Dinwiddie Court House. Thus ten thousand rebel troops now faced more than twice that number of Union soldiers on the Confederate right. Pickett, who had led the doomed uphill charge at Gettysburg, had drawn long odds again. Lee may have suspected the size of the disadvantage, but he was not telling anyone.

The first combats on the far-western front belonged to the rebels. In hot skirmishes against superior forces on March 29 and March 30, the graybacks held fast. They still had plenty of fight in them. At Dinwiddie Court House on March 31, Pickett's force slammed into a roughly equal force of cavalry under the overall command of Phil Sheridan and featuring a glittering array of some of the Union army's most celebrated late-war commanders, including Brigadier General George A. Custer and Brigadier General Wesley Merritt. The rebels sent the Union force reeling in a tactical defeat and caused the normally imperturbable Grant to lose his temper with Sheridan. As of that evening the Army of Northern Virginia had yet to be defeated along its right flank.

But one couldn't argue with numbers. Unfortunately for Lee, Grant had finally learned, once and forever, the fundamental tactical truth of the Civil War: attacking the enemy in uncoordinated assaults was a terrible idea.[5] Fighting with pieces of one's available force gave up numerical advantage — something the Union had held in most major battles in the war. This might seem obvious. But one of the most difficult things a general could do in the mid-nineteenth century was to make all of the units of his army function together, to get his divisions and brigades and regiments on time to the places where they were supposed to be, then to make them move in concert. Even getting five-hundred-man regiments in a three-thousand-man brigade to move together was hard. So many battles were lost because of this failure. Both sides had this problem, though Lee had made a specialty of preying upon it. Grant, who had made this mistake as recently as Cold Harbor, would not make it again. To ensure that his generals moved on time and together, he had placed the strident and preternaturally combative Phil Sheridan in command of the Union left wing. (Grant had also, by the beginning of April, quietly replaced many of his senior commanders in Virginia.)[6] Under Sheridan there would be no vacillation, no dreary excuses for logistical failure. No piecemeal attacks.

On April 1, at around 4:00 p.m., Sheridan launched a head-on assault against Pickett's lines. While his Union men held the rebels in place with their seven-shot repeating carbines — revolutionary weapons that their opponents did not have — Gouverneur Warren's 5th Corps swung round and walloped the Confederate right.* The effect on the rebels was electric: infantry did not respond happily to being shot at from two directions. The result was envelopment. As Sheridan galloped his lines, whooping and cursing and prodding his men forward, Pickett's two divisions collapsed. Half of them threw their weapons down and their hands in the air. The other half ran. With the entire right wing of Lee's army gone, Five Forks was in Union hands. That meant the Yankees would soon control the vital supply and evacuation route, the Southside Railroad, too. Pickett lost four thousand to five thousand men at the Battle of Five Forks, a thousand of whom surrendered after being surrounded.

Grant's blood was up. Five Forks was a victory but not a breakthrough. Petersburg

* Warren was late in moving — for a variety of good reasons. But tardiness or slow-moving advances were no longer tolerated. To Warren's outrage and disbelief, Sheridan relieved him of command that day, with Grant's full support, even though Warren's assault had worked extremely well.

remained unconquered, so this time there would be no pause, no inventory taken, no moment of reflection to wonder what the enemy might do or what action would be best. At 9:00 p.m. on April 1, as the stretcher-bearers and ambulance wagons plied the killing fields at Five Forks, Grant ordered an attack for the next morning against the entire fortified Confederate line south of Petersburg. He would throw everything he had at Lee in one of the largest assaults of the war. The federal artillery began to pound rebel positions an hour later, spitting great streaks of fire and raining shot and shell down on Confederate entrenchments for more than four hours. Grant's infantry — everything and everyone he could muster — would move forward at 4:45 a.m.

The problem with this idea, as anyone in the Union's Petersburg lines could have told you, was that it involved a frontal assault against Lee's fortifications, the same ones that had proven so impenetrable for so long, the same physical structures that in the past year had changed the nature of war itself. The conventional wisdom was that a head-long assault on Lee's works would result in gigantic numbers of casualties. And it would probably not work, either, not even if the federals blew a two-hundred-foot crater in the rebel lines. So the soldiers wrote their names on pieces of paper and pinned them to their clothing, just as they had done at Cold Harbor, in order that their disfigured bodies might later be identified. So great was the fear of such assaults that, two days before, veterans in the 6th Corps had refused to attack the enemy's works. One Pennsylvanian under the command of John Hartranft recalled later that, as he prepared to attack now, thoughts of "God and eternity rushed through my mind."[7] Another was heard to say, "Well, goodbye, boys — this means death." A New Jersey captain wrote, "Some of us are heartsick at the prospect" of crossing into the fortified wastelands.[8]

At first light the Union men got up out of their rifle pits and moved together by the thousands across no-man's-land and directly into the abatis and chevaux-de-frise and tangled telegraph wire, where they came under sharp rifle fire from the fortifications. To veterans of Spotsylvania and Cold Harbor and various assaults on the Petersburg defenses, the moment was horrifically familiar. Rebel engineers had had many months to dig, reinforce, and otherwise perfect their defenses. Union troops went down quickly, and in large numbers. Union major general Horatio Wright's 6th Corps lost eleven hundred men in fifteen minutes.

Then, strangely and miraculously, everything changed. The resistance that had sprung up so fiercely just as suddenly weakened.

There was desperate fighting on the parapets one moment, and the next moment the federals had broken through. Grant's theory — that stretching his lines miles to the west would strain Lee's forces to the breaking point — had been proven correct. As fearsome as those fortifications were, they did not contain very many Confederate soldiers. Soon, amid wild tumult and shouting, federal soldiers along lines south of Petersburg were tearing through obstacles and leaping fortified walls and sweeping their enemies before them. The entire 6th Corps breached rebel defenses en masse. They poured through the empty works in the war's single most important breakthrough, then swung both left and right, rolling up part of the Confederate 3rd Corps line and seizing several forts. The other Union corps were soon through as well across a broad front, as the concentric circles of the rebel defenses collapsed toward the center.

Lee's army was broken, but not yet beaten. His stalwart general James Longstreet strung together a last-ditch line of battle closer to the city's center. He was desperately shorthanded. One of the rebel army's leading generals, A. P. Hill, had been killed in the fight. Upon hearing of his death, Lee said, "He is at rest now, and we who are left are the ones to suffer." Longstreet's few pathetic regiments formed a skirmish line against the entire Union 6th Corps, bravely holding the line while, behind them, the great evacuation began.[9] But Lee was not certain he could hold Grant's army back until nightfall, when the rebel army would have to make its escape from both Richmond and Petersburg. The only way out was to the west, where every soldier in the Army of Northern Virginia would soon be headed. It was not yet noon on Sunday, April 2.

On that same morning thirty miles away in Richmond, His Excellency Jefferson Davis did a curious thing. He went to church. This was not surprising, but its timing was. Davis was fully aware of the steady encirclement of Petersburg, aware of the magnitude of Lee's crushing losses at Fort Stedman and at Five Forks. The Confederate president had been told several times in the last two months that Lee's army might have to abandon Richmond and had pointedly been told the previous evening by Lee that evacuation was imminent. Davis was so alert to the danger that he had sent his wife and children out of the city two days before, so alarmed for their safety that he had given his wife, Varina, a pistol and shown her how to use it, instructing her to "force your assailants to kill you" rather than to suffer unspeakable violation.[10] Most Confederate officials had already fled the capital. Only Davis and his cabinet remained.

Still, Davis went to church. He did so in full view of hundreds of other Richmond residents who out of habit or fear had also turned out to attend services that morning. He sat in his pew at St. Paul's, as he did every Sunday, as though the world of the South were not spinning off its axis, as though a Union army had not crushed the entire right wing of the rebel army the day before, as though he had not received a telegram that morning from Lee with news of yet another unfolding disaster south of Petersburg. As though Davis had not, with unnecessary melodrama, advised his wife that it would be better to die than be captured by the ravening Yankee hordes. Though his fellow parishioners scrutinized his face, his expression, according to Confederate secretary of the navy Stephen R. Mallory, "varied not from that cold, stern sadness which four years of harassing mental labor had stamped upon it." His face was "as impenetrable as an iron mask."[11]

Sometime after 11:00 a.m., while the service proceeded, a man brought Davis a second telegram from Lee. This one was more specific: "I see no prospect of doing more than holding our position here til night. I am not certain that I can do that. If I can I shall withdraw to-night north of the Appomattox, and, if possible, it will be better to withdraw the whole line to-night from James

494

River." Lee explained that the enemy had broken his lines. "I advise that preparation be made for leaving Richmond tonight." Davis, ashen faced and somber, rose from his pew, said nothing to anyone, left the church, and walked back to his office. Lee, in his controlled military prose, had just said, in effect, the end is near, flee for your lives.

To which Davis, in his extreme self-absorption, replied in a wire both testy and oddly perfunctory: "The Secretary of War has shown me your dispatch. To move tonight will involve the loss of many valuables, both for the want of time to pack and of transportation. Arrangements are progressing." Lee, furious with this response, snapped back, "I think it is absolutely necessary that we should abandon our position tonight. I have given all the necessary orders on the subject to the troops."

Still the president of the Confederate States of America, lost in his larger reveries of war, or perhaps praying to God, did not deem it necessary to tell the citizens of his capital city to evacuate. Not until 4:00 p.m. was an official announcement made, some five hours after Davis had received Lee's second telegram. By that time, rumors of the city's imminent fall were everywhere. By mid-afternoon the people had discovered what the president already knew — that the arrival of Northern armies in the Confederate capital was not a matter of days or weeks, but *hours.* A rebel force was already marching *out* of the city.[12] Few people in Richmond, official or otherwise, had anticipated the speed of the collapse. "Although I had all along supposed that the fall of Petersburg would probably be followed by the evacuation of Richmond," wrote former Virginia congressman Alexander Boteler, "I had no idea that the two catastrophes would occur so suddenly, in the same night."[13]

Those who could took flight. They were overwhelmingly white and affluent.* Banks were besieged. Government officials frantically packed up records and archives and hauled them in wagons to the train station. Railcars were loaded with Confederate gold and silver, the sight of which caused even more panic. Crowds jammed the depots on the single remaining rail line, while others clamored for precious spaces on the packet boats heading upriver to Lynchburg. Still others grabbed whatever vehicles they could find — baggage wagons, carts, drays, ambulances — loaded up their belongings and sometimes slaves, too, and trundled off down the James River Canal towpath.[14] Soldiers in hospitals arose from their beds and hobbled forth into the teeming streets. Most of the slaves and

* Many such people had already fled the city, but many had remained, too.

freedmen stayed behind, believing they had nothing to fear from Union soldiers. But for the whites who did remain — largely women, children, and older men — the fear and uncertainty were terrible. They had all read stories in the fearmongering Southern press of Yankee rape and pillage and murder. They had all heard accounts of the ruthlessness of Sherman's men in Georgia and South Carolina. Women stitched valuables into pockets inside their skirts. Pistols were loaded. Doors were locked and curtains drawn.

Stranger sights appeared, too. In Capitol Square soldiers burned huge piles of Confederate currency. It was anyone's guess why keeping the worthless paper out of Union hands was so deeply necessary. At a moment when the institution of slavery was vanishing before everyone's eyes, the streets presented jarring moments. One of the people clamoring for a place on a train was Robert Lumpkin, Richmond's most prominent slave trader, famous for his mistreatment of slaves and the owner of the largest slave lockup in Richmond. During the panic and flight he led fifty shackled slaves through the streets, many of them weeping, and tried to take them with him on the train. Until that very day, a broker with a coffle of slaves would have been a common sight, free to move about as he pleased. Richmond had one of the largest slave markets in the country, where men, women, and children were routinely whipped and tied and chained and families were broken up and "sold south" to distant places. But now a soldier, brandishing a bayonet, told Lumpkin he could not board the train until he let his slaves go.[15] The fall of Richmond was the fall of slavery, too.

Then the real trouble began. Sometime that evening the crowds in the streets of stately Richmond became mobs, the mobs became drunk, and formerly law-abiding citizens began the wholesale looting of the Confederate capital. They were drunk because they had discovered a source of free-flowing liquor: hundreds of barrels of whiskey that the army in its panicky last hours in the city had dumped. Soldiers had staved in the barrelheads and poured the liquid into the gutters, creating a river of alcohol for anyone — black, white, old, or young — who wanted to scoop it up. The gutters were ankle-deep with it.[16] Some people lapped it up with their tongues. Soon the streets were full of thousands of drunken pillagers, looting every store and warehouse, through the night and into the next morning. They also took the belongings of private citizens. Nothing — no one and no force — was there to stop them. They included the poor and the disreputable: escaped prisoners from the penitentiary, stragglers and deserters, riffraff from the bars and the whorehouses and people from the city's slums.

Another element on the streets had a different agenda. Prominent among the looters were slaves, suddenly and gloriously free in a city where the rule of law had completely disappeared. Richmond's wealthy, slave-owning white people, wrote black newsman T. M. Chester, were being "plundered by the people whom they meant to forever enslave." Chester, the only black correspondent for a major daily newspaper, described this aspect of the looting in a way that his white colleagues missed:

The leader of this system of public plundering was a colored man who carried upon his shoulder an iron crow-bar, and as a mark of distinguishment had a red piece of goods around his waist which reached down to his knees. The mob, for it could not with propriety be called anything else, followed him as their leader; moved on when he advanced, and rushed into every passage which was made by the leader with his crow-bar. Goods of every description were seized under these circumstances and personally appropriated by the supporters of an equal distribution of property.[17]

But the drinking and the looting were just the start of the most horrific night in the city's history. In addition to being told to dump liquor, Confederate soldiers had been ordered to destroy all weapons and commodities. The former made a good deal of military sense; the latter, which included the burning of tobacco, cotton, and flour stored in warehouses, did not. The order was egregiously stupid and horrendously destructive. The worst idea of all was to burn four large tobacco warehouses near the city's center. What advantage would destroying tobacco give Robert E. Lee's army? Was it meant to deny Union soldiers free tobacco for their pipes? Deny the immensely wealthy Union the sale of the tobacco? According to Richmond resident Sallie Brock, the tobacco warehouses, if ignited,

> were so situated as to jeopardize the entire commercial portion of Richmond. . . . Mayor Mayo had dispatched, by a committee of citizens, a remonstrance against this reckless military order. But in the mad excitement of the moment the protest was unheeded. The torch was applied, and the helpless citizens were left to witness the destruction of their property.[18]

As the warehouses burned, a strong southerly wind carried embers to the rest of the industrial and business district, and soon a large section of the city was ablaze. Explosive noises of beams snapping, walls collapsing, and roofs falling in rocked the city. The air was filled with flying bricks and broken glass. The earth-shaking detonations of artillery shells in the National Arsenal shattered windows and ripped doors from their hinges in the nearby neighborhood of Shockoe. In four more gigantic, reverberating blasts, Confederates blew up their hulking ironclad ships in the James River.[19] The great spire of the United Presbyterian Church caught fire, swayed precariously for an hour, then plummeted to the ground. All these sounds commingled with the shriek of whistles from departing trains and the shouting of street mobs, and the continuous explosions from the armories. Over four hours, an estimated one hundred thousand shells were detonated by fire. In the neighborhood of French Garden Hill, many of the residents — including most occupants of the city's poorhouse — were killed when a magazine blew up. The military had not bothered to tell them what it was doing.[20] Bridges, arsenals and armories, warehouses, banks, offices, churches, and ships on the river burned. Homes were burning, too. And that "immense crowd of plunderers" was everywhere, wrote Sallie Brock, "moving among the dense smoke like demons."[21]

Jefferson Davis and his cabinet — who left by train around midnight — and thousands of soldiers and citizens saw this blazing, infernal, apocalyptic Richmond on their way out of town. Former legislator Boteler wrote of his final view of the old city that night:

> The three bridges spanning the James River . . . were all on fire. Extensive fires were already raging in the western, central, and eastern sections of the city near the river, which seemed from the reflection to run red with blood. Vast volumes of lurid smoke rolled in billowy clouds across the crimson sky, "blotting out the stars" while innumerable sparks [were] whirling . . . and flakes of fire [were] falling on houses far and near.[22]

The first union infantrymen to enter the city of Richmond were black. Many were former slaves. This epic victory for African Americans was a superb irony and happened in spite of great efforts by white soldiers to prevent it.

At around four thirty the next morning, on the north side of the James River, federal soldiers realized that the deep and deadly Confederate fortifications guarding Richmond had been abandoned. The rebel army was gone. The Yankees, who had expected to fight their way into the city, instead picked their way through the earthworks, obstructions, minefields, and discarded cannons. By 7:00 a.m. they were beyond the fortifications and racing down four roads toward the city.[23]

They were all acutely conscious of what it would mean to be "the first troops into Richmond." They were imagining the stories they would tell for the rest of their lives if they got there first.*

Among them was a brigade of black soldiers consisting of the 36th, 22nd, and 38th regiments of the United States Colored Infantry. They were part of the all-black 25th Corps, and they were anything but ordinary. All three regiments had fought hard and well on the front lines and had suffered abnormally high casualty counts to prove it. (The 22nd had one of the most distinctive regimental battle flags in the army, bearing a detailed rendering of a black soldier mercilessly bayoneting a Confederate soldier.) In their ranks were four winners of the Medal of Honor. Like many black units, they were surprisingly diverse. The brigade included free blacks from New Jersey, slave-camp refugees from Hampton Roads, Virginia, and free black tenant farmers from Maryland. They were under the command of Brigadier General Alonzo Draper, a gung ho Massachusetts abolitionist and brilliant political speaker who had turned down command of white units to lead black troops. He and his men took an early lead in

* Some Union cavalry were in advance of the infantry, so the distinction of being "first" pertains to soldiers on foot.

503

the race but stopped at an intersection short of the city where the mayor tendered the city's surrender. Here one of the war's great scenes unfolded, as the black soldiers cheered and cried and danced and hugged each other at their great good fortune. The 36th's drum corps played "Yankee Doodle" and "Battle Cry of Freedom." Meanwhile Richmond's former slaves and freedmen gathered round them, awestruck by the splendidly equipped army and astounded that the soldiers were *black*. They cheered and hurrahed and waved hats in the air and cried, "You've come at last!" and "Jesus has opened the way!"[24]

Still, the city itself, the great national capital on a hill by the James River, lay unconquered, and a decision had to be made. Only one road led directly into the capital. Who would go first? That was easy: white men. Specifically Brigadier General Edward H. Ripley's brigade from the 24th Corps. Draper's black brigade was ordered to stand aside, and off the white soldiers went, dreaming of glory.

But Draper's men had no intention of giving up so easily. While Ripley's brigade pressed jubilantly forward toward the city, Draper's men took to nearby fields on the "double quick." They covered the three miles to downtown Richmond with such speed that they arrived far in advance of the white soldiers. "It was at least ten to fifteen minutes before a single white regiment came into sight," recalled Draper. "Some of the officers swore heartily at the presumption of the Negroes in outmarching them and entering the city first."[25] Reporter Chester, who was there, recorded the moment in his dispatch to the *Philadelphia Press:* "There may be others who may claim the distinction of being the first to enter the city, but as I was ahead of every part of the force but the cavalry . . . I know whereof I affirm when I announce that General Draper's brigade was the first organization to enter the city limits."[26] Though Ripley and others later contested this assertion, others saw it as cause for celebration. Major General Benjamin Butler described it as "divine retribution."

Chester, an activist from Pennsylvania who had once championed the idea of resettling American blacks in Africa, wrote that dispatch while sitting at the Speaker's desk in the Confederate House of Representatives. While he was writing his report, a paroled Confederate officer saw him, flew into a rage, and demanded that Chester leave the hall. When Chester continued calmly writing, the rebel officer rushed him. Chester met him with a punch that sent him reeling, then returned to the desk and continued writing. The rebel then asked a nearby Union officer for his sword. The officer refused but offered instead to clear an area in the House for a fistfight between the two men. The Confederate officer declined. Chester later wrote of his assault on the Confederate officer, which the day before would have resulted in the reporter's execution, "I thought I would exercise my rights as a belligerent."[27]

Here at last, in a city full of defenseless white women, were the demonic soldiers from a federal army that had allegedly raped, burned, and looted its way across Virginia, Mississippi, Georgia, and the Carolinas. To add to the horror, the Union legions now contained entire divisions of black soldiers, many of them former slaves who presumably burned for vengeance against their oppressors. Nothing, indeed, could stop the federal soldiers from doing whatever they pleased with the city, including treating it as they had much of the state of South Carolina. Many such cities in history — losers in long and bitter civil wars — were put to the sword or the torch, or both.

But instead of facing violence and fire and exile, this vanquished capital city of a slave-holding country was treated with kindness, humility, generosity, and forbearance. The Yankees were on their absolute best behavior. The city they entered was a burning wreck, full of smoke and scorched landscapes and fallen buildings, and they intended to save as much of it as possible. They were determined, too, to let residents know that they were not responsible for the fires and explosions. They did what they could to stop the flames from spreading. They secured food and water. They calmly processed captured Confederate officers and politely handled inquiries from ladies who came to ask for protection for their property. They posted sentinels in private homes and summarily disciplined Union soldiers who got drunk or rowdy.[28] When darkness fell, a brigade of soldiers picketed the city and roamed the suburbs. They enforced a strict curfew: no one, soldier or civilian, was allowed out on the streets after 9:00 p.m. In contrast to the mayhem of the night before, the city was calm, quiet, and orderly. One Richmond lady described the Yankees' behavior as exhibiting "lenity, respect, and even kindness." A Confederate officer later wrote that the occupation was conducted with "mutual understanding and respect."

If this was, historically speaking, strange behavior from the conquering army after a bitter war, stranger still was the unheralded arrival, the following day, of President Abraham Lincoln. He arrived by boat in the early afternoon of April 4, disembarking near the notorious Libby Prison into the ash- and rubble-strewn streets in a silk top hat and long black coat and flanked by a guard of only ten armed sailors. From the beginning of his visit, Lincoln courted immense danger. The steamboat on which he came, the *River*

Queen, had to dodge mines and sunken vessels on the way upstream, and he was eventually forced to take a barge powered by ten oarsmen.[29] But none of this seemed to bother Lincoln. He wanted to see Richmond, so he took the hand of his young son, Tad, and started walking.

He was not prepared for the reception he received on the city's streets. When he first arrived and word got out that "the president" had landed, there were cries of "Hang him!" "Hang him!" "Show him no quarter." Then the people realized *which president* had gotten off that boat, and everything changed. Lincoln had not gotten far when the city's black population, streaming forth from their humble homes and tar-paper shacks, surrounded him. They wept and cried for joy, reached out to touch his hand, but mainly they spoke to him as the man who had set them free. "Glory to God! Glory! Glory! Glory!" repeated one man. "Bless the Lord," others shouted out. "The Great Messiah! I knew him as soon as I saw him. He's in my heart for four long years. Come to free his children from bondage. Glory hallelujah!" Lincoln was uncomfortable with some of this religious adulation, and when one man fell on his knees before the president, Lincoln, looking down at the man, said, "Don't kneel to me. That is not right. You must kneel to God only, and thank Him for the liberty you

508

will enjoy hereafter." Lincoln was right that the blacks would no longer be slaves. Just exactly what they would be was unknown. Many were headed for homeless poverty, for an unfriendly climate and a deeply prejudiced world where those without trade skills faced terribly hard lives.

Most of the crowd was black, and most of the white people hid in their homes, peering out through drawn curtains. But some whites did emerge to celebrate Lincoln's visit. One white teenage girl pushed her way through the crowd and gave Lincoln a bouquet of roses with the message "From Eva to the Liberator of the slaves." A white woman stood by the road prominently waving a Union flag.[30]

Journalist and abolitionist Charles C. Coffin captured the scene best, in the *Boston Journal:*

No written page or illuminated canvas can give the reality of the event — the enthusiastic bearing of the people — the blacks and poor whites who have suffered untold horrors during the war, their demonstrations of pleasure, the shouting, the dancing, the thanksgiving to God, the mention of the name of Jesus — as if President Lincoln were next to the son of God in their affections — the jubilant cries, the countenances

509

beaming with unspeakable joy, the tossing up of caps . . ."[31]

After a mile or so Lincoln was met by a squad of cavalry under the commander of occupied Richmond, Godfrey Weitzel, and escorted to the Confederate White House, which had become the Union's military headquarters. Lincoln seemed anything but elated. He looked tired, wan. He sat down in Jefferson Davis's chair without any particular expression of happiness or relief and requested a glass of water. "There was no triumph in his gesture or attitude," wrote Captain John S. Barnes, who had accompanied Lincoln from the boat. "He lay back in the chair like a tired man whose nerves had carried him beyond his strength." He was so exhausted that, stepping outside onto a balcony to greet the large, cheering crowd that had gathered in the street, he only bowed and did not speak.[32]

Most of the news in the Civil War moved slowly, sometimes shockingly so.

Not this time.

Just before 11:00 a.m. on April 3, Weitzel sent a wire to the War Department in Washington, dated at Richmond, announcing the fall of the rebel capital. The news was so astounding that many simply did not believe it. They were soon enlightened by a series of

War Department bulletins, which found their way into thousands of copies of newspaper extras that were hawked on every corner of Washington. "In a moment of time the city was ablaze with excitement the like of which was never seen before," wrote Noah Brooks, the correspondent for the *Sacramento Daily Union.* "Everybody who had a piece of bunting spread it to the breeze; from one end of Pennsylvania Avenue to the other the air seemed to burn with the bright hues of the flag. The sky was shaken by a grand salute of eight hundred guns."[33]

Soon crowds filled the streets, and everywhere there was laughing and hurrahing and hallooing; men embraced each other, hats were thrown high in the air, songs were sung, parades organized. Black and white, the fraternizing went on. One Vermont man stood on a corner giving out fifty-cent "shinplasters" (paper currency) to every black person who passed, earnestly repeating, "Babylon has fallen." Bands paraded the streets, playing whatever came to mind, including "Yankee Doodle" and "Rally 'Round the Flag," but also "Dixie," until the streets were a great cacophony of shouting and church bells and colliding melodies. There was drinking, too. Prodigious amounts of it.

Mostly, though, people wanted to hear speeches. They wanted to seize the moment and the joy and not let go, and the only way they could do that was by hearing it captured in words. Observed Brooks:

> The American habit of speech-making was never before so consciously exemplified. Wherever a man was found who could make a speech, or who thought he could make a speech, there a speech was made; and a great many men who had never before made one found themselves thrust upon a crowd of enthusiastic sovereigns who demanded something of them by way of jubilant oratory.[34]

Since the fun and jubilation and relief could not be contained in a single day, the celebrations continued into the following evening, when the entire city was alight with illuminations and fireworks of every sort. The great flag-draped government buildings swam in vast eddies of light. At the Corcoran Art Gallery, the opening notes of "The Star-Spangled Banner" were the signal for men, stationed in every window of the building, to light the gas jets, creating, in a time before electricity, a decidedly electric effect, while citizens, beside themselves with joy and relief, continued to drink and sing and dance well into the night.[35]

In a speech by Secretary of War Edwin Stanton, he implored God "to teach us to be humble in the midst of triumph." Everyone applauded this nice sentiment. Though the crowd could not have known it, this spirit was in play in the streets of Richmond at that very moment.

Others, though, when they heard that Richmond was on fire, said simply, "Let her burn."[36]

Chapter Twenty-One: This Bitter Glory

UNION SOLDIERS AT APPOMATTOX COURT HOUSE: *Legends of Union and Confederate troops fraternizing and putting away their bitterness and hatred were just that.*

The great war of the rebellion had been reduced to a footrace. Robert E. Lee had pulled his men out of their earthworks in Petersburg and Richmond and directed them westward toward some new version of the war that no one could yet imagine. They had an eight-hour lead. An army in flight is an ugly thing, lacking its protocols, its formations, its habits of duty and rhythms of march, its sense of purpose. "We moved on in disorder," wrote a North Carolina captain, "keeping no regular column, no regular pace. When a soldier became weary he fell out, ate his scanty rations — if, indeed, he had any to eat — rested, rose, and resumed the march when his inclination dictated. There were not many words spoken. An indescribable sadness weighed upon us."[1] Existence had been reduced to two imperatives: flee, survive.

The rebels at first moved in darkness through a shifting landscape: flat expanses of farm fields, elevated ridges with agonizingly steep slopes, groves of dense forest and underbrush, streams that had flooded their banks, and in the lowlands and river bottoms an endless expanse of mud. Sometimes the road was wide and welcoming; sometimes so narrow an ammunition wagon could barely pass. Bridges were hit-or-miss. The men were cut and scratched, filthy beyond measure, sodden, many of them shoeless. They pressed forward in four columns, stacked north to south between the James and Appomattox Rivers in a band twenty miles across. They were acutely aware that Ulysses S. Grant's great Army of the Potomac, with its promise of death, maiming, or capture, was moving in the wide, rolling country behind them. Already the cavalry of Lee's rear guard and advance Union cavalry units under the command of George Armstrong Custer were fighting. For nine months these rebels had inhabited the dark cloisters of their armored fortifications in Richmond and Petersburg, where they had lived as vermin in dug-out ratholes. Now that world of boundaries had disappeared. They were running free.

Lee's plan was to reunite his army in the village of Amelia Court House, a stop on the Richmond and Danville Railroad about forty miles west of Richmond. There his columns would pick up badly needed rations, then swing south and west along the line of the railroad, always staying ahead of the lead elements of the Army of the Potomac. In that direction lay salvation, or what passed for it in these desperate hours: Joe Johnston's army of twenty thousand, one hundred miles away in North Carolina. There Lee would reorganize and rearm, unite the armies, and stand against Grant, or Sherman, or both. That was the plan. To make it work Lee had to win the race. Grant's objective mirrored Lee's: cut the Confederates off at the Richmond and Danville Railroad, thus preventing their union with Johnston.

Lee arrived at Amelia Court House at midday on April 4 ahead of the five Union infantry corps and cavalry that were chasing him. But his lead was rapidly shrinking. His scattered units had suffered critical delays, mostly from flooding. Just east of the town the rebel columns were supposed to cross the swollen Appomattox River in three places. But the major crossing had been washed out, and pontoons to build a makeshift bridge had never arrived. At another crossing the approaches were swamped. Traffic in some places was funneled down narrow roads to a single bridge. Time was lost. So much that more than a third of Lee's army did not arrive until the following morning.

Adding to these delays was a calamitous logistical mistake. Lee had expected to find 350,000 rations for his famished army waiting at Amelia Court House. But instead of food were boxcars full of ammunition and harnesses. Not a scrap of bacon or cornmeal. Foraging parties had to be sent into the countryside, causing further delay.*

What those failures meant became apparent the following morning, April 5. Lee learned that Sheridan's cavalry along with

* William Marvel in *Lee's Last Retreat: The Flight to Appomattox* (pp. 49ff) makes a convincing argument that the failure at the bridge crossings — as opposed to the failure of the rations — was the main cause of delay since much of Lee's army was not yet even at Amelia Court House on April 4.

UNION PURSUIT OF LEE'S ARMY FROM PETERSBURG AND RICHMOND TO APPOMATTOX, APRIL 1865

Norfolk & Petersburg R.R.

Weldon R.R.

Richmond

Petersburg

1865

James R.

Richmond & Danville R.R.

Appomattox R.

Southside R.R.

FIVE FORKS
April 1

AMELIA SPRINGS
April 5

Sailors?

SAILOR'S CREEK
April 6

Farmville

Richmond & Danville R.R.

VIRGINIA

APPOMATTOX COURT HOUSE
April 8-9

James R.

Lynchburg

0 Miles   20

0 Kilometers   20

Union advance

Confederate retreat

Battle

© 2019 Jeffrey L. Ward

Dec P 189

the entire Union 6th Corps had already occupied Jetersville, the next stop south on the Richmond and Danville line. The Yankees were dug in athwart the railroad line, guns up and battle flags flying. Lee's escape route was now blocked. He would have to head due west, toward Lynchburg, down vastly inferior roads. The great hope that had resided in the unpaved streets of Amelia Court House was gone. Certainly the Union high command thought so. "I feel confident of capturing the Army of Northern Virginia if we exert ourselves," a buoyant Sheridan wired Grant. "I see no escape for Lee."

Still more unsettling to rebel generals was their vanishing army. The fights at Petersburg had caused large numbers of casualties. Now men were deserting at record rates. The Army of Northern Virginia was melting away, especially in the corps commanded by Major General Richard H. Anderson, the army's rear guard. George Pickett's division, one of the army's largest, had lost more than half its men after the fighting on April 1 and 2, many to desertion. One of the best — and worst — examples of what was taking place inside the rebel army was Brigadier General William Wallace's brigade of six South Carolina regiments. As of March 1, it numbered 1,969, respectable strength for a late-war brigade. Wallace had suffered large losses in fights at Fort Stedman on March 25 and at Quaker

Road on March 29. By April 2, Wallace reported to his division commander with a mere 350 men. Where were the others? Most were casualties. Some 300 were lost or straggling. But another 470 had walked away. Eventually those men would either surrender or disappear into the woods. As fighting men they were lost forever to Richard H. Anderson, Robert E. Lee, and the Army of Northern Virginia.[2] Between March 25 and April 9 the Army of Northern Virginia would lose at least 14,400 and perhaps as many as 20,400 troops to desertion.[3]

So the sleepless, hungry, bone-weary rebels were running again, this time toward another place nobody had ever heard of — Farmville — where eighty thousand rations supposedly awaited them. This time everything was worse, more hopeless. The marching was harder. Men plodded down muddy roads that had been churned into a deep, gelatinous ooze. Officers who had not slept for three nights issued nonsensical commands, realizing only later how irrational they had been. Roads merged and diverged and confused everyone; sometimes the army was marching *east,* away from its destination. Men who had fought bravely in the toughest battles of the war sank to their knees, lay down in fields, or simply drifted away from their units in the vague hope of finding food or sleep or safety. They gnawed flower buds off tree branches. As they retreated, they left behind the now-familiar detritus of a used-up army: discarded muskets and bedrolls, empty cartridge boxes, abandoned wagons and ambulances. In this condition, strung out for miles, with an enemy racing up from its southern flank, the army was appallingly vulnerable. They could do nothing about it. Digging in was no longer an option.

Nor was there any relief from Union attacks. Major General Andrew A. Humphreys's 2nd Corps pitched into the Confederate rear in a series of savage little fights that served as reminders of what would happen if the rebels slowed or stopped. "[The attacks went] on and on, hour after hour, from hilltop to hilltop," wrote rebel major general John B. Gordon, commanding the rear. "The lines were alternately forming, fighting, and retreating, making one almost continuously shifting battle."[4] While Humphreys pressed from behind, Sheridan's cavalry and infantry hit the rebels' flank, looking for an opening, searching for a way to cut the line in two, to isolate fragments of the army and destroy them.

In the afternoon of April 6 Sheridan found that opening. In three separate engagements in proximity at Sailor's Creek, Union troops tore into the Confederate column. Sheridan's cavalry surged through gaps in the rebel lines, and many Confederate soldiers suddenly found themselves surrounded. The result was rout, and ruin. Rebel losses were staggering: two thousand casualties and six thousand prisoners. Lee, who viewed from high ground the wreckage in the narrow valley below him — men driving teams of horses without wagons, their traces flapping in the air, hatless and weaponless men moving in "harmless mob" — exclaimed, as though talking to himself, "My God! Has the army been dissolved?"

"No, General," answered Major General William Mahone, who was standing next to him. "Here are troops ready to do their duty."

"Yes," Lee said in a softer voice. "There are some true men left."[5]

But not nearly enough.

Somehow Lee won the race to Farmville. Rations were dispensed. Men built fires, ate, and rested. But their respite was cruelly brief. One of their generals had neglected to blow up a bridge, which meant that the lead units of Grant's army were only four miles away, so near that cavalry were already fighting in the town's streets. So the rebels ran again. In the early evening of April 7, not Lee but Grant was sitting on the veranda of a Farmville hotel watching his soldiers march by in the town's bonfire-lit streets while band music floated on the smoky air. His men were almost jumpy with excitement. When they realized that Grant was on the porch, they instantly erupted, waving torches made from brands, cheering and screaming. During the march west they had been pushed to the limits of their physical endurance. Entire divisions had marched without food.[6] When they were allowed short breaks, the men collapsed in place and fell asleep. Still, many leaped and shouted in the firelight anyway in front of the humble-looking man in the rumpled coat who watched them cross out of town, out of the firelight, and into the cottony darkness above the Appomattox River.

Grant was on the porch when he received a message from Sheridan that Lee's men were hastening to a small town called Appomattox Junction, where rations awaited them. Sheridan said he believed he could get there first, and when Sheridan believed something would happen, it generally happened. If he won that race, Union troops would be on both sides of Lee's army. Lee would be boxed in. Grant immediately gave orders to the Army of the James, under Major General Edward Ord, and the 24th Corps, under Major General John Gibbon, to join Sheridan. Was this the end? Grant wondered. He turned to Gibbon and said, "I have a great mind to summon Lee to surrender."

Thus began the most interesting military correspondence of the war. Grant called for his dispatch book and wrote:

General R. E. Lee
Commanding C. S. Army
General: The results of the last week must convince you of the hopelessness of further resistance on the part of the Army of Northern Virginia in this struggle. I feel it is so, and regard it as my duty to shift from myself the responsibility of any further effusion of blood by asking of you the surrender of that portion of the Confederate States army known as the Army of Northern Virginia.

Very respectfully, your obedient servant,
U. S. Grant, Lieutenant General
Commanding Armies of the United
States

Grant sent the letter under a flag of truce to Lee, who received it around ten o'clock that night. Lee read Grant's letter and handed it to James Longstreet, who read it, handed the paper back, and said, "Not yet." Lee agreed, but added that the letter "must be answered." It is noteworthy that, considering their circumstances, and that prolonging the fight would send thousands more men to their deaths, both men so readily agreed to refuse Grant's proposal. Lee did not yet know that Sheridan was in position to beat the rebel army to Appomattox Junction. Still, one wonders what advantage Lee was hoping to gain. Indeed, advantages could be lost if he was forced to surrender on the battlefield. Longstreet himself wrote of that same dismal night, "Broken down caissons and wagons abandoned and sometimes not even pulled out of the road before they were fired. . . . One of my battery commanders reported his horses too weak to haul his guns."

Lee's reply to Grant was a minor masterpiece of nuance and ambiguity that both closed the door and left it open:

Genl:
I have received your note of this date. Though not entertaining the opinion you express of the hopelessness of further resistance of the Army of N. Va — I reciprocate your desire to avoid the useless effusion of blood, & therefore before considering your proposition, ask the terms you will offer on condition of its surrender.

Very respy your obt. Servt
R. E. Lee, Genl

Grant received Lee's response later that night and answered it the next morning, taking six hours to compose it:

In reply I would say that, peace being my great desire, there is but one condition I

525

would insist upon, viz., that the men and officers surrendered shall be disqualified from taking up arms against the Government of the United States until properly exchanged. I will meet you or will designate officers to meet any officers you may name for the same purpose, at any point agreeable to you, for the purpose of definitely arranging the terms upon which the surrender of the Army of Northern Virginia will be received.

This was far from the "unconditional surrender" Grant had demanded at Fort Donelson and Vicksburg and for which he was justly famous. He was being as generous as he felt he could be. He was writing, and thinking, in the spirit of Abraham Lincoln. If the rebels laid down their arms, they would be free to return to their homes. He had offered to let Lee avoid personal embarrassment by designating others to arrange the surrender. Lee got the message in the late afternoon of April 8 while he was planning to provision his army for a continued retreat. He had even spoken of another major assault, saying of his adversary, "I will strike that man a blow in the morning."

Most of his generals no longer thought that the old reptile instinct of the Army of Northern Virginia — when threatened, attack — was a good idea. That same afternoon half a dozen of them had held a private meeting and decided that the only reasonable course for their army was surrender. They were understandably edgy about putting this to the boss, who was in a foul humor. So they chose Major General W. N. Pendleton, Lee's trusted artillerist, a West Pointer who before the war had been an Episcopal priest, to tell Lee, as Pendleton put it later, that "in our united judgment the cause had become so hopeless we thought it was wrong longer to be having men killed on either side."[7]

Lee, whose army was steadily being engulfed by an ocean of blue and who was probably outnumbered five to one, snapped back, as though the idea were ridiculous:

Surrender? I trust it has not come to that! We certainly have too many brave men to think of laying down our arms. They still fight with great spirit whereas the enemy does not. Besides, if I were to intimate to General Grant that I would listen to terms, he would at once regard it as such an evidence of weakness that he would demand unconditional surrender. And sooner than that I am resolved to die. Indeed, we must all determine to die at our posts.[8]

Though Lee seemed at this moment to be living in an alternate reality, his reply to Grant was measured and diplomatic:

Genl

I received at a late hour your note of today. In mine of yesterday I did not intend to propose the surrender of the Army of N. Va. — but to ask the terms of your proposition. To be frank, I do not think the emergency has arisen to call for the surrender of this Army, but as the restoration of peace should be the sole object of all, I desire to know whether your proposals would lead to that and I cannot therefor meet you with a view to surrender . . . but as far as your proposal may affect the C. S. [Confederate States] forces under my command & tend to the restoration of peace, I shall be pleased to meet you at 10 A.M. tomorrow on the old state road to Richmond between the picket lines of the two armies.

Lee, who refused to surrender his army, was nonetheless ready to talk about the loftier subject of an overall peace between the two nations. Grant, who received the note at midnight while nursing a throbbing migraine, wanted nothing to do with such a conversation. As Grant saw it — correctly — he was not authorized to talk about anything but the surrender of the Army of Northern Virginia. If he was disappointed by Lee's response, Grant's aide John Rawlins was furious, arguing that Lee was only bargaining for time, looking for a way out. As Grant read the letter, he shook his head and said to Rawlins, "It looks like Lee means to fight." Grant was right. But Lee did not yet know what Grant had just learned — that Sheridan's cavalry was already to the west of the rebel army at Appomattox Station, where he had taken prisoners, captured four freight trains loaded with Confederate rations, and seized a number of guns. The divisions of the old Army of the James were on their way to meet him. The head of Lee's army was only a few miles away, at Appomattox Court House.

Grant sent his reply the next morning:

GENERAL: Your note of yesterday is received. I have no authority to treat on the subject of peace; the meeting proposed for 10 A.M. today could lead to no good. I will state, however, General, that I am equally anxious for peace with yourself, and the whole North entertains the same feeling. The terms upon which peace can be had are well understood. By the South laying down arms they will hasten the most desirable event, save thousands of human lives, and hundreds of millions [of dollars] of property not yet destroyed. Seriously hoping that all our difficulties may be settled without the loss of another life, I subscribe myself, etc.,

U. S. GRANT, LIEUTENANT GENERAL

As Grant was writing this, still suffering from his migraine, pressing his hands to his temples in pain, a rebel force under Major General John B. Gordon was doing the only thing left to them: trying to cut their way out through Union lines. It was 5:00 a.m. on Sunday, April 9. Hours and minutes mattered now. Following Lee's orders, Gordon's 2nd Corps, along with cavalry under Lee's nephew Fitz Lee, advanced into the fog and half-light. They scrambled forward and rolled out the old rebel yell as though it were not the last hope of an overmatched and beaten army. Perhaps to their surprise, in this moment of frenzied desperation, these astoundingly brave men from one of the greatest armies in history broke through once again, sweeping the road of Yankees, seizing artillery, advancing to the top of a ridge. There, breathless and in the first flush of victory, they saw what was really waiting for them: in the woods and fields below them thirty thousand men in Union uniforms were stacked in columns two miles wide. Directly in front the rebel soldiers, moving inexorably toward them, was the end of everything. The rebels fought anyway. For what? Honor? Gordon's pride? They were no longer saving the

Confederacy, and they all must have known that. Three hours later Gordon sent a note to Lee that made the obvious official: "I have fought my corps to a frazzle, and I fear I can do nothing." After Lee had read that, he came to the full and final understanding that he was trapped and told his staff, "There is nothing left for me to do but go and see Grant," he said, "and I would rather die a thousand deaths."

Lee met with Generals James Longstreet, William Mahone, and Edward Porter Alexander. The topic was surrender. Alexander, one of Lee's favorite subordinates, suggested that instead of giving up the army might disperse into the woods and hills and continue the war as guerrillas. Jefferson Davis favored this idea and had mentioned it in several speeches, most recently on April 4. This was Grant's, Sherman's, and Lincoln's worst nightmare: a war without end. "We would be like rabbits or partridges in the bushes," said Alexander, "and they could not scatter to follow us." John Singleton Mosby's raiders offered a plausible working model. So, unfortunately, did the depredations of outlaw guerrillas such as William Quantrill and Bloody Bill Anderson in Missouri, where both Unionists and rebel sympathizers had for much of the war butchered one another.

Lee listened carefully, thought about it, and replied:

531

Then, General, you and I as Christian men have no right to consider only how this would affect us. We must consider its effect on the country as a whole. Already it is demoralized by the four years of war. If I took your advice, the men would be without rations and under no control of officers. They would be compelled to rob and steal in order to live. They would become mere bands of marauders, and the enemy's cavalry would pursue them and overrun many wide sections they may never have occasion to visit. We would bring on a state of affairs it would take the country years to recover from.[9]

In a long life filled with many achievements, some of them glorious, this was perhaps Lee's finest moment. He was going against the spoken wishes of his president and the convictions of many of his officers. Fortunately for the South and for the country as a whole, Lee, not Davis, wielded true authority. Lee could not predict his own fate. But he could help determine the immediate fate of his country. He could spare many lives and endless anguish. There would be no guerrilla war in Virginia. He would surrender.

Lee, who had not yet received Grant's letter saying he had no authority "to treat on the subject of peace," rode out with his staff to his picket lines, where he believed he had a 10:00 a.m. appointment with the Union general. But instead of Grant himself, a federal staff officer arrived, professed confusion about any scheduled meeting between the two commanding generals, and instead handed Lee Grant's letter. Lee immediately dictated his reply:

GENERAL: I received your note of this morning on the picket line, whither I had come to meet you and ascertain definitely what terms were embraced in your proposition of yesterday with reference to the surrender of this army. I now request an interview in accordance with the offer contained in your letter of yesterday for that purpose.

Realizing that the Union army was about to renew its attack, Lee dictated another note to Grant requesting a cease-fire, then mounted his horse, Traveller, and rode back to his camp. He was wearing full dress attire: his general's uniform with a red sash, engraved sword, and thread gloves. "I have probably to be General Grant's prisoner today," he told his staff, "and I thought I must make my best appearance."[10]

Events moved quickly now. No one was interested in waiting. It was all Grant could do to keep his attack dog, Phil Sheridan, from encircling the pathetic remnants of Lee's army and finishing them off for good. Any sign of bad faith or dilatory tactics or second thoughts on the part of the rebels would instantly trigger a massively violent response. "Damn them!" Sheridan had said, hearing of the truce. "I wish they had held out an hour longer and I would have whipped the hell out of them." Making a tightly clenched fist, he added, "I've got 'em! I've got 'em like that!"

At 1:00 p.m. Robert E. Lee and his aide Colonel Charles Marshall were escorted through Union lines and into the home of Wilmer McLean, in the middle of the tiny town of Appomattox Court House. Four years earlier McLean had lived near Manassas Junction, where his house had served as Confederate headquarters during the First Battle of Bull Run until a well-placed Yankee artillery shell had wrecked it. So McLean had moved 150 miles south to this somnolent crossroads where, surely, the war would not find him. At 1:30 p.m. Ulysses S. Grant mounted the stairs, followed by Sheridan, Ord, Rawlins, and other staff members, and entered the house.

The contrast between the two generals was startling: the patrician Lee, of the first families of Virginia, straight-backed in an immaculate gray uniform; and the ever-unimpressive Grant, son of a tanner, in a faded coat, mud-splashed private's shirt, and muddy pants tucked into muddy boots. His appearance was as unfortunate as it was unintentional. His baggage had been lost and he had nothing else to wear. He had worried that Lee would see the dirty uniform as a sign of disrespect. The two men shook hands and conversed quietly for a few minutes, remembering their meeting in Mexico two decades before. The conversation was so pleasant that Grant — whose migraine had disappeared — seemed to momentarily forget the reason for the meeting.

Lee, changing the subject, said quietly, "I suppose, General Grant, that the object of our present meeting is fully understood. I asked to see you to ascertain upon what terms you would receive the surrender of my army."

Grant replied, "The terms I propose are those stated substantially in my letter of yesterday, that is, the officers and men surrendered are to be paroled and disqualified from taking up arms again until properly exchanged, and all arms, ammunition, and supplies to be delivered up as captured property."

Grant expressed his hope that this would lead to the end of hostilities and the loss of lives, and Lee suggested that Grant write the terms out.

Grant summoned his order book, lit a pipe,

thought for a long moment, and began writing.

Fortunately his head was already full of words. They had been put there by Abraham Lincoln, who, over two days of informal meetings in late March with Grant, Sherman, and Admiral David Dixon Porter aboard the *River Queen* at City Point, had articulated his version of peace. Unlike many other heads of state after bitter civil wars — France in the wake of its 1789 revolution comes to mind — Lincoln was convinced that the peace should not start with vengeance, retaliation, and military inquisitions. The victors should be stern, yes, but also generous and forgiving. "Let them once surrender and reach their homes, they won't take up arms again," Lincoln told his generals. "Let them all go, officers and all. I want submission and no more bloodshed. Let them have their horses to plow with, and if you like, their guns to shoot crows with. I want no one punished. Treat them liberally all round. We want those people to return to their allegiance to the Union and submit to the laws. Again I say, give them the most liberal and honorable terms."[11]

Grant did that now. With Lincoln's exhortation still ringing in his head, he wrote out one of the more extraordinary documents of military surrender in recorded history. When he finished, he gave it to Lee, who read it intently, pausing to make suggestions for minor changes as he went along. When Grant asked him if that was satisfactory, Lee replied, "Yes, I am bound to be satisfied by anything you offer. It is more than I expected." It was more than most of Lee's officers expected, too. Many believed they would be sent to prison camps. Edward Porter Alexander thought it likely that they would be paraded through the streets of Northern cities. Then the document was handed over to be officially transcribed, by Ely Parker, a Seneca Indian engineer and diplomat. Lee had commented upon meeting him, "I am glad to see one real American here," to which Parker had replied, "We are all Americans."

The document read:

APPOMATTOX COURT-HOUSE, VA.
April 9, 1865

General R. E. LEE:
    In accordance with the substance of my letter to you of the 8th instant, I propose to receive the surrender of the Army of Northern Virginia on the following terms, to wit: Rolls of all the officers and men to be made in duplicate, one copy to be given to an officer to be designated by me, the other to be retained by such officer or officers as you may designate. The officers to give their individual paroles

not to take up arms against the Government of the United States until properly exchanged; and each company or regimental commander sign a like parole for the men of their commands. The arms, artillery, and public property to be parked and stacked, and turned over to the officers appointed by me to receive them. This will not embrace the side-arms of the officers, nor their private horses or baggage. This done, each officer and man will be allowed to return to his home, not to be disturbed by U. S. authority so long as they observe their paroles and the laws in force where they may reside.

U.S. GRANT,
Lieutenant-General

In the final sentence Grant contrived to venture beyond the limits of negotiation imposed upon him and to fully embrace the spirit of what Lincoln had said on the *River Queen.* It meant that no Confederate officers or soldiers — including Lee — would be imprisoned or prosecuted for treason. No lingering lists would be made of traitors or state enemies to be tried and executed or imprisoned. There would, in effect, be a general amnesty.

"This will have a very happy effect upon my army," said Lee, after reviewing it.

Only one more item remained to be dis-

538

cussed, one that Grant, because of the nature of the army he commanded, could not have foreseen. Lee pointed out that in the rebel army cavalrymen and artillerists owned their own horses. He wondered if they might be allowed to keep them. Grant was surprised by this. The idea had never occurred to him. He decided not to rewrite the surrender but instead offered an unofficial accommodation: "I will arrange it this way. I will not change the terms as now written, but I will instruct the officers I shall appoint . . . to let all the men who claim to own a horse take the animals home with them to their little farms."

While federal officers grabbed everything they could lay hands on in the McLean house as souvenirs, Lee was escorted back to his campsite.* As he rode up the hill, a few men whooped and cheered at first, then as they

---

* The Union officers basically took everything that wasn't nailed down, including candlesticks and a doll belonging to McLean's daughter. Some of it they paid for; other items were simply stolen. Wilmer McLean was generally happy to take their money, though his family would later dispute this claim. General Edward Ord got the marble-topped table where Lee had sat. Sheridan, who got the table on which Grant wrote out the terms of the surrender, gave it to George Armstrong Custer's wife, Libbie, as a tribute to her husband's bravery. Horace Porter, who had lent Lee a pencil, kept it as a souvenir. Ely

realized what had happened, the cheers began to multiply and suddenly thousands of soldiers, the survivors of a long war, were cheering deliriously for the gray man on horseback. The cheers were so loud they were audible on the porch of the McLean house, several miles away. There were tears in Lee's eyes as he rode, and many of the hurrahs for him rapidly gave way to sobs.

The following day Grant asked for another meeting with Lee. Grant had followed orders in limiting his negotiations to the surrender of the Army of Northern Virginia, but now that he had the agreement, he felt free to explore a larger objective, if only informally. At nine o'clock on April 10 Grant and a number of staff officers rode to a rise overlooking the Confederate camp, and a few minutes later Lee joined them, alone and unattended. The two men shook hands, then walked away from the group to speak privately. What we know of this less celebrated meeting comes secondhand, from confidants of Lee's and Grant's. The two versions are quite different, though they agree on Grant's overall objective.

In Grant's version, channeled through journalist and author John Russell Young, he

---

Parker kept one of the copies of the surrender terms. See Varon, *Appomattox,* p. 89.

tried to persuade Lee "to use his influence with the people of the South . . . to bring the war to an end." Lee pointed out that his army was the only one capable of making a stand. Said Grant, "I told Lee that this fact only made his responsibility greater, and any further war would be a crime." Grant asked Lee to persuade the South to have all men under arms surrender on the same terms Grant had given the Army of Northern Virginia. In the Grant/Young version, Lee declined, saying he "would not move without [Jefferson] Davis."[12]

Lee's version of the story, rendered through his aide Charles Marshall, featured a more elaborate request.[13] Grant told Lee that he wanted him to meet with President Lincoln. "If you and Mr. Lincoln will agree upon terms," Grant said, "your influence in the South will make the Southern people accept what you accept, and Mr. Lincoln's influence in the North will make reasonable people of the North accept what he accepts, and my influence will be added to Mr. Lincoln's." In this telling, Lee, though pleased by the offer, had to decline, as Grant had before, to speak on behalf of his country, noting, "General Grant, you know that I am a soldier of the Confederacy and cannot meet Lincoln. I do not know what Mr. Davis is going to do, and I cannot undertake to make any terms of that kind." Lee faced an intricate problem: more than 150,000 Confederates remained under arms, from Texas to the Carolinas, none of them had surrendered to anyone, and Jefferson Davis and his cabinet were on the run. (In a letter to Davis ten days later, Lee tried to do what Grant had requested: persuade Davis to give up.)

For now Grant had only put an end to the war in Virginia. As he rode back to his headquarters tent, General Horace Porter asked him if he thought it might not be a good idea to tell people in Washington about the surrender. Grant replied that he had forgotten all about that and dashed off a telegram for Secretary of War Edwin Stanton. The text was perfectly Grant-like. If he wasn't exactly crowing, it was because the war wasn't exactly over:

> General Lee surrendered the Army of Northern Virginia this afternoon on terms proposed by myself. The accompanying additional correspondence will show the conditions fully.
>
> U. S. GRANT,
> LIEUTENANT GENERAL

The events at Appomattox have given rise to many legends. One of the most enduring is that, once the rebel soldiers laid down their arms, soldiers on both sides somehow momentarily forgot their pain and bitterness and suffering and for a brief time brotherhood and mutual respect became the order of the day. In this version, the Yankees saw the rebels as honorable and admirable men who had fought on after all hope was lost, and the rebels saw their foes as magnanimous and humble in victory. Both sides wanted to see themselves this way. Despite moments of genuine goodwill, such characterizations were for the most part false, as were the anecdotes that were deployed to support them.

There was instead a good deal of hostility. Many of the men who cheered Lee and rallied around him when he returned from the McLean house told him that they would fight again for him. Many of them believed it. Up until the surrender, talk on the picket lines had been bitter. Men who were ready to be friends did not talk that way. Nor did the federals refrain from indulging in what might be called exulting and in-your-face triumphalism. When news of the surrender first spread through the ranks, federal artillery near the village of Appomattox Court House began to fire salutes. Grant put a stop to this, reminding his staff that he did not "want them to exult over [the rebels'] downfall." The story of Grant's decency, and this generous gesture, was often told. But his order to desist did not get through to tens of thousands of soldiers with General George G.

Meade a few miles away. These men fell instantly into wild celebration, gunners included. Meade himself went galloping down the road with a squad of cavalry behind him, whooping and waving his hat, while the big guns boomed victory salutes over and over and the air turned black with hats, boots, coats, knapsacks, cartridge boxes, and anything else the soldiers could find to throw. The Union men did not, as one hoary legend had it, walk through rebel camps giving away the contents of their haversacks to the starving johnnies.[14] Instead the Union men danced and screamed and shot their big guns into the air while their bands played "The Star-Spangled Banner" and "Marching Along." They sang "Old Hundredth," a Christian hymn celebrating the blessings of God, which included, at this moment, the demise of the rebel cause.

The closest thing to real fraternization occurred at the second meeting of Lee and Grant, when generals who had accompanied Grant, including Phil Sheridan, were granted permission to enter the rebel camp to find old army friends. They returned in the company of several Confederate generals, including James Longstreet and John B. Gordon, who wanted to meet Grant. Though most of these introductions were stiff and somewhat formal, Grant did manage a kind word for his old friend Longstreet, whom Grant had last seen at that dark moment in his life when he was selling firewood on the streets of St. Louis. Taking Longstreet by the arm, the man who now led the most powerful army in the world said, "Pete, let's have another game of brag to recall the old days."

For the most part, the events at Appomattox Court House — apart from the behavior of Grant and Lee — were neither graceful nor especially honorable. After the surrender General John B. Gordon delivered a defiant rant whose central idea was that his soldiers had not been beaten in a fair fight. They had not really been defeated. They had been forced to give up because they had been outnumbered seven to one by an army with vastly superior resources and ammunition. Other Confederate generals told their troops versions of the same thing: they had lost for reasons far beyond their control. The Union soldiers had not won because of their bravery or fighting skill. They had simply been on the side with the most numbers. None of this smacked of reconciliation.★

The surrender ceremony itself was a minor disaster. Grant and Lee had appointed a "sur-

★ The best-researched debunking of the various Appomattox myths is to be found in William Marvel's definitive Lee's Last Retreat: The Flight to Appomattox. I have generally followed his approach in this section.

render commission" of generals (Longstreet, Gordon, and Pendleton, for the South, Merritt, Gibbon, and Charles Griffin for the North) to oversee the actual surrender. The generals had agreed that the rebel soldiers would march to the center of the tiny town of Appomattox Court House the following morning, stack their weapons and their battle flags, and turn over government-owned horses and mules. This covered about twenty-eight thousand rebels, all that were left after casualties, desertions, and men captured, of the fifty thousand who had left Petersburg and Richmond a week before. (That number did not include the more than six thousand prisoners taken at Sailor's Creek on April 6.)

Nothing of the sort happened. The Union soldiers arrived and stood in ranks to witness the transfer of arms, but not a single rebel showed up. The afternoon passed and the day ended with no sign of Confederate soldiers. Where were they? They were defying the orders of the surrender commission. General Gordon, whose job was to bring the men in to give up their arms, had decided that they would not do any such thing, especially under the haughty, exultant eyes of Grant's men. Gordon and his officers saw this as the deliberate humiliation of a beaten army. So at the appointed time he marched his men out into a field on the other side of the Appomattox River and held what amounted to his own private, unilateral surrender ceremony. He gave another dramatic speech, far from the ears of the Union officers who would have put a stop to it, whose theme was surrender without defeat. The idea was already catching on. The men went forward and stacked their weapons and, having officially "surrendered," went back to their camps.[15]

If Gordon truly believed he had fulfilled his orders from the surrender commission, he was quite wrong. He was informed of this immediately by Union commission member John Gibbon, who told Gordon that he and his men were going to have to go back and do everything again. So the next day they had to march back across the river and into the field, retrieve their weapons, and take them into Appomattox Court House, where the hero of Little Round Top, Joshua Lawrence Chamberlain, was waiting for them at five in the morning, as were some thirty thousand Union soldiers. This time, over the indignant protests of General Gordon, they got it right. The Union's black soldiers were kept out of the way, out of sight. Their absence from the ceremony was yet another symbol of the tension between the two sides. Fraternity among soldiers was a noble idea. So were charity, forbearance, and kindness. No one thought for a minute that these things were possible in the presence of African American soldiers, either former slaves or freedmen. In practice there could not be any such thing.

Chamberlain and Gordon were also featured players in one of the most cherished of the bogus Appomattox stories. In this one, Union soldiers were standing along the sides of the road in Appomattox Court House in the posture "order arms," holding their rifles in one hand with the butts on the ground. As Gordon and his dejected rebels filed by — for this story they must be miserable and beaten down and dejected — Chamberlain ordered the men to change their positions to "carry arms," lifting muskets to their shoulders, a form of salute. This had an immediate, electric effect on the downcast rebels, who brightened up, while Gordon himself whirled about on his horse and bowed to Chamberlain. Such chivalry!

Though this story has moved many people over a century and a half, there is no convincing evidence that it ever happened. None of the thirty thousand other people who saw the surrender noted any such event. The source was Chamberlain, a true hero and, also, in subsequent years, one of the great embellishers of the war. His memoirs are an adjectival orgy, often reflecting the world as he wanted it to be instead of the way it was. For one thing, he did not command the troops at the ceremony, as he claimed, and thus couldn't order the men to salute. His story, moreover, changed significantly over the years. Its staying power was mostly rooted in the fact that Gordon never refuted it. The rebel general apparently liked it, and it reflected well on him, and as time went by Gordon added his own liberal embellishments, including the suggestion that Lee himself had led the army through town. The two generals would clearly have preferred this distinctly Walter Scott–like sequence, described in countless books and memoirs, to the more austere and decidedly less romantic one that actually took place.[16]

When news of the surrender hit Washington, the city erupted again as it had a week before, though this time the citizens were not quite as unrestrained. They were exhausted. One local man, who had been awakened by yet another multihundred-gun salute, commented that he could not take such constant celebration. Still, the muddy streets quickly filled with people who sang and cheered and saluted everybody and wanted all of the speeches they could get. They even got one out of Major General Ben Butler, the great Beast and nemesis of the South, who rose and uttered many remarkably charitable words about his former enemies. At the Treasury Department, employees sang "Old Hundredth" "with thrilling, even tear-compelling effect," according to journalist

Noah Brooks.[17] In late morning an impromptu crowd came barreling up from the Navy Yard dragging six boat howitzers with them, firing them off in the streets and adding new followers, snowball-like, as they continued into the heart of the city. By the time the procession arrived at the White House, the crowd had swelled to huge proportions. The guns were fired again, bands played, and the multitude clamored for a speech.[18]

Finally Tad Lincoln, the president's young son, appeared at the window from which his father usually spoke. The crowd cheered. The president himself then appeared, to more hat-throwing acclamation. He told them he was not prepared to make a speech just then. He was saving it for a more formal celebration. But he asked that the band play one particular tune, not at all the one anyone expected. "I have always thought 'Dixie' to be one of the best tunes I have ever heard," he explained. "Our adversaries . . . attempted to appropriate it, but I insisted yesterday that we fairly captured it. I presented the question to our attorney general, and he gave it as his legal opinion that it is our lawful prize. I now request the band to favor me with its performance."[19] They did, to ringing applause. The president then proposed three cheers for General Grant and disappeared from the window.

CHAPTER TWENTY-TWO:
THE UNBEARABLE WEIGHT
OF HISTORY

Jefferson Davis and Abraham Lincoln, two radically different presidents who faced radically different fates at war's end.

Abraham Lincoln, the complicated man with a broad streak of melancholy who bore his nation's sorrows heavily, was actually happy. His face had lost its look of sickness and fatigue. His friends and associates were amazed to see the change. "The very day after his return from Richmond," Secretary of War Stanton wrote later, "I passed with him some of the happiest moments of my life; our hearts beat with exultation at the victories."[1] Since the fall of Richmond the president had been greeted by madly cheering crowds wherever he went, and though he insisted that all credit for the Union victories go to Grant and the army, Lincoln was clearly pleased with the adulation. On the day after Lee's surrender throngs of singing, shouting, drinking, hat-tossing, banner-waving citizens had twice gathered at the White House to demand a speech, which he finally gave them on the night of April 11.

No one who attended ever forgot the scene at the Executive Mansion. The city's government buildings, including the new Capitol dome, were all bathed in light that was diffused through a faint mist, creating a magical effect. Across the Potomac River, as though stage-managed by some history-conscious director, rose the magnificent columns of Robert E. Lee's former home, Arlington House, also ablaze in light and clearly visible from the White House. Colored lights illuminated the White House lawn, where an enormous crowd had appeared and where former slaves and freedmen sang verse after verse of "The Year of Jubilo."[2]

"[I] never saw such a mass of heads before," recalled Elizabeth Keckley, a former slave who was Mary Lincoln's friend and dressmaker. "It was like a black, gently swelling sea. . . . It was a grand and imposing scene, and when the President, with pale face and his soul flashing through his eyes, advanced to speak, he looked more like a demigod than a man crowned with the fleeting days of mortality."[3] Others, too, noted something out of proportion in the moment. *Sacramento Daily Union* reporter Noah Brooks found the behavior of the manic, welling crowd unsettling, even frightening, writing, "There was something terrible in the enthusiasm with which the beloved Chief Magistrate was received. Cheers upon cheers, wave after wave of applause, rolled up, the President patiently standing quiet until it was all over."[4] Lincoln's speech was less exciting than the mise-en-scène. Instead of crowing about his country's great victory and the glory of the Union, he talked about how he planned to deal equitably with the enormous political, economic, and social entity once known as the Confederate States of America, which had just been dumped into his lap — the process that had come to be known as reconstruction.

Tucked inside his speech, however — the last public speech he would ever give — was a single transformative sentence, one that would have mortal consequences for Lincoln. He had privately expressed support for black voting rights a number of times but had not dared to make that support part of the 1864 campaign. Now he went public with the idea,

553

with a few conditions: "It is . . . unsatisfactory to some that the elective franchise is not given to the colored man. I would myself prefer that it were now conferred on the very intelligent, and on those who serve our cause as soldiers." *I would myself prefer.* Forceful words from an ascendant president. One person in the audience that night — a handsome, successful twenty-six-year-old actor — was especially impressed by those words. "That means nigger citizenship," John Wilkes Booth said to his friend. "Now, by God, I'll put him through! That is the last speech he will ever make."

Lincoln's sunny outlook continued through the week. Unsurrendered rebel forces were still out there, but no one in the Union army or the government thought they would hold out long. Sherman outnumbered Joe Johnston four to one in North Carolina. Major General Kirby Smith's thirty-thousand-man rebel army in the Trans-Mississippi had little chance of surviving in a country whose infrastructure and economy had collapsed and whose capital was in Union hands. The only question was, would the rebels surrender or take to the woods as guerrillas? In a cabinet meeting at 11:00 a.m. on Friday, April 14 — an apparently unexceptional date that no one in the country would ever forget — the president was buoyant. Treasury Secretary Hugh McCulloch recalled, "The weary look which his face had so long worn, . . . even when he was telling humorous stories, had disappeared. It was bright and cheerful." James Harlan, the interior secretary designate, wrote that Lincoln's habitual expression of "indescribable sadness" had been transfigured into "an equally indescribable expression of serene joy."[5]

All of which translated into an unusually happy and relaxed cabinet meeting. Grant, very much the hero of the hour, had come up from City Point the day before and told stories of the Appomattox campaign and Lee's surrender. Everyone wanted to know about Sherman, too, and Grant told the cabinet he was expecting to hear news of rebel commander Joe Johnston's surrender in North Carolina at any moment. Lincoln spoke in a kindly way of Robert E. Lee and other rebel generals and generally held forth against the Radicals' desire to hang them all high while simultaneously rebuilding the social structure of the South in the Radicals' own image. (Lincoln had earlier hinted several times that he would not be unhappy if Jefferson Davis escaped.)

The least orthodox moment of the meeting was Lincoln's description of a dream he had had the night before. He had had the same dream many times, and it always presaged some large piece of news from the war, usually good news. According to Navy Secretary

Gideon Welles, Lincoln said that in the dream "he seemed to be in some singular, indescribable vessel and that he was moving with great rapidity towards an indefinite shore; that he had this dream preceding Sumter, Bull Run, Antietam, Gettysburg, Stones River, Vicksburg, Wilmington, etc." Lincoln was convinced that this dream was an encouraging omen, too, saying, "We shall, judging from the past, have good news very soon. I think it must be from Sherman for my thoughts are in that direction, as are most of yours."[6]

Considering the dream's track record, Lincoln's optimism was curious indeed. Grant pointed out immediately that "Stone [sic] River was certainly no victory" and added that "he knew of no great results which proceeded from it."[7] Grant might have included Fort Sumter, too, from Lincoln's list, a Union defeat that started a four-year war, and Bull Run, both versions of which were humiliating Union defeats.

Seen in retrospect, of course, the event the dream preceded was Lincoln's own death. He had mentioned his death on several occasions, always in conjunction with the end of the war. In July 1864 he had said that, while he believed the Union would win the war, "I may not live to see it. I feel a presentiment that I may not outlast the rebellion. When it is over, my work will be done." He had told his friend Harriet Beecher Stowe, "Whichever way [the war] ends, I have the impression that *I* shan't last long after it's over."[8]

Mary Todd Lincoln was nobody's idea of a good time. Vain, self-centered, and difficult, she was prone to mood swings, fits of temper, and depression. She presented an ongoing social problem for the president, her official handlers, and anyone who was saddled with her company. In March she visited Union headquarters at City Point, just east of Petersburg, where she threw a tantrum because she believed that other generals' wives had been granted privileges she had not been given. When General Grant's wife, Julia, tried to calm her down, Mary erupted at her, too, saying with undisguised spite, "I suppose you think you'll get to the White House yourself, don't you?"*

Julia Grant had such an unpleasant memory of her time with Mary that, when an invitation came to join the Lincolns at Ford's Theatre on the evening of April 14, Julia decided to decline. Ulysses had drawn Mary Lincoln duty the night before. Because Lincoln had a headache — or claimed to — Grant accompanied Mary in a carriage while

* When Mary returned to Washington from City Point, her traveling companion, General Carl Schurz, was so appalled by her vulgar and venomous gossip that he later described it as "outrageous."

she toured the city's illuminations. As they rode through the crowded streets, she quickly decided that Grant was getting too many cheers, and her husband too few. Angry, she ordered the driver to let her out of the carriage. Grant persuaded her to stay. Thus on the following evening Ulysses wanted no more to do with her than Julia did, and the two agreed on the excuse that they would travel by train to see their children in New Jersey. When Secretary of War Edwin Stanton's wife, Ellen, heard of this, she too declined, telling Julia, "I will not sit without you in the box with Mrs. Lincoln." Others passed on the invitation, too, including Speaker of the House Schuyler Colfax.

Thus Lincoln and Mary ended up attending the show — a comedy called *Our American Cousin* — accompanied only by Clara Harris, the daughter of a New York senator, and her fiancé, Major Henry Rathbone. The president had almost no security. At his request no bodyguards had gone to the theater with him, and though two policemen were with his retinue, neither had specifically been asked to guard him. Lincoln had always been lax, even fatalistic, about his safety. His White House visitors entered his office unscreened despite his receipt, since his renomination for president in the summer of 1864, of a constant stream of death threats. He even had a file in his desk labeled "Assassination Letters."

At 10:30 p.m. John Wilkes Booth entered an anteroom behind the president's box, barred the door behind him, stepped forward to the president's rocking chair, and shot him in the back of the head with a single-shot, .44-caliber derringer. Booth slashed Rathbone with a dagger, then leaped from the balcony to the floor of the stage, shouted, *"Sic semper tyrannis!"* (Thus always to tyrants), and fled through a back door.* Lincoln, who was already as good as dead, stopped breathing nine hours later. That night, at home where he was recovering from an accident, Secretary of State William Seward was attacked and stabbed repeatedly by Booth accomplices. Seward survived, but with a permanently scarred face. Grant's decision to visit his children may have saved his life — he was a target of the same conspiracy — but he always regretted his absence. He believed that if he had been in that theater box, he might have protected Lincoln from harm.

As word of the attack on the president spread through the city of Washington, the

* Henry Rathbone recovered from his wounds but not from his failure to stop the assassination. Eighteen years later he fatally shot and stabbed his wife, Clara, then tried unsuccessfully to kill himself. He was sentenced to an asylum for the criminally insane, where he spent the rest of his days.

Grants were on their way to Philadelphia in a private railroad car. They arrived at midnight and went directly to their hotel, where a messenger awaited them with an urgent telegram from the War Department. Grant read it silently, then handed it to his wife:

> The President was assassinated at Ford's Theater at 10:30 tonight and cannot live. The wound was a pistol shot through the head. Secretary Seward and his son Frederick were also assassinated at their residence and are in a dangerous condition. The Secretary of War desires that you return to Washington immediately. Please answer on receipt of this.

Another telegram followed, sent from Assistant Secretary of War Charles A. Dana at 12:50 a.m.:

> Permit me to suggest to you to keep close watch on all persons who come near you in the cars or otherwise; also, that an engine be sent in front of the train to guard against anything being on the track.

Yet another wire suggested the probable assassination of Vice President Andrew Johnson.[9]

Grant returned to the capital that day on a special train. When he arrived, he was stunned

560

by the change in the city. "The joy that I had witnessed among the people in the street and in public places in Washington when I left there," he wrote in his memoirs, "had been turned to grief; the city was in reality a city of mourning."[10] He later told author and journalist John Russell Young that April 15 was "the darkest day of my life. I did not know what it meant. Here was the Rebellion put down in the field, and starting up in the gutters. We had fought it as a war, now we had to fight it as assassination."[11] The man at the head of the victorious army was unable to undo the evil that had been done; indeed, he scarcely understood the nature of that evil. The ground war he had won had somehow gone underground.

Along with the pervasive, almost palpable sadness in the city's streets was panic and rage, too, at what appeared to be a large Confederate conspiracy. Grant, arriving at the War Department in a cold fury, was quickly caught up in it. He was put in charge of the defense and security of the national capital. He was to pay specific attention, said Stanton, to "the large number of Rebel officers and privates, prisoners of war, and Rebel refugees and deserters that are among us."

In that capacity Grant received a message that had been sent the day before from Major General Edward Ord in Richmond, addressed to President Lincoln. Ord was passing on a request from Confederate senator Robert M. T. Hunter and Confederate assistant secretary of war John A. Campbell — two of the three rebel commissioners who had attended the failed February peace conference at Hampton Roads with Lincoln and Seward — to meet with the president. Lincoln had never seen the telegram. Instead, Grant replied. Like so many in the North, he was angry and vengeful. Unlike his countrymen, he wielded immense military power and could act on his feelings. He told Ord:

Arrest J. A. Campbell, Mayor Mayo and the members of the old council of Richmond, who have not yet taken the oath of allegiance, and put them in Libby prison. Hold them guarded beyond the possibility of escape until further orders. Also arrest all paroled officers and surgeons until they can be sent beyond our lines, unless they take the oath of allegiance. . . . Extreme rigor will have to be observed whilst assassination remains the order of the day with the Rebels."[12]

Grant was saying, in effect, round up all the officers and imprison them. This was not only unlike Grant but stood a good chance of reigniting violence. Ord, deeply dismayed by Grant's wire, replied immediately:

The two citizens I have seen [Campbell and Hunter]. They are old, nearly helpless and I think incapable of harm. Lee and staff are in town among the paroled prisoners. Should I arrest them under the circumstance I think the Rebellion would be re-opened. I will risk my life that the present paroles will be kept, and if you will allow me to do so trust the people here who, I believe, are ignorant of the assassination, done I think by some insane Brutus with a few accomplices. Mr. Campbell and Mr. Hunter pressed me earnestly yesterday to send them to Washington to see the President. Would they have done so if guilty? Please answer.

Grant realized immediately that he had overreacted. He replied, far more gently this time:

On reflection I will withdraw my dispatch of this date directing the arrest of Campbell, Mayo and others so far as it may be regarded as an order, and leave it in the light of a suggestion, to be executed only so far as you may judge the good of the service demands.[13]

But Grant remained in a rancorous, obdurate mood. He was preoccupied, as so many were, with the manhunt for the people responsible for the assassination of Lincoln and the attack on Seward.★ A few days later, in response to a request by rebel guerrilla John Singleton Mosby for an additional period of truce, Grant snarled, "If Mosby does not avail himself of the present truce, end it and hunt him and his men down. Guerrillas . . . will not be entitled to quarter."

No quarter. There was no room for tolerance, or negotiation. If Mosby would not fully cooperate, he and his men would be run down and shot. Grant eventually softened his position on that, too, and Mosby would come in peaceably.† But Grant's feelings after Lin-

★ John Wilkes Booth was killed while attempting to flee on April 26. Eight people were found guilty as conspirators on June 30. Of those, four were hanged, three were imprisoned. The other, John Surratt, escaped and was tried later and released.

† After the war Grant and Mosby became friends and close political associates. Mosby wrote in his memoirs about the origins of that relationship: "I had strong personal reasons for being friendly with General Grant. If he had not thrown his shield over me in 1865, I should have been outlawed and driven into exile. When Lee surrendered, my battalion was in northern Virginia, a hundred miles from Appomattox. Secretary of War Stanton invited all soldiers in Virginia to surrender on the same conditions which were offered to Lee's army, but I was excepted. General Grant, who was then all-powerful,

coln's death continued to reflect those of his country at large.‡ Instead of the triumph of only days before, now there was sadness, bit-

---

interposed, and sent me an offer of the same parole that he had given Gen. Lee. Such a service I could never forget. When the opportunity came, I remembered what he had done for me, and I did all I could for him."

‡ Grant would continue to have to deal with feelings of vengeance and retribution, both his own and others'. In May the *New York Times* led a campaign, joined by other papers, to try Robert E. Lee for treason, eventually resulting in a June 7, 1865, indictment of Lee, Johnston, Longstreet, and other rebel generals by a federal grand jury in Norfolk, Virginia. Grant immediately stepped in, protesting that the Appomattox terms had met with Lincoln's and the country's enthusiastic approval and demanding that the judge be ordered to quash all indictments against paroled prisoners of war. When President Andrew Johnson resisted, Grant lost his temper, saying, among other things, "My terms of surrender were according to military law, and so long as General Lee observes his parole, I will never consent to his arrest. I will resign the command of the army rather than execute any order to arrest Lee or any of his commanders so long as they obey the law." Though he was president, Andrew Johnson didn't enjoy anything close to Grant's fame and popularity and understood, correctly, that he was

terness, and helplessness. And darkness. The lights that had illuminated the city since the fall of Richmond had been extinguished. "Everywhere," wrote Noah Brooks, "on the most pretentious residences and on the humblest hovels, were the black badges of grief."[14]

Black was the order of the day, too, at Lincoln's funeral, which was held in the East Room of the White House on April 19. In this cavernous enclosure Lincoln had first welcomed Grant to Washington some thirteen months before. In place of a frenzied, cheering crowd, and the joyous and comic spectacle of William Seward and Ulysses S. Grant standing at bay atop a sofa, was now the domed canopy of Lincoln's catafalque — the black-draped wooden structure that held Lincoln's black-draped coffin. Seated in the room around the catafalque were the president (Andrew Johnson), the Supreme Court, the cabinet, senators, congressmen, and diplomats. At its foot was the Lincoln family's sole representative, his son Robert Lincoln. (Mary Lincoln did not feel up to attending.) At the head of the catafalque, alone, stood Ulysses S. Grant, often weeping openly, the

---

outflanked. He retreated. Grant thus saved Lee et al. (including Mosby) from a public trial for treason.

man who said, of his former boss, "He was incontestably the greatest man I have ever known." From the East Room, Lincoln's body was taken in a solemn procession down Pennsylvania Avenue to the Capitol, where it lay in state until the following night. The procession, which took place amid the ringing of church bells and the booming of minute guns, was led by the 22nd US Colored Infantry, which had fought in several Virginia campaigns. That same day an estimated 25 million Americans attended memorial services for Lincoln in the rest of the country.

From there a nine-car train carried Lincoln's body to Illinois for burial in Springfield, tracing the route Lincoln had taken when he came to Washington in February 1861. More than a million people bid him farewell. In a country that did not yet fully understand what was to become of it, or even whether the war would resume, whole cities found the time to mourn. New York City was so overwhelmed by grief that the city's commerce came to a virtual halt for a full two weeks. In Chicago, one observer remarked, "I have seen three deceased Kings of England lying in state but have never witnessed a demonstration so vast in its proportions, so unanimous and spontaneous, as that which has been evoked by the arrival in the city of the remains of the fallen president."[15]

Grant was back at his desk at the War Department, occupied with the complex winding down of a war that was costing $4 million a day. He had been anxious to hear news from Sherman in North Carolina and got it on April 21: Johnston had signed a surrender agreement with Sherman, a copy of which was sent for approval. With it came a note from Sherman that was fairly bursting with enthusiasm. He believed he had done something great. "If approved by the president," Sherman wrote, "it will produce peace from the Potomac to the Rio Grande."

Grant read the document with growing alarm. He soon concluded that his friend and protégé had made a gigantic mistake.[16]

Through all of this turmoil and uncertainty, the other president, the one on the losing side, who shared few personality traits with his Northern counterpart — stubbornness being the most notable exception — continued to flee southward from Richmond, away from the ruins of the war and toward an unknowable future. Jefferson Davis had left his burning capital by train near midnight on April 2, accompanied by members of his cabinet.[17] Since Confederate legislators and officials had all fled, Davis and his cohort were all that remained of the national government of a country of eleven states containing more than 9 million people and encompassing 770,000 square miles. They reached the town of Danville, Virginia, late in the afternoon of April 3. There Davis promptly established the Confederate government in exile. He set up his "executive offices" at a local hotel and ordered engineers to work on defenses for the city. He had a plan: Lee's army would join Johnston's army. Then Davis would interpose the combined force between Danville and the Yankees and strike a devastating blow against the enemy. On April 4 — five days before Lee's surrender — this still seemed like a reasonable idea.

Whether Davis was still a reasonable, clear-thinking leader was debatable. He was an odd, unlikable man. Though he could be warm and genial in private and tender with his family, he was often cold and aloof in public. Sam Houston's description of him still stands as one of the best summaries of his public persona: "As ambitious as Lucifer, and cold as a lizard." He was by nature uncompromising, self-absorbed, self-righteous, and utterly lacking in humor or the common touch. He considered opposition to his ideas an assault on his integrity. His natural unpleasantness was enhanced by a host of physical ailments that included dyspepsia, chronic pain from a war wound, earaches, and inflammation of the eye. In the past year large components of his country seemed to hate him (he shared that with Lincoln, too). In the winter of 1864, he had been attacked from all sides, and especially in the Richmond press, not only for his constant petty feuding with his generals and mismanagement of the war, but also, ironically, for his exercise of federal power. The man who had once championed localism and states' rights — beliefs at the core of the rebellion — now saw these ideas invoked against him by states that often refused to go along with conscription, procurement, suspensions of habeas corpus, and other arrogations of federal authority. The man who had despised concentrated federal power was now maligned as a nationalist. That he was able to lead his war-torn and politically fractious country for as long as he did was a testament to his iron will and his unshakable belief that the South would triumph.

But now this graduate of West Point, American war hero, former US secretary of war, and senator from Mississippi was on the run. From his makeshift office in Danville he wrote a long letter to his embattled nation, announcing the loss of Richmond and looking to the future. The document is astonishing, both for its otherworldly logic and for its vision of never-ending war. "We have now entered upon a new phase of the struggle, the memory of which is to endure for all ages," he wrote in the baroque style he favored.

Relieved from the necessity of guarding cities and particular points, important but not vital to our defense, with an army free to move from point to point and strike in detail the detachments and garrisons of the enemy, operating on the interior of our own country, where supplies are more accessible, and where the foe will be far removed from his base and cut off from all succor in case of reverse, nothing is now needed to render our triumph certain but the exhibition of our own unquenchable resolve. Let us but will it, and we are free.[18]

Davis's rhetoric sounded like an appeal to conduct the war on the model of John Singleton Mosby: partisan fighting on a national scale. Guerrilla war was to be waged against what Davis proclaimed was a badly faltering nation with "failing resources" whose misguided war "must be abandoned speedily if not brought to a successful close." This statement was either a deliberate lie or the logic of a man living in a land of make-believe. That few people in his country ever read his letter was probably a good thing. While in Danville, Davis found time to meddle in the affairs of his brother-in-law, Major General Richard Taylor, who was still in command in Mississippi. Davis voiced his displeasure with the removal of one of Taylor's subordinates in a small district.

Then came the shattering news of Lee's surrender — Davis had not thought it possible — and His Excellency and his group were in flight again, this time to Greensboro, North Carolina, a forty-six-mile trip by train that took sixteen hours. They received a chilly welcome — Greensboro harbored plenty of Unionist sentiment — and most of Davis's party were forced to camp in a boxcar. They were joined by rebel generals Pierre G. T. Beauregard and Joseph E. Johnston, who told Davis flatly that continuing the war was pointless. Johnston, who had lost the Battle of Bentonville to Sherman's vastly superior army a month earlier, left little room for doubt. "It would be the greatest of human crimes for us to attempt to continue the war," Johnston told Davis. Any blood spilled now would be a pointless, meaningless tragedy. Negotiations with Sherman should begin immediately. The majority of Davis's cabinet concurred. Isolated and outnumbered — only Secretary of State Judah Benjamin was on his side — Davis agreed to ask Sherman for a temporary armistice for discussions. But Davis wanted nothing to do with surrender. He wanted to buy time. He asked a dumbfounded Johnston immediately for his plan of retreat, how he would resupply his army. Davis still intended to rebuild his war machine. He would "fight it out to the Mississippi River." He would keep on fighting "to the end, beyond the end."[19]

Almost everyone but Davis knew by now that this was pure nonsense. The end was near, and neither he nor anyone else could do anything about it. Since Greensboro was no longer safe, the little group took to the road once more, now plodding forward on horseback and in wagons in driving rain and mud. In Charlotte, Davis and his party learned of the assassination of Lincoln. His reaction: "Certainly I have no special regard for Mr. Lincoln. But there are a great many men of whose end I would rather hear than his. I fear it will be disastrous for our people, and I regret it deeply."

In Charlotte, Davis received one of the war's most controversial documents: the signed agreement of surrender between William T. Sherman and Joseph E. Johnston.* The two generals had met in a farmhouse just west of Durham, North Carolina, but instead of arranging a simple surrender of the rebel army — as Grant and Lee had done — they had composed a far-reaching document containing terms and conditions for ending the war everywhere. Davis and his

* Sherman was in Raleigh, North Carolina, with his army, while Johnston was camped in Smithfield, about thirty miles southeast of Raleigh. Davis and his party were in Charlotte, 150 miles west of Raleigh.

cabinet unanimously agreed to accept it. Alone among them, Davis had no intention of surrendering. He still spoke of continuing the war in the Trans-Mississippi. As he saw it, he was buying time. To his colleagues, he looked increasingly like a frail, frustrated old man who had run out of options.

Sherman had sent the document to Grant, and Grant realized two things immediately: first, that Sherman's agreement contained mistakes of nation-altering significance, and second, that Grant needed to show it to his bosses that very night. He wrote a quick message to Stanton:

I have received and just completed reading the dispatches brought by special messenger from General Sherman. They are of such importance that I think immediate action should be taken on them and that it should be done by the president in council with his whole cabinet.[20]

By eight o'clock the cabinet was in full session. Grant read Sherman's "Memorandum and Basis of Agreement" out loud to a stunned and silent group. Sherman had done exactly what Grant had been told not to do at Appomattox: make a general treaty of peace between nations. The agreement covered not only the surrender of all Confederate armies in the field, but also, remarkably, the conditions under which the various Southern states would be admitted back into the Union. Johnston was apparently acting as agent or representative of Jefferson Davis and his cabinet, men who ran a government that neither Lincoln nor Congress had ever recognized as legitimate, and thus lacking the standing to "surrender" anything more than one of their armies in the field.

The document laid out clearly the terms of the end of the war. Confederate soldiers would march to their state capitals, place their weapons in state arsenals, disband, and submit to federal authority. State governments would be recognized as legal and taken back into the Union with full standing as soon as state officials and lawmakers took an oath of allegiance. Courts would reopen, and all Southerners would regain full political rights as well as their "rights of person and property, as defined by the Constitution and of the states, respectively."

Sherman's document, which landed in Washington at the worst possible moment — two days after Lincoln's funeral — was a full-blown disaster. The victor of Atlanta had taken Lincoln's admonitions about forgiveness and leniency and conciliation to heart and had produced an agreement that virtually no Northern politician or general, including Grant and every cabinet member in the room, could support. In the document, rebel armies were allowed the luxury of not surrendering in the field. They only had to walk home and dump their weapons in a state building. Which suggested that if they wanted to, they could simply pick them up and start fighting again. Far worse was the apparently uncritical acceptance of rebel states and their legislatures and officialdom back into the Union in good standing. All it took was an oath of allegiance. Such terms seemed to guarantee that the planter class would be in charge again. The wording even suggested — though this was a more radical interpretation — that slavery might be legalized again. (What did full rights of "person and property" mean?) Lincoln had wanted the South treated gently, but such wholesale forgiveness was out of the question. "The instigators of this monstrous rebellion" had to be punished. States and the leaders of those states whose secession had provoked a bitter civil war in which hundreds of thousands of people had died could not seamlessly reenter the Union. President Johnson and Secretary of War Stanton were so furious with Sherman they accused him of something near treason.

Grant fought them off. But he had a problem that required an immediate solution. He composed a letter to Sherman to tell him that his terms "could not possibly be approved," that there had been "a disapproval of the negotiations altogether," and that hostilities were to recommence "at the earliest moment." Grant then put the letter in his pocket, boarded a steamship, and traveled to Sherman's headquarters in Raleigh to deliver it in person.

Sherman, who had already begun to feel a shift in the political winds, was glad to see his old friend and understood immediately what he had done wrong. He only said that he regretted that he had not seen Stanton's letter to Grant a few months earlier, containing Lincoln's order to deal only with the surrender of the army directly in front of him. "[It] would have saved a world of trouble," wrote Sherman in his memoirs.[21] Events now moved quickly. Grant returned to Washington. Sherman and Johnston signed a new agreement on the Appomattox model. Johnston did so in deliberate defiance of Jefferson Davis, who considered it gross insubordination. But Davis did not matter anymore. No one needed his signature on anything. He existed only as a quarry to be hunted. Rebel armies were poised to surrender all over the South, and even Nathan Bedford Forrest would soon exhort his troops to lay down their arms and advise them their "duty [was] to divest themselves of feelings of hatred and revenge."[22] Since Johnston's army was about to vanish as a fighting unit, Davis and his dwindling party had to move again, ever southward.

■ ■ ■

Major General James Harrison "Harry" Wilson was one of the brightest lights in the Union army. The twenty-seven-year-old cavalry officer had played a major role in routing John Bell Hood's force at Nashville, and in spite of his elevated self-regard and unshakable conviction that his ideas were the only right ones, his military genius was indisputable. He was a leading advocate of using Spencer-carbine-equipped cavalry as mounted infantry. In the late winter of 1865 he persuaded Grant to let him conduct a cavalry raid into the Deep South to destroy the Confederacy's remaining heavy industries and to prevent a last-ditch stand.[23]

He crossed into Alabama on March 22 with a force of more than thirteen thousand men and pushed south, destroying ironworks, cotton gins, factories, and mills as he went. (Alabama produced 70 percent of the Confederacy's iron.) At Selma, on April 1 and 2, he engaged what was left of Forrest's troops, routed them, and took the city along with its gunpowder-making facilities and factories that produced half of the cannons and two-thirds of the fixed ammunition used by rebel armies, along with twenty-seven hundred prisoners. General Forrest would not fight again.[24] On April 12 Wilson took Montgomery without a fight. At Columbus, Georgia, he took another thousand prisoners and burned arsenals and ironworks and five hundred thousand bales of cotton. Those fires raged out of control, and by April 17 much of the city of Columbus had been reduced to ashes. It was the last Civil War battle east of the Mississippi. Two days later Wilson was in Macon, Georgia, where he heard for the first time of Lee's surrender and the armistice between Johnston and Sherman.

By the end of April, Harry Wilson had completed the most successful Union cavalry raid of the Civil War.[25] In twenty-five days he had marched 525 miles, destroyed the remaining industrial capacity of the Deep South, inflicted 1,000 casualties and taken 6,820 prisoners, all at minimal cost to his own force. His achievement, however, went largely unnoticed. Larger events, from the fall of Richmond to the surrender at Appomattox to the death of a president, now occupied center stage.

But Wilson did become famous — quite famous indeed — for an event that took place at the very end of his little-known campaign.

His final assignment was to capture Jefferson Davis and his cabinet, who were thought to be heading to Georgia. Wilson's patrols fanned out, searching across a wide area. To motivate them, Wilson offered $500,000 for Davis's apprehension, to be paid off in gold from the Confederate treasury.

Davis and his ragged little group were more vulnerable than they had ever been. He had once had a cavalry escort of three thousand. Now his band numbered no more than twenty, with only ten soldiers. They pushed on through rain and lightning on faltering horses into a country that was, alarmingly, full of outlaw renegades, the detritus of the long and savage war Davis had helped start. On May 5 Davis disbanded the Confederate government. On May 6 he caught up with his wife, Varina, and the couple's four children, who had been fleeing separately along a more or less parallel path. She had visions of going to England, putting their ten- and eight-year-old children in school there. Like Davis, she had hopes of continuing the war in the Trans-Mississippi.

But they were already out of time. On the morning of May 10, while Davis, Varina, and their children slept soundly in their tents near the town of Irwinville, Georgia, three hundred of Harry Wilson's cavalry approached through the woods. The Davises were awakened by a rifle shot, then came more firing, and soon they realized that their camp was surrounded. Varina persuaded her husband to try to escape. In his dark tent, he had mistakenly grabbed Varina's short-sleeved cloak instead of his own overcoat. As he was leaving, she draped her shawl over his head and shoulders.

He was soon captured and almost instantly recognized. He was shown no respect. The Yankee soldiers ate the breakfast that had been prepared for the Davis children, and the president's aides were stripped of their money, their horses, and their saddles. As the Yankee soldiers rode toward Wilson's headquarters in Macon with their captives, they taunted the Davis family, often in profane language. They sang "We'll hang Jeff Davis from a sour apple tree," a verse from the popular song "John Brown's Body."* Davis, ever the martinet, criticized the commanding officer, Colonel Benjamin Pritchard, for not allowing Davis's family to stay together after dark. When Pritchard answered irreverently, Davis called him a coward and said that Pritchard would not dare speak to Davis that way if he were not a prisoner. Pritchard then questioned the bravery of a man who hid behind women's clothing.[26]

Davis was taken by sea to Fort Monroe in Virginia, where he was imprisoned for two years. He was indicted for treason but never

* The tune for the Civil War song "John Brown's Body" came from folk hymns of the camp-meeting movement in America in the eighteenth and early nineteenth centuries. New lyrics, written by Julia Ward Howe, under the title "Battle Hymn of the Republic," were later adopted for the tune.

581

tried because federal prosecutors doubted they would win and also feared that a judicial ruling might actually validate the constitutionality of secession. He was released on bond in 1867, after which he struggled financially and held a succession of jobs, including as president of the Carolina Life Insurance Company in Memphis. He gave many speeches, wrote a self-justifying, two-volume memoir, and died in Mississippi in 1889 at the age of eighty-one, holding Varina's hand.

CHAPTER TWENTY-THREE: HELL ITSELF

Andersonville Prison, everyone's worst nightmare and Clara Barton's last great challenge.

The war was ending. In the late spring of 1865, Union armies were winding up their terrible work. Violent death would soon cease to be a national way of life. But if the North found joy in its victory, or the South relief that the worst of its suffering was over, the country as a whole was still drowning in grief. How could it be otherwise? Three-quarters of

583

a million men had lost their lives. Another half million at least had been wounded, and many of these had been disfigured in horrible ways. They had lost arms, legs, hands, and feet. They had lost noses and eyes and sex organs. Many would live out their lives in chronic pain. It was impossible to quantify such anguish, to count up the numbers of homes made desolate, families bankrupted and destroyed, lives ruined, spirits forever broken. Americans mourned their fathers and brothers and sons but also the way their lives used to be, the people they used to be, the innocence they had lost.

They looked for meaning in their sorrow, and meaning, as usual, was in short supply. What could possibly redeem such unimaginable suffering? Lincoln had supplied the most compelling answer to that question, one both quantitative and theological. In his Second Inaugural Address in Washington on March 4, 1865, in perhaps the most brilliant sequence of words in a life replete with oratorical brilliance, he explained his notion of why so many had to die:

If we shall suppose that American slavery is one of those offenses which, in the providence of God, must needs come, but which, having continued through His appointed time, He now wills to remove, and that He gives to both North and South this terrible war as the woe due to those by whom the offense came, shall we discern therein any departure from those divine attributes which the believers in a living God always ascribe to Him? Fondly do we hope, fervently do we pray, that this mighty scourge of war may speedily pass away. *Yet, if God wills that it continue until all the wealth piled by the bondsman's two hundred and fifty years of unrequited toil shall be sunk, and until every drop of blood drawn with the lash shall be paid by another drawn with the sword, as was said three thousand years ago, so still it must be said "the judgments of the Lord are true and righteous altogether."* (italics added)

Slavery, the sin of which the North was every bit as guilty as the South, would be atoned by blood, and blood alone, in quantities commensurate with blood shed by slaves over two and a half centuries of bondage.* In Lincoln's fatalistic, Scripture-driven equa-

---

* In some important ways the North bore even more responsibility for slavery than the South, since much of the infrastructure and financing of the slave trade — by which slaves were brought to America from Africa — was done in New York and New England. Newport, Rhode Island, alone launched more than a thousand voyages by which slaves were brought from Africa to North America. And people in the

tion, the Civil War amounted to an inevitable settling of accounts.

Other unpaid blood debts remained, too, at the end of the war. Dead soldiers were scattered across the country's battlefields. Many of them lay unburied, their bones bleaching in the sun. Fully half of the Union dead lay in unidentified graves.[1] "Missing" men had simply vanished from the face of the earth. They included the unaccounted for dead from battles, tens of thousands of soldiers in army prison camps on both sides, as well as soldiers who were still living, their whereabouts unknown.

All of this caused their families acute anguish. The fighting had stopped, but the men were still lost, still unaccounted for. They had died for their countries or had disappeared into prison camps but remained outside the narrative of the war, their stories untold. The coming of peace offered an opportunity to change that. Battle sites and former prison camps could be traveled to. Information once again moved freely. Records could be searched. Missing soldiers, soldiers lying unidentified in unmarked graves, could now be investigated. Didn't the living owe at least that much to the dead?

North owned slaves until the last states abolished it in 1804.

Fortunately, one person, in particular, felt that deep and desperate need. Clara Barton, who had helped revolutionize battlefield medical care, was looking for something else to do as the end of the war approached. In the late winter of 1864–65 she found it. In August 1863 the Union had begun to suspend prisoner exchanges — Grant would end them altogether in April 1864 — because of the Confederacy's refusal to release black prisoners. Since then most captured men had languished — or died — in often horrific conditions in enemy prison camps, North and South. But prisoner exchanges had recently resumed, which meant that thousands of Union soldiers, paroled from Southern prisons, were now spilling out of steamships and into hospitals in Annapolis, Maryland. Because of her work, Barton had become famous as an advocate for common soldiers and had received a continuous stream of letters from people trying to locate missing soldiers. She was amazed, she wrote, by people's "intense anxiety and excitement amounting in many instances nearly to insanity."

In spite of all she had seen on battlefields, what she witnessed on a visit to Annapolis shocked her: former prisoners of war who were so sick and emaciated that they seemed barely human. Many were little more than living skeletons — forty-five-pound men on the verge of death. Others babbled incoherently. Still others had dreamily idiotic faces with thousand-yard stares and vacant, sunken eyes. They stepped onto the wharves clothed in rags and covered in vermin. They had been residents of Libby and Belle Isle Prisons in Richmond, Salisbury Prison in North Carolina, and Andersonville in Georgia.[2]

These men were the lucky ones. Tens of thousands more had perished in the rebel camps, and Barton realized that she might do the nation a great service by finding out what had happened to them. She would have to have government approval to do it, and in spite of her track record she once again faced a fearsome gauntlet of bureaucrats and men who did not believe that women should be in charge of anything. The task was so daunting that she felt she needed the approval of Lincoln himself, which proved exceedingly difficult. In perhaps her most dogged, persistent, and resourceful performance to date, she employed a congressman, a senator, a major general, and the commissioner of Indian affairs to end-run the bureaucracy and get her project approved. Lincoln's note, which secured her an office, a title, and free postage, read, "To the friends of missing persons: Miss Clara Barton has kindly offered to search for the missing prisoners of the war. Please address her at Annapolis, Maryland, giving name, regiment, and company of any missing prisoner. A. Lincoln."

Word of her project spread quickly, and soon she was receiving a hundred letters each day. She hired assistants and purchased stationery with her own money. Her approach was straightforward: use the former inmates themselves as resources. She drew up lists of missing prisoners and posted them in the barracks at Camp Parole, as it was known, in Annapolis, asking for any information about them. She wrote letters and studied camp records. But she found the work difficult and frustrating, finding only about one name in thirty from the rolls at Annapolis.[3] By the end of May most of the former prisoners had moved on, and Camp Parole was closed.

But instead of giving up, Barton, who was still inundated with mail, decided to expand her project. She fully understood this was one of the most important issues in postwar America. Now she would look for *all* missing Union soldiers. She would become the clearinghouse for information about them. Once more she bent the military establishment to her will and got her project approved, this time by President Andrew Johnson and Ulysses S. Grant. With it came permission to use the Government Printing Office. Within two months she published three thousand names, including ones she had gathered while in Annapolis, and posted them in twenty thousand US post offices. These brought even

589

more letters looking for lost men. She was just getting started.[4]

In late June a young Connecticut Yankee named Dorence Atwater walked into a post office in Washington, DC, and saw Barton's list of missing men. He was no ordinary young man. He had been captured after the Battle of Gettysburg and had spent five months in a rebel prison camp at Belle Isle, in Richmond. He had then been transferred to the new Confederate prison camp at Andersonville, Georgia, where he was among the first prisoners. He had spent a year there.[5] Though he was only twenty years old, blue-eyed and beardless, he was badly emaciated and had the wrinkled skin of an old man.

What was most unusual about him, though, was the astounding document in his possession. He had a copy, he told Barton in a letter, "of the Death Register of the Prison at Andersonville, Ga. containing the names of 12,658." He asked her for an interview, which she readily granted. His job at the prison camp had been to record the deaths of all Union soldiers. He had been appalled by the number of deaths in the prison — sometimes more than a hundred per day — and became convinced that Confederate authorities were deliberately mistreating the men to make sure they did not fight again. He thought the Confederates might falsify their records, too, so he kept his own secret copy of the death

590

rolls and smuggled it out when he was released.[6] On it were the names, ranks, and regiments of the men as well as numbers indicating the location of their graves.

His description of the camp was beyond macabre: a world of unimaginable filth, vermin, and disease where prisoners were given so little to eat that they were slowly starving to death. In May of the previous year reports of conditions in Rebel prisons in Richmond — along with photographs of some grotesquely emaciated prisoners — had caused such a scandal that the US Congress had held hearings on the subject. Andersonville was the worst of them, but no one yet knew much about Andersonville.[7] That would soon change.

Atwater's story did not end there. He had dutifully written to Secretary of War Edwin Stanton to tell him about the list, and a month later had been ordered to report to Washington. When he arrived, a colonel named Samuel Breck in the War Department offered him $300 for the list. Atwater, amazed by Breck's response, replied that he did not want money. He simply wanted to publish the list so that the families of the dead men would know what happened to them. Breck then — bizarrely — threatened Atwater, saying that if he tried to publish the list on his own, "we can call it contraband matter and confiscate them." The two then came to an even odder agreement. In exchange for $300 and a job as a clerk at the War Department, Atwater would lend Breck the list so it could be copied. And presumably published. But Breck did nothing, and Atwater believed that the War Department had no intention of publishing his list.

So he had met with Clara Barton. That had spurred Barton, with Atwater in tow, into action. She got an interview with Secretary of War Stanton and proposed an expedition to Andersonville to identify the graves of the dead and to put up individual markers, using Atwater's rolls as a guide. Stanton enthusiastically agreed, and on July 8, 1865, the steamer *Virginia* slipped its moorings in Washington and headed for Savannah with forty workmen, a load of pine lumber, Barton, Atwater, and commanding officer Captain James M. Moore. After an arduous and often unbearably hot seventeen-day journey by land and sea during which Barton was treated rudely by Moore, they finally arrived at Andersonville.

At the camp they found roughly thirteen thousand bodies laid out in trenches that contained between one hundred and one hundred and fifty bodies each. Even in Civil War terms, this was a large number of dead — nearly twice the number killed at the battles of the Wilderness, Spotsylvania, and Cold Harbor combined. Using Atwater's death rolls — as well as the prison's hospital's own incomplete record, which Atwater himself had compiled — the group matched the numbers on the graves to the names on the lists. Then the workmen set to work making white headboards.

The day after their arrival Atwater gave Barton a tour of the camp. As they walked, he described the conditions in which he had lived, and she thus became one of the first outsiders to understand what had happened at Andersonville. The most basic problem was overcrowding. The prison, which had been designed for ten thousand prisoners, was by June 1864 home to twice that many. The Petersburg campaign alone dumped more than a thousand new prisoners a day into the stockade. By the end of June 1864 twenty-five thousand prisoners were crammed into a 26.5-acre enclosure whose habitable area, subtracting a sizable swamp and no-man's-land, was in reality more like 11 acres. This meant that each man had about twenty square feet.[8] By August the population reached thirty-three thousand, making Andersonville both appallingly crowded and the fifth-largest city in the Confederacy. The only shelter consisted of makeshift tents; many soldiers were exposed to the elements, freezing weather in winter and brutal heat in summer. For rations they were supposed to get what the rebel army got: salt beef or fat bacon and cornmeal, with periodic servings of molasses, peas, or rice. In reality they got nothing like that. The war interrupted food supplies. Often days went by with scant or no rations. Much of the corn they got was simply the cob ground up, and they ate virtually no vegetables.

But what made Andersonville a true horror were the filth and disease. Large numbers of prisoners were sick with lethal camp diseases: diarrhea, dysentery, and scurvy. Doctors in the camp's pathetic makeshift hospital were overwhelmed. In the summer of 1864, a Confederate medical inspector reported finding many patients simply lying on the ground without blankets or clothing. Flies and maggots inhabited patients' mouths and laid eggs in open sores. Many of the men, said the doctor, were "literally encrusted with dirt and filth and covered in vermin."[9] The doctors often reused bandages.

Out in the stockade men simply wasted away, excreting huge volumes of liquid with nothing to replace it, starving from lack of food and vitamins. Sometimes they became too sick to move about and lay helpless in the mud while their wounds filled with maggots.[10] Drinking water came from the sluggish, fetid stream that ran through the middle of camp. Heavy rains would flood the ground with human excrement. Even the healthier men suffered from the ghastly effects of chronic vitamin deficiencies. Men with scurvy lost their gums and teeth; their arms and legs swelled nearly to bursting and turned black-purple.[11]

Though Atwater and many others believed that such suffering was mostly the result of deliberate Confederate policies, historical evidence suggests otherwise. Captain Henry Wirz, the Swiss-born officer in charge of the stockade, was not perfect. The small, nervous Wirz, who spoke English with a heavy German accent, was undoubtedly a harsh man, and occasionally cruel. But the overwhelming majority of the camp's problems — its horrendous overcrowding, its lack of food, clothing, medical supplies, and building supplies — were out of his hands, the failings of a failing nation and its incompetent political bureaucracies, and the effects of shortages created by war. It would have been easier in some ways to attribute the horrors of Andersonville to sheer malevolence. But the camp was only the most extreme example of what happened to the four hundred thousand prisoners of war on both sides during the war. "War is cruelty," Sherman had said. "You cannot refine it." Civil War prisons were unrefined cruelty. The Confederacy had no monopoly on it. At the Union prison camp at Point Lookout, Maryland, where four thousand men died, the twenty thousand inmates were more than double the prison's capacity.

In Elmira, New York — better known as Hellmira — horrific overcrowding resulted in a death rate of nearly 25 percent, only a few percentage points behind Andersonville's.[12]

Though Andersonville contained no prisoners when Clara Barton saw it, with the aid of Atwater's narrative she could imagine the suffering that had taken place there. Some of the most dramatic and emotional writings of her later life would be devoted to the subject.[13] "I have looked over its twenty-five acres of pitiless stockade," she said of Andersonville in a speech shortly after the war,

. . . its burrows in the earth, its stinted stream, its turfless hillsides, shadeless in summer and shelterless in winter, its wells and tunnels and caves, its seven forts of death, its balls and chains, its stocks for torture, its kennels for bloodhounds, its sentry boxes and its deadline, and my heart sickened and stood still. My brain whirled, and the light of my eyes went out. And I said, "Surely this was not the gate of hell, but hell itself." And for comfort I turned away to the acres of crowded graves, and I said, "Here at last was rest, and this to them was the gate of heaven."

On August 16, a little more than four months after Lee's surrender at Appomattox, the final grave marker was put in place at the

Andersonville National Cemetery. Atwater's list had enabled the identification of 12,461 dead Union soldiers. Only 451 headboards bore the inscription UNKNOWN U.S. SOLDIER.[14] The following day Captain Moore arranged for a flag-raising ceremony. Though he and Barton had not gotten along, he granted her the honor of raising the colors. In the presence of a small crowd, which included Moore, Dorence Atwater, workmen, soldiers, and reporters from the *Washington Chronicle* and *Harper's Weekly,* Barton and one of the soldiers hauled the American flag up the pole, where it hung limply for a moment and then unfurled majestically in a sudden gust of wind while the crowd sang "The Star-Spangled Banner."

"The work was done," Barton recorded in her diary. "My own hands have helped to run up the old flag on our great and holy ground — and I ought to be satisfied — I believe I am."[15]

She might have noted, too, that the country over which that flag was flying was something entirely new. The United States of America was now a single thing instead of a multiplicity of things, a free, powerful, and coherent unity in place of an aggregation of warring principalities and contingent interests.

The war that had stitched the nation back together had also made a terrible mess of things. As she raised the colors, Clara Barton stood in the midst of a destroyed country whose impoverishment went beyond any reckoning of ledgers and balance sheets. Cities lay in ruins, farms and plantations lay desolated and uncultivated. Money and wealth and physical resources had vanished, and without them how would Richmond or Columbia or Atlanta be rebuilt? How, in the wrecked South, could one even fund a school? Or a hospital? What was the reconstituted nation to do with 4 million freed slaves and hundreds of thousands of starving white refugees? What was to become of all those soldiers, North and South, who were returning to different worlds than the ones they had left? The Union army's rolls alone would drop, astoundingly, from 1 million men to eighty thousand within the year.[16]

In June 1865 a Texas slave owner and former rebel soldier sent for his sixty-six slaves, who had not yet heard that the war had ended. When they had gathered, he said, "I've got something to tell you. You are just as free as I am. You don't belong to nobody but yourselves. We went to war and fought, and the Yankees whipped us, and they say the niggers are free. You can go where you want to go, or you can stay here, just as you like."[17] There it was, right in front of them, the thing dreamed about and so ardently hoped for: freedom, with all of its terrible and thrilling promise.

598

ACKNOWLEDGMENTS

I have had the good fortune of having one of the best editors in the business, Colin Harrison, for my last four books. Colin's fully engaged editorial approach has saved me from countless narrative and structural mistakes, for which I am deeply grateful. He did perhaps his best work on this book. His remarkable ability as a writer of fiction is not insignificant in the nonfiction world. He has an instinct for the craft and is invariably right.

I also offer thanks and deep appreciation to the excellent team at Scribner for all they do: Nan Graham for years of support and guidance, Kate Lloyd for her outstanding publicity ingenuity, Sarah Goldberg for keeping all the balls in the air and on time.

Fauzia Burke, whose company, FSB Associates, handles my online presence and marketing, is the state of the art in that business. Thanks to her for moving my work into the digital age.

I would also like to thank my agent, Amy

Hughes, who has been relentlessly supportive of me and my work and is an extremely important influence in what I do and how I have done it.

Peter Cozzens, my Civil War mentor and one of our finest Civil War historians, has been a guiding light for me in more ways than I can count. His advice has been of inestimable value in the two books I have written about the Civil War. His knowledge of the war is encyclopedic, his suggestions to me always dead on the mark.

Finally, I would like to acknowledge my photo researcher, Drury Wellford, and my mapmaker, Jeff Ward, who have worked on *Rebel Yell* and *Hymns of the Republic* and have done superb and highly creative work. I am indebted to both.

NOTES

Chapter One: The End Begins

1 For anyone wondering how Antietam fits into that assessment, the engagement was a clear tactical victory for Lee, who fought a drawn battle against McClellan with half the troops McClellan had. Lincoln turned Antietam into a strategic victory for the Union by using it as an excuse to issue the Emancipation Proclamation. See S. C. Gwynne, *Rebel Yell: The Violence, Passion, and Redemption of Stonewall Jackson,* 461ff.

2 In modern times, the hotel has become known as the Willard. In the Civil War era, it was universally known as Willard's.

3 Leech, *Reveille in Washington,* 18ff.; Leech's 1941 Pulitzer Prize winner is still the best description of wartime Washington; see also Noah Brooks, *Mr. Lincoln's Washington,* a selection of writings from a reporter, and Kenneth J. Winkle, *Lincoln's Citadel: The Civil War in Washington, D.C.,*

which focuses more on the political side of the capital. For an interesting and entertaining account of Kate Chase's life, see John Oller, *American Queen: The Rise and Fall of Kate Chase Sprague, Civil War "Belle of the North" and Gilded Age Woman of Scandal;* her marriage took place in November 1863.

4 Civil War Washington, website of the Center for Digital Research in the Humanities at the University of Nebraska–Lincoln, directed by Susan C. Lawrence, Elizabeth Lorang, Kenneth M. Price, and Kenneth J. Winkle.

5 Lee had twice crossed the Potomac with the purpose, in part, of threatening Washington, hoping to give political support to anti-Lincoln, antiwar, and anti-Republican sentiment in the North. The results were the battles of Antietam and Gettysburg. The other threatening approach, as noted, was after the Second Battle of Bull Run.

6 Following the Confederate victory at the Second Battle of Bull Run, Jackson had tried unsuccessfully to cut off the retreating Union army, which resulted in the Battle of Chantilly, roughly twenty miles from the capital city.

7 The president's dwelling would not get the official name White House until Teddy Roosevelt's administration in 1901. Prior to that, it was generally referred to as the Executive Mansion, though it was some-

times called the White House.

8 If you add all of the nonpermanent residents, including escaped slaves, soldiers, et al., this number probably exceeded two hundred thousand.

9 Trollope, *North America,* 302.

10 Swisshelm, *Crusader and Feminist,* 269.

11 Civil War Washington website.

12 Maryland, which as a member of the Union was not covered by the Emancipation Proclamation, did not free its slaves until November 1864.

13 Leech, *Reveille in Washington,* 323; Linda Wheeler, "Tame by Comparison," *Washington Post,* May 13, 1999.

14 Leech, *Reveille in Washington,* 261.

15 Brooks, *Lincoln Observed,* 102–3.

16 Grant, "Reminiscences of General U. S. Grant"; Porter, "Lincoln and Grant," 665.

17 Brooks, *Lincoln Observed,* 104.

18 Porter, "Lincoln and Grant," 665.

19 Welles, *Diary,* 539.

20 Nicolay, *Lincoln's Secretary,* 194–95. John Nicolay's notes had a slightly different version of the initial exchange from General Porter's account: "This is General Grant, is it not?"; Brooks, *Lincoln Observed,* 105.

21 The rank of lieutenant general was common in the Provisional Army of the Confederate States. By war's end, eighteen Confederate generals had held that rank.

22 Furgurson, *Freedom Rising,* 285.

23 McClellan was both arriving and passing through, on his way across the Potomac to Virginia at the time of the Second Battle of Bull Run. Chittenden, *Recollections of President Lincoln,* 316.

24 Ibid.

25 An oft-cited story has Grant arriving at the hotel's front desk, asking for a room, and being given something less than grand by a clerk who did not recognize him. After Grant signs the register, the astonished and chastened clerk snaps to and gives the general the elegant rooms that had been reserved for him. The story rests for its effect entirely on the reaction of the clerk. As far as I can tell, the source of this is the generally reliable Lucius Chittenden, who worked for Salmon Chase in the Treasury Department. The problem is, while this is entertaining and dramatic, Chittenden has almost all the other facts wrong. He says it happened in the morning, and that Grant came in with a wave of others from the early Baltimore train. Grant did not arrive until early evening. I have not included the story because the context in which it was told was so completely wrong. More telling was Grant's arrival in the dining room at Willard's hotel — for which there are several good sources — which caused a stir among many people who did not originally recognize him.

26 Grant, "Reminiscences of General U. S. Grant."

27 Brooks, *Lincoln Observed,* 135.

28 Nicolay, *Lincoln's Secretary,* 195.

29 A nice treatment of this moment is in Mc-Feely, *Grant,* 152–53.

30 Wilson, *Life of John A. Rawlins,* 403.

31 Sherman, *Memoirs,* 428–29.

32 Nicolay, *President's Secretary,* 196.

33 Burlingame, *With Lincoln in the White House,* 131.

34 Grant, *Personal Memoirs,* 1:469. The detail about the brass bands and rain comes from Rhea, *Battle of the Wilderness,* 44.

Chapter Two: With Malice Toward All

1 Letter, Achilles V. Clark to Judith Porter and Henrietta Ray, April 14, 1864, in Sheehan-Dean, *Civil War,* 42ff. Clark's account is valuable, both because he has a Confederate point of view and because he is giving an unvarnished first look at what happened.

2 Castel, "The Fort Pillow Massacre," in Castel, *Winning and Losing the Civil War,* 45.

3 Good accounts of the hardening of Union war policy are found in Mark Grimsley, *The Hard Hand of War: Union Military Policy Toward Southern Civilians, 1861–1865;* Charles Royster, *The Destructive War: William Tecumseh Sherman, Stonewall Jackson,*

and the Americans; and James Lee Mc-Donough, *William Tecumseh Sherman: In the Service of My Country: A Life.*

4 Cimprich, *Fort Pillow,* 68ff.

5 Ibid., 74.

6 See the good description of the fort's flaws in the report of Confederate captain Charles W. Anderson in US War Department, *The War of the Rebellion: A Compilation of the Official Records of the Union and Confederate Armies* (hereafter cited as *OR*), ser. 1, vol. 32, pt. 1, 596.

7 Wills, *River Was Dyed with Blood,* 23.

8 Ibid.

9 According to testimony from a member of the 6th Colored Heavy Artillery, Booth and Bradford had initially refused to burn the barracks at all, in spite of recommendations from their troops to do it. *Reports of the Committees of the Senate of the United States,* 38th Cong., 1st Sess. (Washington: Government Printing Office, 1864).

10 The number of rounds comes from "The Fort Pillow Massacre: Report of the Committee on the Conduct of the War, May 5, 1864," *Reports of the Committees of the Senate.*

11 *OR,* ser. 1, vol. 32, pt. 1, 560ff.

12 Castel, "Fort Pillow Massacre," 38; also *OR,* ser. 1, vol. 32, pt. 1, 560ff.; Bradford probably chose to pose as Booth so that

Forrest's troops would not know that the fort's commander was really the local-boy-turned-traitor William Bradford.

13 "Dr. Fitch's Report," *Tennessee Historical Quarterly,* 27–39. This report by a Union army surgeon is one of the best, most detailed, least biased accounts of the incident.

14 Much has been made of statements by Union participants that Forrest took unfair advantage of the truce to make advances on the fort. After more than 150 years of arguing this out, the truth seems to be that some Confederate soldiers likely cheated. But the general conclusion is that such cheating was not significant in the fort's fall. Forrest's men had gained an extremely strong position, in proximity to the fort's breastworks, with or without unauthorized movements under a truce. See John Cimprich's excellent treatment of this in *Fort Pillow: A Civil War Massacre, and Public Memory.*

15 Henry, *Nathan Bedford Forrest,* chap. 17, "Forrest of Fort Pillow."

16 See discussion of this below; Forrest's responsibility for the massacre has been actively debated for a century and a half. Forrest spent much time after the war trying to clear his name. No direct evidence suggests that he ordered the shooting of

surrendering or unarmed men, but to fully exonerate him from responsibility is also impossible.

17 Clark letter to Porter and Ray in Sheehan-Dean, *Civil War,* 44.

18 Report of Captain John G. Woodruff, 113th Illinois Infantry, on the capture of Fort Pillow, dated April 15, 1864, *OR,* ser. 1, vol. 32, pt. 1, 558.

19 Ibid.

20 *OR,* ser. 1, vol. 32, pt. 1, 562.

21 "Dr. Fitch's Report."

22 Cimprich, *Fort Pillow,* 82.

23 Letter from Forrest to Lieutenant Colonel Thomas M. Jack, Assistant Adjutant General, April 15, 1864, *OR,* ser. 1, vol. 32, pt. 1, 610.

24 Testimony before the Committee on the Conduct of the War, in *Reports of the Committees of the Senate.*

25 "Dr. Fitch's Report," *Tennessee Historical Quarterly.*

26 Casualty figures in the Civil War are notoriously sketchy, but here they become even harder because so many bodies were lost in the river, and because it was hard to know what happened to all of the wounded. General Chalmers's report from the Confederate side is remarkably close to the numbers cited, which suggests they are roughly correct.

27 *OR,* ser. 1, vol. 22, pt. 2, 693–94, 702–3, 713–14.

28 Cimprich, *Fort Pillow,* 90.

29 Wills, *River Was Dyed with Blood,* 165.

30 Cimprich, *Fort Pillow,* 90.

31 "Fort Pillow Massacre: Report of the Committee on the Conduct of the War."

32 Cimprich, *Fort Pillow,* 101.

33 Letter from Forrest to Jack.

34 McFeely, *Frederick Douglass,* 212.

35 From "The Prayer of Twenty Millions," August 19, 1862, Greeley's letter to Abraham Lincoln.

36 McPherson, *Struggle for Equality,* 81–82; McPherson's account of this shift in public perception is still the best I have read; McFeely, *Frederick Douglass,* 214.

37 McPherson, *Struggle for Equality,* 73.

38 In Horace Greeley's August 19, 1862, public letter to Abraham Lincoln, entitled "The Prayer of Twenty Millions," he stated, "We think you are strangely and disastrously remiss in the discharge of your official and imperative duty with regard to the provisions of the new Confiscation Act. . . . We complain that the Confiscation Act which you approved is habitually disregarded by your generals, and that no word of rebuke for them from you has yet reached the public ear."

39 Antietam was a drawn battle between Robert E. Lee and George McClellan,

whose Union army outnumbered Lee's two to one. By any measure it was a tactical victory for Lee. Because Lee had to withdraw his depleted army south of the Potomac after the battle, the strategic victory, perforce, went to McClellan.

40 Emancipation Proclamation, January 1, 1863.

41 Lincoln, *Abraham Lincoln,* 490.

42 Tulloch, *Routledge Companion,* 93.

43 John David Smith, "Let Us All Be Grateful That We Have Colored Troops That Will Fight," in Smith, *Black Soldiers in Blue,* 26–45.

44 Burkhardt, *Confederate Rage, Yankee Wrath,* 60–61.

45 Ibid., 60.

Chapter Three: Armies of Spring

1 Various sources were used to construct the scene: Gordon, *Reminiscences of the Civil War,* 235–36; Lyman, *Meade's Army,* 130ff.; Freeman, *Lee's Lieutenants,* 3:343; Rhea, *Battle of the Wilderness,* 25–30; Grimsley, *And Keep Moving On,* 15.

2 Lee had watched Union general John Pope's army from this same vantage point two years before.

3 Gordon, *Reminiscences of the Civil War,* 229.

4 Lee initially underestimated the Army of

the Potomac's effectives, believing he was facing seventy-five thousand. This was in part because the federal 9th Corps under Ambrose Burnside had not yet joined Meade. Lee's own force was still missing Longstreet's 1st Corps, which would have meant that Lee had about fifty-five thousand men on May 2. Thus the illusory twenty-thousand-man gap in strength. Grimsley, *And Keep Moving On,* 15.

5 Stevens, *Three Years in the Sixth Corps,* 300.

6 "Report of the Medical Director," in *Medical and Surgical History,* 148.

7 Bill, *Beleaguered City,* 202.

8 McPherson, *Battle Cry of Freedom,* 691; "Confederate Inflation Rates, 1861–1864," inflationdata.com.

9 Officially, only around three hundred of those men were listed as deserters. Lee had had problems with absenteeism before, notably around the Battle of Antietam, where a significant chunk of his army melted away. Many came back. The sense in 1864 was that a higher percentage of the men did not plan to return.

10 Gallagher, *Fighting for the Confederacy,* 222.

11 Grimsley, *And Keep Moving On,* 14–15.

12 Ibid., 15.

13 Lyman, *Meade's Army,* 131.

14 Ibid.

15 Rhea, *Battle of the Wilderness,* 33.

16 Humphreys, *Virginia Campaign of '64 and '65,* 19–20.

17 Waugh, *Reelecting Lincoln,* 150.

18 *Dayton Daily Empire,* August 21, 1863, in Klement, *Limits of Dissent,* 245.

19 Burlingame, *Abraham Lincoln: A Life,* 2:646; the strategy Grant and Lincoln devised aimed to win the war by the fall elections.

20 Nevins and Halsey, *Diary of George Templeton Strong,* 3:449.

Chapter Four: A Wilderness of Pain

1 This general idea comes from Gordon Rhea, the definitive historian of the Overland Campaign. The Union high command in Virginia had never been known for its perspicacity. But in the Wilderness its commanders seemed unable to think clearly at all. Rhea's phrase was "Something about the Wilderness invariably clouded Yankee minds." *Battle of the Wilderness,* 93.

2 Ibid., 110.

3 Maxwell, *Lincoln's Fifth Wheel,* 250.

4 Grimsley, *And Keep Moving On,* 38.

5 Porter, *Campaigning with Grant,* 72–73.

6 Grimsley, *And Keep Moving On,* 32.

7 Theodore Lyman, May 18, 1864, letter to parents, in Lyman, *Meade's Headquarters,* 99–100.

8 Porter, *Campaigning with Grant,* 70.

9 Wilson, *Life of John A. Rawlins,* 214–17.

10 Chamberlain, *Passing of the Armies,* 29.

11 This description largely follows the account of this era in Jean Edward Smith's *Grant.*

12 Ibid., 91.

13 In a number of accounts of Grant's life, Longstreet is said to have been the best man at Grant's wedding. Since this is mentioned in neither man's memoirs, I have omitted it. The men were certainly close friends.

14 James Longstreet interview with *New York Times,* July 24, 1885.

15 Ibid.

16 Nevins, *War for the Union,* 4:18, citing Hamlin Garland's interview with John M. Schofield.

17 Gordon, *Reminiscences of the Civil War,* 266.

18 Adams, *Reminiscences of the 19th Massachusetts Regiment,* 88.

19 Patrick, *Inside Lincoln's Army,* 369.

20 Rhea, *Battle of Spotsylvania Courthouse.*

21 Horace Porter, in Sheehan-Dean, *Civil War,* 101.

22 Catton, *Stillness at Appomattox,* 92.

Chapter Five: Shovels and Other Weapons of War

1 Robert K. Krick, "The Insurmountable Barrier Between the Army and Ruin: The

Confederate Experience at Spotsylvania's Bloody Angle," in Gallagher, *Spotsylvania Campaign,* 81.

2 The name Spotsylvania was a playful latinization of the last name of Alexander Spotswood, a former Virginia lieutenant governor.

3 Grimsley, *And Keep Moving On,* 64.

4 Gordon C. Rhea, "The Testing of a Corps Commander: Gouverneur Kemble Warren at the Wilderness and Spotsylvania," in Gallagher, *Spotsylvania Campaign,* 84ff.

5 Hess, *Field Armies and Fortifications,* 196, 294; Hess notes, in this excellent study, that the terms *earthworks, breastworks,* and *rifle pits* were often used interchangeably by the soldiers of the day in their correspondence and reports. Technically, breastworks did not involve digging, just the piling of timber or stones aboveground. Earthworks used both dirt and timber or other bolstering materials. For an understanding of what entrenchment theory looked like on the verge of the Civil War, see Mahan, *A Treatise on field fortification.*

6 Gates, *Evolution of Entrenchments,* 13.

7 Lyman, *Meade's Headquarters.*

8 Rable, *God's Almost Chosen Peoples,* 2.

9 Bardeen, *Little Fifer's War Diary,* 137; there are several different versions of this story, but all make the same point, that the staff

officer (Major Hugh Nelson) was suggesting that Dabney did not quite believe in his own preaching.

10 Hess, *Field Armies and Fortifications,* 134.

11 Of this tactical dilemma, Dennis Hart Mahan wrote, "The chief object of entrenchments is to enable the assailed to meet the enemy with success, *by first compelling him to approach under every disadvantage of position,* and then, when he has been cut up, to assume the offensive" (italics mine).

12 Trudeau, "Walls of 1864," 26.

13 Ibid., 24.

14 Jordan, *Happiness Is Not My Companion,* x–xi.

15 Ibid.

16 Rhea, *Battle of Spotsylvania Courthouse.*

17 Carol Reardon, "A Hard Road to Travel: The Impact of Continuous Operations on the Army of the Potomac and the Army of Northern Virginia," in Gallagher, *Spotsylvania Campaign,* 190.

18 Warren had seemed reluctant to attack in the Wilderness, too, so this behavior seemed to Grant and Meade to be more of the same.

19 Grimsley, *And Keep Moving On,* 79.

20 Rhea in Gallagher, *Spotsylvania Campaign,* 67.

21 Michie, *Life and Letters of Emory Upton,* 108–9.

22 Grimsley, *And Keep Moving On,* 79.

23 Trudeau, "Walls of 1864," 27.

24 Brooks, *Washington in Lincoln's Time,* 148.

25 Gordon, *Reminiscences of the Civil War,* 291.

Chapter Six: One Additional Horror

1 Sodergren, *Army of the Potomac,* 19.

2 The major battle histories of the Wilderness and Spotsylvania barely mention the medical catastrophe at Fredericksburg; medical histories address it only briefly, and the odd historian, such as Bruce Catton, has paid it some attention. But it remains untreated in detail by most histories of the period.

3 His name was pronounced *minyay* in France; Americans dropped the accent aigu and pronounced it *minnie.*

4 Adams, *Living Hell,* 68; "Scenes at Fredericksburg," *Harper's Weekly,* June 11, 1864.

5 Adams, *Reminiscences of the 19th Massachusetts Regiment,* 88.

6 Ibid., 91.

7 Rutkow, *Bleeding Blue and Gray,* 13.

8 "Report of the Medical Director," 152.

9 Grant had become impatient with the idea of shipping men from field hospitals to a depot hospital and then to Washington. This was by then normal procedure in the medical department. Grant had decided to skip the depot hospital and — before he changed

his mind — to ship the wounded directly to Washington. See Rutkow, *Bleeding Blue and Gray,* 304.

10 Maxwell, *Lincoln's Fifth Wheel,* 251; the Union army had 813 ambulances, according to Maxwell, nowhere near enough for seven thousand wounded; Oates, *Woman of Valor,* 21.

11 Catton, *Stillness at Appomattox,* 101; Maxwell, *Lincoln's Fifth Wheel,* 253.

12 Maxwell, *Lincoln's Fifth Wheel,* 252.

13 Ibid., 253; a few days later came reports of "six corpses per mile" lying by the roadside where the ambulance drivers had left them.

14 "Report of Edward B. Dalton, Chief Medical Officer of Depot Field Hospital," 1864, *OR,* series 1, vol. 36, pt. 1, 269–70.

15 Rutkow, *Bleeding Blue and Gray,* 304.

16 "Report of the Medical Director," 152.

17 Catton, *Stillness at Appomattox,* 103.

18 James Longstreet, "The Battle of Fredericksburg," in Johnson, *Battles and Leaders* 3:75; he recalled, "Solid shot rained like hail."

19 "Scenes at Fredericksburg," *Harper's Weekly.*

20 "Report of the Medical Director," 156.

21 Jaquette, *South After Gettysburg,* 94–95.

22 "Report of Edward B. Dalton."

23 Ibid., 93.

24 Woolsey, *Hospital Days,* 150.

25 "Report of the Medical Director," 157.

26 Grimsley, *And Keep Moving On,* 163–64.

27 Maxwell, *Lincoln's Fifth Wheel,* 253.

28 Woolsey, *Hospital Days,* 150.

29 "Scenes at Fredericksburg," *Harper's Weekly.*

Chapter Seven: Battlefield Angel

1 Oates, *Woman of Valor,* 59; this was her battlefield uniform, familiar to people who had been with her in various campaigns.

2 After the Battle of Cedar Mountain, Barton had appeared at a field hospital with a wagonload of supplies at a moment of dire need. A surgeon who was there wrote, "I thought that night if heaven ever sent out an . . . angel, she must be one — her assistance was so timely." The newspapers picked up the idea of a battlefield angel.

3 Barton, *Life of Clara Barton,* diary of Clara Barton, May 13, 1864, 1:275; Clara Barton's diary is presented in large, minimally edited chunks in this 1922 "biography," which consists mainly of documents, letters, and diary entries.

4 Ibid., 1:278.

5 Ibid., 1:277.

6 Ibid.

7 Ibid., 1:278.

8 Pryor, *Clara Barton: Professional Angel,* 51.

9 Ibid., 61.

10 Oates, *Woman of Valor,* 13.

11 Grant and Sherman had failed outright in their careers. Jackson had kept his job as a college professor, but was a certifiable failure as a teacher. No one, then or later, disagreed with that assessment.

12 Leech, *Reveille in Washington,* 260–61.

13 Brown, *Clara Barton,* 82.

14 Oates, *Woman of Valor,* 62.

15 Ibid., 69.

16 Ibid., 69ff.

17 Brown, *Clara Barton,* 99.

18 Barton, *Life of Clara Barton,* 1:198; Barton wrote later, "Closely following the guns we drew up where they did, among the smoke of the thousand campfires, men hastening to and fro, and the atmosphere loaded with noxious vapors, till it seemed the very breath of pestilence."

19 Ibid., 1:200.

20 Ibid., 1:202; Barton's own account.

21 Ibid., Barton's diary entry for April 14, 1864.

22 Ibid., 1:279.

23 "Report of the Medical Director," 157.

24 Ibid., 152.

Chapter Eight: A Circus of Ineptitude

1 In 1861 the North had a population of 23,000,000, while the South had only

9,000,000. Of the latter, 5,500,000 were white.

2 Gallagher, *Fighting for the Confederacy,* 347.

3 Burlingame, *Abraham Lincoln: A Life,* 2:647.

4 Ibid., 2:479.

5 Grimsley, *And Keep Moving On,* 95–96.

6 Ibid.

7 Imboden, "Battle of New Market," in Johnson, *Battles and Leaders,* 4:491.

8 Davis, *Battle of New Market,* 131.

9 Report of Lieutenant Colonel S. Shipp, July 4, 1864, in *OR,* ser. 1, vol. 37, pt. 1, 91.

10 Smith, *Grant,* 359.

11 Wheelan, *Terrible Swift Sword,* p. 95.

12 Sigel, "Sigel in the Shenandoah Valley," in Johnson, *Battles and Leaders,* 4:489–90; Sigel claimed that his retreat was orderly and well conducted, and also that the main problem was that he did not have enough men.

13 Cozzens, "Fire on the Mountain."

14 "Report of Brig. Gen. George Crook, U.S. Army Commanding Second Infantry, Division of West Virginia, May 23, 1864," *OR,* ser. 1, vol. 37, pt. 1, 12.

15 Crook bragged in his battle report about his flight to the mountains: "I regard the bringing through of our train as one of the most remarkable features of the expedition." He mentions Lewisburg in his dispatch; his actual destination would be

Meadow Bluff, even farther into the mountains.

16 Nolan, *Benjamin Franklin Butler,* 31ff.

17 Ibid., 50.

18 Butler, a brigadier general of the Massachusetts militia, politicked his way into command of the Massachusetts brigade that went south to protect Washington. He had accomplished that mainly by arranging emergency loans from Boston banks to the State of Massachusetts to finance the trip; with the loans came the banks' endorsements of Butler.

19 Nolan, *Benjamin Franklin Butler,* 83ff.

20 Ibid., 100.

21 Butler, *Butler's Book,* 257; this is Butler's account of the conversation.

22 West, *Lincoln's Scapegoat General,* 83–84.

23 The other major piece of intelligence was the Union discovery of Lee's Special Orders 191 in September 1862. Because the capture of Richmond and the advent of thirty thousand or more soldiers in Lee's rear might plausibly have ended the war, I give the Van Lew material a slight edge. In both cases, Union generals failed to capitalize on their advantages.

24 Hughes-Wilson, *Secret State,* 176.

25 Butler, *Butler's Book,* 640.

26 Grimsley, *And Keep Moving On,* 124; Trefousse, *Ben Butler,* 148.

27 Wells, *Bermuda Hundred Campaign,* 103;

Butler, *Butler's Book,* 641.

28 Butler, *Butler's Book,* 642; Nolan, *Benjamin Franklin Butler,* 269–70.

29 Wells, *Bermuda Hundred Campaign,* 115.

30 *OR,* ser. 1, vol. 36, pt. 2, 587ff.

31 Grimsley, *And Keep Moving On,* 124–25.

32 *OR,* ser. 1, vol. 36, pt. 2, 586.

33 Grimsley, *And Keep Moving On,* 138.

34 The so-called Battle of Old Men and Young Boys, June 9 and 15, 1864, at Petersburg; and the fiasco at Fort Fisher in December.

Chapter Nine: The Persuasive Logic of Gunpowder

1 What enabled soldiers to be protected while they dug or improved trenches was known as a sap roller. This was a large wicker cylinder filled with dirt and rolled into place. In siege warfare, the sap roller enabled the attacking side to move its trenches forward.

2 Sodergren, *Army of the Potomac,* 175.

3 Trudeau, *Last Citadel,* 287.

4 Ibid., 288.

5 Glatthaar, *General Lee's Army,* 278–81.

6 Ibid., 292.

7 Burkhardt, *Confederate Rage, Yankee Wrath,* 160–61.

8 Testimony of Lieutenant Colonel Henry Pleasants, "Explosion of the Mine Before

Petersburg," 2.

9 Meade testified before the Official Court of Inquiry on the Mine, "The mine . . . was commenced . . . without any sanction obtained from general headquarters. . . . I never considered that the location of General Burnside's mine was the proper one. . . . It is a very unusual way of attacking field fortifications. I do not think there was any reasonable chance of success by such an attack." Because Burnside reported to Grant, not Meade, Meade could not order Burnside to stop.

10 Trudeau, *Last Citadel,* 101, citing testimony of both Lieutenant Colonel Pleasants and Major Oliver Bosbyshell.

11 Ibid., 161.

12 Claxton and Puls, *Uncommon Valor,* 133ff.

13 Testimony of Ambrose Burnside, "Explosion of the Mine Before Petersburg."

14 Wilson, *Campfires of Freedom,* 13.

15 The 23rd Regiment, which had been recruited in Baltimore and Washington, DC, had fought in a May 15 skirmish near Spotsylvania. Source: regimental records.

16 This is part of a graphic in the May 1, 1864, *Chicago Tribune* story about unequal pay.

17 Cornish, *Sable Arm,* 187.

18 Douglass, *Life and Times,* 423.

19 Wilson, *Campfires of Freedom,* 42.

20 Glatthaar, *Forged in Battle,* 114.

21 Ibid., 115.

22 John David Smith, "Let Us All Be Grateful That We Have Colored Troops That Will Fight," in Smith, *Black Soldiers in Blue,* 43.

23 Letter dated April 4, 1863, "Letters of Dr. Seth Rogers, 1862–1863," in *Proceedings of the Massachusetts Historical Society* 43:386.

24 Ibid., 43:89.

25 Reid, "Government Policy, Prejudice."

26 Cornish, *Sable Arm,* 257; Cornish notes that as of October 1864, 140 black regiments were in federal service with a total strength of 101,950. To this number he added losses by casualty, discharge, desertion, and disease, which totaled 33,139, bringing the grand total to 135,089.

27 Wilson, *Campfires of Freedom,* 215–17.

28 Catton, *Stillness at Appomattox,* 230, citing the Reverend Frederic Denison's *Shot and Shell: The 3rd Rhode Island Heavy Artillery Regiment in the Rebellion* (Charleston, SC: Nabu Press, 2010), 214, 229.

29 The 29th and 31st Regiments enlisted in later April 1864; the 39th and 43rd had enlisted in March. The earliest enlistments were from late 1863; source: regimental records.

30 Rhea, *Cold Harbor,* 312–13.

31 Ibid., 314; Rhea's analysis is, as always, excellent.

32 Grimsley, *And Keep Moving On,* 214.

Chapter Ten: An Elaborate Slaughter

1 Furgurson, *Not War but Murder.*
2 McFeely, *Grant,* 158.
3 Letter from Dana to Stanton, July 7, 1864, *OR,* ser. 1, vol. 40, pt. 1, 35.
4 In congressional testimony, Meade said he thought the troops were too inexperienced, which was why he did not have confidence in them. His true feelings were evident in the duties he gave the 4th Division in the Overland Campaign. He never wanted them on the front lines.
5 William Glenn Robertson, "From the Crater to New Market Heights," in Smith, *Black Soldiers in Blue,* 181–82.
6 Weld, *War Diary,* 311–12.
7 Letter from Charles Francis Adams Jr. to his father, August 5, 1864, in Ford, *Cycle of Adams Letters,* 2:172.
8 Ibid., 2:353.
9 Byron Cutcheon of the 20th Michigan, in Trudeau, *Last Citadel,* 107.
10 Ibid.
11 Aide to James Ledlie, ibid., 108.
12 Testimony of O. Cubb, surgeon with 20th Michigan, "Explosion of the Mine Before Petersburg," 192.
13 Ibid., 196; Weld, *War Diary,* 353; Weld notes that the rebel countercharge "[drove]

the negroes head over heels into us, trampling down everyone, and adding still more to the confusion."

14 Thomas H. Cross, "The Crater Battle," *Philadelphia Weekly Times,* September 10, 1881, in Cozzens and Girardi, *New Annals of the Civil War,* 392.

15 Weld, *War Diary,* 354.

16 Robertson and Pegram, "Boy Artillerist," 243.

17 Blackett, *Thomas Morris Chester,* 146.

18 Captain R. G. Richards, in Trudeau, *Last Citadel,* 121.

19 Testimony of Ambrose Burnside, "Explosion of the Mine Before Petersburg," 176.

20 Letter from Adams Jr. to his father, 2:172.

21 Theodore Bowers, in Chernow, *Grant,* 430.

22 Letter from Adams Jr. to his father, 2:172.

23 Burkhardt, *Confederate Rage, Yankee Wrath,* 160.

24 Ibid., 159.

Chapter Eleven: The Man Who Lost Everything

1 McPherson, *Battle Cry of Freedom,* 742.

2 Davis, *Crucible of Command,* 420; Lee's decision to take troops from his defensive lines was quite daring, since it left him with only twenty-five thousand men in Petersburg facing Grant's sixty-five thousand.

3 Brooks, *Washington in Lincoln's Time,* 159.

4 Leech, *Reveille in Washington,* 337–38.

5 Burlingame, *Abraham Lincoln: A Life,* 2:655–56.

6 Brooks, *Washington, in Lincoln's Time,* 159.

7 Burlingame, *Abraham Lincoln: A Life,* 2:656.

8 Lewis, "When Washington Came Close," *Smithsonian,* July 1988.

9 Baker, "Burning of Chambersburg."

10 Grant, *Personal Memoirs,* 1:614.

11 Burlingame, *Abraham Lincoln: A Life,* 2:656.

12 Brooks, *Washington in Lincoln's Time,* 157.

13 Strong, *Diary of George Templeton Strong,* 476.

14 Leech, *Reveille in Washington,* 346; McPherson, *Battle Cry of Freedom,* 760.

15 McPherson, *Battle Cry of Freedom,* 742.

16 Letter from J. K. Herbert to General Benjamin Butler, August 11, 1864, in Ames, *Private and Official Correspondence,* 5:35; this is one of those secondhand quotations, Herbert telling Butler what Lincoln told Herbert. But it rings true as Lincoln's belief of the moment.

17 Arlington House was confiscated by the federal government for delinquent taxes in January 1864. US quartermaster Montgomery Meigs turned it into a cemetery, making sure to locate graves of prominent Union officers in proximity to the house and garden. Robert E. Lee and his wife,

Mary, tried and failed to reclaim it. Finally, in December 1882, twelve years after Lee's death, the US Supreme Court ruled 5–4 in favor of the claim of their son Custis. Arlington House was restored to the family, which meant that the federal government, now officially a trespasser, would have to abandon a fort on the grounds, relocate residents of the Freedmen's Village, and disinter the bodies of twenty thousand Union soldiers. Or Robert E. Lee's former adversary could buy it. In 1883 Custis sold Arlington House to the federal government for $150,000, its fair market value. It is today the site of Arlington National Cemetery, and the mansion is officially known as Arlington House: The Robert E. Lee Memorial.

18 Poole, "How Arlington National Cemetery Came to Be"; Lee had arranged for a friend to pay the debt, but the government had insisted that Mary Lee, its owner, come in person to pay it.

19 Thomas, *Robert E. Lee,* 175ff.

20 Letter from Robert E. Lee to Mary Lee, December 27, 1856, in Jones, *Life and Letters of Robert E. Lee,* 82.

21 Ibid., 156.

22 Lee, *Recollections and Letters of Robert E. Lee,* 59.

23 Thomas, *Robert E. Lee,* 315.

24 Pryor, "Thou Knowest Not the Time."

25 Anyone who finds Lee's position extreme or hypocritical need only look at the viewpoint of religious Americans during World War II. The overwhelming majority of them had no doubt that God was on their side, and they could justify the killing of enemy soldiers — and indeed the mass bombing of innocent civilians — in the service of their righteous cause. As Lincoln pointed out in his Second Inaugural, both sides in the Civil War read the same Bible.

26 Connelly, *Marble Man,* 191.

27 Letter from Robert E. Lee to Anne Carter Lee, March 2, 1862, in Jones, *Life and Letters of Robert E. Lee,* 65.

28 Letter from Robert E. Lee to Mary Lee, February 8, 1862, ibid.

29 Cox, *Religious Life of Robert E. Lee,* 184.

30 Letter from Mary Lee to Robert E. Lee, May 9, 1861, ibid., 178–79.

31 Letter from Robert E. Lee to Mary Lee, May 25, 1864, in Jones, *Life and Letters of Robert E. Lee,* 32.

32 Connelly, *Marble Man,* 182.

33 Thomas, *Robert E. Lee,* 332.

Chapter Twelve: The Mind of Ulysses S. Grant

1 Letter from Rawlins to T. T. Eckerts, July 15, 1864, *OR,* ser. 1, vol. 37, pt. 2, 331.

2 Smith, *From Chattanooga to Petersburg,* 174–75.

3 Catton, *Grant Takes Command,* 334; an account of this incident is also in Chernow, *Grant,* 421–24.

4 Wilson, *Life of John A. Rawlins,* 249.

5 Letter from Rawlins to T. T. Eckerts, July 15, 1864.

6 Sheridan, *Memoirs of Philip H. Sheridan,* 2:459.

7 Davis, *Crucible of Command,* 431–32; Davis accurately describes Grant's former attitude toward slavery as "near indifference."

8 Grant, *Personal Memoirs,* 1:615.

9 This can only be surmised. But we know from Sheridan's memoirs (p. 463) that Lincoln had initially opposed Sheridan's appointment, and we know the contents of the wire traffic that followed the meeting, showing that Lincoln had changed his mind.

10 Grant, *Personal Memoirs,* 1:615.

11 Letter from Halleck to Sherman, July 16, 1864, *OR,* ser. 1, vol. 36, pt. 5, 151.

12 Lyman, *Meade's Headquarters,* 81.

13 Grant, *Personal Memoirs,* 1:616.

14 Ibid., 1:614.

15 Sheridan, *Memoirs of H. Sheridan,* 461.

16 Letter from Bowers to Rawlins, August 10, 1864, in Wilson, *Life of John A. Rawlins,* 257.

17 Catton, *Grant Takes Command,* 354.

18 McFeely, *Grant,* 175.
19 Letter from Charles Francis Adams Jr. to his mother, August 27, 1864, in Ford, *Cycle of Adams Letters,* 2:185.
20 The general in question was John G. Foster.
21 Letter from Grant to Elihu Washburne, August 16, 1864, in Simon, *Papers of Ulysses S. Grant,* 12:16–17.

Chapter Thirteen: The War Against Lincoln

1 Hart, *Salmon P. Chase,* 82–83.
2 Hay and Nicolay, "Abraham Lincoln," 38:279.
3 Weik, *Real Lincoln,* 287.
4 Hay, *Lincoln and the Civil War,* 53.
5 Kathleen A. Frankovic, "Opinion Polls and the Media in the United States," in Holtz-Bacha and Stromback, *Opinion Polls and the Media,* 113–34.
6 Nevins, *War for the Union,* 4:114; there was so much anti-Lincoln language that *Harper's* magazine in 1864 compiled a catalog of it.
7 Waugh, *Reelecting Lincoln,* 140.
8 McFeely, *Frederick Douglass,* 234.
9 Ibid., 55.
10 Ibid., 40, citing the account of Elizabeth Keckley, Mary Lincoln's seamstress and friend.
11 Burlingame and Ettlinger, *Inside Lincoln's*

White House, 93.

12 Waugh, *Reelecting Lincoln,* 115.

13 Zornow, *Lincoln and the Party Divided,* 26–27.

14 Letter from Dewitt C. Chipman to Abraham Lincoln, February 29, 1864, transcribed and annotated by Lincoln Studies Center, Knox College.

15 Hay and Nicolay, "Abraham Lincoln," 38:282.

16 Burlingame, *Abraham Lincoln: A Life,* 2:619.

17 Blue, *Salmon P. Chase,* 223.

18 McPherson, *Struggle for Equality,* 271.

19 Waugh, *Reelecting Lincoln,* 192.

20 Burlingame, *Abraham Lincoln: A Life,* 2:661.

21 Lincoln, "Proclamation of Amnesty and Reconstruction."

22 Vorenberg, " 'Deformed Child,' " 243.

23 Waugh, *Reelecting Lincoln,* 54.

24 Burlingame, *Abraham Lincoln: A Life,* 2:662.

25 Vorenberg, " 'Deformed Child,' " 244.

26 "From Washington," *New York Times.*

27 Wade-Davis Manifesto.

28 Waugh, *Reelecting Lincoln,* 260.

29 Burlingame, *Abraham Lincoln: A Life,* 663.

30 Waugh, *Reelecting Lincoln,* 262.

31 Conversation between Lincoln, part of cabinet, and Henry Raymond, recorded by John Hay, in Basler, *Collected Works of Abraham Lincoln,* 7:518.

Chapter Fourteen: Politics of the Not Quite Real

1 Kinchen, *Confederate Operations,* 155ff.
2 Castleman, *Active Service,* 132–33; Castleman was part of the larger group of Confederate agents in Canada.
3 Nelson, *Bullets, Ballots, and Rhetoric,* xi.
4 McPherson, *Battle Cry of Freedom,* 595.
5 Weber, *Copperheads,* 5.
6 Neely, *Fate of Liberty,* 53.
7 Ibid.
8 Ibid., 54.
9 Waugh, *Reelecting Lincoln,* 158.
10 Ibid., 158, 208.
11 Ibid., 150.
12 Nelson, *Bullets, Ballots, and Rhetoric,* 87.
13 McPherson, *Battle Cry of Freedom,* 764.
14 Williams, *Horace Greeley,* 252.
15 Greeley to Lincoln, July 7, 1864, and Lincoln to Greeley, July 9, 1864, in Basler, *Collected Works of Abraham Lincoln,* 7:435.
16 Waugh, *Reelecting Lincoln,* 253.
17 McPherson, *Battle Cry of Freedom,* 769.
18 Vorenberg, " 'Deformed Child,' " 248.
19 Greeley to Lincoln, August 9, 1864, in Basler, *Collected Works of Abraham Lincoln.* 7: 476.
20 Albert Castel, "The Atlanta Campaign and the Presidential Election of 1864: How the South Almost Won by Not Losing," in

Castel, *Winning and Losing in the Civil War,* 18.

21 Weber, *Copperheads,* 99.

22 Memorandum of Clement C. Clay, in Basler, *Collected Works of Abraham Lincoln,* 7:460.

23 Long, *Jewel of Liberty,* 155.

24 McPherson, *Battle Cry of Freedom,* 789.

25 Long, *Jewel of Liberty,* 166.

26 Ibid., 157.

27 Ta-Nehisi Coates, "The Miscegenation Ball," *Atlantic,* July 14, 2010.

28 Long, *Jewel of Liberty,* 60; Waugh, *Reelecting Lincoln,* 320.

29 McFeely, *Frederick Douglass,* 234.

30 McClellan to Lincoln, July 7, 1862, in Sears, *Civil War Papers,* 344–45.

31 Text of the 1864 Democratic platform from the American Presidency Project, University of California, Santa Barbara.

32 Nevins, *War for the Union,* 4:102.

33 Nelson, *Bullets, Ballots, and Rhetoric,* 113.

34 McPherson, *Battle Cry of Freedom,* 761.

35 Letter from Grant to Sherman, August 18, 1864, in Simon, *Papers of Ulysses S. Grant,* 34.

36 McDonough, *William Tecumseh Sherman,* 540.

37 Castel, "Atlanta Campaign," 25.

38 Grant, *Personal Memoirs,* 1:511.

39 Diary entry dated September 21, 1864, in Woodward, *Mary Chesnut's Civil War,* 645.

Chapter Fifteen: Valley of Fire

1 Paul Andrew Hutton, *Phil Sheridan and His Army* (Lincoln: University of Nebraska Press, 1985), 2.
2 Wheelan, *Terrible Swift Sword,* 104.
3 Early, *Memoir of the Last Year,* 79.
4 Smith, *Grant,* 384.
5 Grant, *Personal Memoirs,* 1:621.
6 Ibid., 1:620–21.
7 Catton, *Grant Takes Command,* 363.
8 Nicolay and Hay, *Abraham Lincoln,* 9:306.
9 Sheridan, *Personal Memoirs,* 1:484ff.
10 Ibid., 2:56.
11 Wheelan, *Terrible Swift Sword,* 130–31.
12 The army had been ordered to spare the homes of Mennonites and Dunkers, pacifists who were known to support the Union. Not all of them were spared, but most were, and some sought Union protection after the army had departed.
13 Custer was a lieutenant colonel by brevet. His rank was captain.
14 Wheelan, *Terrible Swift Sword,* 129.
15 As noted in an earlier chapter, parts of the valley had been treated harshly by David Hunter in May and June 1864. But the scale was quite limited.
16 Mackey, *Uncivil War,* 115.

17 *OR,* series 1, vol. 43, pt. 1, 560; in his report Early also noted Sheridan "has laid waste nearly all of Rockingham and Shenandoah [counties]."

18 Prior to his engagements with Early, Sheridan had carried out orders in mid-August to burn parts of Loudoun County in northern Virginia, specifically to deter guerrillas. He then suspended such activity until he had beaten Early at Fisher's Hill on September 22, 1864. Sheridan resumed the burning campaign in earnest in early October. By contrast, the burning of barns in Loudoun County was a minor affair.

19 Greiner, *General Phil Sheridan,* 314.

20 Sheridan, *Personal Memoirs,* 1:487–88.

21 Wiggins, *Journals of Josiah Gorgas,* 120.

22 Wheelan, *Terrible Swift Sword,* 131.

23 The army would have been either Pope's or McClellan's around the time Mosby first suggested the idea.

24 Ramage, *Gray Ghost,* 50.

25 Ibid., 57.

26 Wert, *Mosby's Rangers,* 26.

27 Mackey, *Uncivil War,* 75.

28 Wert, *Mosby's Rangers,* 132–33.

29 Ibid., 149.

30 Russell, *Memoirs of Colonel John S. Mosby,* 284.

31 Ramage, *Gray Ghost,* 68.

32 Russell, *Memoirs of Colonel John S. Mosby,* 175ff.

33 Ramage, *Gray Ghost,* 73.

34 Allmon, "Desperate Battle of Allatoona Pass."

35 *The Life of Francis Marion,* by William Gilmore Simms, published in 1840; *The Life of General Francis Marion,* by M. L. Weems, published in 1809. The former was relatively factual. The latter — the one Mosby loved — was richly embellished. ("Parson" Weems was the same writer who came up with the apocryphal cherry-tree story about George Washington.)

36 Simms, *The Life of Francis Marion,* 19.

37 Wachtell, "Author of the Civil War."

38 Ibid.

39 Turner Ashby and Jeb Stuart were also prominent examples of these ideals.

40 Mackey, *Uncivil War,* 82.

41 For a twentieth-century rendering of this chivalric version of the old South, read Margaret Mitchell's *Gone with the Wind.*

42 Twain, *Life on the Mississippi,* 418.

43 Wert, *Mosby's Rangers,* 292.

44 Burkhardt, *Confederate Rage, Yankee Wrath,* 205.

45 Ibid., 204.

46 Ibid., 117; one such placard on a corpse read SUCH THE FATE OF ALL FORAGERS.

47 In Sheridan's memoirs, he cites four major guerrilla leaders in the valley area: "Mosby,

White, Gilmore, and [John Hanson] Mc-Neill."

48 Russell, *Memoirs of Colonel John S. Mosby,* 283.

49 Sheridan, *Personal Memoirs,* 2:99.

50 Ramage, *Gray Ghost,* 193.

51 Though this order was not carried out, it was not rescinded, either.

52 Sheridan to Grant, August 19, 1864, *OR,* series 1, vol. 43, pt. 1, 822ff.

53 Ramage, *Gray Ghost,* 199.

54 Wert, *Mosby's Rangers,* 245.

55 Russell, *Memoirs of Colonel John S. Mosby,* 302–3.

56 Ramage, *Gray Ghost,* 212.

57 Waugh, *Reelecting Lincoln,* 329.

58 Vorenberg, " 'Deformed Child,' " 240.

Chapter Sixteen: Back Roads to Fame

1 I note later on that Sherman was a talented administrator and a talented manager of armies, including their supply lines. He just did not fight well. In this sense he is like George McClellan and Joseph Hooker, both of whom knew how to handle, train, and transport armies, but did less well on the battlefield.

2 Henry Halleck, who graduated third in the class of 1839, was one obvious exception.

3 William T. Sherman to Ellen Ewing, November 10, 1847, Sherman Family Papers,

Notre Dame Archives.

4 O'Connell, *Fierce Patriot,* xii.

5 Sherman letter to Henry S. Turner, March 4, 1858, Ohio Historical Society.

6 Kennett, *Sherman,* 95.

7 I have left P. G. T. Beauregard off this list. He became quickly famous in spite of his remarkable incompetence, then just as quickly fell from grace.

8 Kennett, *Sherman,* 98–100, citing various contemporaneous descriptions of Sherman in 1861.

9 Sherman, *Memoirs,* 227.

10 Michael Fellman, "Sherman's Demons," *New York Times,* November 9, 2011.

11 Kennett, *Sherman,* 138.

12 Ibid.

13 Hart, *Sherman,* 106.

14 Marszalek, *Sherman,* 160–63.

15 What exactly brought on Sherman's nervous breakdown is unclear. His wife, Ellen, noted that she had seen him in a similar state before, once when his bank had failed in San Francisco. One of his uncles was described as "melancholic," a condition associated in modern times with bipolar disorder.

16 Marszalek, *Sherman,* 165.

17 Ibid., 207.

18 Ibid., 154–55.

19 McDonough, *William Tecumseh Sherman,* 444; Marszalek, *Sherman,* 244–45.

Chapter Seventeen: The Moralist from Hell

1 The term *total war* is often connected to Sherman's theory and practice. I have not used it here because the meaning has changed so much over the years. In the twentieth century *total war* meant the deliberate killing of large numbers of civilians, as the Allies did in Dresden, Tokyo, Hiroshima, and elsewhere during World War II. Neither Sherman nor the Union armies did any such thing. Military targets during the Civil War expanded to include civilian property, but never civilian lives.

2 An excellent analysis of Sherman's need to explain himself is in Grimsley, *Hard Hand of War,* 172; see also O'Connell, *Fierce Patriot,* xii.

3 Davis's speech in Jackson, Mississippi, December 26, 1862, in Davis, "To the People of the Confederate States."

4 Davis speech to the Congress of the CSA, Richmond, May 2, 1864, in Crist, *Papers of Jefferson Davis,* vol. 10.

5 "New Lesson on Dying," *New York Times.*

6 Marszalek, *Sherman,* 200–201.

7 Sherman, *Memoirs,* 286.

8 Marszalek, *Sherman,* 194.

9 Berlin and Simpson, *Sherman's Civil War,* 292.

10 Jones, *Tennessee in the Civil War,* 109.

11 Ibid.

12 Ibid.

13 Sherman, *Memoirs,* 295.

14 Ibid., 300.

15 Grimsley, *Hard Hand of War,* 158ff.

16 Royster, *Destructive War,* 341.

17 Letter from Sherman to H. W. Hill, September 7, 1863, *OR,* ser. 1, vol. 30, pt. 3, 402.

18 Foster, "Sherman's First Campaign," 61.

19 Marszalek, *Sherman,* 254.

20 "Treatment of the Inhabitants," *New York Times.*

21 This and the quotations that follow are all from Sherman's letter to Major R. M. Sawyer, Assistant Adjutant General, Army of the Tennessee, Huntsville, Alabama, April 28, 1864, in the *New York Times* of that date.

Chapter Eighteen: Uncle Billy's Book of Moments

1 Kennett, *Sherman,* 101.

2 Porter's descriptions of Sherman all come from Porter's 1897 book, *Campaigning with Grant,* 290ff.

3 Ibid.

4 Marszalek, *Sherman,* 285.

5 Sherman, *Memoirs,* 599.

6 Letter from Sherman to Mayor James M. Calhoun and E. E. Rawson and S. C. Wells of the Atlanta city council, September 12,

1864, *OR,* series 1, vol. 39, pt. 2, 417.

7 Ibid.

8 Ibid.

9 Marszalek, *Sherman,* 296.

10 Sherman, *Memoirs,* 628.

11 Grimsley, *Hard Hand of War,* 191.

12 Marszalek, *Sherman,* 300.

13 Special Field Orders no. 120, November 9, 1864, *OR,* ser. 1, vol. 39, pt. 3, 713–14.

14 McDonough, *William Tecumseh Sherman,* 567.

15 Ibid., 568.

16 Hitchcock, *Marching with Sherman,* 161–62.

17 Historian Noah Andre Trudeau found that only one victim of supposed rape was known by name. Historian Joseph T. Glatthaar could find only one example of a soldier being prosecuted for rape during the march to the sea.

18 Grimsley, *Hard Hand of War,* 199.

19 Kennett, *Sherman,* 107.

20 Anne J. Bailey, "The USCT in the Confederate Heartland," in Smith, *Black Soldiers in Blue,* 229.

21 Royster, *Destructive War,* 345.

22 Ibid.

23 Ibid., 346.

24 Letter from Henry Halleck to Sherman, December 30, 1864; in it Halleck describes the "certain class" of politicians in Washington who were telling Lincoln that Sherman

"was not willing to carry out the wishes of the Government in regard to [slaves]."

25 Sherman, *Memoirs,* 725–27; this account comes from notes taken by Stanton, the army's Adjutant General Edward Townsend, and presumably their assistants. Sherman reproduces the official documents along with Stanton's twelve questions and the answers to them. Sherman also comments on the meeting extensively in his own memoir.

26 Carr, "General Sherman's March," 31.

27 Bailey, *War and Ruin,* 117.

28 *New York Herald,* December 22 and 27, 1864.

29 Letter from Sherman to Major General George H. Thomas, January 21, 1865, *OR,* ser. 1, vol. 45, pt. 2, 622.

30 "Major General W. T. Sherman's Report of the Campaign of Georgia," January 1, 1865, *Executive Documents of the House of Representatives,* 39th Cong., 1st Sess., vol. 3, pt. 2, 1186.

31 Letter from Halleck to Sherman, December 18, 1864; letter from Sherman to Halleck, December 24, 1864, *OR,* ser. 1, vol. 44, 741, 799.

32 McPherson, *Battle Cry of Freedom,* 827.

33 Journal of William C. Pritchard, entry for February 23, 1865, in Grimsley, *Hard Hand of War,* 202.

34 McPherson, *Battle Cry of Freedom,* 827.

35 Marszalek, Sherman, 324–25.

36 McDonough, *William Tecumseh Sherman,* 608.

37 Ibid., 613.

38 *National Freedman,* April 1, 1865, in Sterling, *Trouble They Seen,* 1.

Chapter Nineteen: Death Ahead of Them, Death Behind Them

1 Trudeau, *Last Citadel,* 343.

2 Luther Rice Mills, letter to John Mills from the Petersburg front dated March 2, 1865, in Sheehan-Dean, *Civil War,* 610.

3 Marvel, *Lee's Last Retreat,* 11.

4 Gordon, *Reminiscences of the Civil War,* 410.

5 Trudeau, *Last Citadel,* 350.

6 McPherson, *Battle Cry of Freedom,* 826.

7 The *Lee paradox* is my term for this phenomenon, first discussed in chapter 11.

8 Duncan Rose, "Why the Confederacy Failed," in Johnson, *Battles and Leaders,* 6:570.

9 Peter Cozzens, "Nation of Nomads: When War Landed on Their Doorsteps, Southern Refugees Fought Their Own Battle for Survival," *America's Civil War,* September 2015, 34.

10 McPherson, *Battle Cry of Freedom,* 817.

11 Boteler, "Beginning of the End."

12 Bill, *Beleaguered City,* 265.

13 Ibid.

14 From one of Chester's dispatches from the James River front to the *Philadelphia Press,* in Blackett, *Thomas Morris Chester,* 171.

15 Taylor, *Four Years with General Lee,* 145–46.

16 Mills, letter to John Mills.

17 Bill, *Beleaguered City,* 261.

18 Nevins, *War for the Union,* 4:280.

19 McPherson, *Battle Cry of Freedom,* 824.

20 Pollard, *Observations in the North,* 131.

21 Confederate diarist Mary Chesnut had mentioned the idea, which she favored, as early as 1861.

22 Cleburne, "Patrick Cleburne's Proposal."

23 Ibid.

24 Davis, *Jefferson Davis,* 597.

25 Winik, *April 1865,* 57.

26 Letter from Lee to "Hon. E. Barksdale," *Scribner's* 50 (July–December 1911): 584.

27 Winik, *April 1865,* 61.

28 Ibid., 61–62.

29 I am largely following Noah Andre Trudeau's detailed account of the fight. See Trudeau, *Last Citadel,* 348ff.

30 Ibid., 354.

Chapter Twenty: Richmond Is Burning

1 Gallagher, *Fighting for the Confederacy*, 513.
2 Encyclopedia Virginia/Virginia Humanities online resource, in partnership with the Library of Virginia.
3 From an article in the *New Orleans Democrat*, July 5, 1881.
4 Estimates of troop strength near the end of the war vary widely, in part because Confederate military people and South-leaning historians tend to underestimate rebel strength while greatly exaggerating Union troop numbers. Lee was never, for example, outnumbered six to one during the war's final campaign, as has often been asserted. It remains difficult to make definitive assessments of troop strength. The numbers used in this chapter are rough estimates based on excellent research by historian William Marvel. See his book *Lee's Last Retreat*, particularly appendix A.
5 Gallagher, *Fighting for the Confederacy*, 512; Porter Alexander also noted that Grant had learned another lesson that he put into practice at Petersburg: not to send his cavalry off on a wild-goose chase, as he had done in the Wilderness, and as Hooker had done at Chancellorsville.
6 Smith, *Grant*, 399.
7 Trudeau, *Last Citadel*, 363.
8 Marvel, *Lee's Last Retreat*, 16; Catton, *Still-*

ness at *Appomattox,* 360.

9 Marvel, *Lee's Last Retreat,* 22.

10 Davis, *Jefferson Davis,* 601.

11 Stephen R. Mallory, "The Last Days of the Confederate Government," in Johnson, *Battles and Leaders,* 5:666.

12 Bill, *Beleaguered City,* 270.

13 Boteler, "Beginning of the End."

14 McGuire, *Diary of a Southern Refugee,* 344.

15 Tucker, "Digging Up the Past."

16 Bill, *Beleaguered City,* 272.

17 T. M. Chester's dispatch to the *Philadelphia Press,* April 4, 1865.

18 Brock, *Richmond During the War,* 365.

19 McGuire, *Diary of a Southern Refugee,* 345.

20 Chester dispatch, April 4, 1865.

21 Brock, *Richmond During the War,* 365.

22 Boteler, "Beginning of the End."

23 Erickson, "Black Troops from Hampton Roads."

24 Chester dispatch, April 4, 1865.

25 Erickson, "Black Troops from Hampton Roads."

26 Chester dispatch, April 4, 1865.

27 Blackett, *Thomas Morris Chester,* 42.

28 McGuire, *Diary of a Southern Refugee,* 348.

29 Burlingame, *Abraham Lincoln: A Life,* 2:789.

30 Bill, *Beleaguered City,* 280.

31 Burlingame, *Abraham Lincoln: A Life,* 2:789.

32 Ibid., 2:790.

33 Brooks, *Washington in Lincoln's Time,* 219.

34 Ibid.

35 Leech, *Reveille in Washington,* 378.

36 Ibid.

Chapter Twenty-One: This Bitter Glory

1 Smith, *Grant,* 395.

2 Marvel, *Lee's Last Retreat,* 42.

3 Ibid., 205.

4 Gordon, *Reminiscences of the Civil War,* 423.

5 Longstreet, *From Manassas to Appomattox,* 614–15.

6 Catton, *Stillness at Appomattox,* 372.

7 W. N. Pendleton, "Personal Recollections of General Lee," *Southern* 15 (July–December 1874): 633.

8 Ibid.

9 Alexander, *American Civil War,* 605.

10 Winik, *April 1865,* 169.

11 Porter, *Incidents and Anecdotes,* 314–15; Sherman's version of the meeting diverges in places from Porter's, which is frequently gossipy and inaccurate, but on this point there is general agreement.

12 Young, *Around the World,* 2:458.

13 Marshall, *Aide-de-Camp of Lee,* 275.

14 Marvel, *Lee's Last Retreat,* 189.

15 Ibid., 191ff.

16 Ibid., 194–95.

17 Brooks, *Washington in Lincoln's Time,* 224.

18 Ibid.

19 Burlingame, *Abraham Lincoln: A Life,* 2:801.

Chapter Twenty-Two: The Unbearable Weight of History

1 Burlingame, *Abraham Lincoln: A Life,* 2:800.

2 Brooks, *Washington in Lincoln's Time,* 225.

3 Keckley, *Behind the Scenes,* 176.

4 Brooks, *Washington in Lincoln's Time,* 226.

5 Burlingame, *Abraham Lincoln: A Life,* 2:806.

6 Beale, *Diary of Gideon Welles,* 2:281 (his entry for April 14, 1865); Welles, who wrote the entry three days later, was the only one with this description.

7 Ibid.; note that in current usage the name of the battle is Stones River.

8 Both quotes are in Burlingame, *Abraham Lincoln: A Life,* 2:799.

9 Grant, *Personal Memoirs,* 2:750.

10 Ibid.

11 Young, *Around the World,* 2:355.

12 Letter from Grant to Ord, 4:00 p.m., April 15, 1865, *OR,* ser. 1, vol. 46, pt. 3, 762.

13 Ord to Grant, April 15, 1865, ibid.

14 Brooks, *Washington in Lincoln's Time,* 231.

15 Burlingame, *Abraham Lincoln: A Life,* 2:825.

16 Smith, *Grant,* 412.

17 Secretary of War John Breckinridge was

not with them. He would join them later.

18 Davis's letter from Danville, Virginia, April 4, 1865, in Davis, "To the People of the Confederate States."

19 Davis, *Jefferson Davis,* 611.

20 Letter from Grant to Stanton, April 21, 1865, *OR,* ser. 1, vol. 47, pt. 3, 263.

21 Sherman, *Memoirs,* 2:847–48.

22 Forrest's Final Address to His Troops, May 9, 1865, *OR,* ser. 1, vol. 49, pt. 2.

23 Cozzens, "Irresistible Force."

24 Ibid.

25 Ibid.

26 Davis, *Jefferson Davis,* 640–41.

Chapter Twenty-Three: Hell Itself

1 Oates, *Woman of Valor,* 309.

2 Ibid., 295–97.

3 Barton, *Life of Clara Barton,* 1:306–7.

4 Ibid., 305ff.

5 Mackintosh, "Were It Not for Dorence Atwater," 20.

6 Pryor, *Clara Barton,* 138.

7 Ransom, *John Ransom's Andersonville Diary,* 262.

8 Marvel, *Andersonville,* 110.

9 Oates, *Woman of Valor,* 324.

10 Ransom, *John Ransom's Andersonville Diary,* 92.

11 Oates, *Woman of Valor,* 324.

12 Flavion, "Suffering and Survival."

13 Pryor, *Clara Barton,* 140.

14 Oates, *Woman of Valor,* 335.

15 Atwater's story was still not over. He remained locked in a struggle with various military bureaucrats over possession of his list. On September 20, barely a month after the raising of the flag over Andersonville cemetery, Atwater was tried and convicted of, in effect, stealing his own death rolls. Though he was completely innocent, he spent several months in jail. Through the considerable help of Clara Barton, Atwater was finally able to publish those lists in the *New-York Tribune* on February 14, 1866, in a pamphlet that included Atwater's personal story in addition to Clara Barton's full report to Secretary of War Edwin Stanton on the Andersonville project. Atwater, who was exonerated in the public eye, somehow managed in 1868 to secure an appointment as American consul in the Seychelles Islands. Three years later he became US consul in Tahiti, where he married a princess and became rich from his vanilla and coffee plantations and pearl fisheries.

16 McPherson, *Battle Cry of Freedom,* 853.

17 Harrigan, *Big Wonderful Thing,* 306.

BIBLIOGRAPHY

Books

Adams, George Worthington. *Doctors in Blue: The Medical History of the Union Army in the Civil War.* New York: Henry Schuman, 1952.

Adams, John G. B. *Reminiscences of the 19th Massachusetts Regiment.* Boston: Wright and Potter, 1899.

Adams, Michael C. C. *Living Hell: The Dark Side of the Civil War.* Baltimore: Johns Hopkins Press, 2014.

Alexander, Edward Porter. *The American Civil War: A Critical Narrative.* London: Siegle, Hill, 1908.

———. *Memoirs of a Confederate: A Critical Narrative.* New York: Charles Scribner and Sons, 1907.

Allen, Stanton P. *Down in Dixie: Life in a Cavalry Regiment in the War Days from the Wilderness to Appomattox.* Boston: D. Lothrop Company, 1893.

Anonymous. *The Lincoln Catechism: Wherein*

the Eccentricities and Beauties of Despotism Are Fully Set Forth — a Guide to the Presidential Election of 1864. New York: J. F. Feeks, 1864.

Ash, Stephen V. *When the Yankees Came: Conflict and Chaos in the Occupied South, 1861–1865.* Chapel Hill: University of North Carolina Press, 1995.

Bailey, Anne J. *War and Ruin: William T. Sherman and the Savannah Campaign.* Wilmington, DE: SR Books, 2003.

Bardeen, Charles William. *A Little Fifer's War Diary.* Syracuse, NY: C. W. Bardeen, 1910.

Barton, William E. *The Life of Clara Barton: Founder of the American Red Cross.* Boston and New York: Houghton Mifflin, 1922.

Basler, Roy P., ed. *The Collected Works of Abraham Lincoln.* Springfield, IL: Abraham Lincoln Association, 1955.

Beale, Howard K., ed. *The Diary of Gideon Welles.* Vol. 2 (of 3). New York: W. W. Norton, 1960.

Berlin, Jean V., and Brooks D. Simpson. *Sherman's Civil War: Selected Correspondence of William T. Sherman, 1860–1865.* Chapel Hill: University of North Carolina Press, 1999.

Bill, Alfred Hoyt. *The Beleaguered City: Richmond 1861–1865.* New York: Alfred A. Knopf, 1946.

Blackett, R. J. M. *Thomas Morris Chester,*

Black Civil War Correspondent: His Dispatches from the Virginia Front. Baton Rouge: LSU Press, 1989.

Blair, William Alan, ed. *A Politician Goes to War: The Civil War Letters of John White Geary.* University Park: Penn State University Press, 1995.

Blight, David W. *Frederick Douglass: Prophet of Freedom.* New York: Simon & Schuster, 2018.

Blue, Frederick J. *Salmon P. Chase: A Life in Politics.* Kent, OH: Kent State University Press, 1987.

Bradley, Mark. *Last Stand in the Carolinas: The Battle of Bentonville.* Campbell, CA: Savas Woodbury, 1996.

Brands, H. W. *The Man Who Saved the Union: Ulysses S. Grant in War and Peace.* New York: Doubleday, 2012.

Brock, Sallie A. *Richmond During the War: Four Years of Personal Observation by a Richmond Lady.* New York: G. W. Carleton, 1867.

Brooks, Noah. *Washington in Lincoln's Time.* Chicago: Quadrangle Books, 1971.

Brownlee, Richard S. *Gray Ghosts of the Confederacy: Guerrilla Warfare in the West, 1861–1865.* Baton Rouge: LSU Press, 1958.

Bryant, James K., II. *The 36th Infantry United States Colored Troops in the Civil War: A His-*

tory and Roster. Jefferson, NC: McFarland, 2012.

Burkhardt, George S. *Confederate Rage, Yankee Wrath: No Quarter in the Civil War.* Carbondale: Southern Illinois University Press, 2007.

Burlingame, Michael. *Abraham Lincoln: A Life.* 2 vols. Baltimore: Johns Hopkins University Press, 2008.

———, ed. *Abraham Lincoln: The Observations of John G. Nicolay and John Hay.* Carbondale: Southern Illinois University Press, 2007.

———, ed. *Lincoln Observed: Civil War Dispatches of Noah Brooks.* Baltimore: Johns Hopkins University Press, 1998.

———, ed. *With Lincoln in the White House: Letters, Memoirs and Other Writings of John G. Nicolay.* Carbondale: Southern Illinois University Press, 2000.

Burlingame, Michael, and John R. T. Ettlinger, eds. *Inside Lincoln's White House: The Complete Civil War Diary of John Hay.* Carbondale: Southern Illinois University Press, 1999.

Butler, Benjamin F. *Butler's Book: A Review of His Legal, Political, and Military Career.* Boston: A. M. Thayer, 1892.

Carter, Dan T. *When the War Was Over: The Failure of Self-Reconstruction in the South, 1865–1867.* Baton Rouge: LSU Press, 1985.

Carter, Gari. *Troubled State: Civil War Journals of Franklin Archibald Dick.* Kirksville, MO: Truman State University Press, 2008.

Carter, Robert G. *Four Brothers in Blue: Sunshine and Shadows of the War of the Rebellion; a Story of the Great Civil War from Bull Run to Appomattox.* 1913. Reprint, Austin: University of Texas Press, 1978.

Castel, Albert. *Winning and Losing in the Civil War: Essays and Stories.* Columbia: University of South Carolina Press, 1996.

Castel, Albert, and Thomas Goodrich. *Bloody Bill Anderson: The Short, Savage Life of a Civil War Guerrilla.* Mechanicsburg, PA: Stackpole Books, 1998.

Castleman, John Breckinridge. *Active Service.* Louisville, KY: Courier-Journal Job Printing, 1917.

Catton, Bruce. *Grant Moves South.* Boston: Little, Brown, 1960.

———. *Grant Takes Command.* Boston: Little, Brown, 1968.

———. *Mr. Lincoln's Army.* New York: Pocket Books, 1951.

———. *A Stillness at Appomattox.* Garden City, NY: Doubleday, 1953.

———. *This Hallowed Ground.* New York: Washington Square Press (Pocket Books), 1961.

Chamberlain, Joshua Lawrence. *The Passing of the Armies: An Account of the Final Cam-*

paign of the Army of the Potomac Based upon *Personal Reminiscences of the Fifth Army Corps*. 1915. Reprint, New York: Skyhorse, 2013.

Chernow, Ron. *Grant*. New York: Penguin Press, 2017.

Chittenden, Lucius Eugene. *Personal Reminiscences, 1840–1890: Including Some Not Hitherto Published of Lincoln and the War*. New York: Richmond, Croscup, 1893.

———. *Recollections of President Lincoln and His Administration*. New York: Harper & Brothers, 1904.

Cimprich, John. *Fort Pillow: A Civil War Massacre, and Public Memory*. Baton Rouge: LSU Press, 2005.

Claxton, Melvin, and Mark Puls. *Uncommon Valor: A Story of Race, Patriotism, and Glory in the Final Battles of the Civil War*. Hoboken, NJ: John Wiley & Sons, 2006.

Coggins, Jack. *Arms and Equipment of the Civil War*. Mineola, NY: Dover Publications, 1962.

Connelly, Thomas. *The Marble Man: Robert E. Lee and His Image in American Society*. New York: Alfred A. Knopf, 1977.

Cornish, Dudley Taylor. *The Sable Arm: Black Troops in the Union Army, 1861–65*. Lawrence: University Press of Kansas, 1987.

Cox, R. David. *The Religious Life of Robert E. Lee*. Grand Rapids, MI: William B. Eerdmans Publishing Co., 2017.

Cozzens, Peter. *The Shipwreck of Their Hopes: The Battles for Chattanooga.* Urbana: University of Illinois Press, 1994.

Cozzens, Peter, and Robert L. Girardi. *The New Annals of the Civil War.* Mechanicsburg, PA: Stackpole Books, 2004.

Crist, Linda Lasswell, ed. *The Papers of Jefferson Davis.* Vol. 10, *October 1863– August 1864.* Baton Rouge: LSU Press, 1999.

Cunningham, H. H. *Doctors in Gray: The Confederate Medical Service.* Baton Rouge: LSU Press, 1958.

Cushman, Stephen. *Reflections on a Civil War Battle.* Charlottesville: University of Virginia Press, 1999.

Davis, Burke. *To Appomattox: Nine April Days, 1865.* New York: Rinehart, 1959.

Davis, William C. *The Battle of New Market.* Garden City, NY: Doubleday, 1975.

———. *Crucible of Command: Ulysses S. Grant and Robert E. Lee: The War They Fought, the Peace They Forged.* Boston: Da Capo Press, 2014.

———. *Jefferson Davis: The Man and His Hour.* New York: Harper Collins, 1991.

Dennett, Tyler, ed. *Lincoln and the Civil War: In the Diaries and Letters of John Hay.* New York: Dodd Mead, 1939.

Douglass, Frederick. *Life and Times of Freder-*

ick Douglass, Written by Himself. Cleveland, OH: 1883.

Early, Jubal A. *A Memoir of the Last Year of the War for Independence in the Confederate States of America.* Lynchburg, VA: Charles W. Bunton, 1867.

Eby, Cecil D., Jr. *A Virginia Yankee in the Civil War: The Diaries of David Hunter Strother.* Chapel Hill: University of North Carolina Press, 1989.

Egerton, Douglas R. *Thunder at the Gates: The Black Civil War Regiments That Redeemed America.* New York: Basic Books, 2016.

Erwin, James W. *Guerrillas in Civil War Missouri.* Charleston, SC: History Press, 2012.

Faust, Drew Gilpin. *This Republic of Suffering: Death and the American Civil War.* New York: Alfred A. Knopf, 2008.

Fellman, Michael. *Citizen Sherman: A Life of William Tecumseh Sherman.* New York: Random House, 1995.

———. *Inside War: The Guerrilla Conflict in Missouri During the American Civil War.* New York: Oxford University Press, 1989.

Fisher, Noel C. *War at Every Door: Partisan Politics and Guerrilla Violence in East Tennessee, 1860–1869.* Chapel Hill: University of North Carolina Press, 1997.

Foner, Eric. *Reconstruction: America's Unfinished Revolution, 1863–1877.* New York:

Harper and Row, 1988.

Foote, Shelby. *The Civil War: A Narrative.* 3 vols. New York: Random House, 1974.

Ford, Worthington Chauncey, ed. *A Cycle of Adams Letters: 1861–1865.* Vol. 2. Boston: Houghton Mifflin, 1920.

Foster, Buck T. *Sherman's Mississippi Campaign.* Tuscaloosa: University of Alabama Press, 2006.

Frank, Lisa Tendrich. *The Civilian War: Confederate Women and Union Soldiers During Sherman's March.* Baton Rouge: LSU Press, 2015.

Freeman, Douglas Southall, ed. *Lee's Dispatches: Unpublished Letters of General Robert E. Lee, C.S.A., to Jefferson Davis and the War Department of the Confederate States of America, 1862–1865.* Baton Rouge: LSU Press, 1957.

————. *Lee's Lieutenants: A Study in Command.* 3 vols. New York: Charles Scribner's Sons, 1944.

————. *R. E. Lee: A Biography.* 3 vols. New York: Charles Scribner's Sons, 1946.

Furgurson, Ernest B. *Freedom Rising: Washington in the Civil War.* New York: Alfred A. Knopf, 2004.

————. *Not War But Murder: Cold Harbor 1864.* New York: Vintage Civil War Library (Random House), 2000.

Gallagher, Gary, ed. *Fighting for the Confed-*

eracy: The Personal Memoirs of General Edward Porter Alexander. Chapel Hill: University of North Carolina Press, 1989.

————, ed. *The Spotsylvania Campaign.* Military Campaigns of the Civil War (series). Chapel Hill: University of North Carolina Press, 1998.

Glatthaar, Joseph T. *Forged in Battle: The Civil War Alliance of Black Soldiers and White Officers.* New York: Free Press, 1990.

————. *General Lee's Army: From Victory to Collapse.* New York: Free Press, 2008.

————. *The March to the Sea and Beyond: Sherman's Troops in the Savannah and Carolinas Campaigns.* New York: New York University Press, 1985.

Goodman, Sergeant Thomas M. *A Thrilling Record: Founded on the Facts and Observations Obtained During Ten Days' Experience with Col. Wm. T. Anderson.* 1868. Reprint, Maryville, MO: Rush Printing, 1960.

Gordon, John Brown. *Reminiscences of the Civil War.* New York: Scribner, 1903.

Grant, Ulysses S. *Personal Memoirs and Selected Letters, 1839–1865.* 2 vols. New York: Library of America, 1990.

Greiner, Captain Henry C. *General Phil Sheridan as I Knew Him: Playmate, Confidant, Friend.* Chicago: J. S. Hyland, 1908.

Grimsley, Mark. *And Keep Moving On: The Virginia Campaign, May–June 1864.* Lincoln:

University of Nebraska Press, 2002.

———. *The Hard Hand of War: Union Military Policy Toward Southern Civilians, 1861–1865.* Cambridge, UK: Cambridge University Press, 1995.

Guelzo, Allen C. *Abraham Lincoln: Redeemer President.* Grand Rapids, MI: W. B. Eerdmans, 1999.

Gwynne, S. C. *Rebel Yell: The Violence, Passion, and Redemption of Stonewall Jackson.* New York: Scribner, 2014.

Hagerman, Edward. *The American Civil War and the Origins of Modern Warfare: Ideas, Organization, and Field Command.* Bloomington: Indiana University Press, 1988.

Hall, Richard H. *Women on the Civil War Battlefront.* Lawrence: University Press of Kansas, 2006.

Hargrove, Hondon B. *Black Union Soldiers in the Civil War.* Jefferson, NC: McFarland, 1988.

Harrigan, Stephen. *Big Wonderful Thing: A History of Texas.* Austin: University of Texas Press, 2019.

Hart, Albert Bushnell. *Salmon P. Chase.* New York: Chelsea House, 1980.

Hart, B. H. Liddell. *Sherman: Soldier, Realist, American.* New York: Da Capo Press, 1993.

Hay, John. *Lincoln and the Civil War: Diaries and Letters of John Hay.* New York: Dodd,

Mead, 1939.

Hearn, Chester G. *When the Devil Came Down to Dixie: Ben Butler in New Orleans.* Baton Rouge: LSU Press, 1997.

Henry, Robert Selph. *Nathan Bedford Forrest: First with the Most.* Wilmington, NC: Broadfoot, 1987.

Hess, Earl J. *Field Armies and Fortifications in the Civil War: The Eastern Campaigns, 1861–1864.* Chapel Hill: University of North Carolina Press, 2005.

Hitchcock, Henry. *Marching with Sherman: Passages from the Letters and Campaign Diaries of Henry Hitchcock, Major and Asst. Adjutant General of Volunteers, November 1864–May 1865.* Edited by M. A. DeWolfe Howe. Lincoln: University of Nebraska Press, 1995.

Holtz-Bacha, Christina, and Jesper Stromback, eds. *Opinion Polls and the Media: Reflecting and Shaping Public Opinion.* London: Palgrave McMillan, 2012.

Holzer, Harold. *The Civil War in 50 Objects.* New York: Viking, 2013.

Hughes-Wilson, John. *The Secret State: A History of Intelligence and Espionage.* New York: Pegasus Books, 2017.

Humphreys, Andrew A. *The Virginia Campaign of '64 and '65: The Army of the Potomac and the Army of the James.* New York: Charles Scribner's Sons, 1883.

Jaquette, Henrietta Stratton. *South After Gettysburg: Letters of Cornelia Hancock, 1863–1868.* 1937. Reprint, New York: Thomas Y. Crowell, 1956.

Johnson, David Alan. *Decided on the Battlefield: Grant, Sherman, Lincoln and the Election of 1864.* Amherst, NY: Prometheus Books, 2012.

Johnson, Robert Underwood, ed. *Battles and Leaders of the Civil War.* 4 vols. New York: Century, 1884–88.

Jones, James B., Jr. *Tennessee in the Civil War.* Jefferson, NC: McFarland, 2011.

Jones, James Pickett. *Yankee Blitzkrieg: Wilson's Raid Through Alabama and Georgia.* Athens: University of Georgia Press, 1976.

Jones, Reverend J. William. *Life and Letters of General Robert E. Lee: Soldier and Man.* New York and Washington: Neal Publishing, 1906.

———. *Personal Reminiscences of General Robert E. Lee.* Richmond, VA: United States Historical Society Press, 1989.

Jordan, David. *Happiness Is Not My Companion: The Life of G. K. Warren.* Bloomington: University of Indiana Press, 2011.

Keckley, Elizabeth. *Behind the Scenes: Thirty Years a Slave and Four Years in the White House.* New York: G. W. Carleton, 1868.

Keegan, John. *The American Civil War: A*

Military History. New York: Alfred A. Knopf, 2009.

Kennett, Lee. *Marching Through Georgia: The Story of Soldiers and Civilians During Sherman's Campaign.* New York: Harper Collins, 1995.

————. *Sherman: A Soldier's Life.* New York: Harper Collins, 2001.

Kinchen, Oscar. *Confederate Operations in Canada and the North.* North Quincy, MA: Christopher Publishing House, 1970.

Klement, Frank L. *The Limits of Dissent: Clement L. Vallandigham and the Civil War.* Lexington: University Press of Kentucky, 1970.

Lane, Mills, ed. *"War Is Hell!": William T. Sherman's Personal Narrative of His March Through Georgia.* Savannah, GA: Beehive Press, 1974.

Lee, Captain Robert E. *Recollections and Letters of Robert E. Lee.* New York: Doubleday, Page, 1904.

Leech, Margaret. *Reveille in Washington, 1860–1865.* 1941. Reprint, New York: Time, 1962.

Lemire, Elise. *"Miscegenation": Making Race in America.* Philadelphia: University of Pennsylvania Press, 2002.

Lincoln, Abraham. *Abraham Lincoln, Speeches and Writings, 1859–1865: Speeches, Letters, Miscellaneous Writings,* and *Proclamations.* New York: Library of America, 1989.

Long, David E. *The Jewel of Liberty: Abraham Lincoln's Re-election and the End of Slavery.* Mechanicsburg, PA: Stackpole Books, 1994.

Longstreet, James. *From Manassas to Appomattox: Memoirs of the Civil War in America.* Philadelphia: J. B. Lippincott, 1896.

Lyman, Theodore. *Meade's Army: The Private Notebooks of Lt. Col. Theodore Lyman.* Edited by David Lowe. Kent, OH: Kent State University Press, 2007.

———. *Meade's Headquarters, 1863–1865.* Freeport, NY: Books for Libraries Press, 1970.

Mackey, Robert R. *The Uncivil War: Irregular Warfare in the Upper South, 1861–1865.* Norman: University of Oklahoma Press, 2004.

Mahan, Dennis Hart. *A Treatise on field fortification, containing instructions on the methods of laying out, constructing, defending, and attacking intrenchments, with the general outlines also of the arrangement, the attack, and defense of permanent fortifications.* New York: J. Wiley, 1856.

Marshall, Charles. *An Aide-de-Camp of Lee.* Boston: Little, Brown, 1927. Available through Lee Family digital archive.

Marshall, Jessie Ames, ed. *Private and Official Correspondence of General Benjamin F. Butler, During the Period of the Civil War.* Vol. 5. Norwood, MA: Plimpton Press, 1917.

Marszalek, John F. *Sherman: A Soldier's Passion for Order.* New York: Free Press, 1993.

————. *Sherman's March to the Sea.* Abilene, TX: McWhiney Foundation Press, 2005.

Marvel, William. *Andersonville: The Last Depot.* Chapel Hill: University of North Carolina Press, 1994.

————. *Lee's Last Retreat: The Flight to Appomattox.* Chapel Hill: University of North Carolina Press, 2002.

Maxwell, William Quentin. *Lincoln's Fifth Wheel: The Political History of the United States Sanitary Commission.* New York: Longmans, Greene, 1956.

McClure, Alexander K. *Lincoln and Men of War-Times.* Lincoln: University of Nebraska Press, 1997.

McDonough, James Lee. *William Tecumseh Sherman: In the Service of My Country: A Life.* New York: W. W. Norton, 2016.

McFeely, William S. *Frederick Douglass.* New York: W. W. Norton, 1991.

————. *Grant: A Biography.* New York: W. W. Norton, 1980.

McGuire, Judith White. *Diary of a Southern Refugee During the War.* New York: E. J. Hale and Son, 1868.

McKnight, Brian D. *Contested Borderland: The Civil War in Appalachian Kentucky and Virginia.* Lexington: University Press of Kentucky, 2006.

McPherson, James M. *Battle Cry of Freedom: The Civil War Era.* New York: Oxford University Press, 1988.

———. *The Struggle for Equality: Abolitionists and the Negro in the Civil War and Reconstruction.* Princeton, NJ: Princeton University Press, 1964.

———. *The War That Forged a Nation: Why the Civil War Still Matters.* New York: Oxford University Press, 2015.

Michie, Peter S. *The Life and Letters of Emory Upton.* New York: D. Appleton, 1885.

Neely, Mark E., Jr. *The Fate of Liberty: Abraham Lincoln and Civil Liberties.* New York: Oxford University Press, 1991.

Nelson, Larry E. *Bullets, Ballots, and Rhetoric: Confederate Policy for the United States Presidential Contest of 1864.* Tuscaloosa: University of Alabama Press, 1980.

Nevins, Allan. *War for the Union.* 4 vols. New York: Konecky and Konecky, 1971.

Nevins, Allan, and Milton Halsey, eds. *Diary of George Templeton Strong, 1835–1875.* 4 vols. New York: Macmillan, 1952.

Nichols, Bruce. *Guerrilla Warfare in Civil War Missouri.* Vol. 3, *January–August 1864.* Jefferson, NC: McFarland, 2014.

————. *Guerrilla Warfare in Civil War Missouri. Vol. 4, September 1864–June 1865.* Jefferson, NC: McFarland, 2014.

Nicolay, Helen. *Lincoln's Secretary: A Biography of John G. Nicolay.* New York: Longmans, Green, 1949.

Nicolay, John G., and John Hay. *Abraham Lincoln: A History.* Vol. 9. New York: Century, 1890.

Nolan, Alan T. *Lee Considered: General Robert E. Lee and Civil War History.* Chapel Hill: University of North Carolina Press, 1991.

Nolan, Dick. *Benjamin Franklin Butler: The Damnedest Yankee.* Novato, CA: Presidio Press, 1991.

Oates, Stephen B. *A Woman of Valor: Clara Barton and the Civil War.* New York: Free Press, 1994.

O'Connell, Robert L. *Fierce Patriot: The Tangled Lives of William Tecumseh Sherman.* New York: Random House, 2014.

Oller, John. *American Queen: The Rise and Fall of Kate Chase Sprague, Civil War "Belle of the Ball" and Gilded Age Woman of Scandal.* Boston: Da Capo Press, 2014.

Page, Charles A. *Letters of a War Correspondent.* Boston: L. C. Page, 1899.

Patrick, Marsena Rudolph. *Inside Lincoln's Army: The Diary of Marsena Rudolph Patrick, Provost Marshal General, Army of the Potomac.* New York: T. Yoseloff, 1964.

Pollard, Edward A. *Observations in the North: Eight Months in Prison and on Parole.* Richmond, VA: F. W. Ayres, 1865.

Porter, David Dixon. *Incidents and Anecdotes of the Civil War.* New York: D. Appleton, 1885.

Porter, Horace. *Campaigning with Grant.* New York: Century, 1897.

Pryor, Elizabeth Brown. *Clara Barton: Professional Angel.* Philadelphia: University of Pennsylvania Press, 1998.

Rable, George C. *The Confederate Republic: A Revolution Against Politics.* Chapel Hill: University of North Carolina Press, 1994.

―――. *God's Almost Chosen Peoples: A Religious History of the American Civil War.* Chapel Hill: University of North Carolina Press, 2010.

Ramage, James A. *Gray Ghost: The Life of Col. John Singleton Mosby.* Lexington: University Press of Kentucky, 1999.

Ransom, John. *John Ransom's Andersonville Diary: Life Inside the Civil War's Most Infamous Prison.* New York: Berkeley Books, 1994.

Rhea, Gordon C. *The Battle of the Wilderness, May 5–6, 1864.* Baton Rouge: LSU Press, 1994.

―――. *Cold Harbor: Grant and Lee, May 26–June 3, 1864.* Baton Rouge: LSU Press, 2002.

────────. *To the North Anna River: Grant and Lee, May 13–May 25.* Baton Rouge: LSU Press, 2000.

Royster, Charles. *The Destructive War: William Tecumseh Sherman, Stonewall Jackson, and the Americans.* New York: Vintage Books, 1991.

Ruhlman, R. Fred. *Captain Henry Wirz and Andersonville Prison: A Reappraisal.* Knoxville: University of Tennessee Press, 2006.

Russell, Charles Wells, ed. *The Memoirs of Colonel John S. Mosby.* Boston: Little, Brown, 1917.

Rutkow, Ira M. *Bleeding Blue and Gray: Civil War Surgery and the Evolution of American Medicine.* New York: Random House, 2005.

Scott, Robert Garth. *Into the Wilderness with the Army of the Potomac.* Bloomington: Indiana University Press, 1985.

Sears, Stephen W., ed. *The Civil War Papers of George B. McClellan: Selected Correspondence, 1860–1865.* New York: Da Capo Press, 1992.

Sensing, Thurman. *Champ Ferguson: Confederate Guerrilla.* Nashville, TN: Vanderbilt University Press, 1942.

Sheehan-Dean, Aaron, ed. *The Civil War: The Final Year by Those Who Lived It.* New York: Library of America, 2014.

Sheridan, Philip. *Personal Memoirs of P. H. Sheridan, General, United States Army.*

New York: Da Capo Press, 1992.

Sherman, William Tecumseh. *Memoirs of General W. T. Sherman.* New York: Library of America, 1990.

Simms, William Gilmore. *The Life of Francis Marion.* 1840. Reprint, Philadelphia: G. G. Evans, 1860.

Simon, John Y., ed. *The Papers of Ulysses S. Grant.* Vol. 12, *August 16–November 15, 1864.* Carbondale: Southern Illinois University Press, 1984.

Simson, Jay W., *Custer and the Front Royal Executions of 1864.* Jefferson, NC: McFarland, 2009.

Smith, Jean Edward. *Grant.* New York: Simon & Schuster, 2001.

Smith, John David. *Black Soldiers in Blue: African Troops in the Civil War Era.* Chapel Hill: University of North Carolina Press, 2002.

Smith, William Farrar. *From Chattanooga to Petersburg Under Generals Grant and Butler: A Contribution to the History of the War and a Personal Vindication.* Boston and New York: Houghton Mifflin, 1893.

Sneden, Robert Knox. *Eye of the Storm: A Civil War Odyssey.* Edited by Charles E. Bryan Jr. and Nelson D. Lankford. New York: Free Press, 2000.

Sodergren, Steven. *The Army of the Potomac in the Overland & Petersburg Campaigns:*

Union Soldiers and Trench Warfare, 1864–1865. Baton Rouge: LSU Press, 2017.

Starr, Stephen Z. *The Union Cavalry in the Civil War.* Vol. 2, *The War in the East from Gettysburg to Appomattox, 1863–1865.* Baton Rouge: LSU Press, 1979.

Steere, Edward. *The Wilderness Campaign.* 1960. Reprint, Harrisburg, PA: Stackpole, 1987.

Sterling, Dorothy. *The Trouble They Seen: Black People Tell the Story of Reconstruction.* Garden City, NY: Doubleday, 1976.

Stevens, George Thomas. *Three Years in the Sixth Corps: A Concise Narrative of Events in the Army of the Potomac.* Bedford, MA: Applewood Books, 1866.

Stewart, John. *Jefferson Davis's Flight from Richmond.* Jefferson, NC: McFarland, 2015.

Straudenras, P. J., ed. *Mr. Lincoln's Washington: Selections from the Writings of Noah Brooks, Civil War Correspondent.* South Brunswick, NJ: T. Yoseloff, 1967.

Strong, George Templeton. *Diary of George Templeton Strong.* Seattle: University of Washington Press, 1988.

Sutherland, Daniel E. *A Savage Conflict: The Decisive Role of Guerrillas in the American Civil War.* Chapel Hill: University of North Carolina Press, 2009.

Swisshelm, Jane Grey. *Crusader and Feminist:*

Letters of Jane Grey Swisshelm. Edited by Arthur Larsen. St. Paul: Minnesota Historical Society, 1934.

Switzler, William F. *History of Boone County, Missouri.* St. Louis: Western History, 1882.

Taylor, Richard. *Destruction and Reconstruction.* Nashville, TN: J. S. Sanders, 1998.

Taylor, Walter H. *Four Years with General Lee.* 1877. Reprint, Bloomington: Indiana University Press, 1962.

————. *General Lee, His Campaigns in Virginia, 1861–1865, with Personal Reminiscences.* Dayton, OH: Press of Morningside Bookshop, 1975.

Thomas, Emory M. *The Confederate State of Richmond: A Biography of the Capital.* Austin: University of Texas Press, 1971.

————. *Robert E. Lee.* New York: W. W. Norton, 1995.

Trefousse, Hans L. *Ben Butler: The South Called Him BEAST.* New York: Twayne, 1957.

Trollope, Anthony, *North America.* New York: Harper & Brothers, 1862.

Trudeau, Noah Andre. *The Last Citadel: Petersburg, June 1864–April 1865.* Hills, CA: Savas Beatie, 1991.

————. *Southern Storm: Sherman's March to the Sea.* New York: Harper Collins, 2008.

Tulloch, Hugh. *The Routledge Companion to the American Civil War Era.* New York:

Routledge, 2006.

Twain, Mark. *Life on the Mississippi*. London: Chatto and Windus, 1883.

Varon, Elizabeth R. *Appomattox: Victory, Defeat, and Freedom at the End of the Civil War.* New York: Oxford University Press, 2014.

Von Borcke, Heros. *Memoirs of the Confederate War for Independence.* Philadelphia: J. B. Lippincott, 1867.

Waugh, John C. *Class of 1846 — from West Point to Appomattox: Stonewall Jackson, George McClellan and Their Brothers.* New York: Ballantine Books, 1994.

————. *Reelecting Lincoln.* New York: Crown Publishing, 1997.

Weber, Jennifer L. *Copperheads: The Rise and Fall of Lincoln's Opponents in the North.* New York: Oxford University Press, 2006.

Weems, M. L. *The Life of General Francis Marion.* 1809. Reprint, Baltimore: J. Hagerty, 1815.

Weik, Jesse W. *The Real Lincoln: A Portrait.* Lincoln: University of Nebraska Press, 2002.

Weld, Stephen Minot. *War Diary and Letters of Stephen Minot Weld, 1861–1865.* Boston: Massachusetts Historical Society, 1979.

Welles, Gideon. *Diary of Gideon Welles, Secretary of the Navy Under Lincoln and Johnson.* Vol. 1. New York and Boston:

Houghton Mifflin, 1911.

Wells, Bruce R. *The Bermuda Hundred Campaign: The Creole and the Beast.* Charleston, SC: History Press, 2011.

Wert, Jeffrey D. *From Winchester to Cedar Creek: The Shenandoah Campaign of 1864.* Carlisle, PA: South Mountain Press, 1987.

————. *Mosby's Rangers.* New York: Simon & Schuster, 1990.

West, Richard S., Jr. *Lincoln's Scapegoat General: A Life of Benjamin F. Butler.* Boston: Houghton Mifflin, 1965.

Wheelan, Joseph. *Terrible Swift Sword: The Life of General Philip. H. Sheridan.* Cambridge, MA: Da Capo Press, 2012.

Widmer, Ted, ed. The New York Times *Disunion: A History of the Civil War.* New York: Oxford University Press, 2016.

Wiggins, Sarah Woolfolk, ed. *The Journals of Josiah Gorgas, 1857–1878.* Tuscaloosa: University of Alabama Press, 1995.

Williams, Robert C. *Horace Greeley: Champion of American Freedom.* New York: NYU Press, 2006.

Wills, Brian Steel. *The River Was Dyed with Blood: Nathan Bedford Forrest and Fort Pillow.* Norman: Oklahoma University Press, 2014.

Wilson, James Harrison. *The Life of John A. Rawlins; Lawyer, Assistant Adjutant-General, Chief of Staff, Major General of Volunteers,* and Secretary of War. New York: Neale, 1916.

Wilson, Keith P. *Campfires of Freedom: The Camp Life of Black Soldiers During the Civil War.* Kent, OH: Kent State University Press, 2002.

Winik, Jay. *April 1865: The Month That Saved America.* New York: Harper Collins, 2001.

Winkle, Kenneth J. *Lincoln's Citadel: The Civil War in Washington, D.C.* New York: W. W. Norton, 2013.

Woodward, C. Vann, ed. *Mary Chesnut's Civil War.* New York: Book of the Month Club's Essential Classics of the Civil War, 1981.

Woodworth, Steven E. *Davis and Lee at War.* Lawrence: University Press of Kansas, 1995.

———. *While God Is Marching On: The Religious World of Civil War Soldiers.* Lawrence: University Press of Kansas, 2001.

Woolsey, Jane Stuart. *Hospital Days.* New York: D. Van Nostrand, 1870.

Wyeth, John Allen. *The Life of Nathan Bedford Forrest.* New York: Harper & Brothers, 1908.

Young, John Russell. *Around the World with General Grant: A narrative of the visit of General U. S. Grant, ex-president of the United States, to various countries in Europe, Asia, and Africa, in 1877, 1878, and 1879, to which are added certain conversations with*

General Grant on questions connected with American Politics and History. Vol. 2. New York: American News, 1927.

Zornow, William Frank. *Lincoln and the Party Divided.* Westport, CT: Greenwood Press, 1972.

Articles

Bacon-Foster, Corra. "Clara Barton, Humanitarian." *Records of the Columbia History Society* 21:278–356.

Baker, Liva. "The Burning of Chambersburg." *American Heritage Magazine* 24, no. 5 (August 1973).

Boteler, Alexander. "The Beginning of the End." *Philadelphia Weekly Times* 2, no. 25 (August 17, 1878).

Carr, Matt. "General Sherman's March to the Sea." *History Today,* November 2014, 29.

Cozzens, Peter. "Fire on the Mountain." *Civil War Times,* October 1997.

———. "Irresistible Force: 'Harry' Wilson's Ruthless 1865 Raid Extinguished Confederate Hopes in the Southern Heartland." *America's Civil War,* July 2017.

Devine, Shauna. "Intensely Human: The Health of the Black Soldier in the American Civil War." *Canadian Bulletin of Medical History* 26, no. 1 (April 2009).

"Dr. Fitch's Report on the Fort Pillow Massacre." Edited by John Cimprich and Paul Manafort. *Tennessee Historical Quarterly* 44, no. 1 (1985): 27–39.

Erickson, Mark St. John. "Black Troops from Hampton Roads Among the First Union Forces to Occupy Richmond." *Newport News (VA) Daily Press,* April 2, 2015.

Foster, Buck T. "Sherman's First Campaign of Destruction." *MHQ: The Quarterly Journal of Military History,* Summer 2007, 58.

French, Steve. "Greenback Raid Builds Mosby's Legend." *Washington Times,* November 12, 2004.

"From Washington; Proclamation by President Lincoln; His View on Reconstruction." *New York Times,* July 10, 1864.

Geiger, Mark. W. "Indebtedness and the Origins of Guerrilla Violence in Civil War Missouri." *Journal of Southern History* 75, no. 1 (February 2009).

Grant, Frederick Dent. "Reminiscences of General U. S. Grant." *Journal of the Illinois State Historical Society* 7, no. 1 (April 1914).

Hay, John, and John G. Nicolay. "Abraham Lincoln, a History: The Pomeroy Circular — the Cleveland Convention — the Resignation of Chase." *Century Illustrated Monthly, May 1889 to October 1889,* vol. 38. New York: Century, 1889, 279.

Horton, Scott. "How Walter Scott Started

the American Civil War." *Harper's*, July 29, 2007.

Hunter, Robert M. T. "The Peace Commission of 1865." *Philadelphia Weekly Times* 1, no. 4 (March 24, 1877).

Imboden, John D. "The Battle of New Market." In Johnson, *Battles and Leaders*, vol. 4.

Lewis, Thomas A. "When Washington Came Close to Being Conquered by Confederates." *Smithsonian*, July 1988.

Livingston, Jonathan, et al. "Freedom's Soldiers: The Black Military Experience in the Civil War." *Journal of Negro History* 85, no. 4 (2000).

Mackintosh, Fiona J. "Were It Not for Dorence Atwater, Many Union Dead at Andersonville Would Remain Unknown." *America's Civil War*, May 2005.

Merritt, Major General Wesley. "Sheridan in the Shenandoah Valley." In Johnson, *Battles and Leaders*, vol. 4.

Murphy, Brian J. "The Truth Behind U. S. Grant's Yazoo River Bender." *America's Civil War*, January 2005.

Poole, Robert M. "How Arlington National Cemetery Came to Be." *Smithsonian*, November 2009.

Porter, General Horace. "Lincoln and Grant." *National Magazine* 29 (October 1908–March 1909): 665. Published in collection by the Chapple Publishing Company, Boston.

Pryor, Elizabeth Brown. "Thou Knowest Not the Time of Thy Visitation." *Virginia Magazine of History and Biography* 119, no. 3 (July 1, 2011).

Reid, Richard. "Government Policy, Prejudice, and the Experience of Black Civil War Soldiers and Their Families." *Journal of Family History* 27, no. 4 (October 2002).

———. "North Carolina's Black Soldiers in the Civil War." *Journal of American History* 95, no. 3 (December 2008).

Robertson, James I., Jr., and William Pegram. "The Boy Artillerist: Letters of Colonel William Pegram, C.S.A." *Virginia Magazine of History and Biography* 98, no. 2 (April 1990).

Ryan, Daniel J. "Lincoln and Ohio." *Ohio Archaeological and Historical Quarterly,* 1923.

Samito, Christian D. "The Intersection Between Military Justice and Equal Rights: Mutinies and Court-Martials and Black Soldiers." *Civil War History* 53, no. 2 (October 2007).

Sanders, Stuart W. "Bloody Bill's Centralia Massacre." *America's Civil War,* March 2000.

Sears, Stephen W. "Civil War Generals: Overrated and Underrated." *American Heritage*

50, no. 3 (1999): 47.

Sigel, Franz. "Sigel in the Shenandoah Valley." In Johnson, *Battles and Leaders,* vol. 4.

Trudeau, Noah Andre. "The Walls of 1864: Field Entrenchments Saved Robert E. Lee's Army — and Grant's as Well." *MHQ: The Quarterly Journal of Military History* 6, no. 2 (Winter 1994).

Tucker, Abigail. "Digging Up the Past at a Richmond Jail." *Smithsonian,* March 2009.

Vorenberg, Michael. " 'The Deformed Child': Slavery and the Election of 1864." *Civil War History* 47, no. 3 (2001).

Wachtell, Cynthia. "The Author of the Civil War." *New York Times,* July 6, 2012.

Wade-Davis Manifesto. *New-York Daily Tribune,* August 5, 1864.

Willis, Deborah. "The Black Civil War Soldier: Conflict and Citizenship." *Journal of American Studies* 51, no. 2 (May 2017).

Wukovits, John F. "John Mosby and George Custer Clash in the Shenandoah Valley." *America's Civil War,* March 2001.

Young, John Russell. Interview with Grant. *New York Herald,* July 24, 1878.

Lectures

Cozzens, Peter. "George Crook and Rutherford B. Hayes: A Friendship Forged in

War." Hayes Lecture on the Presidency, February 20, 2000.

Internet Sources

Allmon, William B. "The Desperate Battle of Allatoona Pass." Warfare History Network, October 20, 2015.

"Clara Barton's Missing Soldiers Office." Missing Soldiers Office Museum.

Cleburne, Patrick. "Patrick Cleburne's Proposal to Arm Slaves." January 2, 1864. American Battlefield Trust.

Davis, Jefferson. "To the People of the Confederate States of America." Danville, VA, April 4, 1985. *The Papers of Jefferson Davis,* Rice University.

Encyclopedia Virginia/Virginia Humanities, in partnership with the Library of Virginia.

Flavion, Gary. "Suffering and Survival." Overview of Civil War Camps. American Battlefield Trust.

"Fredericksburg, City of Hospitals." Containing transcriptions of official records, contemporaneous letters from 1864, Christian Commission reports, and memoirs. University of Mary Washington.

Lehrman Institute. Collected papers on Abraham Lincoln.

Lincoln, Abraham. "The Proclamation of Amnesty and Reconstruction." Freedmen & Southern Society Project.

Longacre, Edward G. *Was Grant a Drunk?* History News Network, September 9, 2007.

"A New Lesson on Dying in the Last Ditch." *New York Times,* August 22, 1864.

Rhea, Gordon. *The Battle of Spotsylvania Courthouse.* Essential Civil War Curriculum.

Sears, Stephen W. "The Dahlgren Papers Revisited." Historynet.

Simpson, Brooks D. "Grant and Drinking Revisited." Crossroads, March 13, 2011.

"Treatment of the Inhabitants of the South by Our Military Commander: A Noteworthy Letter from Major-Gen. W. T. Sherman." *New York Times,* April 28, 1864.

Woolley, John T., and Gerhard Peters. The American Presidency Project. University of California, Santa Barbara.

Zeiser, Dan. "The Most Overrated General." Cleveland Civil War Roundtable, 2008.

Miscellaneous

Gates, Lieutenant Colonel John M. *Evolution of Entrenchments During the American Civil War: A Vision for World War I Leaders.* Program paper published by US Army War College, Carlisle Barracks, Pennsylvania, 1991.

Government Documents

"Explosion of the Mine Before Petersburg." *Official Court of Inquiry on the Mine.* In *Reports of the Committees of the Senate of the United States,* 38th Cong., 2nd Sess.

Proceedings of the Massachusetts Historical Society 43. Boston: Massachusetts Historical Society, 1910.

"Report of the Medical Director of the Army of the Potomac, from January 14 to July 31, 1864, by Surgeon Thomas A. McParlin." In *The Medical and Surgical History of the War of the Rebellion, Appendix to Part I: Reports of Medical Directors and Other Documents.*

US War Department. *The War of the Rebellion: A Compilation of the Official Records of the Union and Confederate Armies.* Washington, DC: Government Printing Office, 1880–1901.

ILLUSTRATION CREDITS

Insert

1 Fort Totten, 1863, Prints and Photographs Division, Library of Congress, LC-DIG-ppmsca-32734

2 Arlington House, June 29, 1863, Prints and Photographs Division, Library of Congress, LC-DIG-ppmsca-08246

3 Willard Hotel, Robert N. Dennis Collection of Stereoscopic Views, the Miriam and Ira D. Wallach Division of Art, Prints and Photographs: Photography Collection, The New York Public Library

4 Frederick Douglass, Randolph Linsly Simpson, African-American Collection. Yale Collection of American Literature, Beinecke Rare Book and Manuscript Library

5 Abraham Lincoln, February 1865, Alexander Gardner, National Portrait Gallery, Smithsonian Institution: Frederick Hill Meserve Collection

6 Fort Pillow Massacre, chromolithograph,

courtesy of Tennessee State Library and Archives

7 Spotsylvania dead Confederates, Prints and Photographs Division, Library of Congress, LC-DIG-ppmsca-32912

8 Edwin Stanton, Brady Studios, Prints and Photographs Division, Library of Congress, LC-DIG-cwpbh-02151

9 George B. McClellan, December 1862, Case and Getchell, Prints and Photographs Division, Library of Congress, LC-DIG-ppmsca-41848

10 Henry Halleck, 1861, Brady Prints and Photographs Division, Library of Congress, LC-DIG-cwpb-06956

11 Joseph E. Johnston, National Archives (111-B-1782)

12 Jubal A. Early, Cook Collection, The Valentine

13 John Bell Hood, National Archives (111-B-5274)

14 Horace Greeley, 1869, Sarony, National Portrait Gallery, Smithsonian Institution; gift of Robert L. Drapkin

15 Robert E. Lee on Traveller, Petersburg, VA, 1864–65, probably Rockwell & Cowell, public domain

16 City Point supply wagons, wharves, Union ships, Prints and Photographs Division, Library of Congress, LC-DIG-ppmsca-33258

17 Dutch Gap, VA. Picket station of Colored

troops near Dutch Gap canal, Prints and Photographs Division, Library of Congress, LC-DIG-cwpb-01930

18 Grant's Headquarters City Point, VA, Prints and Photographs Division, Library of Congress, LC-DIG-ppmsca-33025

19 Interior of Fort Sedgewick, Petersburg, 1865, Prints and Photographs Division, Library of Congress, LC-DIG-ppmsca-32436

20 114th Pennsylvania Infantry, Co. G, Petersburg, April 1864, Timothy O'Sullivan, Prints and Photographs Division, Library of Congress, LC-DIG-cwpb-03857

21 Atlanta rolling mills, public domain

22 Atlanta rolling mills ruins, Prints and Photographs Division, Library of Congress, LC-DIG-ppmsca-33492

23 Atlanta Union Depot, Prints and Photographs Division, Library of Congress, LC-DIG-cwpb-02220

24 Atlanta Depot ruins, Prints and Photographs Division, Library of Congress, LC-DIG-cwpb-02226

25 Abraham Lincoln of Illinois. Andrew Johnson of Tennessee. No. 37, Prints and Photographs Division, Library of Congress, LC-DIG-ppmsca-19255

26 Lincoln giving Second Inaugural Address, Prints and Photographs Division, Library of Congress, LC-DIG-ppmsc-02928

38 Flag at Andersonville, Prints and Photographs Division, Library of Congress, LC-DIG-ppmsca-05602

Interior

p. 13 Abraham Lincoln, 1864, Gardner, National Portrait Gallery, Smithsonian Institution

p. 34 Nathan Bedford Forrest, public domain

p. 65 Robert E. Lee, 1864, Julian Vannerson, Prints and Photographs Division, Library of Congress, LC-DIG-ppmsca-35446

p. 81 Ulysses Grant seated, Brady, Prints and Photographs Division, Library of Congress, LC-DIG-cwpb-06947

p. 105 George G. Meade, Brady, Prints and Photographs Division, Library of Congress, LC-DIG-ppmsca-19398

p. 128 Wounded at Spotsylvania, public domain

p. 143 Clara Barton, 1865, C.R.B. Claflin, Prints and Photographs Division, Library of Congress, LC-DIG-ppmsca-56384

p. 163 Benjamin Butler, Brady, Prints and Photographs Division, Library of Congress, LC-DIG-cwpb-04894

p. 190 View of tent with four USCT, Randolph Linsly Simpson, African-American Collection. Yale Collection of American Literature, Beinecke Rare Book and Manuscript Library

Capitol, National Archives (165-SC-53)

p. 460 Dead Confederates in trench, Fort Mahone, Petersburg, VA, Prints and Photographs Division, Library of Congress, LC-DIG-ppmsca-32918

p. 483 Philip Sheridan, National Portrait Gallery, Smithsonian Institution

p. 514 Appomattox Court House, Prints and Photographs Division, Library of Congress, LC-DIG-ppmsca-32918

p. 551 Jefferson Davis, National Archives (111-B-4146)

p. 551 Abraham Lincoln, 1863, Alexander Gardner, Prints and Photographs Division, Library of Congress, LC-DIG-ds-07061

p. 583 Andersonville Prison, Prints and Photographs Division, Library of Congress, LC-DIG-ppmsca-33768

ABOUT THE AUTHOR

S. C. Gwynne is the author of the *New York Times* bestsellers *Empire of the Summer Moon,* which was a finalist for the Pulitzer Prize and the National Book Critics Circle Award; *Rebel Yell,* which was also a finalist for the National Book Critics Circle Award and was shortlisted for the PEN Literary Award for biography; and *The Perfect Pass.* He is an award-winning journalist whose work has appeared extensively in *Time,* for which he worked as a bureau chief, national correspondent, and senior editor from 1988 to 2000, and in *Texas Monthly,* where he was executive editor. His work has also appeared in *Outside* magazine, the *New York Times,* the *Dallas Morning News,* the *Los Angeles Times,* the *Los Angeles Herald Examiner, Harper's,* and *California* magazine. He lives in Austin, Texas, with his wife, the artist Katie Maratta.

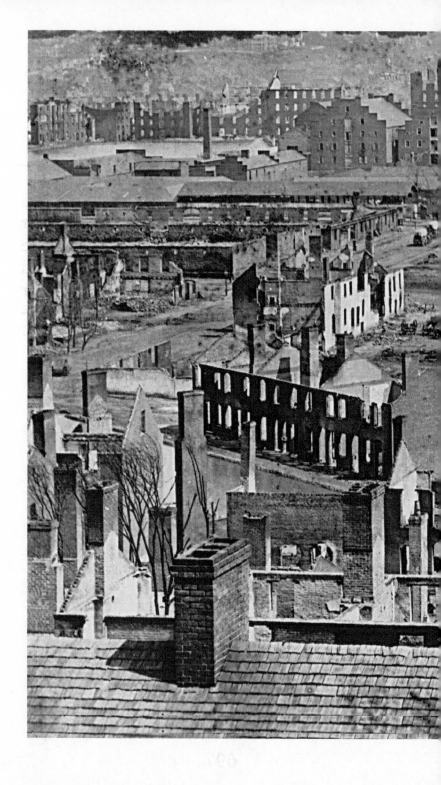